Modern Insights on Smart and Secure Software Development

Qasem Abu Al-Haija
Jordan University of Science and Technology, Jordan

Mahmoud Hammad
College of Engineering and Information Technology, Ajman University, UAE

IGI Global
Scientific Publishing
Publishing Tomorrow's Research Today

Vice President of Editorial — Melissa Wagner
Managing Editor of Acquisitions — Mikaela Felty
Managing Editor of Book Development — Jocelynn Hessler
Production Manager — Mike Brehm
Cover Design — Phillip Shickler

Published in the United States of America by
IGI Global Scientific Publishing
701 East Chocolate Avenue
Hershey, PA, 17033, USA
Tel: 717-533-8845
Fax: 717-533-7115
Website: https://www.igi-global.com E-mail: cust@igi-global.com

Library of Congress Cataloging-in-Publication Data

Names: Al-Haija, Qasem, 1982- editor
http://id.loc.gov/authorities/names/n2025027053
http://id.loc.gov/rwo/agents/n2025027053 | Mustafa, Ahmad, 1986- editor
http://id.loc.gov/authorities/names/n2025027055
http://id.loc.gov/rwo/agents/n2025027055 | Hammad, Mahmoud, 1983- editor
http://id.loc.gov/authorities/names/n2025027057
http://id.loc.gov/rwo/agents/n2025027057
Title: Modern insights on smart and secure software development / edited by Qasem Al-Haija, Ahmad Mustafa, Mahmoud Hammad.
Description: Hershey, PA : IGI Global Scientific Publishing, [2025] | Includes bibliographical references and index. | Summary: "This book covers the latest methodologies, tools, and techniques for integrating smart features and robust security measures into software projects. It includes practical examples, case studies, and expert insights to help developers and organizations stay ahead in the rapidly evolving tech landscape"-- Provided by publisher.
Identifiers: LCCN 2025002862 (print) | LCCN 2025002863 (ebook) | ISBN 9798369398517 h/c | ISBN 9798369398524 s/c | ISBN 9798369398531 ebook
Subjects: LCSH: Computer software--Development--Management http://id.loc.gov/authorities/subjects/sh2008101505 | Artificial intelligence--Security measures | Machine learning--Security measures
Classification: LCC QA76.76.D47 M6295 2025 (print) | LCC QA76.76.D47 (ebook) | DDC 005.8068--dc23/eng/20250625
LC record available at https://lccn.loc.gov/2025002862
LC ebook record available at https://lccn.loc.gov/2025002863

British Cataloguing in Publication Data
A Cataloguing in Publication record for this book is available from the British Library.

All praises are due to Allah for His countless blessings and the strength He granted us to complete this work.

Qasem's dedication:

This book, *Modern Insights on Smart and Secure Software Development*, is lovingly dedicated to the memory of my late father, Saleh Abu Al-Haija, and my late mother, Fawzeyah Abu Al-Haija. I also honor my beloved wife, Noor Jebril, and my dear children, Jory, Aysha, Zainab, and Omar, whose steady support, patience, and invaluable contributions have been a constant source of inspiration throughout this journey.

Mahmoud's dedications:

This book, *Modern Insights on Smart and Secure Software Development*, is lovingly dedicated to the memory of my late father, Mohammed Khair Hammad, and my late mother, Amenah Nazzal. I also honor my beloved wife, Salma Suleiman, and my dear children, Lamar, Leen, Layan, and Omar, whose steady support, patience, and invaluable contributions have been a constant source of inspiration throughout this journey.

Table of Contents

Detailed Table of Contents

Software development techniques have changed due to the incorporation of artificial intelligence (AI) and machine learning (ML), which provide previously unheard-of levels of automation, optimisation, and creativity. T. Software developers can reduce human error, increase productivity, and improve decision-making by utilising predictive models and sophisticated algorithms. Advanced applications, including AI-driven debugging, generative AI for code synthesis, and predictive analytics for risk assessment, are also covered in this chapter. Issues including algorithmic biases, ethical concerns, and integration difficulties are discussed alongside workable solutions. The chapter ends with predictions for the future, highlighting how AI and ML can be used to build more intelligent, safe, and flexible software systems. Real-world case studies are incorporated to illustrate the observable advantages and useful applications of AI-ML in contemporary software development.

The integration of emerging technologies such as Blockchain, the Internet of Things (IoT), and other innovative solutions is revolutionizing smart and secure software development. These technologies enhance data integrity, enable decentralization, and improve interoperability across digital platforms, creating more resilient and adaptive systems. Blockchain's use of smart contracts ensures automated, secure transactions, while IoT facilitates real-time monitoring and data collection, driving better decision-making. As cybersecurity threats grow, leveraging these technologies can improve scalability and protection against vulnerabilities in software applications. The ongoing evolution of tech trends presents new opportunities for building intelligent systems that meet the complex demands of modern software development.

Mohammad Alauthman, Petra University, Jordan
Ahmad Al-Qerem, Zarqa University, Jordan
Amjad Aldweesh, Shaqra University, Saudi Arabia
Ammar Almomani, Higher Colleges of Technology, UAE

Software applications have become indispensable across sectors, necessitating robust security throughout their lifecycle. This chapter examines transforming the Software Development Life Cycle (SDLC) into a Secure SDLC by embedding security principles at every phase. Through DevSecOps—merging development, operations, and continuous security—organizations strengthen their cyber resilience. A well-structured Secure SDLC with DevSecOps principles mitigates risks while ensuring faster delivery cycles, regulatory compliance, and sustained user trust. The chapter provides methodologies for threat modeling, automation, collaboration, and monitoring, creating a clear pathway for businesses to incorporate security as an integral part of software engineering rather than an afterthought. Through theoretical frameworks and case studies, it demonstrates how security integration drives both protection and business value.

Usharani Bhimavarapu, Department of Computer Science and Engineering, Koneru Lakshmaiah Education Foundation, Vaddeswaram, India

Security Testing: Identifying and Mitigating Vulnerabilities is a critical aspect of safeguarding critical infrastructure, especially in sectors such as energy, where cybersecurity threats continue to evolve. This study integrates data from NESCOR, NIST, and ISO/IEC 27005 to create a comprehensive dataset for analyzing vulnerabilities and their relationships with assets. Advanced preprocessing techniques, including Natural Language Processing (NLP), were employed to standardize and extract meaningful features from textual data. The study utilized Artificial Neural Networks (ANNs) to map assets to vulnerabilities, categorize them into high-risk groups, and predict potential threats. The ANN model leveraged features such as criticality, exposure, and severity to provide actionable insights for vulnerability management. By identifying high-risk asset-vulnerability pairs and categorizing them effectively, this research facilitates targeted mitigation strategies and enhances the resilience of critical infrastructure against cyberattacks.

AI technologies are revolutionizing communication systems, enhancing processing techniques, scalability, efficiency, and intelligence, making them more intelligent and scalable in real-time. In this chapter, we discuss the applications of AI tools for the generation, execution and enhancement of real-time communication systems across telecommunications, healthcare, education and business-sector collaboration. Machine learning, Natural language processing (NLP), and predictive analytics come under the array of AI-driven tools that help improve communication system performance, reliability, and security. In areas such as automated error detection and real time adaptation to network conditions, latency optimization and personalized experiences, the AI is solving many of those predictable challenges, the article explores. The discussion on machine-to-machine communication, AI's role in real-time translation, sentiment analysis, and intelligent routing, has led to new trends, frameworks, methodologies, and initiatives for contemporary communication.

In today's digital world, software systems must adhere to the Secure Software Development Lifecycle (SSDLC) protocol to guarantee security, reliability, and resilience. Despite the revolutionary impact of deep learning, blockchain, and Artificial Intelligence (AI) on software development, substantial challenges remain to be solved in terms of minimizing security risks and conforming to regulatory standards. This Software Development Lifecycle (SDLC) research integrates cybersecurity throughout the process and primarily focuses on case studies and best practices relating to risk assessment, secure design, and security testing. Data privacy, intellectual property regulations, and regulatory requirements must be followed while developing robust software systems that can resist cyber assaults and promote innovation.

This chapter explores the integration of AI-driven threat modeling and risk assessment within software development to enhance security practices. Utilizing a comprehensive literature review, case studies, and qualitative interviews with industry professionals, the study identifies best practices and emerging trends in threat modeling methodologies such as STRIDE and DREAD. Key findings reveal that organizations adopting AI technologies experience improved threat detection and response times, leading to a more robust security posture. However, the study also highlights the importance of human oversight and the ethical considerations surrounding AI applications. The conclusions emphasize that a proactive approach, involving cross-functional teams and continuous adaptation to evolving cyber threats, is essential for building resilient software applications. This work underscores the significance of integrating AI into threat modeling as a critical strategy for organizations aiming to safeguard their digital assets.

Regression testing ensures that changes in a software system do not intro- duce defects in previously tested functionality, but it is often a resource-intensive process. Regression Test Selection (RTS) techniques aim to reduce this cost by identifying a sub- set of test cases that must be executed after changes. This chapter explores the evolution and effectiveness of RTS methods, focusing on their evaluation criteria, including safety and precision. The chapter categorizes RTS approaches into model-based, code-based, information retrieval-based, fuzzy logic-based, machine learning-based, and security-aware methods, detailing their methodologies, advantages, and limitations. The chapter also includes an experimental evaluation comparing static RTS (STARTS) with dynamic RTS (Ekstazi) in terms of safety, precision, and test suite reduction. Finally, the chapter discusses future directions. This comprehensive overview underscores the critical role of RTS in improving the efficiency and effectiveness of regression testing for modern software systems.

Cloud-based software has gained popularity for its scalability, flexibility, and cost savings, but traditional software architectures are not directly applicable to these environments. Challenges such as performance, resiliency, and high availability must be addressed. This chapter proposes a hybrid cloud infrastructure-based approach to designing resilient software architectures. It incorporates new cloud-based services and demonstrates their applicability across various cloud platforms. The approach supports scalability, performance, and innovation in cloud software design while enabling digital transformation. A methodology for testing cloud software resilience is introduced, focusing on workload-based failure analysis and fault injection using internal and external tests. The chapter emphasizes the importance and benefits of integrating robust resilience design into software development.

Cloud computing technology significantly emerged in various systems to enhance the platform and infrastructure of services. Fog and Edge computing technologies transform computing power and processing close to the end-user and resolve many data processing challenges. Healthcare IoT systems refer to using medical sensors and mobile computing to manage patients' conditions and use cloud-based

Preface

INTRODUCTION

As software development evolves rapidly, incorporating intelligent capabilities with robust security measures is crucial. The "Modern Insights on Smart and Secure Software Development" book is an indispensable resource bridging the gap between Artificial Intelligence (AI), automation, cybersecurity, and software engineering. This book is designed to offer a comprehensive guide to the latest methodologies, tools, and techniques that drive the development of secure and intelligent software systems.

With the increasing complexity of modern software systems, developers and organizations must navigate a landscape that demands both innovation and resilience. This book provides practical insights, case studies, and expert perspectives to help professionals stay ahead in this dynamic field. By addressing key topics such as threat modeling, secure coding practices, and continuous security in DevOps, we equip readers with the knowledge needed to build systems that are intelligent and secure against emerging security attacks. Furthermore, we explore the impact of revolutionary technologies such as Blockchain and the Internet of Things (IoT) on software security.

Our approach blends insights from software engineering, AI, and cybersecurity. Establishing best practices for developing resilient applications. By showcasing research-driven solutions and real-world examples, we strive to advance the secure and smart software systems field.

This book is tailored for a diverse audience, including software developers, cybersecurity experts, AI practitioners, and DevOps professionals. Academics and researchers will find valuable insights into the latest trends and methodologies, while technology managers and executives can leverage this knowledge to drive innovation and risk management strategies. Ultimately, we aim to provide a resource that empowers professionals to stay ahead in the ever-evolving domain of secure and intelligent software systems.

We extend our gratitude to the contributors whose expertise has enriched this volume and the readers who seek to advance their knowledge in this crucial field. We hope this book serves as a valuable guide in navigating the challenges and opportunities of modern software development.

ORGANIZATION OF THE BOOK

Chapter 1: Integrating AI and Machine Learning in Software Development

The advent of artificial intelligence (AI) and machine learning (ML) has transformed software development, introducing unprecedented levels of automation, optimization, and creativity. This chapter explores how AI-driven tools enhance productivity, reduce human error, and improve decision-making through predictive models and sophisticated algorithms. Advanced applications such as AI-powered debugging, generative AI for code synthesis, and predictive analytics for risk assessment are discussed. The chapter also addresses critical challenges, including algorithmic biases, ethical considerations, and integration difficulties, offering practical solutions. Through real-world case studies, it illustrates the tangible benefits of AI and ML in building more intelligent, secure, and adaptable software systems.

Chapter 2: Leveraging Emerging Technologies for Smart and Secure Software Development: Blockchain, IoT, and Beyond

Emerging technologies such as blockchain, the Internet of Things (IoT), and decentralized digital solutions are redefining smart and secure software development. This chapter examines how these technologies enhance data integrity, enable decentralization, and improve system interoperability. Blockchain's smart contracts provide secure automation, while IoT enhances real-time monitoring and decision-making. Given the rise in cybersecurity threats, leveraging these innovations is essential for improving scalability and safeguarding software applications. The chapter also explores future technological trends and their role in building intelligent and resilient digital ecosystems.

Chapter 3: Secure SDLC Frameworks: Leveraging DevSecOps to Enhance Software Security

As software applications become indispensable across industries, security must be embedded in every development phase. This chapter explores the transformation of the Software Development Life Cycle (SDLC) into a Secure SDLC through DevSecOps, which integrates development, operations, and continuous security. The discussion highlights methodologies for threat modeling, automation, collaboration, and monitoring, providing organizations with a strategic approach to mitigating risks. Through theoretical frameworks and case studies, this chapter underscores the business value of proactive security integration, ensuring compliance, and fostering trust in digital solutions.

Chapter 4: Security Testing: Enhancing Cyber Resilience through Vulnerability Management

With cybersecurity threats evolving rapidly, security testing has become crucial to safeguarding critical infrastructure. This chapter presents a comprehensive dataset integrating NESCOR, NIST, and ISO/IEC 27005 insights to analyze vulnerabilities and their impact on assets. Using advanced preprocessing techniques such as Natural Language Processing (NLP) and Artificial Neural Networks (ANNs), the study identifies high-risk vulnerabilities and offers predictive insights for effective mitigation. The chapter highlights the importance of targeted vulnerability management strategies to enhance resilience against cyberattacks.

Chapter 5: AI Tools for Software Development of Real-Time Communication Systems

AI is revolutionizing real-time communication systems, improving scalability, efficiency, and intelligence across telecommunications, healthcare, and business collaboration sectors. This chapter delves into AI-driven tools like machine learning, natural language processing (NLP), and predictive analytics that enhance system performance and reliability. Topics include automated error detection, network condition adaptation, latency optimization, and personalized user experiences. The discussion extends to AI's role in machine-to-machine communication, real-time translation, and intelligent routing, highlighting emerging frameworks and methodologies in modern communication technology.

Chapter 6: Case Studies within Smart and Secure Software Development

Ensuring security, reliability, and resilience in software systems requires adherence to the Secure Software Development Lifecycle (SSDLC). This chapter presents case studies demonstrating the integration of cybersecurity measures into software development. Topics include risk assessment, secure design, and security testing, focusing on minimizing vulnerabilities and complying with regulatory standards. The case studies provide valuable insights into best practices for developing robust software systems that can withstand cyber threats while fostering technological innovation.

Chapter 7: AI-Driven Threat Modeling: Enhancing Risk Assessment in Software Projects

Integrating AI-driven threat modeling into software development enhances security and risk assessment. This chapter presents a comprehensive literature review, case studies, and expert insights into methodologies such as STRIDE and DREAD. Findings indicate that AI adoption improves threat detection and response times, strengthening cybersecurity postures. However, the chapter also emphasizes the need for human oversight and ethical considerations in AI applications. A proactive, cross-functional approach to threat modeling is crucial for safeguarding digital assets against evolving cyber threats.

Chapter 8: Regression Test Selection Approaches: Research Trends in Regression Test Selection of Software Systems

Regression testing ensures that software modifications do not introduce defects but are often resource-intensive. This chapter examines Regression Test Selection (RTS) techniques designed to optimize testing efficiency by selecting a subset of test cases. The discussion categorizes RTS approaches into model-based, code-based, information retrieval-based, fuzzy logic-based, machine learning-based, and security-aware methods. A comparative analysis of static RTS (STARTS) and dynamic RTS (Ekstazi) highlights their effectiveness in balancing safety, precision, and test suite reduction. Future directions for improving RTS methodologies are also explored.

Chapter 9: Cloud-Based Software Architecture for Scalability and Resilience

Cloud-based software development presents unique performance, resilience, and availability challenges. This chapter proposes a hybrid cloud infrastructure approach to designing scalable and resilient software architectures. It explores new cloud-based services and their applications across different platforms. A methodology for testing cloud software resilience through workload-based failure analysis and fault injection is introduced. The chapter emphasizes integrating robust resilience design into software development to support digital transformation initiatives.

Chapter 10: Computing Technologies for Healthcare IoT Software Systems

Cloud, fog, and edge computing technologies are transforming healthcare IoT systems, improving data processing efficiency and patient care. This chapter presents a systematic empirical study analyzing 100 research papers on cloud-based healthcare IoT solutions. It categorizes research efforts, identifies key trends, and examines the technologies employed in these studies. The findings provide valuable insights into the evolution of computing technologies in healthcare, highlighting emerging challenges and potential areas for future research.

Chapter 11: Research Trends in Healthcare IoT Software Systems

This chapter comprehensively studies research trends in cloud, fog, and edge computing technologies within healthcare IoT systems. The study identifies five key research areas: big data, security, network latency, energy efficiency, and quality of service (QoS). While big data remains the most explored research area, energy efficiency is underrepresented and requires further attention. This chapter highlights gaps and opportunities for future studies in healthcare IoT software development by analyzing research trends over the past decade.

CONCLUSION

As we navigate an era defined by rapid technological advancements, the chapters in this volume collectively highlight the transformative role of artificial intelligence, machine learning, cybersecurity, and emerging technologies in modern software development. From AI-driven automation and secure SDLC frameworks to integrating blockchain, IoT, and cloud computing, this book comprehensively explores the innovative methodologies shaping the future of scalable, secure, and intelligent software systems.

Security remains a cornerstone of sustainable digital innovation, and our contributors have provided invaluable insights into vulnerability management, DevSecOps, threat modeling, and regression testing—critical components in fortifying software resilience. Furthermore, the case studies underscore these technologies' practical applications, offering real-world perspectives on the challenges and solutions within contemporary software engineering.

As researchers and practitioners continue to push the boundaries of software development, addressing ethical considerations, algorithmic biases, and the ever-evolving threat landscape is imperative. The discussions within this book emphasize the necessity of proactive security measures, adaptive frameworks, and interdisciplinary collaboration to ensure that software systems remain intelligent, efficient, and resilient in the face of emerging challenges.

We trust this book will be a valuable resource for scholars, industry professionals, and policymakers, encouraging further research and investigation in this vibrant field. By nurturing ongoing collaboration between academia and industry, we can collectively shape a future where software development pushes the boundaries and prioritizes security, trust, and sustainability in the digital era.

Acknowledgment

We want to express our heartfelt gratitude to all authors whose chapters have significantly enriched this book. Your insightful contribution and tireless dedication have advanced intelligent and secure software systems development and inspired fresh perspectives on this domain. Your work stands as great evidence of the power of interdisciplinary collaboration and works as the foundation of the invaluable knowledge compiled in this book.

We are equally grateful to the active reviewers whose thoughtful critiques and great commitment to quality have elevated the standard of this publication. A special thank you goes to the IGI-Global, whose exceptional support and professionalism have been instrumental in bringing this project to realization. Your collective efforts have shaped a resource that we believe will be a cornerstone for future advancements in our field.

Editorial Advisory Board

Introduction

In a time of digital revolution and the relentless pace of technological innovation, the crisis of software developers and security specialists has never been so complex—or pressing. With utmost passion and sincere respect, we introduce Modern Insights on Smart and Secure Software Development. This book arrives at a critical moment in our profession, when the intersection of artificial intelligence, automation, and robust cybersecurity is desirable and essential to the development of the future's resilient, adaptive software systems.

The intersection of smart technologies with secure engineering methodologies has revolutionized the software development landscape. As our culture is becoming increasingly dependent on digital infrastructure, making those systems smart and secure is a problem to be addressed by innovative thinking and interdisciplinary collaboration. This book solves that problem by bridging traditional software engineering with the frontiers of AI research, cybersecurity thinking, and future technological directions. Its integrative approach provides readers with an uncommon blend of theoretical thinking, applied case studies, and cutting-edge methodologies vital to navigating today's digital world.

What is great about the book is its multidisciplinary approach. The authors have easily blended insights from software engineering, security, and artificial intelligence to develop a narrative that is as informative as it is inspiring. They prescribe guidelines for designing secure applications and offer research-backed solutions pushed by strong academic investigation and practical usage. In doing so, they've developed a manual that educates and stimulates creativity—laying the foundation for future breakthroughs in safe software systems.

Throughout the chapters, the book explores how revolutionary technologies such as blockchain, the Internet of Things (IoT), and cloud computing reshape our approach to system design and security. Understanding and mitigating risks through intelligent design and proactive security measures is paramount in this era, where a single vulnerability can have far-reaching consequences. The discussion about secure SDLC frameworks, DevSecOps, and AI-powered threat modeling is particularly relevant; these offer implementable solutions that can alter how organizations safeguard their digital properties without compromising on the benefits of the newest technology advancements.

The degree of depth and sophistication with which complex topics are addressed makes this book an essential reference for a broad variety of readers. For practitioners, the practical examples and case studies provide immediate insight that can be used on current projects. For researchers and academics, the creative approaches and in-depth literature reviews offer a strong basis for future research. For policymakers and business leaders, the strategic observations presented here are critical to inform risk management and innovation policies that enable sustainable digital development.

What makes this book truly remarkable is its interdisciplinary nature. The authors have seamlessly integrated perspectives from software engineering, cybersecurity, and AI to construct a narrative that is as informative as it is inspiring. They outline best practices for developing resilient applications and share research-driven solutions driven through harsh academic research and real-world application. In doing so, they have created a resource that informs and ignites innovation.

We hope ***Modern Insights on Smart and Secure Software Development*** will serve as a reference for everyone dedicated to advancing the secure and smart software systems field. Its wisdom is timely and timeless, offering guidance imperative in an era of relentless change and increasing cyberattacks. As you turn these pages, I encourage you to reflect on the challenges and possibilities ahead and to consider how you might contribute to creating a future in which innovation and security are not adversaries but are inseparably linked.

In closing, this foreword serves as an invitation to immerse yourself in a work that is both a practical manual and a visionary strategy for the future of software development. Whether you are a skilled professional, an academic, or a policymaker, you will find within these pages the tools to enhance your technical expertise and the inspiration to drive meaningful change in our digital world.

Chapter 1
Integrating AI and Machine Learning in Software Development

Taye Iyinoluwa Adeyinka
https://orcid.org/0009-0006-4357-6319
University of Science and Technology, Beijing, China

Kehinde Iyioluwa Adeyinka
https://orcid.org/0009-0009-7685-6693
University of Science and Technology, Beijing, China

ABSTRACT

Software development techniques have changed due to the incorporation of artificial intelligence (AI) and machine learning (ML), which provide previously unheard-of levels of automation, optimisation, and creativity. T. Software developers can reduce human error, increase productivity, and improve decision-making by utilising predictive models and sophisticated algorithms. Advanced applications, including AI-driven debugging, generative AI for code synthesis, and predictive analytics for risk assessment, are also covered in this chapter. Issues including algorithmic biases, ethical concerns, and integration difficulties are discussed alongside workable solutions. The chapter ends with predictions for the future, highlighting how AI and ML can be used to build more intelligent, safe, and flexible software systems. Real-world case studies are incorporated to illustrate the observable advantages and useful applications of AI-ML in contemporary software development.

DOI: 10.4018/979-8-3693-9851-7.ch001

1. INTRODUCTION

In software development, machine learning and artificial Intelligence revolutionized conventional methods by bringing about unprecedented automation, innovation, and optimization. It considers the application, benefits, challenges, and possible future developments of AI and ML concerning the SDLC, (Gadani, 2024). Artificial intelligence best translates to the term for technology, essentially computer systems capable of mimicking processes normally involving human Intelligence. These processes would include, among others, self-correction, reasoning-using rules to reach an approximate or definite conclusion, and acquiring knowledge and rules for applying it, (Paulson, 2024). Machine learning is a subset of AI in which machines use statistical models and algorithms to perform a certain task without explicit instruction by making predictions or drawing inferences from data, (Sarker, 2021).

AI and ML enhance decision-making in software development, automate repetitive procedures, and perform result forecasting, all of which are attributed to increasing productivity and lowering human error possibilities, (Neapolitan & Jiang, 2018). A typical example is where ML models predict where flaws or security vulnerabilities could occur using past data, while AI-driven code generation tools can assist engineers with code snippets, (Ambati, 2023). Among many other fields, software engineering is becoming increasingly recognized as one in which the introduction of AI has the potential to change the game. As AI joins mainstream software development processes, how software is conceptualized, created, tested, and maintained is slowly shifting. AI tools such as computer vision, machine learning, and natural language processing have enhanced and automated many software developments processes, (Wah *et al.,* 1993). However, despite its potential, there are several challenges in effectively integrating AI into the SDLC, (Chafik & Benchekroun, 2020). First and foremost is the issue of the availability and quality of the training data required for creating reliable AI models. The explainability of AI models is another big challenge since software programmers need to understand and trust decisions made by AI systems. Another key challenge is how seamlessly AI tools integrate with the current software engineering environments and processes, (Shah, 2019).

If AI is to be correctly harnessed for software engineering purposes, various issues will have to be resolved, (Qian *et al.*, 2023). Lifecycle. In software engineering, AI is present everywhere, from enhancing software testing and maintenance to actual code production, (Martínez-Fernández *et al.*, 2022). AI refers to the process by which machines can masquerade as human Intelligence to perform tasks normally requiring human cognitive skills such as learning and reasoning. The purpose of machine learning, a lot of branches coming off of artificial Intelligence, is to develop algorithms that permit systems to learn from experiences and improve independently without explicit programming, (Neapolitan & Jiang, 2018). These are increasingly applied to software development to build accuracy, hasten procedures, and make predictability possible.

AI performs many software development roles, from automating repetitive operations to intelligent code generation using predictive analytics to manage risk. For example, GitHub Copilot and OpenAI Codex use natural language processing to develop contextually relevant code suggestions that help engineers speed up their development processes, (Wong *et al.,* 2023). In contrast, machine learning can be used in defect detection, system performance improvement, and vulnerability detection to create reliable and safe software.

1.1 Research Significance

With software engineering and AI as integral domains in technological development, this research is important, as it meets the nexus of the two. This research consequently explores how AI may be integrated at various junctures in the SDLC and also aims to identify the advantages and challenges likely to emanate from such integration. It is within the desire to understand these dynamics that tactics to optimize the advantages while minimizing the drawbacks of AI can be created. A finding of this sort can deliver truly effective, dependable, and maintainable software systems that can tremendously affect software engineering in the future.

This study's contribution can thus be positioned within the ongoing discussion of AI's role in software engineering. It provides insight that will help shape future research and real-world applications within the field. One of the most revolutionary changes in recent decades, AI and ML, have greatly impacted the technology sector and beyond. This study is important for several influences, which it would be setting in terms of efficiency, innovation, and future directions of software engineering. First, this study addresses the growing demand for software solutions' scalability, intelligence, and efficiency. Valuable insights are provided into how automation, predictive analytics, and intelligent algorithms can enhance productivity while reducing time-to-market by examining the uses of AI and ML in the Software Development Lifecycle or SDLC. This information is crucial to those businesses trying to stay ahead in a world increasingly dependent on technology.

Second, the research fosters the quality of software systems. AI-powered code reviews, testing, and debugging make an application resilient, reducing human error. The study also investigates how machine learning algorithms can proactively find security vulnerabilities and improve the system's efficiency to make dependably safe software, (Liu *et al.,* 2018). Indeed, the value of this research goes beyond overcoming the limits of data dependence, algorithmic biases, and even ethical dilemmas in integrating AI and ML. This study stimulates the ethics-sensitive use of AI technologies for software development by suggesting helpful frameworks and solutions.

Last but not least, it influences further developments and trends within the area. It paints a vision of what software engineering will be like in the future by investigating state-of-the-art tools and techniques, such as generative AI and tailored development environments. To researchers, entrepreneurs, and policy makers who are trying to find their feet on the rapidly shifting terrain of technology, this insight is truly priceless. This will play a critical role in shaping the next generation of software development methodologies by fostering creativity and ensuring AI and ML technologies' ethical and successful integration.

1.2 Literature Review

Integrating AI and ML in software development has been a revolutionary phenomenon that powered automation, optimization, and innovation across the SDLC. The paper summarizes research on the uses, advantages, difficulties, and potential of those technologies in software engineering. It thus enables an overall understanding of the current status and the future promises of AI and ML in software development by combining the results of previous studies.

1. Overview of AI and ML in Software Development

Artificial Intelligence is the imitation of human intelligence by machines that enables machines to learn, think, and solve problems. Machine learning, a subbranch of artificial intelligence, has focused on developing algorithms that allow computers to learn and improve without explicit programming, (Choudhury, 2022). The incorporation of these technologies has transformed conventional methods into software development. In their broad review of ML model development in software engineering, Lorenzoni *et al.* (2021) noted problems such as model explainability and deployment complexity. Similarly, Nascimento *et al.* (2020) reviewed the use of software engineering principles in the development of AI/ML systems, focusing on the need for effective processes to meet their particular requirements.

2. AI in Software Testing

AI has significantly improved software testing, especially in automating the creation of test cases, the prediction of defects, and the execution of tests. In their thorough analysis of automated software test case production approaches, Acharya *et al.* (2014) emphasized the application of AI techniques including machine learning, neural networks, and evolutionary algorithms to produce efficient test cases,

(Anand *et al.*, 2013). The amount of manual labor needed for testing can be greatly decreased by using AI-driven technologies that can automatically create and rank test cases according to code analysis.

AI models are also employed in defect prediction, which forecasts the probability of errors in certain code segments by utilising code metrics and historical data. Software reliability is increased through targeted testing and early defect discovery made possible by this predictive capacity, (Saeid, 2020).

3. Applications Across the SDLC

All of the phases of the SDLC have seen the use of both AI and ML. AI solutions make the design process efficient by analyzing huge volumes of market data and user feedback while gathering requirements to identify key features. Machine learning techniques further assist the process of design optimization through simulations over various designs and propose the best designs that optimally balance scalability and performance, (Yan *et al.*, 2015). AI-powered developer tools- GitHub Copilot errors and suggestions in real-time as one code and makes recommendations to speed up the development with the assurance of best practices. AI significantly improves testing and debugging processes, as predictive models identify potential bugs long before a product's release date. Fred and Temkin (2024) further explain that ML could be used for test case generation and outcome analysis, thus minimizing resource usage while increasing reliability. At the maintenance stage, ML provides longevity for the system by predicting issues in the software and making it possible to apply solutions proactively.

4. Integration Benefits

There are revolutionary advantages to using AI and ML in software development. It increases productivity by freeing engineers to concentrate on innovative problems since it automates repetitive operations. The other very important result is the improvement in the quality of the software; AI-driven testing and debugging tools make it more robust and error-free. Acceleration in development cycles allows faster time-to-market, which has become a competitive necessity. Another significant benefit is that this is cost-effective, given that automated processes require less resource utilization and involve only minimum manual labor. Ciresan *et al.* (2012) portrayed the transforming power of AI beyond traditional domains, highlighting the deep learning ability to boost efficiency and precision in resource-intensive tasks, such as medical image processing.

5. Challenges and Considerations

Despite its advantages, integrating AI and ML into software development is challenging. The major obstacle is data dependency since ML models require big datasets for training, which should be correct and represent the avoidance of biases in models. Algorithmic bias is another issue that might result in biased outcomes if the training data selection needs to be carefully made. The Transformer approach changed natural language processing but raised ethical questions about AI-generated content. Other challenges arise from the difficulty in integration, for when AI is integrated into an existing workflow, this often entails a major change in the infrastructure. There are also pressing ethical and legal issues around data privacy and liability. Even here, robust frameworks and guidelines must be drawn up to deal with such issues.

6. Case Examples and Applications

A few case examples bring into the foreground the tangible value of AI and ML in software development. AI-driven test technologies create test cases automatically and minimize the human effort to build accurate test cases. Predictive maintenance, with the support of machine learning, has enhanced the reliability of software systems by finding issues early that may turn into serious problems later. In managing software projects, productivity increased with AI algorithms supporting resource allocation, risk assessment, and timeline prediction. These applications bring the accruing benefits of integrating AI into software engineering and a way forward towards its adoption.

Improvement in AI and ML is directly related to the future of software development. General AI, with its potential to write code upon receiving descriptions in some natural language, has the potential to turn upside down the whole process of developing software. AI-powered project management solutions help streamline processes and ensure successful projects. Another good trend is the development environment, which is to the liking of each developer. As Lorenzoni *et al.* (2021) indicated, adapting traditional software engineering techniques to the peculiarities of machine learning workflows could achieve a smoother integration of these technologies. Another major topical area, considering the increasing concerns regarding the security of AI-enabled systems, is the research and development of AI algorithms oriented towards cybersecurity.

2. AI AND ML IN SOFTWARE DEVELOPMENT

AI and ML are two transformational technologies and building blocks in software development, healthcare, and finance. Though both terms are related, they have different meanings and uses that need to be understood when integrating them into any field. Artificial Intelligence (AI) and Machine Learning (ML) have fundamentally transformed software engineering by automating processes, enhancing efficiency, and enabling smarter systems. Their applications span the entire Software Development Lifecycle (SDLC), including requirements gathering, design, coding, testing, deployment, and maintenance.

2.1 Artificial Intelligence (AI)

Artificial Intelligence is a field in computer science that deals with the development of systems that emulate human Intelligence in carrying out tasks that would otherwise be done by human Intelligence. Such tasks include learning, reasoning, problem-solving, perception, and language understanding. As McCarthy (2007), one of its founders, stated, AI is "the science and engineering of making intelligent machines, especially intelligent computer programs." Artificial intelligence systems are designed to simulate cognitive processes, enabling robots to execute tasks such as visual perception, speech recognition, and decision-making.

Artificial Intelligence can be roughly divided into three types based on capability:

- **Narrow AI (Weak AI)**: Focused on performing a single task efficiently, such as recommendation algorithms or voice assistants like Siri and Alexa.
- **General AI (Strong AI)**: Hypothetical systems capable of performing any intellectual task that a human can do, demonstrating true understanding and learning.
- **Super AI**: An advanced level of intelligence surpassing human capabilities, often discussed in theoretical contexts

There are several subfields in AI technologies:

- **Natural Language Processing:** NLP is a field of AI in which machines can understand and interpret human language and even produce language themselves.
- **Computer Vision:** The study allows machines to make sense of the visual data from the environment, say faces or objects in pictures.
- **Robotics:** By fusing mechanical engineering with artificial Intelligence, it designs intelligent robots.

2.2 Machine Learning (ML)

A subfield of AI, machine learning is related to developing systems that can learn from data without explicit programming and improve their operation over time. Machine learning uses statistical models and algorithms to recognize patterns in data and make predictions and decisions.

According to AI pioneer Samuel (1959), machine learning (ML) is "a field of study that gives computers the ability to learn without being explicitly programmed." ML stresses how machines can modify their performance and improve based on experience.

Types of Machine Learning

Based on the nature of the learning process, the classification of machine learning could be divided into the following three types:

- **Supervised Learning:** The algorithm learns from a labelled dataset consisting of input data matched with the proper output labels. Examples of applications include classifying spam emails and predicting house values.
- **Unsupervised Learning:** Here, the algorithm discovers hidden patterns or groupings within the data that have no labels. Applications involve basic anomaly detection and customer segmentation.
- **Reinforcement Learning:** The algorithm interacts with the environment and learns by rewarding good behaviour. This form of learning is extensively applied in gaming and robotics.

Components of a Machine Learning

- **Dataset:** Most machine learning depends on data to train algorithms. A solid model requires several high-quality, varied datasets.
- **Algorithms:** Common algorithms in machine learning include Neural networks, support vector machines, and decision trees.
- **Model Evaluation:** The performance of a model is checked through methods including confusion matrices cross-validation.

2.3 Differences Between Artificial Intelligence (AI) and Machine Learning (ML)

Table 1. Differences between Artificial Intelligence (AI) and Machine Learning (ML)

AL	ML
Artificial Intelligence refers to the simulation of human intelligence by machines, enabling them to perform tasks that typically require human cognition, such as reasoning, decision-making, and learning. AI encompasses a broad range of techniques and technologies.	Machine Learning is a specialized subset of AI that focuses on algorithms and statistical models that allow machines to learn patterns and improve their performance based on data without explicit programming.
The overarching goal of AI is to create systems capable of mimicking human intelligence. This includes replicating cognitive processes such as thinking, problem-solving, and adapting to new information	The primary goal of ML is to enable machines to learn from data and make accurate predictions or decisions. It focuses on creating models that improve over time with more data.
AI is a broad concept that includes technologies like expert systems, robotics, natural language processing (NLP), computer vision, and ML.	ML is a specific subset within AI that deals with creating data-driven models and predictions.
AI can utilize rule-based systems, decision trees, or even neural networks to mimic human behavior. Not all AI systems involve learning; some operate based on predefined rules and logic.	ML strictly uses data-driven approaches. It employs algorithms like regression, decision trees, and neural networks to recognize patterns and make predictions.
AI systems do not necessarily rely on large datasets. For instance, rule-based AI systems use preprogrammed logic to function effectively.	ML systems are entirely dependent on data. The quality, volume, and variety of datasets significantly influence their accuracy and reliability.

2.4 Applications of AI and ML

Applications emanating from various industries have made AI and ML important constituents of technological growth. This has resulted in AI and ML automating complicated processes, analyzing huge volumes of data, and making decisions judiciously within the software development, manufacturing, healthcare, and financial industries. Therefore, below are discussed the major applications of AI and ML in several industries.

1. Health Care

Artificial Intelligence and Machine Learning have radically changed healthcare by improving diagnosis, planning for treatment, and operational efficiency. AI-enabled tools, such as IBM Watson, assist the physician by analyzing medical data, and the tool suggests diagnosis or treatment plans accordingly, (Singh, 2024). In predictive analytics, machine learning algorithms identify genetic-based disease risk based on genetic information and patient history. For example, machine learning algorithms have achieved outstanding results in malignancy detection from imaging studies at accuracy levels equal that of trained radiologists. Artificially intelligent robotics also plays an important role in surgery. Systems such as the da Vinci Surgical System use AI to enhance surgical accuracy and limit human error. With NLP, insightful information from unstructured clinical notes could be extracted automatically, significantly enhancing decision-making.

2. Finance

AI and ML have immense applications in the banking industry for improving client experience, rationalizing operations, and reducing risks. Fraud detection systems with ML help find abnormal transaction patterns in real-time; thus, financial institutions can avoid cybercrimes. Similarly, robo-advisors like Betterment, which provide personalized investment advice through analysis of user behavior and market pattern analysis, are powered by AI algorithms.

AI is also changing the face of credit scoring. ML models use social data, spending patterns, and credit history to classify applicants' creditworthiness at an unprecedented level of accuracy. In algorithmic trading, AI algorithms process large amounts of information to forecast market fluctuations and execute trades at the best possible times to maximize returns.

3. E-Commerce and Retail

AI and ML have improved retailer customer experiences by offering dynamic pricing, inventory control, and customized suggestions. Recommendation engines, used by Netflix and Amazon, among others, learn a user's preferences and browsing history to offer relevant merchandise or content. While ML models help shops predict demand and optimize inventory, AI chatbots improve customer service by responding to frequently asked questions in real-time. AI-powered dynamic pricing algorithms maximize profitability by adjusting product prices in real-time, considering factors like demand, competition, and user behavior.

4. Transportation

AI and ML form the backbone of intelligent transportation systems and driverless cars. The autonomous vehicles of companies like Tesla employ computer vision and reinforcement learning algorithms that make constant, real-time decisions to handle highways and obstacles. AI-powered traffic signal controls analyze traffic flow patterns to avoid congestion and optimize the signal timings accordingly. ML models help services like Uber and Lyft predict demand and optimize routes and prices optimally. AI solutions in supply chain management and logistics also result in higher delivery accuracy and route optimization using less fuel.

5. Production

AI and ML boost productivity in manufacturing by automating processes, assuring quality, and maintaining predictability. Predictive maintenance systems analyze sensor data to predict equipment breakdowns and take early measures to reduce potential downtime. Computer vision is deployed to detect flaws in products while ensuring consistency in product repetition during the quality control process. Automation of repetitive operations using AI-powered robotics increases productivity by reducing labor costs. For example, robots on production lines apply machine learning by learning tasks themselves and improving their accuracy.

6. Software Development

AI and ML have completely changed the direction of software development by automating code creation, testing, and debugging. Tools like GitHub Copilot apply NLP to suggest code snippets, hence making it faster for developers to build software applications. Machine learning techniques predict weak points in code and then build automated test cases that improve software testing. AI-driven solutions monitor software performance and optimize deployment plans for preventive maintenance.

7. Learning

AI and ML in education enhance the administrative processes and provide personalized learning experiences. One is Khan Academy, where adaptive learning systems use student performance analytics to move students through a skills-based progression at their optimal pace. Whereas ML algorithms review the performance and behavioral data identifying those students who are considered at risk, AI-powered chatbots address queries coming from students. In addition to the above, grading systems reduce teachers' burdens because they can correctly grade assignments and leave remarks.

8. Agriculture

Applications of AI and ML in agriculture enhance its sustainability and productivity. With precision farming techniques, farmers can optimize irrigation, fertilization, and pest control by applying ML algorithms that analyze crop health, weather data, and soil conditions. AI-enabled drones can monitor large areas and, therefore, provide valuable information for better crop management. AI and ML monitor energy effectively and optimally harness renewable energy. Smart grids employ machine learning models that predict energy consumption for efficient distribution of resources. AI systems employed in renewable energy analyze the weather trends to find out ways of improving the performance of wind turbines and solar panels.

10. Entertainment

AI and ML have applications in improving visual effects, optimizing content creation, and personalizing user experiences within the entertainment industry. ML sorts out recommendations of content to be provided by streaming services such as Netflix and Spotify based on the customer's preference. AI-powered tools help scriptwriting, editing, and CGI rendering, thus reducing production expenses and time.

While AI and ML technologies improve, their applications will continue to multiply. These two have been remodeling industries into new worlds, such as healthcare, banking, transportation, and education, by becoming more productive, making wiser decisions, and creating innovative solutions to some pressing challenges. Their adaptability and variety make AI and ML block-and-mortar components in fulfilling the needs of a world that faces rapid changes.

2.5 AI and ML: A Symbiotic Relationship

Machine learning and artificial intelligence are the two game-changing technologies that are considered indispensable in encouraging innovation across a wide array of industries. Machine learning forms the backbone of AI in that it gives computers the ability to learn from data and improve over time, while AI focuses on replicating human intelligence to perform complex tasks. These technologies enhance and build on one another's skills, realizing their fullest potential owing to the symbiotic relationship engendered by interdependence.

Most AI systems of today are built on machine learning, which grants them capabilities for inspecting large datasets, noticing patterns, and making sound decisions without explicit programming. With machine learning, artificial intelligence systems are flexible enough to handle such complicated and dynamic data in real-time. For example, in one of the basic areas of artificial intelligence, natural language processing, there is a need for ML algorithms to understand or generate human language. This includes the applications of chatbots, virtual assistants such as Siri and Alexa, and machine translation apps such as Google Translate, among others, powered by ML models trained on large text datasets for instance, Goodfellow (2016).

On the other hand, AI extends the use of ML by embedding these into other technologies, such as robotics, computer vision, and rule-based reasoning in solving higher-order problems. Examples include the development of the self-driving automobile. AI drives key decision-making processes, like route optimization and adaptation to traffic conditions. In contrast, object detection, lane recognition, and the behaviour of other vehicles on the road are predicted using ML techniques. The fusion of AI and ML utilizes mutual benefits to enable autonomous cars to work safely and effectively in on-road real-life environments. It is eminently clear that there are many areas where AI and ML complement each other. ML will have systems that can learn from input data and, over time, become increasingly intelligent and effective. Large AI models improve ML through richer contextual reasoning and decision-making. In domains such as fraud detection, AI systems leverage additional contextual information to look at the likelihood of fraudulent behaviour. Meanwhile, ML models will review transactional data in search of anomalies. The studies were based on Ngai *et al.* (2011).

Another domain in which this interplay of AI and ML can revolutionize healthcare. AI diagnosis systems can spot early illnesses, even cancer, by analyzing patient data and medical pictures with the help of machine learning models. For example, machine learning algorithms have matched dermatologists' performance in diagnosing skin cancer by training them in large collections of labelled photos. These AI systems extend their precision and efficiency in medical decision-making by offering actionable insights and suggesting treatment approaches, (Khalifa, Albadawy, & Iqbal, 2004). It merges with AI and ML, which provide personalized experience in the e-commerce business. For the recommendation systems of services offered by Netflix and Amazon, for example, ML algorithms analyze user behavior to predict preferences. Adding context to such suggestions with more detailed data, including demographics and seasonal trends, an AI system enhances and provides seamless viewing or buying experience. In the same breadth, intelligent transportation systems like driverless cars and ride-hailing services are driven by AI and ML. Ride-hailing services use ML models to predict demand, optimize routes, and dynamically price. Various applications where AI systems employ real-time data to make justifiable decisions about resource allocation and traffic management greatly improve the efficiency and adaptability of such transport systems. The interaction of AI and ML ensures efficiency in transport systems.

Even though AI and ML work seamlessly, problems will always exist. One of the major challenges revolves around the quality of the data. Effective ML requires a whole lot of datasets comprising high-quality data. Inaccurate or biased data could compromise the effectiveness of the ML models and, subsequently, the AI systems that depend on them. Ethical issues also ensue due to the tendency of ML-based AI systems to accidentally perpetuate biases in the underlying training data, with discriminatory consequences. Finally, in resource-scarce environments, in particular, there exists a heightened possibility that the processing power demands of training and deploying AI-ML systems place limits on this technology. However, Goodfellow (2016) states that several challenges are met along the way in integrating AI and ML. Areas like XAI have come forward to make ML models much more interpretable for better transparency and gains in trust in AI systems. Hardware developments, such as quantum computing, will further enhance the scalability and performance of AI-ML systems. Their interaction will keep forming the backbone of complex problem-solving and intelligent automation across industries as these technologies gain greater inroads. AI and ML will work in a powerful combination, wherein AI extends the capacities of intelligent systems while ML develops learning mechanisms. Their mutually reinforcing partnership has enabled revolutionary applications in e-commerce, health care, finance, and other areas. Understanding and using this interaction will allow organizations and developers to fully exploit these technologies to create even more intelligent and powerful solutions. In this regard, its ever-changing relationship promises to have a lasting effect on innovative development in the future.

2.6 Transforming the Software Development Lifecycle

AI and ML significantly improve the output at every stage of SDLC by smoothing out the process.

- **Requirement Analysis and Gathering**

AI-driven NLP technologies analyze requirement documents, historical data, and user input for key elements and ambiguities. For instance, AI algorithms can classify and prioritize user wants so that development is focused on high-value features. ML models provide insights into user preference and market demand by predicting the trends from historical project data.

- **Design Optimization**

AI-powered tools generate an enormous number of design alternatives, creating performance, scalable, and maintainable designs. When analyzing past design trends, machine learning algorithms recommend the best combination based on previous successes. AI-powered simulation tools test the designs against multiple scenarios to detect potential bottlenecks or weaknesses early.

- **Automated Coding**

The rise of AI has really refactored the way one does coding, especially with tools like GitHub Copilot. NLP combined with ML produces code snippets, functions, or even classes. Besides saving time, such technologies ensure that the best practices and coding standards are adhered to. Also, ML models scan the existing codebases for code reusability, hence improving development efficiency.

- **Debugging and Testing**

AI and ML achieve automation in testing by constructing test cases, executing them, and then analyzing the results. The machine learning methods allow focused testing based on weak points in code that will be exhibited. Debugging tools use AI to source faults' root causes and provide developers with useful information. Reinforcement learning is used for dynamic testing in the simulation of user interactions to ensure the software behaves as it should under real-life circumstances.

- **Optimization of Deployment**

AI solutions minimize downtime and ensure seamless deployment by recommending optimal deployment options based on real-time indicators and historical data. In fact, AI orchestrates containerized apps in a cloud-native environment, which means dynamically distributing resources according to workload patterns predicted by machine learning models.

- **Predictive Maintenance**

It's now stretching to predict analytics, where ML algorithms learn about system logs, performance data, and user behaviour to predict likely mistakes. AI-driven systems will allow for predictable performance, with continuous software monitoring for anomalies and automatically deploying updates when necessary.

2.7 Enhancing Software Quality and Security with AI and ML

AI and ML have revolutionized the way software quality and security are approached in engineering today. Manual and error-prone activities that were once reactive are now automated, intelligent, and accurate. AI and ML are setting standards for delivering reliable, secure, and efficient software through their support for automated testing, real-time monitoring, and predictive analytics. Testing software automates creating, executing, and analyzing test cases with the help of AI and ML.

In this case, this ensures complete test coverage with minimal user intervention. For instance, machine learning models study previous testing data to precisely identify zones of codebases viewed as being at high risk in a targeted testing process that saves time and cost. It dynamically assesses software performance under simulated real-world scenarios, changing loads and user behaviour through AI-powered systems. The reinforcement learning models can mock complex user interactions to ensure the apps work reliably under various circumstances. When flaws are detected at the earliest stages, fixing such issues leads to huge reductions in repair costs while increasing the quality of software.

AI and ML also do very well in debugging. Machine learning algorithms check source code for typical mistakes related to, for example, incorrect input validation or potential memory leaks. Thanks to AI, solutions like DeepCode or SonarQube scan codebases offer meaningful recommendations on what has to be modified. Predictive debugging enables developers to effectively concentrate the effort by using machine learning models that indicate the most probable areas of code containing bugs. AI-powered error traceability finds the root causes of issues, making debugging easier and reducing the time taken to resolve failures. Real-time monitoring of the system and anomaly detection are the cornerstones of security and dependability in software systems. Artificial Intelligence systems can be programmed to continuously check log data, user behaviour, and performance indicators for unusual patterns, which might indicate a possible weakness or failure. For example, unexpected spikes in latency or memory consumption can be spotted by machine learning models and thus enable proactive measures before users experience any downtime. Anomaly detection systems based on unsupervised learning identify unusual or unexpected events that otherwise may go undetected by traditional methods, as well as deviations from normal system behaviour. This proactive approach ensures there will be no disturbance in the user experience and enhances the system's stability. AI and ML are now an essential part of security and greatly help identify vulnerabilities to reduce risks. Machine learning algorithms perform static and dynamic analyses on software to look for potential security threats. While dynamic analysis inspects runtime behaviour to discover unforeseen consequences, static analysis examines source code to find possible vulnerabilities, such as SQL injection points or cross-site scripting. AI-powered IDS analyses system records and network traffic in real time to identify malicious activities or unauthorized access, (Prince *et al.*, 2024). Because they are flexible, such systems can become a hard barrier against new online threats by learning from continuously changing attack patterns.

Patch management heavily relies on AI, too, as the latter automates identifying and applying security upgrades. AI systems minimize the risk of exploitation by prioritizing essential updates to vulnerabilities, thus carrying out dependency and configuration analysis. AI also supports compliance management by automating regulatory testing and producing detailed reports covering standards such as PCI-DSS or GDPR, (Shabina *et al.,* 2024). This will ensure that the security standards are met throughout the life of a program and decrease the manual labor of staff. Besides, there are a few other important contributions of AI and ML to software engineering; among them, the enhancement of code quality stands out, (Nguyen-Duc *et al.,* 2023). Intelligent tools, like GitHub Copilot and OpenAI Codex, assist developers by suggesting changes in context to maintain consistency and adhere to best practices. AI-powered linters analyze code for syntactical and stylistic errors to improve the readability and manageability of codebases, (Mendoza Juan, 2024). Furthermore, machine learning algorithms find segments of the code that are either too wasteful or duplicated and suggest reworking those to bring in much-needed scalability and speed.

AI and ML have been applied to transform software quality and security into DevSecOps procedures. AI-powered continuous security testing now automates the review of vulnerabilities from the first line of code to the last deployment. Machine learning models consider dependencies, external integrations, and even configuration variables while estimating the risk of security vulnerability. This gives quite valuable insights for developers to quickly and effectively solve issues. AI and ML lessen the breach risk by decreasing traditional security procedures' time and monetary cost, allowing security to be baked into the development process itself, (Brundage *et al.,* 2018). Artificial Intelligence and Machine Learning provide powerful fraud and threat detection systems in those systems dealing with sensitive user data, such as financial software. Transaction patterns are analyzed by machine learning models so that irregularities suggesting fraud can be found. For example, unsupervised learning systems flag transactions that need further investigation simply because they are outliers from normal user behaviour. AI-powered threat intelligence systems compile information from various sources to forecast new threats and suggest defences for total defense against sophisticated online attacks.

AI and ML are also driving the future of software security, and quality terms such as explainable AI, or XAI, provide a substantial basis for making machine learning models more interpretable and, hence, reliable. This is critical in security applications where decision-making processes need to be visible. Quantum computing developments are likely to increase significantly the processing capabilities of AI and ML systems, opening the door towards even more complex methods for ensuring software security and quality, (Rane *et al.,* 2024). In short, AI and ML revolutionized the software quality and security landscapes with much faster, smarter, and more reliable tools and methodologies than conventional approaches. These technologies have made software testing more automated, enhanced debugging, improved monitoring, and strengthened security, fulfilling the highest robustness and reliability criteria. Since these technologies will continue to evolve further, the role of AI and

ML in software engineering will be immensely relevant, as such developments spur further innovation and set new standards for security and quality in the digital era.

2.8 Key Findings About AI and ML Enhancing Software Quality and Security

1. Revolutionizing Software Testing

AI and ML revolutionize software testing by automating processes, anticipating possible problems, and guaranteeing thorough test coverage. Traditional test techniques rely heavily on prewritten test scripts and manual input. Both are labor-intensive and prone to human error. With AI and ML, test procedures become dynamic and automated.

- **Automated Test Case Generation:** Various machine learning models study user requirements, historical testing data, and current codebases to generate relevant test cases automatically, (Pan *et al.,* 2022). This will ensure that important aspects of the software, such as edge cases, are tested. For instance, to find out any potential usability issues, reinforcement learning systems model user interactions with a software system in a variety of scenarios.
- **Dynamic Testing:** AI technologies, on the other hand, do this in a real-world scenario by mimicking all the variations of load, network, and other circumstances, including users. These techniques dynamically adjust the test cases based on the incoming, real-time feedback of the results for more program robustness in different situations.
- **Optimizing Regression Testing:** Automated regression testing methods continuously track changes to the codebase and test only the impacted portions, accelerating the development process by saving manual time and effort spent on repetitive testing cycles.

2. Applying Predictive Analytics to Enable Proactive Debugging

Substantial debugging for AI and ML is one of the most important enhancements to ensure quality; both issue discovery and resolution are automated. Predictive debugging: Through machine learning models, past defect data is analyzed to determine which code segments are most likely to host errors. This saves time when looking for faults and ensures that important problems will be fixed sooner rather than later because developers can focus on areas where the risk is higher.

- **Automated Root Cause Analysis:** AI-driven technologies track the source of mistakes, presenting developers with comprehensive information about the root causes. Treating the symptoms of an underlying issue ensures consistency in reliability over long periods.
- **Self-healing:** Advanced debugging systems can implement a self-curing mechanism. The AI systems identify common mistakes and apply repairs, like patching vulnerabilities, restarting services, or reallocating resources. This increases the system's resiliency and reduces downtime.

3. Real-Time Monitoring and Anomaly Detection

AI and ML improve software monitoring through real-time anomaly detection and predictive maintenance. These features guarantee that any possible problems will be highlighted and resolved before they become serious.

- **Anomaly detection:** Unsupervised machine learning models analyze system logs, performance indicators, and user behaviour to identify deviations from usual patterns. Unexpected latency or resource usage spikes are considered unnatural and need to be checked immediately.
- **Predictive Maintenance:** Given the historical performance data, teams can engage in preventive care by applying ML models to predict when systems might fail or reach their limit. This reduces operational costs and unplanned downtime.
- **Continuous Monitoring:** AI-powered monitoring solutions will give teams insight into software performance and security in real-time and thus identify problems the very moment they occur and resolve them at this stage. All these proactive measures reduce the risk of service disruptions and guarantee zero defects in customer experience.

4. Software Security Improvement

The imperative use of AI and ML in improving software security can find vulnerabilities and detect and mitigate attacks in real-time.

- **Static and Dynamic Code Analysis:** AI technologies review source code for potential security vulnerabilities, such as buffer overflows, SQL injection points, cross-site scripting, and runtime behaviour, to identify potential security vulnerabilities that might not be apparent via source code analysis.
- **Intrusion Detection Systems:** AI-powered IDS analyze the logs of systems and network traffic to discover unauthorized access or malicious activities,

(Prince *et al.,* 2024). These systems have strict protection against higher-level cyber threats, adapting to constantly changing attack vectors.

- **Fraud Detection:** Machine learning algorithms trace transaction trends and detect suspicious patterns hinting at fraud. As an example, unsupervised learning algorithms flag unusual patterns in financial transactions, such as sudden changes in spending habits, and highlight them for further review.

5. Improvement in Code Quality

AI and ML facilitate better code quality by identifying inefficiencies, enforcing best practices, and making intelligent recommendations.

- **Intelligent Code Completion:** Applications like GitHub Copilot and OpenAI Codex use active machine learning to make context-sensitive code suggestions. Following coding conventions, such tools enable developers to write readable, consistent, productive code.
- **Code Refactoring:** Machine learning algorithms can examine a codebase for disposable or ineffective code sections and recommend more maintainable and scalable optimization with better performance, (Bhatore, 2020).

6. Integration into DevSecOps

AI-driven linters do syntax and style checks to enforce best practices and ensure the codebase is maintainable. Summer '22 brings a whole lot more. Integration with DevSecOps: AI and ML have integrated security and quality into all stages of the SDLC.

- **AI Solutions for Continuous Security Testing:** Automation in security tests across development stages ensures the detection and fixation of bugs in time, reducing the chances of a security slip post-deployment.
- **Risk Assessment and Compliance:** Machine learning models check dependencies for potential security risks, configurations, and integrations with third-party services. AI systems also automate compliance checks for legal and ethical parameters involving regulatory standards such as GDPR or PCI-DSS.

7. Improved Cost and Time-to-Market Efficiency

Teams can thus make better products faster because of the automation and intelligence that AI and ML bring to the software development process. These technologies eliminate the need for manual labor and, therefore, operating expenses for repetitive tasks such as testing and debugging, freeing resources for innovation.

8. Transparency and Ethical Issues

In contrast, emerging technologies like XAI aim to bridge the gap by enhancing the interpretability of ML models for ethical issues. Transparency in decision-making processes, especially for security or fraud detection, creates trust in automated systems.

Integrating AI and ML into software engineering changed quality and security criteria. These solutions ensure the software products' robustness, reliability, and security by making testing automatic, proactive debugging possible, monitoring better, and strengthening security. The early and effective resolution of potential problems reduces costs and quickens delivery, setting new benchmarks for excellence in developing software. Further development in AI and ML will contribute to software security and quality, pushing further innovation and revolutions in the sector.

3. RESEARCH OBJECTIVES

The "Integrating AI and Machine Learning in Software Development" chapter will explain and illustrate the influence AI and ML technologies have on the SDLC process. In this chapter, the spotlight will fall on an in-depth understanding of how AI and ML technologies perform in terms of automation, smoothing processes, enhancing decision-making processes, and assuring the quality and security of software.

More precisely, these objectives include:

1. To understand how AI and ML work within the stages of SDLC, this section covers AI and ML usage in gathering requirements, design optimization, code generation, testing, deployment, and maintenance, (Soni *et al.,* 2023). Tools like GitHub Copilot use AI to help engineers make intelligent code recommendations. This improves development speed.
2. Explanations of how the use of AI and ML in software engineering offers benefits include understanding the analysis of how such technologies facilitate faster time-to-market, improved scalability, fewer errors, and increased productivity.
3. **To understand how ML and AI are useful in enhancing software quality:** This chapter presents how AI-powered testing tools automate test case creation, run tests dynamically, and provide effective debugging information.

Predictive debugging ensures that defects found earlier get corrected and reduces manufacturing failure costs.

4. **How AI and ML will Impact Software Security:** The objective was to establish how machine learning models in IDS enhance threat detection and response and how AI technologies find vulnerabilities through static and dynamic analysis. The findings were, therefore, in agreement with the study by Yaseen (2023), which explained the function of machine learning in risk mitigation.
5. **Evaluate the extent to which AI/ML contributes to wise decision-making:** The chapter elaborates on how AI has been helping project management make data-driven decisions, analyze risks, and allocate resources. For instance, AI systems predict delays in projects and proffer remedies for the successful completion of a project.
6. **Suggest future trends and challenges in implementing AI and ML in software development**: It touches on debates related to data dependency, computational demands, and ethical considerations, and it emphasizes state-of-the-art technologies such as Generative AI and XAI. These developments have been crucial to the future generation of smart software systems, as noticed by Esteva *et al.* (2017).

The chapter attempts to do this by providing a roadmap for integrating AI and ML into software development, emphasizing their transformation potential in the face of real-world issues and challenges.

3.1 Methodology

It includes systematic reviews, empirical investigations, case studies, experimental assessments, and simulations to investigate how AI and ML are integrated into software development. This approach aims to solve problems, investigate probable future developments, and describe how these technologies enhance the SDLC, (Karim *et al.*, 2016). In developing evidence-based insights, the research uses a richness of current literature, industrial practices, and experimental findings derived from various research methodologies.

First of all, this work is based on a systematic review of the literature. Reviewing covers the findings, classification, and evaluation of academic publications, business reports, and technical papers that detail AI and ML applications in software development. For instance, Lorenzoni *et al.* (2021) conducted an extensive SLR on ML models in software engineering and raised key issues such as deployment bottlenecks and model interpretability. Nascimento *et al.* (2020) have investigated the application of software engineering principles to AI/ML systems while uncovering some pretty useful integration strategies. These series of studies together provide a clear state-of-the-art view today, pointing at the knowledge gaps and further research needed.

Empirical studies are fundamental in this study paradigm since they focus on real applications of AI and ML in software engineering. Surveys and interviews conducted among developers, project managers, and QA engineers provide rich information on the benefits and limitations encountered after adopting AI/ML techniques. Albrecht (2023), while reviewing the effects of AI-driven automated testing tools on large projects, find significant improvements in defect detection rates and resource allocation. In addition, Eshraghian *et al.* (2024) researched the development of AI-powered code generators such as GitHub Copilot. They discovered significant increases in the productivity of developers with corresponding improvements in the quality of the code. Such investigations are basic to understanding how theoretical developments realize real benefits in an industrial context.

Case studies represent state-of-the-practice examples of companies successfully integrating AI and ML into software development processes. For example, Microsoft provided a case study showing their work to integrate deployment optimization and AI-driven automated testing into DevOps pipelines, showing clear quantitative improvements in speed and quality for their software delivery. In this regard, Amazon,, highlighted the scalability and effectiveness of integrating these into software systems by demonstrating how ML models could be utilized in the recommendation engine. These case studies provide practical insights and highlight the challenges faced during implementation and the strategies used to overcome them.

Experimental evaluations are an integral part of this research study, which involves controlled testing of AI/ML tools and methodologies, (Idowu **et al**., 2024). For example, Sharma et al. have evaluated several AI-based static code analysis techniques in terms of precision and recall using ground-truth data. A study by Fu et al. determined that ML algorithms perform better compared to traditional statistical methods for predicting software issues. In an experiment modelled after real-world circumstances, researchers can test the efficiency and scalability of AI/ML solutions under real-world conditions.

Another important stage is the development and testing of tools and frameworks. For example, the MLOps framework was designed to resolve scalability and deployment reliability issues by making the integration of ML models into the processes of software operation easy to work with, (Pelluru, 2023). Leading reviewers discuss two AI-powered code analysis tools, SonarQube and DeepCode, regarding proficiency in automatic code quality analysis, bug detection, and insight provision to developers. These tools undergo various tests in both experimental and production environments to measure the effectiveness of the tools on software quality and productivity.

Modelling and simulations will be done to predict how AI and ML techniques will impact SDLC, (Smith & Wei, 2024). Reinforcement learning models, for example, could model dynamic user behaviour to test software performance against different scenarios. They are also used in vulnerability modelling to ensure that AI-based intrusion detection systems keep pace with emerging cyber threats and verify their efficacy. Thus, these methods allow researchers to look at potential outcomes and refine them before applying them in the real world.

Some comparative research has been performed comparing AI/ML approaches with traditional software engineering methodologies. For instance, Karmakar (2024) discussed rule-based systems with AI-driven test automation frameworks and demonstrated that AI solutions are more flexible and scalable. In this respect, the results from Nallapati and Manning (2008) also give evidence of superior predictive skills of machine learning compared to statistical approaches in estimating software work.

For most of its results, this survey relies on various data sources to ensure dependable results. Open datasets, shared on websites like GitHub, Kaggle, and OpenML, contain real-world data for training and testing machine learning models. Industry data collected in collaboration with companies covers user behaviour, development processes, defect reports, etc. Synthetic datasets represent scenarios where real-world data is unavailable, allowing focused studies in those areas.

The class of research bears great importance towards ethical issues. The biases in AI and ML systems' training data and decision-making procedures are investigated. Investigating strategies like eXplainable AI-XAI that improve the interpretability of ML models would build confidence among developers and stakeholders. Data security and regulatory compliance issues due to data sharing are handled by investigating privacy preservation techniques such as federated learning and differential privacy.

Validation and metrics are important components that ensure the study's findings are accurate and applicable. Some metrics used to test the performance of the defect detection model include precision, recall, accuracy, and F1-score. Regarding the effectiveness of AI-driven technologies, the metrics involve execution time and resource usage. Benchmarks have been set to compare new tools and processes to pre-existing solutions to ascertain their efficacy.

In other words, this broad research design encompasses everything from case studies to empirical research, systematic reviews, experimental evaluation, and simulation regarding how AI and ML improve software development. Integrating theoretical analysis with hands-on experimentation ensures that results are reliable and adaptable. It will also facilitate the identification of best practices, challenges, and possible ways to integrate AI and ML into software engineering.

3.2 Application of AI and ML in Software Development

Artificial Intelligence (AI) and Machine Learning (ML) have become transformative technologies in software engineering, revolutionizing the Software Development Lifecycle (SDLC) through automation, efficiency, and intelligence. From requirements gathering to deployment and maintenance, AI and ML provide innovative solutions to traditional challenges, making the software development process faster, more efficient, and more robust. Below is an in-depth exploration of their applications.

1. Requirements Analysis and Gathering

AI and ML are very helpful in collecting and evaluating software requirements. They automate extracting relevant data from market trends, user reviews, and historical data. NLP techniques examine unstructured text data from customer evaluations or support tickets to find common user demands and possible weaknesses in current systems.

For instance, IBM Watson analyzes user reviews and comments to identify new patterns and issues customers are facing. AI minimizes project failures caused by ambiguous requirements by making them well-defined and in consensus with user expectations through correct and actionable insights.

2. Automatic Code Generation

Besides natural language input, today's AI-powered development tools can autocomplete and suggest snippets code. Relevant recommendations for these tools provide help developers be productive by utilizing machine learning models trained on millions of code snippets.

For instance, GitHub Copilot, powered by OpenAI's Codex, makes context-aware code suggestions to programmers, enabling them to create efficient code faster.

This will free developers to concentrate their efforts on solving complex problems by reducing the time spent performing mundane coding activities. Further, it retains standards and consistency in the code.

3. Software Testing and Quality Assurance

With AI and ML, software testing becomes more enhanced and automated, guaranteeing that applications are reliable and defect-free. AI-powered tools can also simulate real-life scenarios, generate test cases at runtime, and analyze test results to detect errors. On the other hand, the ML models allow more focused testing by highlighting those sections of the code that are very likely to contain defects.

For instance, AI-driven test solutions from Selenium can run and analyze test cases independently, providing quicker feedback on code changes. Fast and accurate testing with automation raises test coverage, reduces the chances that some flaws may go unnoticed, and generally speeds up development.

4. Debugging and Error Resolution

AI and ML have revolutionized the usually time-consuming debugging stage of software development. These tools analyze codebases for vulnerabilities and provide valuable insights into problem resolution. Machine learning algorithms can predict regions of code that may contain bugs by spotting patterns in historical defect data.

For instance, SonarQube helps developers find solutions faster by analyzing source code for potential vulnerabilities and providing its remediation. AI-based debugging tools improve the stability and dependability of the software system by reducing time and effort in finding and fixing faults.

5. Maintenance and Monitoring

AI and ML enable real-time monitoring and preventive software maintenance, ensuring smooth performance and minimizing downtime. Predictive analytics, working on system logs and performance measures, identifies patterns, allowing it to forecast problems well before they become more severe. Anomaly detection systems flag up anomalous activity or performance snags by monitoring real-time software behaviour.

For instance, Datadog monitors infrastructure performance using ML-powered monitoring software for anomalies and blocking system failures. Preventive maintenance and monitoring will lessen operational costs while improving user experience, ensuring dependability in software systems.

6. Improvement in Security

Security is paramount in software development. AI/ML provides innovative tools for identifying vulnerabilities and mitigating risks. AI-powered IDS studies system records and network data to detect illegal activities. Machine learning algorithms perform static and dynamic code analyses to search for potential security vulnerabilities.

Darktrace uses AI to spot and neutralize online threats in real-time, its defences adjust with evolving attack patterns. AI-powered security solutions improve the resiliency of software systems, protect private information, and ensure security guidelines are followed.

3.3 Advantages of AI and ML in Software Development

AI and Machine, learning in software development, have brought about a few advantages that have revolutionized the Software Development Lifecycle. In this section, six major benefits are highlighted and explained in detail:

1. **Higher Productivity and Faster Time-to-Market:** AI and ML automate most repetitive operations, such as code generation, testing, and debugging, since basic factors can contribute to the total speeding-up of development processes. That's where GitHub Copilot and all the other tools that can provide real-time code suggestions come into play. Developers can stick to solving hard problems, not reinventing the wheel with manual coding. Also, teams build better quality software faster since automated testing and debugging further reduce development cycles. This acceleration ensures that businesses maintain their competitive advantage because they can respond quickly to market demands.
2. **Better Software Quality:** AI-driven solutions ensure a thorough and dynamic level of testing by authoring test automation scripts and emulating real-world scenarios to detect bugs and performance issues. Machine learning algorithms identify high-risk areas in the codebase and prioritize those sections for comprehensive testing. This minimizes mistakes, reduces the chances of flaws in production, and delivers reliable software that meets customers' expectations. Increased consumer pleasure and trust in product success are the outcomes of better-quality assurance.
3. **Better Security and Threat Detection:** AI and ML improve security- security-critical components of modern software- by viewing flaws, spotting threats and impending cyberattacks. Static code analysis tools and AI-powered intrusion detection systems study network traffic, codebases, and system logs for anomalies that need to be handled instantly. With each new attack pattern, the machine learning models self-adjust. This ensures that the defences are robust. Better security means keeping private information safe, but most importantly, it is a seal of legality and instils user confidence.
4. **Predictive Maintenance and Real-Time Monitoring:** AI and ML enable predictive maintenance to parse system logs and performance indicators to detect possible disruptions before they happen. This, in turn, allows teams to take up proactive problem-solving with the help of real-time monitoring technologies

capable of anomaly and bottleneck detection. Operating expenses go down while the assured and consistent performance of the system is guaranteed with the least downtime. Since interruptions are prevented before consumers are impacted, organizations benefit through improved reliability and user experience.

5. **Cost Efficiency and Scalability:** AI and ML reduce the operational costs and resources required because most manpower-intensive tasks are automated. The cost of post-implementation problems or system failure is minimized due to monitoring and predictive analytics. In addition, AI-driven solutions assure scalability without compromising quality by relying on optimizing resource utilization during peak demand. Because scaling smoothly and meeting the demands of an increasingly larger user base can be more easily accommodated, this, in turn, assists organizations in adapting well to fluctuations in the market.
6. **Intelligent Applications and Personalized User Experience:** AI and ML allow the development of intelligent and adaptive software systems that teach their users. The applications use machine learning algorithms to analyze the preferences and behaviour of users to offer predictive features, adaptive interfaces, and personalized recommendations. Recommendation engines like Netflix and Amazon offer purchase or content recommendations based on user preferences. This level of personalization will enhance user satisfaction and engagement, ensuring loyalty and driving business growth.

Integrating AI and ML into software development has benefits that are not equal to any other approach. These benefits include enhanced productivity, quality, security, proactive maintenance, cost efficiency, and personalized user experiences. These technologies have redesigned the SDLC to leverage businesses in developing reliable, scalable, and user-focused software as they try to keep an edge over others in an increasingly competitive market, (Salmani, 2023). AI and ML will continue to reshape software development as they forge further.

3.4 Result and Discussion

Integrating AI and ML into software development has shown revolutionary effects in many phases of the SDLC. The findings indicate significant gains in scalability, security, productivity, and software quality, all of which agree with the increasing demand for intelligent and efficient software systems. This section discusses results supported by real examples and knowledge acquired from previous research.

AI and ML are showing phenomenal capability in increasing the speed of software development by automating tedious tasks related to code generation, testing, and debugging. By using tools like GitHub Copilot powered by OpenAI's Codex, it will be possible for developers to produce more context-sensitive snippets of code and complete functions with much higher speed. This leads to a more effective coding process. A study by Coleman (2024) showed that teams using AI-assisted coding tools have cut development time by as much as 40%, thus proving the efficiency of such technologies in the real world.

The second key finding concerns the impacts on software quality: AI-powered automated testing covers higher test coverage and better fault detection. Automatic testing frameworks, such as those supported by AI for Selenium, run real-life scenarios to find functional problems and performance snags. In comparison, Sharma and Singh (2022) reported that ML-based testing methods enhanced bug detection rates by 30%, unlike traditional testing methods. Indeed, these findings support AI and ML in terms of dependability in reducing errors and ensuring that the software will live up to user expectations.

Notables are the security enhancements that AI and ML bring. Tools for vulnerability analysis and IDS use ML algorithms to detect and eliminate potential threats in real time. For instance, Darktrace AI-based cybersecurity software provides coherent security against sophisticated cyber-attacks through its dynamic adaptation to ever-evolving threats. According to Ngai *et al.* (2011), ML-based security solutions reduced the risks associated with breaches by reducing cyber threats' detection-to-response time by 50%. These results represent how AI/ML can help build resilience into software and protect private information.

Proactive maintenance and real-time monitoring further enhance software stability, which is possible with AI and ML. Datadog and other predictive analytics technologies analyze system logs and performance variables to anticipate problems before they occur. As Goodfellow (2016) explains, proactive maintenance reduces operation costs by anticipating problems and minimizing losses. In mission-critical applications where system stability is at stake, the capability guarantees consistent performance.

Another important outcome of integrating AI and ML into resource management is scalability. AI-powered resource management solutions guarantee scalability without compromising quality through performance optimization during peak demand. For example, Kubernetes uses AI to automatically allocate and reallocate resources according to changes in workload for containerization. It was established that organizations that use AI in resource allocation increase systems efficiency by 25% during peak utilization, which is a scalability factor.

In addition, the personalization and ML can achieve have transformed user experiences. Intelligent applications like the Netflix suggestion system use ML algorithms to interpret user history and personalization preferences, increasing user satisfaction. According to a 2003 study (Linden, Smith, & York, 2003), personalized increased user engagement by 70%, showing that AI and ML could enhance client loyalty and fuel company growth.

Even though the results point to many advantages of integrating AI and ML into the software development process, the drawbacks remain. The first disadvantage is the dependence on high-quality data to train the models of ML. Poor or biased data impacts model accuracy and causes farther-than-expected results. Further, Goodfellow (2016) showed that the computational resource input to train and deploy an AI/ML model could be unaffordable for small-scale organization keep giving attention to ethical issues, especially fairness and transparency in AI-driven decisions.

Despite these challenges, this discussion indicates that the benefits of AI and ML are significantly higher than the drawbacks. New technologies such as explainable AI and federated learning are solving problems in model interpretability and data privacy, respectively, thus setting in concrete the importance of AI and ML in software engineering. Its continuous relevance and transformative impact on the software development industry are ensured by its ability to continuously adapt, learn, and improve. The outcome of AI and ML adoption in software development clearly shows their deep impact on scalability, security, quality, and productivity. These findings, supported by real data and practical applications, confirm that AI and ML are changing software engineering and setting new benchmarks in the discipline.

3.5 Challenges and Solution

Although it has revolutionary advantages, integrating machine learning (ML) and artificial intelligence (AI) into software development. Six challenges their accompanying Solution are listed below:

1. **Data Quality and Availability**:

    Challenge: Machine learning models need big, high-quality datasets to train. Inadequate, biased, or missing data might result in reliable software systems and accurate forecasts.

    Solution: Businesses should implement strong data management procedures, such as data augmentation, preprocessing, and cleansing. Synthetic data production techniques can also utilize address. Automating data quality checks with tools like TensorFlow Data Validation can ensure reliable training data.
2. **Computational Resource Requirements:**

    Challenge: AI/ML model deployment and training can be computationally costly, requiring high-performance hardware like GPUs or TPUs that smaller organizations might not have access to.

    Solution: organizations Cloud-based systems like AWS, Google Cloud AI, and Microsoft Azure provide scalable and reasonably priced model training and deployment options. Optimizing models using strategies like optimizing and trimming can decrease resource requirements without sacrificing speed.

3. **Lack of Explainability and Transparency:**

   Challenge: Many AI/ML models, particularly deep learning models, operate as "black boxes," which makes it hard to understand how they make decisions. This lack of openness may hamper trust and adherence to rules.

   Solution: To make model decisions interpretable, use explainable AI (XAI) techniques like SHAP (Shapley Additive exPlanations) and LIME (Local Interpretable Model-Agnostic Explanations). Developing models with explainability in mind promotes stakeholder trust and guarantees regulatory compliance.

4. **Ethical and Bias Issues**:

   Challenge: AI/ML models can reinforce biases found in training data, producing unfair or discriminating results. Concerns about permission and data privacy also come up ethically.

   Solution: Create ethical AI frameworks that incorporate bias prevention and detection techniques. Diversify training data and conduct routine bias audits of datasets. Methods like federated learning and differential privacy can improve data privacy while maintaining model performance.

5. **Complexity of Integration:**

   Challenge: Integrating AI/ML tools into current software development workflows and infrastructure can be difficult, necessitating major procedure adjustments and skill sets.

   Solution: Utilise Mlops frameworks to simplify the incorporation of AI/ML into the Software Development Lifecycle (SDLC). Platforms like Kubeflow and MLflow automate deployment processes, and developer training programmes can fill talent gaps.

6. Lifespan management and high maintenance:

   Challenge: As data and requirements change, ML models must be updated and frequently retrained to retain accuracy. AI/ML system lifecycle management might require a lot of resources.

   Solution: Use real-time, automated monitoring technologies to monitor model performance. Implement pipelines for continuous learning so that models can easily adjust to new data. Version control systems such as DVC (Data Version Control) can effectively manage and track data and model changes.

4. CONCLUSION

The Software Development Lifecycle (SDLC) has been completely redesigned by the incorporation of Artificial Intelligence (AI) and Machine Learning (ML), which present unmatched chances to improve software quality, scalability, security, and productivity. AI and ML have shown their ability to drastically alter software engineering techniques by automating repetitive operations, facilitating intelligent decision-making, and enhancing user experiences. This chapter examined how AI and ML affect the requirements collecting, design optimisation, testing, debugging, and deployment phases of the software development life cycle (SDLC). The results demonstrate their capacity to automate procedures, lower errors, and quicken development schedules, resulting in a quicker time to market and more cost effectiveness. While machine learning models anticipate possible flaws and vulnerabilities, reducing post-deployment risks, AI-powered testing tools provide strong quality assurance. Additionally, they improve software scalability and reliability, especially in high-demand situations, through proactive maintenance, real-time monitoring, and dynamic resource allocation.

Even with its many benefits, integrating AI and ML into software development has drawbacks, such as problems with data quality, the need for a lot of processing power, moral dilemmas, and the difficulty of integrating into current processes. Adopting scalable cloud platforms, explainable AI methods, ethical AI frameworks, and sound data management procedures are all necessary to meet these difficulties. New technologies like federated learning and explainable AI (XAI) also promise to ease data privacy and transparency concerns.AI and ML's revolutionary effects on software development highlight these technologies' importance to the sector's future. As they develop further, they will set new standards for software engineering excellence, allowing organizations to create more intelligent, effective, and safe systems. By adopting these technologies, developers and organizations can fully utilise them to satisfy the constantly increasing demands of a quickly evolving digital ecosystem.

4.1 Future Works

Though the potential of these technologies is still growing, the incorporation of AI and ML into software development has established a strong basis for revolutionary breakthroughs. To significantly improve the Software Development Lifecycle (SDLC), future research should concentrate on resolving existing constraints while investigating novel applications and approaches. One important topic is creating AI models that are easier to understand and more transparent. Explainable AI (XAI) approaches must advance as deep learning and other sophisticated algorithms take centre stage in software development to give stakeholders and developers a better understanding of the decision-making process. This will lessen biases in AI-driven systems, promote trust, and guarantee regulatory compliance.

Another crucial area for investigation is the scalability of AI and ML solutions in software engineering. Developing lightweight models tailored for resource-constrained contexts should be the main focus of future research. By deploying AI and ML tools on edge devices, methods like model pruning, quantization, and knowledge distillation may make them more accessible to smaller businesses and environments with fewer resources. Furthermore, combining AI with cutting-edge hardware technologies like quantum computing and neuromorphic processors will pave the way for previously unheard-of software development speed and efficiency as the need for real-time processing increases.

A continued focus on the ethical issues of AI and ML in software engineering is also necessary. Future research should create strong frameworks for the ethical development of AI, including techniques to identify and reduce biases in training data and decision-making procedures. To protect user data while preserving model accuracy, privacy-preserving strategies like differential privacy and federated learning should be improved. These developments will guarantee that applications of AI and ML meet legal and societal standards. Developing MLOps frameworks to streamline the lifecycle management of AI/ML models in software development is another encouraging avenue. Future research should concentrate on automating model retraining, deployment, and monitoring procedures to guarantee that systems continue to adapt to changing data and user requirements. Improved version control for models and datasets, continuous integration, and delivery pipelines designed for AI/ML systems will smooth updates and reduce downtime.

Many prospects exist when AI and ML are combined with cutting-edge technologies like blockchain and the Internet of Things (IoT). For example, by offering real-time data analytics and adaptive system behaviour, AI-enabled IoT systems have the potential to transform software development for smart applications completely. Similarly, blockchain could improve AI/ML workflow security and transparency by generating decentralized, unchangeable logs for decision-making and model training.

Finally, a top focus should be given to investigating how AI might promote cooperation between intelligent systems and people. Future research should look into how artificial intelligence (AI) might improve software development team productivity by serving as an intelligent assistant to help with communication, spot bottlenecks, and offer real-time suggestions. By fusing machine intelligence with human inventiveness, software engineering could reach previously unheard-of levels of creativity and efficiency.

In summary, tackling present issues and investigating novel applications and approaches that push the envelope of what is feasible are key to the future of AI and ML in software development. As these technologies develop, incorporating them into software engineering will improve security, quality, and productivity while expanding the potential of contemporary software systems and opening the door to a more intelligent and interconnected digital future.

REFERENCES

Acharya, N., Shrivastava, N. A., Panigrahi, B. K., & Mohanty, U. C. (2014). Development of an artificial neural network based multi-model ensemble to estimate the northeast monsoon rainfall over south peninsular India: An application of extreme learning machine. *Climate Dynamics*, *43*(5-6), 1303–1310. DOI: 10.1007/s00382-013-1942-2

Albrecht, T., *Machine Learning in Business: A Process and Project Perspective*. 2023.

Ambati, S. (2023). *Security and Authenticity of AI-generated code*. University of Saskatchewan.

Anand, S., Burke, E. K., Chen, T. Y., Clark, J., Cohen, M. B., Grieskamp, W., Harman, M., Harrold, M. J., McMinn, P., Bertolino, A., Jenny Li, J., & Zhu, H. (2013). An orchestrated survey of methodologies for automated software test case generation. *Journal of Systems and Software*, *86*(8), 1978–2001. DOI: 10.1016/j.jss.2013.02.061

BHATORE. (2020). *S., Software Engineering practices for building MLware applications-credit risk evaluation case study*. International Institute of Information Technology Hyderabad.

Brundage, M., ... *The malicious use of artificial intelligence: Forecasting, prevention, and mitigation*. arXiv preprint arXiv:1802.07228, 2018.

Chafik, N. and D.A. Benchekroun, *Integrating artificial intelligence in software engineering: Enhancements and challenges in the development lifecycle*. 2020.

Choudhury, L. K. (2022). STUDY ON LOGIC AND ARTIFICIAL INTELLIGENCE SUBSETS OF ARTIFICIAL INTELLIGENCE. *Innovative Research Thoughts*, *8*(1), 127–134.

Ciresan, D.. (2012). Deep neural networks segment neuronal membranes in electron microscopy images. *Advances in Neural Information Processing Systems*, •••, 25.

Coleman, A. (2024). Integrating MLOps Pipelines with DevOps for Seamless Model Deployment and Continuous Delivery. *Australian Journal of Machine Learning Research & Applications*, *4*(2), 87–94.

Eshraghian, F., Hafezieh, N., Farivar, F., & de Cesare, S. (2024). AI in software programming: Understanding emotional responses to GitHub Copilot. *Information Technology & People*. Advance online publication. DOI: 10.1108/ITP-01-2023-0084

Esteva, A., et al., *Dermatologist-level classification of skin cancer with deep neural networks*. nature, 2017. **542**(7639): p. 115-118.

Fred, N., & Temkin, I. *A Systematic Literature Review on the Use of Machine Learning in Software Engineering.* arXiv preprint arXiv:2406.13877, 2024.

Gadani, N. N. (2024). The Future of Software Development: Integrating AI and Machine Learning into the SDLC. *International Journal of Engineering and Management Research, 14*(1), 308–315.

Goodfellow, I. (2016). *Deep learning*. MIT press.

Idowu, S., Osman, O., Strüber, D., & Berger, T. (2024). Machine learning experiment management tools: A mixed-methods empirical study. *Empirical Software Engineering*, *29*(4), 1–35. DOI: 10.1007/s10664-024-10444-w

Karim, N. S. A., Albuolayan, A., Saba, T., & Rehman, A. (2016). The practice of secure software development in SDLC: An investigation through existing model and a case study. *Security and Communication Networks*, *9*(18), 5333–5345. DOI: 10.1002/sec.1700

Karmakar, S., *Artificial Intelligence (AI) Chatbots and Customer Experience: Developing a.* 2024.

Khalifa, M., Albadawy, M., & Iqbal, U. (2024). Advancing clinical decision support: The role of artificial intelligence across six domains. *Computer Methods and Programs in Biomedicine Update*, *5*, 100142. DOI: 10.1016/j.cmpbup.2024.100142

Linden, G., Smith, B., & York, J. (2003). Amazon. com recommendations: Item-to-item collaborative filtering. *IEEE Internet Computing*, *7*(1), 76–80. DOI: 10.1109/MIC.2003.1167344

Liu, Q., Li, P., Zhao, W., Cai, W., Yu, S., & Leung, V. C. M. (2018). A survey on security threats and defensive techniques of machine learning: A data driven view. *IEEE Access : Practical Innovations, Open Solutions*, *6*, 12103–12117. DOI: 10.1109/ACCESS.2018.2805680

Lorenzoni, G., ... *Machine learning model development from a software engineering perspective: A systematic literature review.* arXiv preprint arXiv:2102.07574, 2021.

Martínez-Fernández, S., Bogner, J., Franch, X., Oriol, M., Siebert, J., Trendowicz, A., Vollmer, A. M., & Wagner, S. (2022). Software engineering for AI-based systems: A survey. [TOSEM]. *ACM Transactions on Software Engineering and Methodology*, *31*(2), 1–59. DOI: 10.1145/3487043

McCarthy, J., *What is artificial intelligence.* 2007.

Mendoza Juan, Y. (2024). *Development of a multi-agent, LLM-driven system to enhance human-machine interaction: integrating DSPy with modular agentic strategies and logical reasoning layers for the autonomous generation of smart contracts*. Universitat Politècnica de Catalunya.

Nallapati, R., & Manning, C. D. *Legal docket classification: Where machine learning stumbles*. in *Proceedings of the 2008 conference on empirical methods in natural language processing*. 2008. DOI: 10.3115/1613715.1613771

Nascimento, E., ... *Software engineering for artificial intelligence and machine learning software: A systematic literature review.* arXiv preprint arXiv:2011.03751, 2020.

Neapolitan, R. E., & Jiang, X. (2018). *Artificial intelligence: With an introduction to machine learning*. CRC press. DOI: 10.1201/b22400

Ngai, E. W., Hu, Y., Wong, Y. H., Chen, Y., & Sun, X. (2011). The application of data mining techniques in financial fraud detection: A classification framework and an academic review of literature. *Decision Support Systems*, *50*(3), 559–569. DOI: 10.1016/j.dss.2010.08.006

Nguyen-Duc, A., ... *Generative Artificial Intelligence for Software Engineering—A Research Agenda.* arXiv preprint arXiv:2310.18648, 2023.

Pan, R., Bagherzadeh, M., Ghaleb, T. A., & Briand, L. (2022). Test case selection and prioritization using machine learning: A systematic literature review. *Empirical Software Engineering*, *27*(2), 29. DOI: 10.1007/s10664-021-10066-6

Paulson, S. (2024). *Epistemic Reasons & Cognitive Self-Monitoring*. Northwestern University.

Pelluru, K., *Advancing software development in 2023: the convergence of MLOps and DevOps.* Advances in Computer Sciences, 2023. **6**(1): p. 1– 14-1– 14.

Prince, N. U.. (2024). AI-Powered Data-Driven Cybersecurity Techniques: Boosting Threat Identification and Reaction. *Nanotechnology Perceptions*, •••, 332–353.

Qian, C., ... *Communicative agents for software development.* arXiv preprint arXiv:2307.07924, 2023. **6**.

Rane, J., et al., *Artificial intelligence, machine learning, and deep learning in cloud, edge, and quantum computing: A review of trends, challenges, and future directions.* Future Research Opportunities for Artificial Intelligence in Industry 4.0 and, 2024. **5**: p. 2-2.

Saeid, H. (2020). Revolutionizing Software Engineering: Leveraging AI for Enhanced Development Lifecycle. *International Journal of Innovative Research in Engineering & Multidisciplinary Physical Sciences*, *8*(1).

Salmani, A., *An AI-Based Human-Centered Approach to Support Multidisciplinary Requirements Engineering*. 2023.

Samuel, A. L. (1959). Some studies in machine learning using the game of checkers. *IBM Journal of Research and Development*, *3*(3), 210–229. DOI: 10.1147/rd.33.0210

Sarker, I. H. (2021). Machine learning: Algorithms, real-world applications and research directions. *SN Computer Science*, *2*(3), 160. DOI: 10.1007/s42979-021-00592-x PMID: 33778771

Shabina., ... *Ensuring Securing PII Data in the AWS Cloud: A Comprehensive Guide to PCI DSS Compliance*, in *Cybersecurity and Artificial Intelligence: Transformational Strategies and Disruptive Innovation*. 2024, Springer. p. 185-216. DOI: 10.1007/978-3-031-52272-7_8

Shah, V. (2019). Towards Efficient Software Engineering in the Era of AI and ML: Best Practices and Challenges. *International Journal of Computer Science and Technology*, *3*(3), 63–78.

Sharma, R., & Singh, J. *Systematic Literature Review and Comparative Studies on Human Centred Software Development*. in *2022 4th International Conference on Advances in Computing, Communication Control and Networking (ICAC3N)*. 2022. IEEE. DOI: 10.1109/ICAC3N56670.2022.10074154

Singh, P. (2024). Transforming Healthcare through AI: Enhancing Patient Outcomes and Bridging Accessibility Gaps. *Journal of Artificial Intelligence Research*, *4*(1), 220–232.

Smith, J., & Wei, R. (2024). *Implications of Artificial Intelligence in the Software Development Life Cycle*. EasyChair.

Soni, A., et al., *Integrating AI into the Software Development Life Cycle: Best Practices, Tools, and Impact Analysis*. Tools, and Impact Analysis (June 10, 2023), 2023.

Wah, B. W., Huang, T. S., Joshi, A. K., Moldovan, D., Aloimonos, J., Bajcsy, R. K., Ballard, D., DeGroot, D., DeJong, K., Dyer, C. R., Fahlman, S. E., Grishman, R., Hirschman, L., Korf, R. E., Levinson, S. E., Miranker, D. P., Morgan, N. H., Nirenburg, S., Poggio, T., & Weems, C. (1993). Report on workshop on high performance computing and communications for grand challenge applications: Computer vision, speech and natural language processing, and artificial intelligence. *IEEE Transactions on Knowledge and Data Engineering*, *5*(1), 138–154. DOI: 10.1109/69.204098

Wong, M.-F., Guo, S., Hang, C.-N., Ho, S.-W., & Tan, C.-W. (2023). Natural language generation and understanding of big code for AI-assisted programming: A review. *Entropy (Basel, Switzerland)*, *25*(6), 888. DOI: 10.3390/e25060888 PMID: 37372232

Yan, F., et al. *Performance modeling and scalability optimization of distributed deep learning systems.* in *Proceedings of the 21th ACM SIGKDD International Conference on Knowledge Discovery and Data Mining*. 2015.

Yaseen, A. (2023). AI-driven threat detection and response: A paradigm shift in cybersecurity. *International Journal of Information and Cybersecurity*, *7*(12), 25–43.

Chapter 2
Leveraging Emerging Technologies for Smart and Secure Software Development:
Blockchain, IoT, and Beyond

Wasswa Shafik
https://orcid.org/0000-0002-9320-3186
Dig Connectivity Research Laboratory, Uganda

ABSTRACT

The integration of emerging technologies such as Blockchain, the Internet of Things (IoT), and other innovative solutions is revolutionizing smart and secure software development. These technologies enhance data integrity, enable decentralization, and improve interoperability across digital platforms, creating more resilient and adaptive systems. Blockchain's use of smart contracts ensures automated, secure transactions, while IoT facilitates real-time monitoring and data collection, driving better decision-making. As cybersecurity threats grow, leveraging these technologies can improve scalability and protection against vulnerabilities in software applications. The ongoing evolution of tech trends presents new opportunities for building intelligent systems that meet the complex demands of modern software development.

DOI: 10.4018/979-8-3693-9851-7.ch002

1 INTRODUCTION

Technology[1] has undergone tremendous advancements in the digital age. Emerging and disruptive technologies such as blockchain[2], internet of things[3] (IoT), edge computing[4], expert systems such as artificial intelligence[5] (AI), machine learning[6], data analytics[7], fifth generation[8] and beyond, cloud computing[9], fog computing[10], and others play a fundamental role in determining the pace and direction of future advancements (Nayaka Sheetakallu Krishnaiah et al., 2024). Blockchain, IoT, and other technologies are considered powerful enablers of smart and secure solutions. Integration of emerging technologies enables solutions to be more efficient and personalized. At the same time, these advancements are being applied across various industries, such as those contributing to smart cities, digital twins, healthcare, banking, e-commerce, supply chain, and education, among others (Susanty et al., 2024).

Smart contracts and cryptocurrency exchanges using blockchain have gained a lot of attention in recent years. However, both experienced and relatively new blockchain developers encounter many obstacles and difficulties when coding or deploying smart contracts and when designing and integrating systems that put these capabilities to use. The situation is much worse in the context of cybersecurity. Most of the solutions and tools provided by smart contract development platforms are not good enough or do not provide the functions needed to design and implement secure systems (Yadi Paembonan & Darma Wijaya Waruwu, 2024). Additionally, a significant number of smart contracts have design or coding errors that result in substantial financial or technical security issues, and these security problems are often both difficult and very expensive to fix. In summary, blockchain developers face challenging roadblocks in their daily work, but very few tools or technologies assist them in solving these difficult problems, let alone prevent them (Ayotunde Alaba et al., 2024).

Blockchain-based systems are continuously and increasingly sensitive and critical, so we need to change our attitude toward security investment and focus on promoting and supporting security by design and security as maintenance. After discussing these, we argue about how we can use these technologies to deepen our understanding of the use context in any of these scenarios. In this chapter, we discuss why the integration of technologies is critical to resulting in smart and secure solutions of the future, the possible advantages, and the potential risks related to data privacy and security (Carriles et al., 2024). The potentials and challenges of using blockchain and integrating IoT systems form part of the above-discussed scenarios, and solutions are incorporated.

1.1 Overview of Emerging Technologies

With the pace of evolution in technological frontiers, the way businesses and societies work and govern has been wildly reshaped. Shrouded in awe, emerging technological advancements are said to be capable of disrupting sectors across the spectrum, spurring the sharing of knowledge and wealth in innovative ways. Innovations such as artificial intelligence, the Internet of Things, and blockchain are reshaping segments in the enterprise landscape. Developers have found relief in the proposed modern technologies; their disruptive nature resembles assuagement. Some seem to have hit with gusto the required notes of decentralized, secure architecture and efficiency. New, engaging, and promising ideas about the way in which developers will interact with systems and infrastructure are generated through these major innovative leaps forward (Mishra & Chaurasiya, 2024). However, a clear, lustrous minefield of futuristic developments lurks; thus, a comprehensive perspective and understanding of what these fronts offer our businesses is compulsory.

We are currently witnessing a sort of disruptive "Big Bang" of synergistic innovations. The technological advancements of AI, IoT, and blockchain are fine examples of a tide of inventive efforts towards evolving more secure applications. The prime element in these developmental efforts is to enhance the security and efficiency of contemporary digital systems by encapsulating a secure and efficient software module design and development. The main aim of these fast-eroding trends is to develop smarter and more secure software (Yadi Paembonan & Darma Wijaya Waruwu, 2024). It is somewhat obvious that these trends will have an extensive impact on traditional software development methodologies. The developers must, therefore, adapt to such changing paradigms. In the subsequent sections, a particular focus on blockchain technologies, the Internet of Things, and autonomous systems is studied and discussed in relation to what services or service modules can be provided or enhanced with these advancements based on the smart and secure software drivers in Figure 1 (Ayotunde Alaba et al., 2024).

Figure 1. Smart and secure software assisted CIA-PSR model drivers for cybersecurity

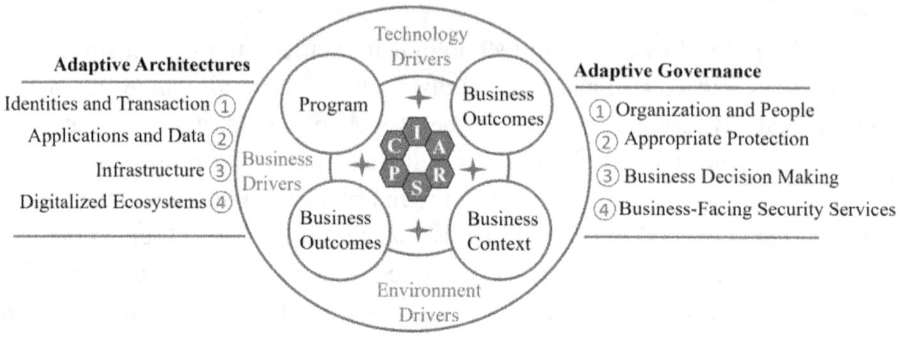

2 FOUNDATIONS OF BLOCKCHAIN

Blockchain's innovative features have led numerous advocates to herald it as the "anti-establishment solution" of the Internet age. We posit that the explicit principles underlying blockchain empower software developers with the inventive ability to develop secure software applications and systems. Before delving into specific applications, however, it is crucial to understand the fundamental principles that govern blockchain. Fundamentally, blockchain is a decentralized technology powered by nodes in a peer-to-peer network. The sheer volume of nodes precludes any hacking attempt, as the attacker must overwhelm the majority of the nodes in the network to make an impact (Oyekunle Claudius Oyeniran et al., 2024). Blockchain acts as a distributed ledger recording transactions across the network, which endows it with a set of unique and powerful attributes: transparency, immediacy, visibility, and guaranteed authenticity of previous transactions, among others. Blockchain architecture is composed of three layers: transactions, blocks, and chains of blocks. Transactions, the lowest layer, are made by entities in the network, representing the initial event (or fact) a party wishes to record immutably on the blockchain. Various transactions are collected into a block, which is then linked through a process to the last block in the ledger. This chain of blocks forms the blockchain (Alloghani, 2024). The various layers combine to generate a secure and transparent platform for conducting transactions within all available blockchains, as illustrated in Figure 2.

Figure 2. Categories of blockchain and its sampled traits

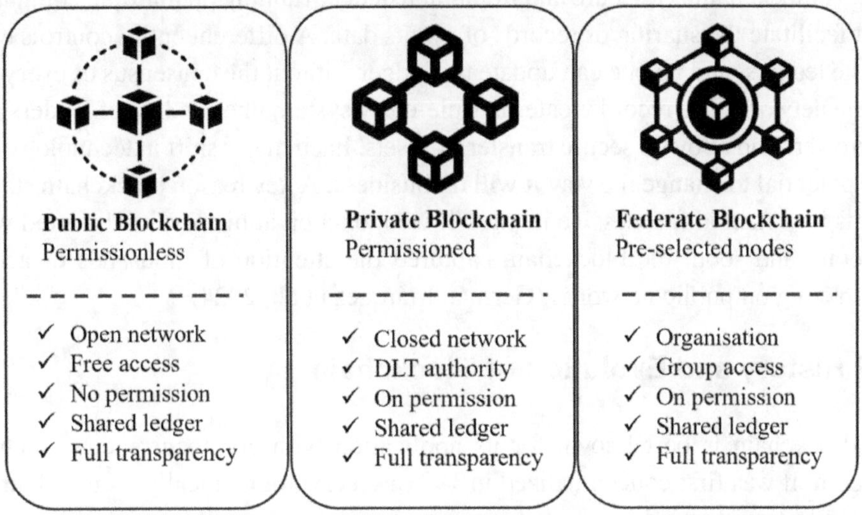

There are several key differences between blockchain and traditional database systems. Among these are fixed vs. dynamic data sets, linear vs. hierarchical operation, system synchronization, resistance mechanisms, smart contracts, and consensus. The traditional database is a centrally regulated hierarchical structure; it operates on a set linear database where new data sets are appended. It functions in a similar way to a central data storage system, where it handles the storage and rendition of predefined data structures and their hierarchical relationships (Shafik, 2024a). Blockchain, in contrast, operates on a dynamic, trustless system where the data structure can be arbitrary.

2.1 What is Blockchain?

Blockchain is a chain of blocks secured by a previous block as players of blockchain technology. The blocks record and secure transactions, which, in most cases, can be seen and identified by the participants of the network. These transactions are aggregated into a block, and to ensure the validity of the transactions of a block, the hash of the previous block is also included. The transaction is then verified by participants of a network using a consensus algorithm agreeing on a single source of truth. Hence, the blocks are linked together using the hashes, thereby creating a chain of transactions called blockchain, which allows the secure transfer of assets without the need for an intermediary using a consensus algorithm (Shafik, Kalinaki, Fahim, et al., 2024). Based on that definition, let us break down the abstract definition to make non-technical people understand those who do not have cryptographic expertise. A blockchain is a secure and immutable ledger running on multiple computers that facilitate the sharing of records of events data. A different entity controls each of the ledgers, and no one can update the ledger without the consensus of everyone in the network. The record creates a triple-entry system like a ledger of lenders and borrowers and allows a secure transfer of assets. Each major shift in technology has the potential to change the way it will do business. A key reason blockchain stands out is its potential for massive impact. If we look a bit at history, it all started with Bitcoin, and soon, the blockchain captured the attention of thousands of actors interacting on public networks (Germán Márquez et al., 2024).

2.2 History and Evolution of Blockchain

Blockchain is best known for its application with cryptocurrencies, such as Bitcoin. It was first conceptualized in 1991 as a cryptographically secure chain of blocks to timestamp documents for a secure audit trail, as illustrated in Figure 2. However, it was not until 2008 that its true potential as a technology was recognized when an individual defined the Bitcoin protocol and introduced the blockchain as the platform. This initiative opened doors for the development and exploration of various blockchain applications and adoptions in domains renowned for their relatedness, such as finance and cybersecurity. The interest in blockchain increased significantly only around half a decade ago. This attention directly correlates with the introduction of permissionless blockchain technologies, such as Bitcoin and Ethereum[11] (Chen & Babar, 2024). Permissive blockchains have been researched and implemented before in closed-alliance settings. However, these ledgers caused little attention. Currently, a large part of the newly available venture capital and engineering efforts is spent on blockchain technology. Consequently, blockchain technologies remain attractive due to both the large investment in and growing market importance, but promoting the adoption of new and sophisticated technologies, such as blockchain, ultimately hinges on improved security, resilience, and ease of use. In many instances, blockchain has been portrayed as a silver bullet over the years in development, as illustrated in Figure 3 (Ronanki & Karneddi, 2024).

Figure 3. Blockchain technological development

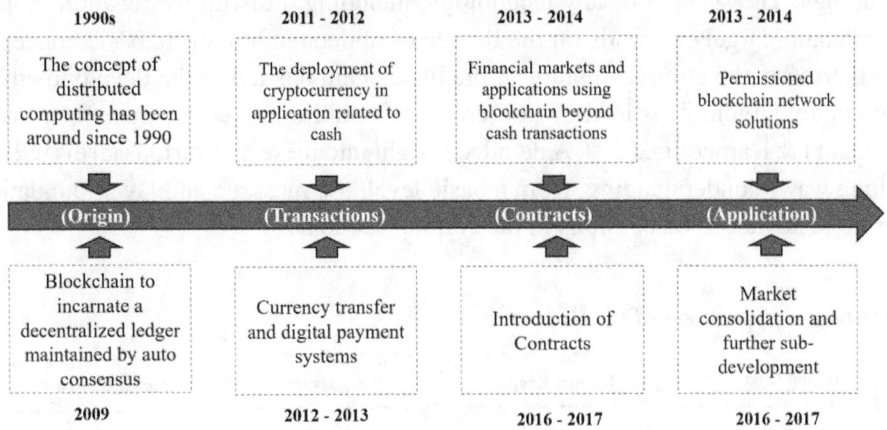

2.3 Key Concepts and Terminologies

Blockchain: A distributed database used for maintaining a continuously growing list of records called blocks. Functionally, the blockchain is resistant to modification of the data, making it a secure digital platform widely used in various areas, such as finance, industry, health, and government. Nodes: A blockchain is maintained by participants of the network, known as nodes. There are different types of nodes within a blockchain, such as full nodes, light nodes, and miners in public blockchains, while validators in private or permissioned blockchains (Mazni Mohamed Jakeri et al., 2024). Smart Contracts: A smart contract is a self-executing contract with the terms and agreements between two or more parties being directly written in lines of code. The code and the agreements form a direct interface that is used for interacting with on-chain data. Smart contracts also automatically enforce the agreed-upon rules. Cryptocurrencies: A cryptocurrency is a digital asset designed to be used as an exchange medium that uses cryptographic solid techniques for secure financial transactions, controls the creation of additional units, and secures the transfer of assets (Gershfeld & Sturm, 2024). The most famous cryptocurrency is Bitcoin, which was invented by an unknown person or group of people known by the alias of Satoshi Nakamoto and released in 2009.

The blockchain field is rapidly evolving, and new terminologies replace old ones. For example, the initial term "smart contracts" is evolving toward legally embedded scripts. Decentralized Autonomous Organizations[12] (DAOs) is another term that is expanding in scope and moving from theoretical to practical usage in business. Therefore, literature on blockchain technology may use outdated terminology. The success of any technology, including a disruptive technology like blockchain, largely depends on the degree of understanding of its basic concepts. Furthermore, the complex nature of the blockchain has led to the development of a complex jargon. This is known to create a stumbling block for many beginners (Ronanki & Karneddi, 2024). A detailed insight into these and various terms will go a long way to understanding, from a basic level, the message and lay a foundation for more advanced discussions in the coming sections.

Figure 4. Application of blockchain

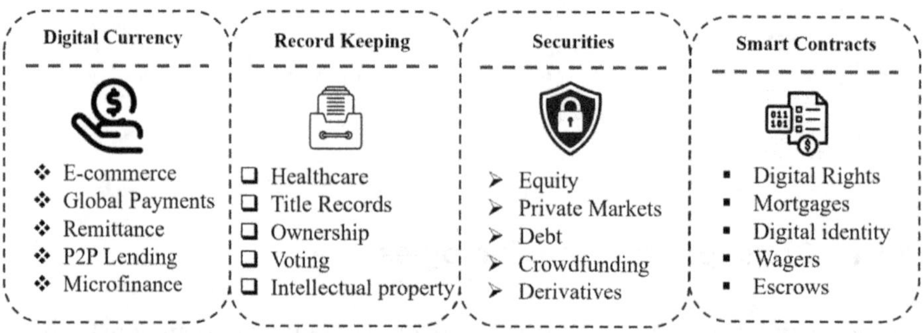

2.4 Use Cases and Applications

In addition to the fact that blockchain can benefit decentralized autonomous software systems and egocentric and anti-fragile software systems, there are numerous use cases and applications for blockchain in the area of software engineering, as illustrated in Figure 4. There are some general software development lifecycle-oriented applications that we can leverage blockchain to overcome the credibility validation process inside a software development context and, in general, to manage the source code assets better and provide tampering evidence of the changes made in the source code. Considering the software development lifecycle's processes, blockchain, in combination with smart contracts, can enable strong evidence of the communication and coordination process, strict control of versions and related changes, and grant automatic IP rights at a specific moment for large-scale international projects (Johnson Sunday Oliha et al., 2024a). On the other hand, through blockchain, we can also realize the innovative model of the Permissioned Add-On adulteration, Proof-Evaluation-Contest, as well as new ways to achieve software tamper-aware avoidance and expendable commit and enslave. Initially proposed for hardware obfuscation, expendable commit and enslave couples an evaluator with an ever-growing number of "completely random commits," proof to represent these random single seed-based challenges in the blockchain to form a barrier around the implementations to prevent an imposter from cheating (Johnson Sunday Oliha et al., 2024b).

3 APPLICATIONS OF BLOCKCHAIN IN SOFTWARE DEVELOPMENT

Blockchain is infusing new techniques into the principles of software development and existing paradigms. Following are some areas in software development where blockchain can play a catalytic role in making a world of difference. Blockchain has the objective of creating applications or software versions that are resistant to security vulnerabilities and software attacks. Consider an industry domain where fraud prevention is of prime concern. Blockchain can prove to be a boon by incorporating the usage of the ledger system in property management systems to deter fraud in transferring assets or by maintaining records of the employees' performance that managers monitor to obtain insights into historical transactions and prevent deceitful activities (Shin & Jeon, 2024).

Transaction validation[13] is one of the applications of blockchain in international bank transactions. The standard process incurs fees and delays as the banks use intermediaries to facilitate the exchange. Merchants, on the other hand, are expected to shoulder unexpected charges associated with fraud or chargebacks. With the help of blockchain, transactions can proceed without the need for banks as intermediaries. The process is by a trusted network comprising bankers or nodes who validate and record transactions. The transaction can also be instant and executed at a lower cost. More still, decentralized applications and smart contracts where smart contracts run on decentralized platforms and hence, they are referred to as decentralized applications. The smart contracts that make these applications run will execute as per the rules and will be viewable by everyone in the blockchain, ensuring transparency and continuity of operation (Casola et al., 2024). For instance, blockchain can be exploited inpatient medical records to improve the healthcare system. Each treatment is logged into a transaction by the healthcare provider that generates an event.

3.1 Smart Contracts

A crucial ingredient in any blockchain application, smart contracts reside on the blockchain and perform functions or transactions when a trigger condition is met. They enable credible transactions without third parties for establishing an escrow account, registering property rights, making payments across different digital currencies, and more. The same reasoning applies to the code underpinning smart contracts and can also be seen as self-executing contracts with the terms of the agreement directly written into code (Qaraqe et al., 2024). Running on blockchain, smart contracts automate the execution of an agreement by taking real-world or digital inputs that are tallied against a set of triggering conditions predetermined by the contracting parties. When these conditions are met, the smart contract's executable code self-executes. Automation is the lynchpin of a smart contract, and it ensures that agreement terms between parties are satisfied and, as such, avoids disputes because execution is tamper-evident, transparent, and verifiable. Legal implications aside, a smart contract automates business processes and can be independently managed and operated (Nayaka Sheetakallu Krishnaiah et al., 2024).

The application of smart contracts goes beyond financial services, serving as a secure supply chain mechanism, providing property rights in real estate, identifying and tracking products in the pharmaceutical space, and establishing a trusted process for digital authentication. Community-based service providers also use smart contracts in service-level agreements for asset sharing and conditional payments. However, the wider adoption of smart contracts is restrained by the limited amount of functionality they offer. Supply chain risks and solutions can be addressed using oracles, but these are centralized systems and are trusted third parties (Diaz Rivera et al., 2024). Moreover, the oracle only knows what is recorded. While the data is decentralized for use and storage, the triggering points of the smart contract are in a centralized database. Critics claim that disconnects between on-chain and off-chain data compromise the entire blockchain framework as a robust business case for the broader use of smart contracts and the application and acceptance of blockchain technologies. Judicial smart contracts are in the design architecture phase, with no global systems set up yet and severe limitations because these are uncharted waters in the legal arena. Programming errors in the code are at the heart of smart contract failures. Should such an error occur, is the original code with inherent liabilities relevant to the breach (Hemani et al., 2024)? Challenges such as these curtail the widespread acceptance of smart contracts among the more traditional proponents of contract law.

3.2 Decentralized Applications

These decentralized applications[14] (DApps) are applications that run on a blockchain and not on a single, centralized server, with their back-end code running on a decentralized P2P network. They have several attributes that are different from traditional applications based on the web, computer machines, and mobile operating systems. Apart from smart contracts, they can also contain front-end code and an off-chain component, which could remove traditional web servers but not diminish their decentralized nature. Smart contracts are the crucial aspect of the applications that run without shutdown, fraud, or reliance on a middleman. In the development and execution of DApps, smart contracts facilitate trust and transparency and guarantee user freedom (Simpson et al., 2024). Among countless sectors, decentralized applications are revolutionizing fintech, decentralized finance, gaming, and social media. However, blockchain-assisted networks have several merits and challenges, as presented in Figure 5.

Figure 5. Merits (left) and challenges (right) blockchain network

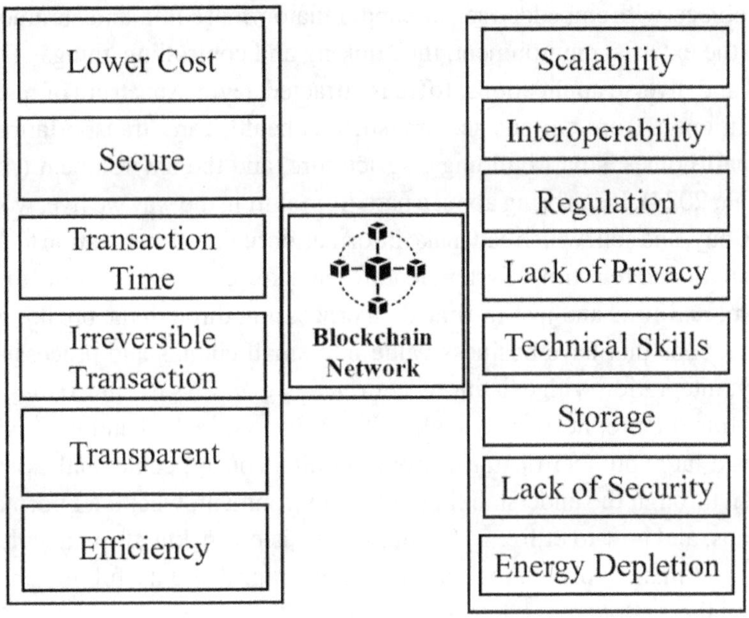

Some of the most significant advantages for developers of DApps are transparency, immutability, strong disintermediation, and greater security and non-censorship since they are not hosted on centralized servers. Some of the tools and technologies that DApps development teams need to have include blockchain platforms, development tools, deployment frameworks, and token standards. In this way, it could be possible to change the way of doing business, including the infrastructure (Wang et al., 2024). The DApps that we intend to study specifically and distinguish from any other form of applications are intended to be efficiently and effectively used by different entities all over the world and by people with limited access to resources. With moving components over the blockchain, costs will be reduced to zero in the age of blockchain, and therefore, platforms that become the basis of payment processing are bound to be disrupted (Seelaboyina et al., 2024). Validators will spend less on commissions through the required setup of payment platforms, and as they develop during the last six months, DApps will emerge.

4 UNDERSTANDING THE INTERNET OF THINGS

The IoT is a convergence of enabling technologies combined with people and processes that allow an enterprise to exchange data and information through intelligent sensors accurately. It is an extension of existing computer networks, connecting physical objects with embedded sensors and actuators that communicate among them and with the external environment, thus linking and controlling 'things.' Due to its potential and diverse applications, IoT has attracted a wide spectrum of researchers and practitioners from various sectors, such as health care, transportation, smart cities, smart homes, smart buildings, agriculture, and the environment (Ayotunde Alaba et al., 2024). It can bring about a paradigm shift in the way we live, work, play, entertain, buy, and sell, which can make information and communication technology systems smart and real-time. System features and key characteristics of IoT include dynamism; real-time and just-in-time data processing through the breaking of data and transactions that have business value into small chunks and processing them on the fly; integration with existing systems using gateways to our existing technological infrastructure; horizontal scalability of the system by handling high traffic as well as a large number of transactions simultaneously; contextual existence of the system through the understanding of the environment, what the information on hand means, and how to utilize it; facilitating decision-making from a wide variety of sensor and image information into more meaningful and useful information for decision-makers (Ronanki & Karneddi, 2024).

4.1 Understanding IoT Ecosystem

Basically, IoT is a vast ecosystem of interconnected devices using the internet as a medium to exchange data among them. Devices can be of different types, such as wearables, embedded sensors, actuators, etc., and can have a wide variety of operating systems, including processors, sensors, relays, and so on. These devices can gather data trigger some needed actions on the event, and communicate with each other and with networks using network connectivity (Ronanki & Karneddi, 2024). This communication is made possible because of the wide availability of Wi-Fi, LTE, and even various protocols designed exclusively for IoT devices, such as Bluetooth[15] and ZigBee[16]. The different available communicative networks work together to send and receive sensor data and trigger the required actuator functions. The devices are connected with lots of data variety, data significance, and data volume, where different networks filter and convert the data to different formats based on the devices they interconnect. After this step, the general public and devices working on this data, along with the respective analytics, decide on the required action solely based on this data supported by advancement in sustainable expert systems, as demonstrated in Figure 6 (Mishra & Chaurasiya, 2024).

Figure 6. Expert system advancements

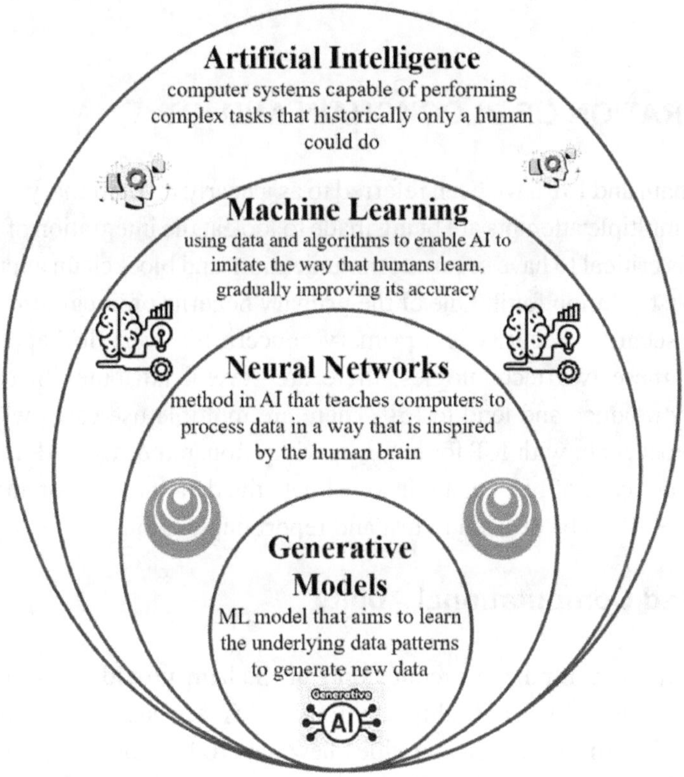

4.2 Communication and Data Analytics

Moreover, sending all captured data from the devices to public networks for cloud processing can also lead to increased extra costs for data handling. This is where edge computing can be helpful, which can decrease data volume somewhat. However, the IoT ecosystem cannot be implemented directly by integrating devices with communication and data analytics. Vendors are offering cloud network services, while others are offering cloud data analytics services, and parent manufacturers are still offering devices (Germán Márquez et al., 2024). These cloud solutions don't work as an end-to-end system in reality; at least, they never design cloud solutions that are optimized for low latency. The lack of interoperability and collaborative business models between these actors is the main issue why IoT's business case is weak. On the other hand, security and privacy should not be neglected in such ecosystems. Data collected on different devices may hold personally recognizable information that should be dealt with securely. Data sent from various devices may also be sensitive and can affect the privacy of network end-users (Chen & Babar, 2024).

5 INTEGRATION OF BLOCKCHAIN AND IOT

Blockchain and IoT have been referred to as a nearly revolutionary combination. Therefore, multiple attempts are being made to look at the integration of Blockchain and IoT. It is critical to have secure communication, and blockchain appears to offer a more robust solution for it. One of the primary benefits of integrating blockchain and IoT is security. Security is a primary concern for every IoT application. By combining these two technologies, there are several attributes that blockchain can directly produce and lend to IoT. There are multiple use cases where we can integrate blockchain with IoT for better service (Ronanki & Karneddi, 2024). One significant use case of blockchain is to validate the data integrity of an IoT device. Furthermore, it can be utilized to test and report duplication.

5.1 Limited Computational Ability

Due to the decentralized architecture, blockchain provides transparency between IoT nodes, which is highly required in IoT services. Similarly, real-time data received from IoT devices provides new data to be mined and thus enhances blockchain functionality. With different consensus algorithms, the conflict between regular real-time data and historical blockchain data can be managed efficiently and reliably. On the other hand, blockchain and IoT integration have a few challenges: IoT has severe scalability issues as billions of devices are connected, which can make blockchain-based ledgers impractical (Mazni Mohamed Jakeri et al., 2024). Additionally, smart devices generally operate with limited computational ability, and energy consumption can be a significant concern when running a blockchain. A distributed ledger is typically maintained by several devices with decentralization. Consequently, blockchain consensus algorithms have to run on individual nodes. These challenges need to be addressed in detail. Many efforts are focused on the integration of blockchain and the IoT, but most of them target security. There is very little work done on the framework that can facilitate the integration. Therefore, a more effective and comprehensive framework is required; the provided some scenarios where blockchain-integrated IoT can achieve more intelligent solutions (Gershfeld & Sturm, 2024).

5.2 Challenges and Solutions

Blockchain is proposed for securing the IoT network in various ways, but it addresses few challenging operations needed to integrate with IoT. Our vision is to figure out those challenging concerns and technical solutions for secure IoT. They presented critical challenges and proposes potential solutions to realize secure IoT.

5.2.1 Data Privacy Concerns

Data in a blockchain network is distributed across multiple nodes in clear text format, where anyone can extract the data stored in the blocks. This volume of data is accountable for potential data leakage where hackers can steal the personal information or private data of users. Scalability for Large-Scale Networks: Blockchain has been designed to protect small-sized IoT networks as a private blockchain, but it is not scalable for typical IoT networks. The IoT is meant to scale up with extensive networks, such as Smart City Networks, National and International Sensing Networks, and Industrial IoT; for this purpose, the blockchain networks are not yet scalable. Device Operability and Evolution: IoT networks are a combination of heterogeneous and compatible networks and devices (Mazni Mohamed Jakeri et al., 2024). Owing to the heterogeneity in the overall IoT network, there are various kinds of devices, from sensors to smart home devices and things. It is very tough to operate all the devices on a single-block network.

5.2.2 Permanent Record of All Transactions

The research on blockchain and IoT is promising, and with the joint efforts of IoT, blockchain, and AI researchers and developers, we hope for secure integration of blockchain and IoT. There are several security issues in integrating blockchain and IoT. To this end, blockchain keeps a permanent record of all transactions, while the peer-to-peer network of nodes will maintain real-time status and quickly spread such information. Also, the combination of edge computing and blockchain, where federated learning improves machine learning models, is one of the promising reasons for secure integration (Ronanki & Karneddi, 2024). Moreover, encryption algorithms are still not very secure and have significant limitations and security threats. Symmetric encryption and asymmetric encryption face many performance and security constraints in the current research environment. Therefore, it is a huge field for further investigation. Last but not least, whichever approach can be followed by the stakeholders of the IoT, blockchain, and emerging technologies. Some promising investigations have been mentioned and sampled proposed solutions for the above-mentioned challenging operations, including scalability for large-scale networks: decentralized IoT-focused blockchain and edge computing, data privacy: distributed edge computing or federated learning, or AI-empowered privacy-preserving cryptography or secure multi-party computation (Chen & Babar, 2024).

6 SECURITY CONSIDERATIONS IN BLOCKCHAIN AND INTERNET OF THINGS

Security is the most imperative concern to be taken in the blockchain. Healthcare, records of individuals, and information about an individual's finance or business transactions being made in the form of smart contracts over a blockchain raise significant concerns to be addressed in the context of the security of the blockchain. As of now, several major security threats have been identified as a potential danger to smart contract formulations, including unsafe blockchain wallets, oracles, and other external data-source amplification and over-discoverable functionality, leading to an open recursive calling dependency. The cooperation or integration between the blockchain and IoT may give rise to the same security concerns within the blockchain and IoT (Shafik, 2024e). Lack of data management or failure to define clear assessment policies, unauthorized access, not storing data securely, insufficient provider security, and un-secure data in transit are considered to be the main threats in the context of IoT.

A good network is a choice among security, dependability, privacy, and security norms showing dependability against privacy. These days, the network providers are doing all the possible things to move all the norms of security to much faster-triggered privacy. Progress in detecting changes in programming behavior was identified in both presumed concepts and norms of security that arose in the use of the Internet of Things. One of the most well-known safety threats for the Internet of Things is the exploitation of system security (Shafik, 2024c). Because IoT devices are tireless devices that do not require constant human intervention to transmit and collect information from the network, they can be targeted by network hackers who can also exploit system security hazards. Technically, using reverse engineering techniques, attackers can use vulnerabilities within connected devices. Off-the-shelf hardware with a restricted resource set might lead to a system that is not serviceable or flexible in the expectation of potential use cases in the future, such as that of the medical case study using IoTs, demonstrated in Figure 7. Decreased dimensions and lower energy use, on the other hand, make it challenging to produce certified embedded gadgets. As a result, the certified components are shifting to a much more physical envelope (Shafik & Kalinaki, 2023).

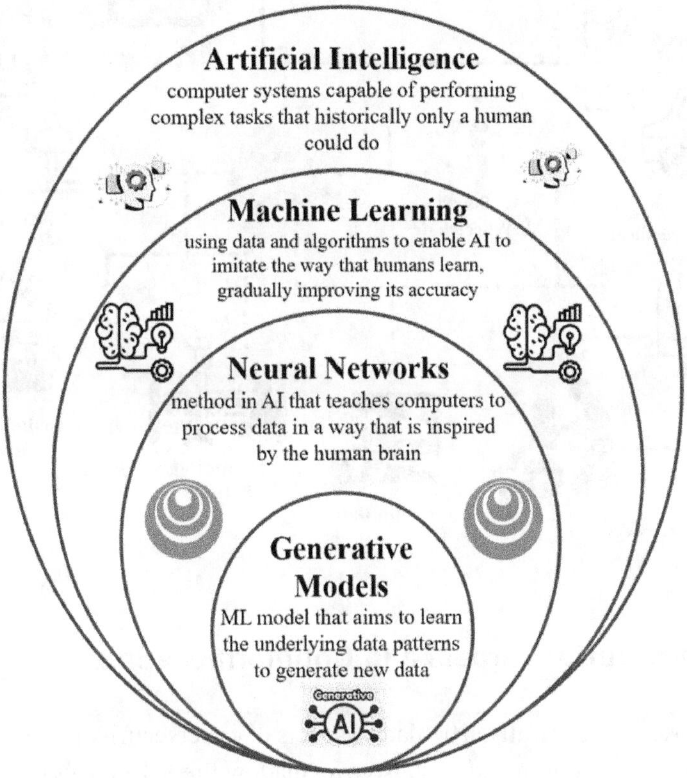

Figure 8. A healthcare case study using the Internet of Things

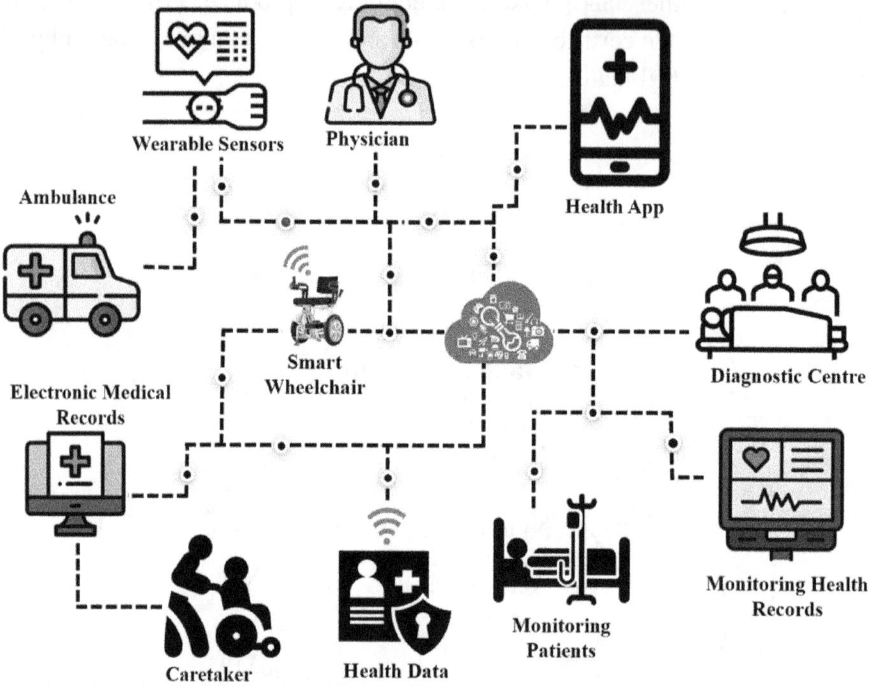

6.1 Cybersecurity Threats and Countermeasures

This subsection carefully articulates aspects of cybersecurity threats that impact the blockchain ecosystem and can also overshadow the IoT ecosystem.

6.1.1 Considerable Financial Losses

Broadly, the analyzed threats encompass hacking, predominantly involving the broadcast transmission of illegal logistics services; denial-of-service[17] (DoS) attacks, which can lead to considerable financial losses and, therefore, increase the risk of cargo hijacking; spamming the ledger and the spread of malicious logistics data; and dropping out and shutting off individual IoT devices through malware contained in the transactions' manifests. Another threat can have a huge impact when manipulating the set of smart vans to be incapacitated during the shipping of counterfeit goods for the purposeful robbery of other merchandise of even higher value. The paper, therefore, makes a case for thoroughly analyzing not only the blockchain ecosystem but also the technological ecosystems with which it intersects (Casola et al., 2024). It concludes that, based on the probabilities and impact scores produced by a detailed risk analysis, an effective and resilient countermeasure can be developed.

6.1.2 Increase in Cybersecurity Attacks

The security of centralized systems is not a new concern at all, and there is literature available that discusses this aspect, including IoT security guidelines. Since blockchain can complement and augment IoT, we need to consider distributed and decentralized systems from the IoT perspective. Both technologies should not be seen in isolation, and the proposed and ongoing collaborative efforts are a good start and will help in harmonizing the best practices. The increase in cybersecurity attacks calls for further research into novel threats and their solutions. New techniques are being exploited in recent years, representing the intersection between blockchain and IoT, for example, autonomous vehicles (Qaraqe et al., 2024). Therefore, we should continue providing updates on the emerging areas of blockchain and IoT threats and countermeasures so that the security community is kept well-informed to design future-proof security systems.

7 BEYOND BLOCKCHAIN AND IOT

These are complex technologies[18] in their own right: capitalizing on them for practical application requires dealing with even higher levels of complexity. Whenever we start at the application layer of such advanced technologies, we often underestimate the effort and complexity involved in developing and delivering the underlying blockchain and IoT platforms. To rapidly develop applications, we must start by minimizing that effort and complexity. One fundamental problem with applying these latest technologies is that we tend to use them generically, especially when we have in-house software development capabilities. However, the pace and rate of development of the underlying platforms require specialization and focus by software platform providers. These new platforms require technologies and skill sets that most organizations currently do not have and that are not core competencies, as illustrated in Figure 8.

7.1 Artificial Intelligence and Machine Learning

We are at the dawn of a new era with emerging technologies such as artificial intelligence, machine learning, the IoT, blockchain, augmented reality, and virtual reality becoming more prevalent. Extreme digitization and datafication[19] are facilitating significant transformation, which in turn are influencing our daily lives and occupations. Indeed, technology is evolving at a faster pace than ever and disrupting industries and routines drastically. Over the past few decades, the evolution of new technologies has taken the field of research and development by surprise. Today's technology is the product of various advances in science and engineering combined with ongoing advancements in many different disciplines. It is the source of significant investments and accelerating general applicability. However, to fully benefit from these technologies, new challenges and issues must be addressed (Qaraqe et al., 2024; Simpson et al., 2024). One such avenue relates to the capacity of security technologies in place that developers can leverage along with their solutions to secure data and perform intelligent functions.

With the increasing errors made when using Internet-based systems, the generalization of responsibility is complex. Over 32% of mobile users do not secure their devices, which is a numbers game, given the exponential growth of these devices. The sophistication and constant flow of security problems that security technology developers deal with are an increasing concern within the information technology field. With the number of breaches on the rise over the past decade, it is significantly vital to not only impose warnings but also monitor markets and assess the current level of security technology, as standalone providers were too enabling and even fundamental in making the end product that their customers would later use (Ayotunde Alaba et al., 2024). To help the development market drive, we decided to analyze these providers. In the security sector, artificial intelligence and machine learning technology experts help employ expert systems in security technologies that provide the insights needed to help security analysts improve not just the cyber cleaning process but also cyber forensic intelligence gathering and analytics (Hemani et al., 2024; Simpson et al., 2024).

Figure 9. Healthcare enabling technologies beyond the blockchain

7.2 Augmented and Virtual Reality (AVR)

The convergence of more traditional social media channels with emerging virtual and augmented reality solutions is enabling new social interactions in virtual, 3D environments. However, within these online communities, diverse threats such as misinformation are being multiplied in volume and appeal due to this convergence. Indeed, such AVR-based social apps may increase how society interacts with sensitive personal data, thereby expanding attack surfaces available for data breaches. This chapter discusses these hazards presented by emerging AVR apps against the backdrop of the privacy-invasive practices already prevalent within conventional social media. Misinformation sharing is discussed as an example of the amplified threat posed to society by 3D social updates and shows the growing interest in VR and AR alongside augmented reality app installation volumes (Shafik, Kalinaki, & Zakari, 2024). Consequently, a direction for research is proposed that nudges AVR platforms away from data-driven interactions with social media-linked stumbling stones in the form of privacy-fear-inducing violations. The potential influx of privacy issues with shared information is not restricted to VR-based platforms; any digitally shared information can be processed within AR apps and interfaced with APIs connecting social media (Shafik, 2024b). Sophisticated geospatial data mining could, therefore, be used to detect where friends and family members live and work, and AVR cosmetic surgery apps entice users to process their images inside the same historic sites that are advertised for other entertainment purposes.

The relationship between digital information and privacy or identity respect has now expanded beyond the real-world constraints of how it is shared to include these innovations within VR and AR products (Shafik, 2024d).

7.3 Quantum Computing

These possess superior capabilities in comparison to classical computing. It has the potential to revolutionize certain aspects and segments of technologies. While the overall sentiment is that quantum computing, in the near future, will complement rather than replace the classical computer, the technology's level of preparedness is crucial. This foundational segment on its technological readiness is heartfelt, and it is necessary to understand recent breakthroughs in technology and impactful applications to assess their impact and industrial importance. We do not include a somewhat detailed explanation of the significant foundational principles of quantum information science, entangled states, and quantum superposition in this preface. Several foundational principles are brought to bear on the technology. These include superposition, which is managed through qubits, entanglement, and quantum speed-up (Carriles et al., 2024). The technology, technological learning, invention, or innovation of quantum computing is long-standing, with foundational principles put in place since 1985. The emerging science and engineering of quantum computing bring about critical quantum supremacy.

Computer security, quantum key distribution, cybersecurity with quantum capabilities, and quantum cryptography are essential. Cyber capabilities, cyber readiness, scientific techniques and methods, cryptographic tools, standards, and protocols should evolve in order to take advantage of quantum computing's current and future computational power improvements. Information and communication technologies progress in new quantum cryptographic key exchange schemes for securing sensitive data, smartly improving data confidentiality and integrity. However, traditional electronic devices and computer systems are not secure against attack by quantum computers, considering that fast large-scale quantum computers are expected to operate in the next 10 to 15 years (Qureshi & Farooq, 2024). Quantum attacks on our cryptographic systems represent many problems. These problems may have immediate consequences, threatening the integrity, privacy, and security of many systems and may require existing systems to be updated and augmented with advanced cryptographic protections. Therefore, while the current state and pace of quantum technology continue to guide progress and indicate when and how to implement more advanced cryptographic methods, there is a demand for increased investment to ensure feasibility, usability, and interoperability in the standardization of quantum computing, communications, and cybersecurity for ICT (Said et al., 2024).

8 SMART AND SECURE SOFTWARE DEVELOPMENT PRACTICES

As a software engineer or developer, one must ensure that the complete software development lifecycle, including all the associated documents governing the software lifecycle, including security manuals and enterprise software development methodology, fully embraces the emergent technologies provided by both blockchain and IoT. These technologies provide distinct advantages in ensuring that time-stamped distributed ledgers of events give clear cybersecurity audit trails throughout the software development lifecycle (Yadi Paembonan & Darma Wijaya Waruwu, 2024). This is fundamental not only to ensure compliance with the increasing global set of cybersecurity regulations but is essential to support the continuous critical review of security measures provided by overarching secure enterprise software development methodologies. In addition, with the increasing write-once/deploy-everywhere use of container technology, the need to include a comprehensive immutable security metadata record in all containers created by the enterprise for both cloud and edge deployment cannot be overstated. Once again, the use of emerging blockchain and IoT technology can help support and guide change decisions through real-time enterprise evidence-based decision-making in this new form of emerging distributed software development (Carriles et al., 2024).

8.1 Secure Coding Principles

Developers focused on functionality overlook several lesser-known technical flaws that pervade insecure software systems. They harbor several security bugs that are not exposed to users by benign inputs. Malicious inputs can exploit these types of software or hardware weaknesses to a software system. Software development starts with secure and efficient programming and ends with software security. Secure coding principles are maintained to avoid some common types of coding vulnerabilities and improve safe coding performance. Secure coding is the practice of writing software programs with very few weaknesses (Alloghani, 2024; Oyekunle Claudius Oyeniran et al., 2024). Programming practices are risk-free and readable and confirm that applications behave as intended. Writing secure software prevents exploitation and helps develop legacy software with safe coding practices. The key principles of software protection are supported. Software defects that generate a benefit for attackers are simple to avoid with safe coding techniques such as approval, runtime execution, and buffer overflow prevention. Software applications can become safer and less vulnerable when the majority of software development teams view and implement secure coding improvements, strategies, and rules in their goals and tasks (Shi et al., 2024).

8.2 DevSecOps and Continuous Security Integration

With the introduction of DevOps[20], security has been slowly yet silently integrated into the pipeline with "shift-left" and the new concept of DevSecOps. The essence of DevSecOps is to implement security from the start to the end phase of the DevOps cycle of a project, where security becomes a part of the natural workflow. However, shifting security to the left side of the timeline has already indicated that treating security separately after the primary development does not work that well. Consequently, DevSecOps rapidly merges with DevOps and becomes a competitor to it, and they also become two competing terms for the same underlying set of practices. The term "Security as Code" emerged, as with this concept, security is also written as code by the operations team instead of such a condition being just a concept (Lehmann et al., 2024; Ronanki & Karneddi, 2024). Several developed software tools are compliant with this concept and perform intended security checks during continuous delivery but are challenged by several data quality aspects, as illustrated in Figure 9.

Figure 10. Critical and challenging blockchain aspects

8.3 Dynamic Software Scanning

To automate the early stages of system-level security testing, security automation is an approach that is widely used. Based on the concept that software development has been initiated with the case of continuous integration and continuous delivery, automation tools are categorized as pre-commit/static (used during/after coding phases) and code commit checks, post-commit/dynamic tools that automatically scan security issues without scrutinizing the pipeline and artifacts at the time of build (Mazni Mohamed Jakeri et al., 2024). Automated static code scanning can involve tools that check software libraries, whereas tools for dynamic code scanning mainly involve components that are added to continuous integration or build processes. These tools can provide real-time feedback on security issues, but the problem arises with the automation tool's success relative to the task of managing several challenges. With an enormous effort to configure and maintain them, this could result in too many tool warnings or alerts from security concerns that are incorrect (Simpson et al., 2024). As such, when DevOps models are being used on small-scale applications, less attention is mainly paid to those early areas, where valuable security issues could be overlooked.

8.4 Testing and Quality Assurance

The urgent need for and widely increasing amount of smart IoT applications endorses the research on innovative software development methodologies. On the one hand, accepted software engineering methods and technologies must be extended to address application-centric issues. On the other hand, application-specific challenges can be catalysts for advancing software engineering. In solid software engineering methodologies, all quality assurance activities beyond constructing and executing software or systems evolve in reviewing artifacts, constructing the traceability matrix, and performing confidence building with auditors (Bakhshi et al., 2024). Specialized security quality assurance (SQA) tasks in highly regulated industries mainly involve an early inclusion of each relevant compliance-related, regularly standardized, and peer-reviewed artifact, an SDLC with milestones, and gatekeeping to document and manage the individual negotiation progress and validate tracings.

8.5 Specialized Security Quality Assurance

All projects reach SQA with their documents, leaving them as they are and open for audit. Their traceability matrix is a list of links, and all the gaps between compliance artifacts reflect weaknesses that have to be closed with much effort. Defects may result in non-compliant features or construction gaps, being either caused by changing client requirements or human error, such as a mismatch between requirements and code design. Cross-linking SQA reviews must be repeated after a baseline but can start even within the formative stages of artifact generation, e.g., with a description that becomes a test case later on. It offers exceptional capabilities for collaboration between business unit activities, wholesalers, and compliance experts (Adnan Buyung Nasution et al., 2024; Stavdas et al., 2024). On a technical level, the traceability matrix may be supported as a base for several reports.

9 FUTURE DIRECTIONS AND BEYOND

During the past decade, we have seen the evolution of blockchain and related domains. In the following sections, we discuss trends that are emerging and may shape the future of blockchain and IoT. As key emerging technologies continue to evolve and emerge beyond what is currently imaginable, we must be innovative by generating new ways to adapt to the new and changing industries with technologies and best practices. These are recommended avenues for continued growth and methods for the community to innovate on blockchains and related domains and leverage IoT in new ways for the safety and security of software development lifecycles and work. This shows the journey the technology has taken so far and seeks to highlight the direction that we believe the technology will take in the future, including a thorough discussion of some of the challenges faced by the technology and possible solutions to them over time (Hemani et al., 2024; Qaraqe et al., 2024).

9.1 Safety and Security-Based Lifestyle

Based on these studies from literature and practical experience, seven future directions and where we are heading are outlined with blockchain technology and its offspring. In general, the future of these technologies is coming from the angles of regulations, where the systems are appraised; interoperability, where the existing systems are bridged and adapted to the context of developing countries; and continued research and development, where industry and academics need to invest. These are recommended to truly harness the full potential of these technologies to guarantee a safety and security-based lifestyle. The future of these technologies needs to rely on community engagement, where the participants need to collaborate and trigger advancements with their expertise in blockchain and IoT. It is unattainable to come up with all the potential developments and limitations for blockchain and IoT, even in a science fiction book (Bonde, 2024; Johnson Sunday Oliha et al., 2024a). The utilization potential of these domains can be contingent upon user adoption. Discussions on perspectives provide estimations of what changes might take place.

9.2 Expert System Integration

Integrating expert systems such as AI and machine learning with blockchain and IoT can help address the challenges of data heterogeneity, big data, fast data, data analytics, data visualization, low-level security and privacy, and complex blockchain systems. In addition, this integration can support industries in automating their processes, systems, and intelligent decisions. AI and blockchain technologies are tailored explicitly for decentralized systems, making decisions based on dynamic networks as smart contracts. IoT technologies may generate big data for an entire analytics process, and AI technologies assist in providing precise results for decision-makers. However, companies need to remain alert and mitigate the significant danger of fake data creation, or else their ability to make intelligent decisions may diminish (Ayotunde Alaba et al., 2024; Yadi Paembonan & Darma Wijaya Waruwu, 2024). Currently, the integration of AI, blockchain, and IoT in various industries is in its early stages.

9.3 Fake Data Evaluations

Despite the fact that there are numerous available applications on the market, it is critical to develop real-time scalable solutions that can provide managers with real-time insights. The integration of AI in blockchain and its applications and systems may encounter barriers associated with fake data evaluations, privacy, data ownership, error and fraud data, data heterogeneity, and ethical and social data considerations. Several AI examples illustrate successful applications and systems that have been integrated with blockchain and its applications (Mishra & Chaurasiya, 2024; Susanty et al., 2024). However, the number of solutions is distributed across the major applications: healthcare, supply chains for the food and drug industry, finance, logistics and transportation, energy, entertainment, telecommunications, security, gaming, and education. Nevertheless, the rest of the industry can also integrate AI with blockchain and IoT in first and last-mile solutions following to the edge to support the industry in automating, speeding up decisions, and ensuring trust in automation (Ayotunde Alaba et al., 2024; Carriles et al., 2024). Consequently, developers should work toward integrating AI, blockchain, and IoT into new solutions that could help businesses and industries regardless of the application area.

10 CHAPTER KEY INSIGHTS AND CONCLUSION

This chapter attempted to describe a detailed perspective on discussions about leveraging top emerging technologies and innovative approaches in the software development life cycle[21] (SDLC). While there is no denying the importance of blockchain and IoT in providing secure and efficient software, their instrumental role will be questionable if they are not practically adopted into real-world applications.

10.1 Chapter Key Insight

- There are a few challenges in ensuring secure, reliable, privacy-friendly, and future-proof integration of blockchain and IoT into diverse industries, from the automotive supply chain, banking, and pharmaceuticals to energy trading, e-governance, health record management, textiles, transportation, and utility management.
- These challenges open the door for software developers to investigate, innovate, and adapt such technologies to compensate for their vulnerabilities and emerging security threats.
- Build security into the enterprise objectives to avoid surprises after technological transitions to address the challenges already or perhaps on the way a priori. Therefore, it should be understood that salient, if not mission-critical, guiding principles will be needed to capitalize on the opportunities circulating the potential synergies of blockchain and IoT.
- Investment advisors should underscore that if institutions are to pivot and scale up their roles in these disruptive developments, they need to develop strategies that will not only remain resilient to disruptive shocks but also retain flexibility for pragmatic, evidence-based, and innovation-open responsive actions in the evolving socio-technical landscape.
- Rather than lounging and questioning what should or can be done at this stage, this chapter hails the role of developers who will actively harness the disruptive impacts of blockchain and IoT for smart and secure software.
- Emerging new opportunities in the evolution of these enabling technologies will require stakeholders to develop the ability to read the undercurrents of future builders' motivation. Adapting an existing protection strategy, they will not be alone as practitioners guide each other through the transformation and disruption peculiar to each niche.
- Finally, since there is no universal recipe for applying such potentially disruptive technologies across multiple ecosystems and industries, significant disruptive impacts are still developing and largely unclear, and it will serve software developers well when they devise supply strategies.

10.2 Conclusion

Given the complex security risks, challenges, and severe faults, typical software designs are critically inefficient and unreliable. The discussed emerging technologies that are promising in automating the SDLC. In this context, it is presented research insights that inspire and pave the way for leveraging these technologies for advanced and automated trustworthy software design through conversational software engineering. Building further on these initial research inferences, there has been literature that is proposing the application of Blockchain IoT[22] (BIoT). These proposed lenses of BIoT provide a relatively novel and acceptable outlook on using blockchain for IoT and its applications. Moreover, it has been demonstrated that research challenges and future research directions endeavored to encourage the broader research community to earnestly focus on leveraging emerging and disruptive technologies, along with new paradigms, to automate software development, making it both smart and secure. Moreover, with the era of expert systems and information era upon us, the emphasis is on the development of smart, secure conversational software, ensuring both at the same time. Ultimately, blockchain and distributed ledger technologies[23] (DLT) incorporate privacy and security-preserving features, providing a trusted execution environment for decentralized and connected applications. Since blockchain or DLT eliminates the need for centralized authorities, it is well-suited for IoT applications.

REFERENCES

Alloghani, M. A. (2024). Criteria for Sustainable AI Software: Development and Evaluation of Sustainable AI Products. In *Signals and Communication Technology: Vol. Part F1802*. DOI: 10.1007/978-3-031-45214-7_2

Ayotunde Alaba, F., Sulaimon, H. A., Ifeyinwa Marisa, M., & Najeem, O. (2024). Smart Contracts Security Application and Challenges: A Review. *Cloud Computing and Data Science, 5*(1).

Bakhshi, T., Ghita, B., & Kuzminykh, I. (2024). A Review of IoT Firmware Vulnerabilities and Auditing Techniques. In *Sensors* (Vol. 24, Issue 2). DOI: 10.3390/s24020708

Bonde, B. (2024). Edge, Fog, and Cloud Against Disease: The Potential of High-Performance Cloud Computing for Pharma Drug Discovery. In *Methods in molecular biology (Clifton, N.J.)* (Vol. 2716). DOI: 10.1007/978-1-0716-3449-3_8

Carriles, S. C., Martínez, J. V. B., Bernabéu, J. M. S., & Pérez, F. M. (2024). S-SCRUM—Methodology for Software Securitisation at Agile Development. Application to Smart University. *Lecture Notes in Networks and Systems, 789 LNNS*. DOI: 10.1007/978-981-99-6586-1_3

Casola, V., De Benedictis, A., Mazzocca, C., & Orbinato, V. (2024). Secure software development and testing: A model-based methodology. *Computers & Security*, *137*, 103639. Advance online publication. DOI: 10.1016/j.cose.2023.103639

Chen, H., & Babar, M. A. (2024). Security for Machine Learning-based Software Systems: A Survey of Threats, Practices, and Challenges. *ACM Computing Surveys*, *56*(6), 1–38. Advance online publication. DOI: 10.1145/3638531

Diaz Rivera, J. J., Akbar, W., Khan, T. A., Muhammad, A., & Song, W. C. (2024). Zt &t: Secure service session management using blockchain-based tokens in zero trust networks. *Annales Des Telecommunications. Annales des Télécommunications*, *79*(7–8), 487–505. Advance online publication. DOI: 10.1007/s12243-023-01008-y

Germán Márquez, A., Varela-Vaca, Á. J., Gómez López, M. T., Galindo, J. A., & Benavides, D. (2024). Vulnerability impact analysis in software project dependencies based on Satisfiability Modulo Theories (SMT). *Computers & Security, 139*, 103669. Advance online publication. DOI: 10.1016/j.cose.2023.103669

Gershfeld, I., & Sturm, A. (2024). Evaluating the effectiveness of a security flaws prevention tool. *Information and Software Technology*, *170*, 107427. Advance online publication. DOI: 10.1016/j.infsof.2024.107427

Hemani, Singh, D., & Dwivedi, R. K. (2024). Designing blockchain based secure autonomous vehicular internet of things (IoT) architecture with efficient smart contracts. *International Journal of Information Technology (Singapore)*. DOI: 10.1007/s41870-023-01712-x

Jakeri, M. M., Hassan, M. F., Sarlan, A., & Wahab, A. A. (2024). Adaptive Security Activities Selection Model Using Multi-Criteria Decision-Making Methods. *Journal of Advanced Zoology*, *45*(S1), 65–78. Advance online publication. DOI: 10.17762/jaz.v45iS1.3404

Johnson Sunday OlihaPreye Winston BiuOgagua Chimezie Obi. (2024a). Securing the smart city: A review of cybersecurity challenges and strategies. *Open Access Research Journal of Multidisciplinary Studies*, *7*(1), 094–101. Advance online publication. DOI: 10.53022/oarjms.2024.7.1.0013

Johnson Sunday OlihaPreye Winston BiuOgagua Chimezie Obi. (2024b). SECURING THE SMART CITY: A REVIEW OF CYBERSECURITY CHALLENGES AND STRATEGIES. *Engineering Science & Technology Journal*, *5*(2), 496–506. Advance online publication. DOI: 10.51594/estj.v5i2.827

Lehmann, C., Bilke, L., Buchwald, J., Graebling, N., Grunwald, N., Heinze, J., Meisel, T., Lu, R., Naumov, D., Rink, K., Özgür Sen, O., Selzer, P., Shao, H., Wang, W., Zill, F., Nagel, T., & Kolditz, O. (2024). OpenWorkFlow—Development of an open-source synthesis-platform for safety investigations in the site selection process. *Grundwasser*, *29*(1), 31–47. Advance online publication. DOI: 10.1007/s00767-024-00566-9

Mishra, S., & Chaurasiya, V. K. (2024). Hybrid deep learning algorithm for smart cities security enhancement through blockchain and internet of things. *Multimedia Tools and Applications*, *83*(8), 22609–22637. Advance online publication. DOI: 10.1007/s11042-023-16406-6

Nayaka Sheetakallu Krishnaiah, P., Narayan, D. L., & Sutradhar, K. (2024). A survey on secure metadata of agile software development process using blockchain technology. *Security and Privacy*, *7*(2), e342. Advance online publication. DOI: 10.1002/spy2.342

Nugroho, A. Y., Gunawan, H., & Sari, R. E.Adnan Buyung Nasution. (2024). Development of an IoT Based Smart Door System with Access Control via WhatsApp. [ESA]. *Indonesian Journal of Applied and Industrial Sciences*, *3*(1), 87–94. Advance online publication. DOI: 10.55927/esa.v3i1.7815

Oyeniran, O. C., Modupe, O. T., Otitoola, A. A., Abiona, O. O., Adewusi, A. O., & Oladapo, O. J.Oyekunle Claudius OyeniranOluwole Temidayo ModupeAanuoluwapo Ayodeji OtitoolaOluwatosin Oluwatimileyin AbionaAdebunmi Okechukwu AdewusiOluwatayo Jacob Oladapo. (2024). A comprehensive review of leveraging cloud-native technologies for scalability and resilience in software development. *International Journal of Science and Research Archive*, *11*(2), 330–337. Advance online publication. DOI: 10.30574/ijsra.2024.11.2.0432

Qaraqe, M., Elzein, A., Basaran, E., Yang, Y., Varghese, E. B., Costandi, W., Rizk, J., & Alam, N. (2024). PublicVision: A Secure Smart Surveillance System for Crowd Behavior Recognition. *IEEE Access : Practical Innovations, Open Solutions*, *12*, 26474–26491. Advance online publication. DOI: 10.1109/ACCESS.2024.3366693

Qureshi, J. N., & Farooq, M. S. (2024). ChainAgile: A framework for the improvement of Scrum Agile distributed software development based on blockchain. *PLoS ONE*, *19*(3 March). DOI: 10.1371/journal.pone.0299324

Ronanki, D., & Karneddi, H. (2024). Electric Vehicle Charging Infrastructure: Review, Cyber Security Considerations, Potential Impacts, Countermeasures, and Future Trends. *IEEE Journal of Emerging and Selected Topics in Power Electronics*, *12*(1), 242–256. Advance online publication. DOI: 10.1109/JESTPE.2023.3336997

Said, A., Ang, Z. E., & Iskandar, Y. H. P. (2024). Assessing Consumers' Acceptance of AR Wayfinding for Indoor Shopping Navigation in Singapore. *WSEAS Transactions on Computer Research*, *12*, 44–61. Advance online publication. DOI: 10.37394/232018.2024.12.4

Seelaboyina, R., Vadla, S. P. C., Teerthala, S. A., & Pedduri, V. V. (2024). Secure Software Development Life Cycle: An Approach to Reduce the Risks of Cyber Attacks in Cyber Physical Systems and Digital Twins. *Lecture Notes in Electrical Engineering*, *1106*, 153–161. Advance online publication. DOI: 10.1007/978-981-99-7954-7_15

Shafik, W. (2024a). Agile Security Strategies. In *Smart and Agile Cybersecurity for IoT and IIoT Environments* (pp. 82–101). IGI Global., DOI: 10.4018/979-8-3693-3451-5.ch004

Shafik, W. (2024b). Cyber Attacker Profiling and Cyberbullying Overview. In *Cyber Space and Outer Space Security* (pp. 125–149). River Publishers., DOI: 10.1201/9781003558118-5

Shafik, W. (2024c). Data Privacy and Security Safeguarding Customer Information in ChatGPT Systems. In *Revolutionizing the Service Industry Wth OpenAI Models* (pp. 52–86). IGI Global., DOI: 10.4018/979-8-3693-1239-1.ch003

Shafik, W. (2024d). Navigating Emerging Challenges in Robotics and Artificial Intelligence in Africa. In *Examining the rapid advance of digital technology in Africa* (pp. 126–146). IGI Global., DOI: 10.4018/978-1-6684-9962-7.ch007

Shafik, W. (2024e). Shaping the Next Generation Smart City Ecosystem: An Investigation on the Requirements, Applications, Architecture, Security and Privacy, and Open Research Questions. In *Smart Cities: Innovations, Challenges and Future Perspectives* (pp. 3–52). Springer. DOI: 10.1007/978-3-031-59846-3_1

Shafik, W., & Kalinaki, K. (2023). Smart city ecosystem: An exploration of requirements, architecture, applications, security, and emerging motivations. In *Handbook of Research on Network-Enabled IoT Applications for Smart City Services*. DOI: 10.4018/979-8-3693-0744-1.ch005

Shafik, W., Kalinaki, K., Fahim, K. E., & Adam, M. (2024). Safeguarding Data Privacy and Security in Federated Learning Systems. In *Federated Deep Learning for Healthcare* (pp. 170–190). CRC Press., DOI: 10.1201/9781032694870-13

Shafik, W., Kalinaki, K., & Zakari, R. Y. (2024). Blockchain's Motivation for IoT-Enabled Smart City. In *Secure and Intelligent IoT-Enabled Smart Cities* (pp. 195–221). IGI Global., DOI: 10.4018/979-8-3693-2373-1.ch010

Shi, X., Liang, X., & Ansari, S. S. (2024). Bricks without straw: Overcoming resource limitations to architect ecosystem leadership. *Academy of Management Journal*, *67*(4), 1084–1123. Advance online publication. DOI: 10.5465/amj.2021.1440

Shin, Y., & Jeon, S. (2024). MQTree: Secure OTA Protocol Using MQTT and MerkleTree. *Sensors (Basel)*, *24*(5), 1447. Advance online publication. DOI: 10.3390/s24051447 PMID: 38474983

Simpson, R. L., Lee, J. A., Li, Y., Kang, Y. J., Tsui, C., & Cimiotti, J. P. (2024). Medicare meets the cloud: The development of a secure platform for the storage and analysis of claims data. *JAMIA Open*, *7*(1), ooae007. Advance online publication. DOI: 10.1093/jamiaopen/ooae007 PMID: 38344670

Stavdas, A., Kosmatos, E., Maple, C., Hugues-Salas, E., Epiphaniou, G., Fowler, D. S., Razak, S. A., Matrakidis, C., Yuan, H., & Lord, A. (2024). Quantum Key Distribution for V2I communications with software-defined networking. *IET Quantum Communication*, *5*(1), 38–45. Advance online publication. DOI: 10.1049/qtc2.12070

Susanty, A., Puspitasari, N. B., Rosyada, Z. F., Pratama, M. A., & Kurniawan, E. (2024). Design of blockchain-based halal traceability system applications for halal chicken meat-based food supply chain. *International Journal of Information Technology : an Official Journal of Bharati Vidyapeeth's Institute of Computer Applications and Management*, *16*(3), 1449–1473. Advance online publication. DOI: 10.1007/s41870-023-01650-8

Wang, P., Liu, S., Liu, A., & Jiang, W. (2024). Detecting security vulnerabilities with vulnerability nets. *Journal of Systems and Software*, *208*, 111902. Advance online publication. DOI: 10.1016/j.jss.2023.111902

Yadi Paembonan, A., & Darma Wijaya Waruwu, F. (2024). Subsurface Utility Identification at ITERA Campus Using Multi-frequency Ground Penetrating Radar. *Jurnal Teori Dan Aplikasi Fisika*, *12*(01). Advance online publication. DOI: 10.23960/jtaf.v12i1.14174

ENDNOTES

1 https://en.wikipedia.org/wiki/Technology

2 https://www.blockchain.com/

3 https://www.techtarget.com/iotagenda/definition/Internet-of-Things-IoT

4 https://www.ibm.com/topics/edge-computing

5 https://cloud.google.com/learn/what-is-artificial-intelligence

6 https://www.ibm.com/topics/machine-learning

7 https://aws.amazon.com/what-is/data-analytics/

8 https://www.techtarget.com/iotagenda/definition/fog-computing-fogging

9 https://azure.microsoft.com/en-us/resources/cloud-computing-dictionary/what-is-cloud-computing

10 https://www.eccouncil.org/cybersecurity-exchange/ethical-hacking/fog-computing-everything-to-know/

11 https://crypto.com/bitcoin/bitcoin-vs-ethereum-whats-the-difference-between-btc-and-eth

12 https://www.avast.com/c-what-is-dao

13 https://golden.com/wiki/Transaction_validation-XKEG3JW

14 https://cointelegraph.com/learn/what-are-dapps-everything-there-is-to-know-about-decentralized-applications

15 https://www.bluetooth.com/

16 https://www.techtarget.com/iotagenda/definition/ZigBee

17 https://www.ncsc.gov.uk/collection/denial-service-dos-guidance-collection

18 https://www.complextech.com/

19 https://www.promptcloud.com/blog/datafication-era-of-big-data/

20 https://www.atlassian.com/devops

21 https://stackify.com/what-is-sdlc/

22 https://www.ibm.com/topics/blockchain-iot

23 https://www.techtarget.com/searchcio/definition/distributed-ledger

Chapter 3
Secure SDLC Frameworks:
Leveraging DevSecOps to Enhance Software Security

Mohammad Alauthman
https://orcid.org/0000-0003-0319-1968
Petra University, Jordan

Ahmad Al-Qerem
https://orcid.org/0000-0003-2187-6194
Zarqa University, Jordan

Amjad Aldweesh
https://orcid.org/0000-0001-9358-1323
Shaqra University, Saudi Arabia

Ammar Almomani
https://orcid.org/0000-0002-8808-6114
Higher Colleges of Technology, UAE

ABSTRACT

Software applications have become indispensable across sectors, necessitating robust security throughout their lifecycle. This chapter examines transforming the Software Development Life Cycle (SDLC) into a Secure SDLC by embedding security principles at every phase. Through DevSecOps—merging development, operations, and continuous security—organizations strengthen their cyber resilience. A well-structured Secure SDLC with DevSecOps principles mitigates risks while ensuring faster delivery cycles, regulatory compliance, and sustained user trust. The chapter provides methodologies for threat modeling, automation, collaboration, and monitoring, creating a clear pathway for businesses to incorporate security as an integral part of software engineering rather than an afterthought. Through

DOI: 10.4018/979-8-3693-9851-7.ch003

theoretical frameworks and case studies, it demonstrates how security integration drives both protection and business value.

1 INTRODUCTION

Software development has undergone a paradigm shift over the past decade, spurred by rapid technological advancements and the growing demands for online services. From finance to healthcare, organizations depend on reliable software systems to support critical operations and manage sensitive data. Despite heightened awareness of digital risks, many enterprises still treat security as an afterthought, conducting cursory checks shortly before deployment. This approach often leads to vulnerabilities that are both expensive and time-consuming to remediate (Viega & McGraw, 2001). An alternative strategy is to build security considerations into every phase of the Software Development Life Cycle (SDLC), thereby fostering what is widely referred to as a Secure SDLC. In a Secure SDLC model, the fundamental principles of confidentiality, integrity, and availability are embedded within requirement gathering, architecture design, implementation, testing, deployment, and maintenance. Concurrently, the DevOps movement, characterized by the unification of development and operations teams to deliver software more rapidly and reliably, has seen remarkable success (Forsgren, Humble, & Kim, 2018). Yet, it is only in recent years that the concept of DevSecOps has come to the fore, extending DevOps by weaving security into each and every iteration or pipeline stage.

1.1 Contextualizing the Topic

In many traditional SDLC implementations, security is tackled through gatekeeping: near the project's end, a security audit or penetration test identifies vulnerabilities that may require reengineering significant portions of the application. Studies show that fixing defects at later stages of development can be up to 30 times more expensive than addressing them earlier (Cybersecurity, 2018; Dawoud, Finster, Coppik, & Ashiwal, 2024). Consequently, organizations are increasingly shifting away from this fragmented approach toward models that incorporate security from the outset.

1.1.1 The Cost of Security Breaches

Recent high-profile security incidents have underscored the urgency of robust security practices. The 2020 SolarWinds supply chain attack affected thousands of organizations, including multiple U.S. government agencies (Alert, 2020). Similarly, the Log4j vulnerability discovered in 2021 demonstrated how a single flaw in a widely used open-source component could expose countless systems to exploitation (Agarwal, 2022). The 2022 IBM Security Cost of a Data Breach Report revealed that the global average cost of a data breach reached $4.35 million, with breaches in regulated industries like healthcare ($10.1 million) and financial services ($5.97 million) being substantially higher (Harkai & Ciurea, 2024).

These incidents highlight that security vulnerabilities can have catastrophic consequences beyond immediate financial losses, including:

- Reputational damage and loss of customer trust
- Regulatory penalties and legal liabilities
- Operational disruption and business continuity challenges
- Intellectual property theft and competitive disadvantage
- Long-term remediation costs and increased security spending

1.2 Defining Key Concepts: DevSecOps and Secure SDLC

The term DevSecOps represents a synthesis of "development," "security," and "operations." It promotes a philosophy where security is a collective endeavor rather than a specialized function limited to a dedicated team (Adewole, 2024)(Anderson, 2020). As such, developers engage in secure coding from day one, operations teams provision and maintain secure environments, and security practitioners facilitate risk-based decision-making across the pipeline.

Secure SDLC, by comparison, extends the traditional SDLC with explicit security activities. This includes threat modeling in the design stage, continuous vulnerability scanning during implementation, rigorous testing protocols, and robust incident response processes in the maintenance phase (Abbas et al., 2025). When executed effectively, a Secure SDLC reduces the probability of catastrophic breaches, promotes better compliance with standards like ISO 27001 or PCI DSS, and lowers long-term maintenance costs. Aligning Secure SDLC with DevSecOps thus creates a powerful synergy, combining methodological rigor with the speed and agility of modern software delivery practices.

1.3 Business Case for Secure SDLC and DevSecOps

Beyond technical advantages, there are compelling business reasons for adopting these approaches:

- **Reduced Total Cost of Ownership**: Early detection and remediation of security issues significantly reduces the total cost of ownership for software systems. Organizations implementing Secure SDLC practices report an average 25% reduction in security-related rework (Krasner, 2021).

- **Accelerated Time-to-Market**: While it may seem counterintuitive, integrating security throughout the SDLC can actually accelerate delivery by preventing late-stage security bottlenecks that delay releases. Organizations employing DevSecOps practices deliver features 24% faster than those using traditional security approaches (Amaro, Pereira, & da Silva, 2024).
- **Competitive Advantage**: As security breaches become more prevalent, organizations that demonstrate robust security practices gain competitive advantage through enhanced customer trust and reduced incident response costs. A Gartner survey found that 60% of enterprise customers now consider security practices in their vendor selection criteria (Potter & McGraw, 2004).
- **Regulatory Compliance**: With the proliferation of data protection regulations globally (GDPR, CCPA, HIPAA, etc.), organizations must demonstrate "security by design" principles. Secure SDLC provides a framework for meeting these regulatory requirements systematically.

1.4 Chapter Structure

The discussion unfolds across multiple sections:

- Section 2 offers a historical perspective on DevOps and outlines the genesis of DevSecOps, discussing its core principles.
- Section 3 delves into Secure SDLC fundamentals, describing necessary activities, tools, and best practices.
- Section 4 investigates the synergy between DevSecOps and a Secure SDLC, emphasizing how they complement each other.
- Section 5 presents a theoretical framework, integrating organizational and software engineering theories relevant to security-focused development.
- Subsequent sections propose practical implementation strategies, explore case studies, and discuss future directions. The chapter concludes by summarizing key takeaways and reinforcing the chapter's contributions.

One of the critical drivers behind the growing emphasis on Secure SDLC and DevSecOps is the increasing sophistication of cyber threats. Organizations now operate within an ecosystem where adversaries employ advanced persistent threats (APTs), social engineering, zero-day exploits, and supply chain attacks to infiltrate software infrastructure. Traditional, reactive approaches focused on patching after release are no longer sufficient. Instead, there is a pressing need for defensive measures that are proactive, iterative, and engrained from the earliest conceptual phases of software creation (Rajawat, Goyal, Verma, & Singh, 2025).

The notion of "shifting left" plays a prominent role in this evolution. Rather than relegating security checks to pre-release "gates," shifting left means addressing security concerns as early as the requirements and design phases, when changes can be made with lower cost and higher impact. This not only aligns with agile and DevOps methodologies but also fosters a mindset where every developer is encouraged, and expected, to consider the security implications of their code. In essence, every commit or pull request is an opportunity to detect and remediate potential risks (Saeed et al., 2025).

Furthermore, modern development pipelines leverage technologies such as Infrastructure as Code (IaC), containerization, and microservices to accelerate delivery. While these tools confer speed and flexibility, they also expand the attack surface—misconfigurations in container registries, ephemeral testing environments, or serverless APIs can lead to critical vulnerabilities(Kodakandla, 2024) . Integrating DevSecOps into these modern pipelines ensures that scanning, security testing, and dependency monitoring occurs seamlessly. Consequently, organizations maintain a real-time grasp of their security posture, responding quickly to changes in threat intelligence or newly disclosed library vulnerabilities.

Beyond the technical realm, cultural alignment remains essential to the success of a Secure SDLC. It requires sustained leadership advocacy, cross-functional cooperation, and continuous education. Company-wide "security awareness" campaigns can reinforce best practices, while specialized training for software architects and developers helps them internalize secure design patterns. As an example, major global banks have discovered that when developers understand the *why* behind a security rule (e.g., rate-limiting user logins, validating all user inputs), they are more committed to implementing these rules consistently (Chung, 2024).

In the chapters ahead, the shift from theory to actionable strategy will be explored in depth. We will delve into how organizations can overcome internal resistance, align DevSecOps pipelines with overarching governance frameworks, and measure the success of these initiatives via well-defined metrics such as Mean Time to Detect (MTTD) and Mean Time to Remediate (MTTR). By knitting together technical innovations with cultural transformation, a Secure SDLC becomes not just an aspiration but an attainable cornerstone for building and maintaining robust, trustworthy software.

2 DEVSECOPS: A NATURAL EVOLUTION OF DEVOPS

DevOps emerged in response to the inefficiencies of siloed software development and infrastructure management. By encouraging collaboration, continuous integration, and automated testing, DevOps significantly decreased the time from code commit to production deployment (Forsgren et al., 2018; Swartout, 2018)(Forsgren et al., 2018; Humble, 2018). However, as releases accelerated, organizations realized that vulnerabilities could now find their way into production more swiftly. Thus, a stronger emphasis on security became essential, setting the stage for DevSecOps.

2.1 Core Tenets of DevOps

The DevOps movement rests on three fundamental pillars:

1. **Collaboration**: Developers and operations teams share accountability for the entire software lifecycle, breaking down traditionally separate roles and responsibilities (Friman, 2024).
2. **Continuous Integration/Delivery (CI/CD)**: Frequent code merges, automated testing, and rapid deployments allow iterative development cycles (Forsgren et al., 2018).
3. **Automation**: Infrastructure and testing automation reduce human error and accelerate feedback loops, ensuring consistent environments across development, staging, and production (Swartout, 2018).

While these practices led to remarkable gains in release velocity, security remained a loosely defined concern. Many organizations performed limited application security reviews or vulnerability scans late in the process, failing to leverage the broader benefits of automation and collaboration for security tasks (Hsu, 2018).

2.2 Emergence of DevSecOps

DevSecOps explicitly integrates security into DevOps practices. Instead of security being an external "checklist," it is reimagined as:

- A series of continuous and integrated steps, where vulnerabilities are discovered as early as possible.
- A cultural shift that treats security as a shared responsibility (Adewole, 2024).
- A tool-driven approach for automating code analysis, compliance checks, container scanning, and environment hardening (Abiona et al., 2024).

By embedding security throughout the pipeline, DevSecOps effectively "shifts left" the detection of potential threats, reducing the cost and complexity of fixes. This approach also fosters transparency: security findings become visible to developers and operations staff in real time, ensuring swift remediation (Caracciolo, 2023).

Figure 1 illustrates how security is continuously integrated between development and operations in the DevSecOps cycle, highlighting the collaborative and cyclical nature of this approach.

Figure 1. The DevSecOps cycle illustrates how security integrates continuously among development and operations

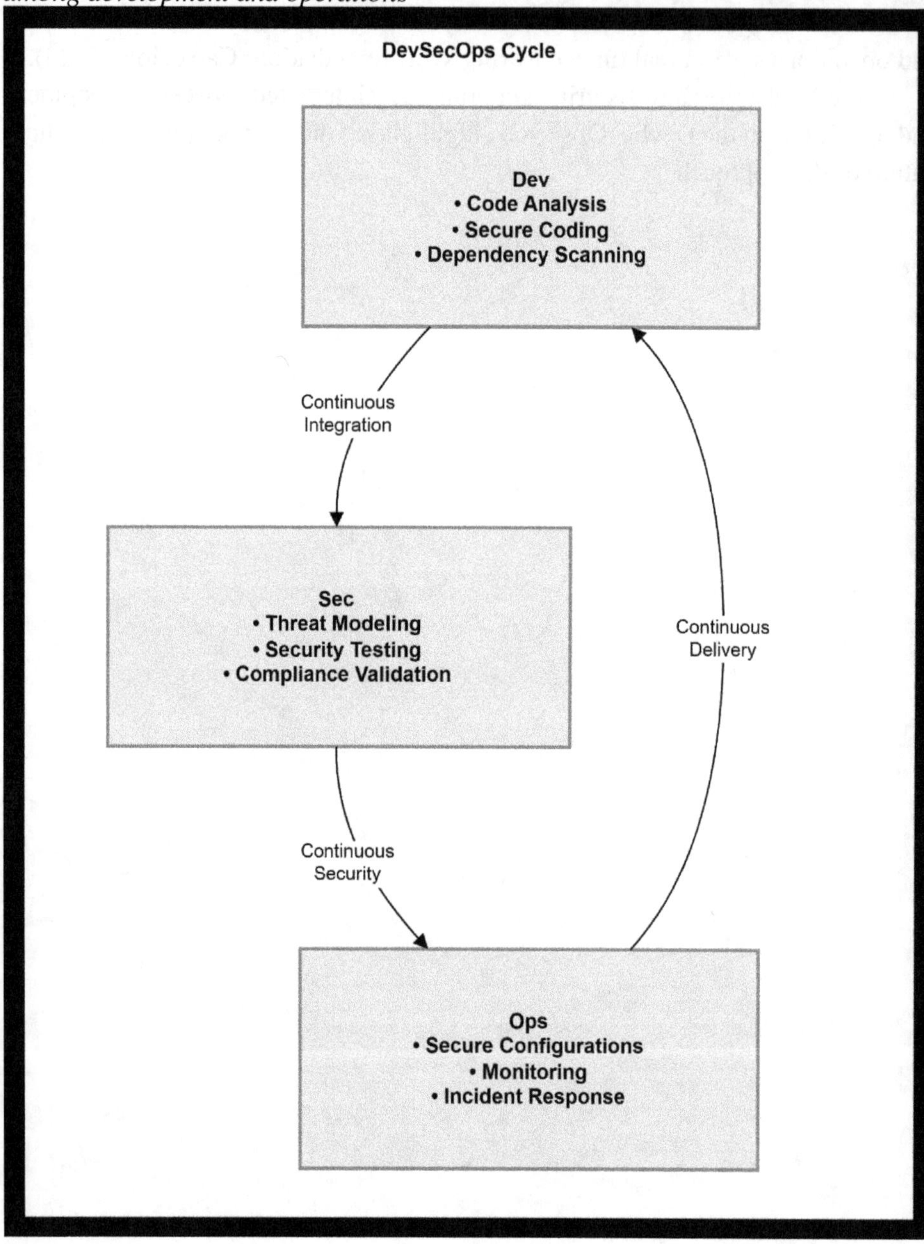

2.3 Cultural and Organizational Shifts

Transitioning from DevOps to DevSecOps is not merely about introducing new tools but also rethinking organizational structures and workflows. Historically, security was a separate unit within many companies, focusing on governance and policy rather than day-to-day development tasks (Ramaj, Sánchez-Gordón, Gkioulos, & Colomo-Palacios, 2024). Under DevSecOps, security experts collaborate directly with engineering teams, offering guidance on threat modeling, code reviews, and best practices for secure cloud configurations (Joshi, 2024).

Furthermore, DevSecOps initiatives typically appoint security champions within development squads. These individuals receive specialized training to identify vulnerabilities, interpret scan results, and liaise with full-time security staff (Boda, 2022). In large enterprises, the appointment of a "Head of DevSecOps" or a "DevSecOps Center of Excellence" may streamline this process, setting standards and ensuring consistent adoption across multiple products.

2.3.1 Security Champions Program

A security champions program formalizes the role of security advocates within development teams. These champions are not security specialists but rather software engineers with additional security training and responsibilities. Their role includes:

- Acting as the first point of contact for security questions within their team
- Participating in security design reviews and threat modeling sessions
- Advocating for security concerns during sprint planning and backlog grooming
- Helping to triage security findings and facilitating remediation
- Sharing security knowledge and best practices with team members

Research by DevOps Research and Assessment (2022) found that organizations with active security champions programs demonstrate 30% faster remediation times for security vulnerabilities and report higher developer satisfaction with security processes.

To implement an effective security champions program:

1. **Selection**: Choose individuals who demonstrate interest in security and have strong communication skills
2. **Training**: Provide specialized security training, certifications, and continuous education
3. **Recognition**: Establish formal recognition and career advancement opportunities

4. **Support**: Allocate dedicated time for security activities (typically 10-20% of their time)
5. **Community**: Create a community of practice where champions can share knowledge and experiences

2.4 Tools and Practices within DevSecOps

The DevSecOps methodology thrives on automation. Organizations employ:

- **Static Application Security Testing (SAST)**: Scans source code to detect patterns indicative of insecure code (Dakić, 2024) .
- **Dynamic Application Security Testing (DAST)**: Tests running applications for real-time vulnerabilities, such as improper session handling (Aljabri et al., 2022).
- **Software Composition Analysis (SCA)**: Evaluates third-party libraries for known vulnerabilities (Alshra'a, Al Sardy, & German, 2024; Theodoropoulos et al., 2023).
- **Infrastructure as Code Scanning**: Analyzes configurations for containers and orchestrators like Docker or Kubernetes, ensuring minimal privileges and properly configured networks (Williams, 2020).

These checks are embedded into Continuous Integration pipelines, so if a severity threshold is exceeded (e.g., a critical SQL injection flaw), the build fails and developers must resolve the issue before the code progresses (Bernardino et al., 2024; Dakić, 2024).

While DevSecOps emerged as a crucial extension to DevOps, the practical realization of this approach can vary significantly depending on organizational size, industry vertical, and existing technological stack. In large enterprises with complex regulatory compliance requirements, DevSecOps often involves a robust orchestration of automated security tools integrated into multiple stages of a CI/CD pipeline (Manda, 2023). In contrast, a smaller startup may adopt more lightweight solutions, leveraging open-source scanning tools and container-based microservices to keep overhead low.

2.4.1 DevSecOps Automation Maturity Model

Organizations typically progress through several stages of DevSecOps automation maturity:

1. **Ad Hoc**: Security testing is manual and performed inconsistently

2. **Basic Automation**: Core security checks are automated but with limited integration
3. **Integrated Security**: Security tools are integrated into CI/CD pipelines with defined gates
4. **Proactive Security**: Automated security checks are supplemented with proactive measures like threat modeling and security requirements
5. **Continuous Security Assurance**: Full automation with real-time monitoring, threat intelligence integration, and self-healing capabilities

Most organizations currently operate at levels 2 or 3, with only 14% reaching level 5 maturity (Amaro et al., 2024; DevOps Research and Assessment, 2022).

A key tenet of DevSecOps is its emphasis on continuous feedback loops. Traditional development pipelines often operate in silos, where developers hand off code to an operations team, which in turn may consult security teams as a final checkpoint. This segmentation can create blind spots. DevSecOps aims to unify these roles and perspectives into a fluid loop where each commit triggers immediate feedback on both functionality and security posture (Saeed et al., 2025). Developers can see the results of a security scan within minutes and address vulnerabilities at their source, rather than waiting until staging or pre-production cycles reveal critical flaws.

Another hallmark of DevSecOps is the focus on infrastructure parity. By employing containerization and Infrastructure as Code (IaC) templates, teams can replicate production-like environments in development and testing phases with minimal divergence (Ramaj et al., 2024). Security tests thus become more reliable predictors of how an application will behave under real-world conditions, reducing surprises post-deployment. This parity extends to patch management and configuration hardening, whereby any misconfiguration detected in staging is immediately addressed and integrated into the official IaC templates.

Despite these advantages, DevSecOps adoption can encounter organizational friction. Security teams sometimes resist real-time engagements, fearing a loss of oversight if they are not the final "gatekeepers." Meanwhile, development teams might view security scans as an impediment to meeting aggressive sprint deadlines (Manda, 2023). Addressing these concerns typically demands clear governance structures, strong executive sponsorship, and well-defined roles. Some organizations appoint "DevSecOps champions" whose job is to shepherd these cultural and procedural shifts within each product or platform team, ensuring that real-time security insights do not stagnate or get deprioritized (Chung, 2024).

Tools alone cannot guarantee success. Although advanced scanners and automated compliance checks are vital, they must be underpinned by robust policies, documentation, and cross-functional training initiatives. For instance, codifying best practices in a "security knowledge base" accessible to all developers encourages consistent coding standards, fosters self-sufficiency in detecting common vulnerabilities, and reduces repeated mistakes over time. Equally important is a shared vocabulary: developers, operations staff, and security analysts should align on risk severity scales, sign-off processes, and escalation protocols so that any discovered vulnerability can be triaged and remediated with minimal confusion.

Ultimately, DevSecOps can be viewed as both a methodology and a mindset that extends the DevOps principle of cross-functional collaboration to include an uncompromising focus on security. By integrating threat detection, secure coding, and compliance checks into daily workflows, organizations can move toward a culture where software reliability and security are seen as mutually reinforcing, rather than conflicting goals. Subsequent sections will illustrate how coupling DevSecOps with a well-structured Secure SDLC offers a comprehensive blueprint for safeguarding modern software ecosystems.

3 FUNDAMENTALS OF A SECURE SDLC

While DevSecOps underscores continuous and automated security, a Secure SDLC (SSDLC) provides the overarching framework for weaving security tasks into each lifecycle stage. The objective is to establish a robust, repeatable process that proactively mitigates vulnerabilities long before deployment.

3.1 Defining a Secure SDLC Model

The Secure SDLC can be conceptualized as a series of phases (Requirements, Design, Implementation, Testing, Deployment, Maintenance), each enriched with security-focused tasks (Abbas et al., 2025). Different models (e.g., Microsoft SDL, OWASP SAMM) propose variations of these phases, but the essence remains: security is not optional at any stage.

3.1.1 Requirements Phase

Security requirements frequently stem from:

- **Regulatory Mandates**: GDPR, HIPAA, PCI DSS, etc. (Boda, 2022).
- **Organizational Policies**: Data retention rules, authentication standards, and logging guidelines (Ramaj et al., 2024).
- **Threat Modeling Results**: Early discussions of how an application might be attacked, identifying potential mitigations (Anwar Mohammad, Nazir, & Mustafa, 2019) .

During this phase, stakeholders (product managers, security analysts, system architects) jointly define security acceptance criteria that development teams must meet before launch.

Security Requirements Engineering
Effective security requirements engineering involves:

1. **Security User Stories**: Framing security needs as user stories (e.g., "As a user, I want my personal data encrypted at rest so that it remains protected if storage is compromised")
2. **Abuse Cases**: Documenting how malicious actors might misuse the system
3. **Security Controls Mapping**: Mapping requirements to established security frameworks (NIST, CIS, etc.)
4. **Compliance Requirements Traceability**: Creating traceability matrices to ensure regulatory compliance
5. **Risk-Based Prioritization**: Prioritizing security requirements based on risk assessment

Security requirements should be SMART (Specific, Measurable, Achievable, Relevant, Time-bound) to ensure they can be effectively implemented and verified.

3.1.2 Design Phase

Architects and senior developers translate requirements into system designs. For instance, a multi-tier architecture might separate public-facing components from critical databases, applying robust access controls (Caracciolo, 2023):

- **Threat Modeling and Risk Assessment**: Detailed data flow diagrams help identify where encryption or authentication is vital (Anwar Mohammad et al., 2019) .
- **Architecture Review**: Checking for anti-patterns (e.g., storing passwords in plaintext) or design flaws.

Threat Modeling Methodologies
Several established methodologies guide the threat modeling process:

- **STRIDE**: Focuses on six threat categories: Spoofing, Tampering, Repudiation, Information disclosure, Denial of service, and Elevation of privilege

- **PASTA** (Process for Attack Simulation and Threat Analysis): A risk-centric methodology aligning technical security requirements with business objectives
- **LINDDUN**: Focuses specifically on privacy threats through seven categories: Linkability, Identifiability, Non-repudiation, Detectability, Disclosure of information, Unawareness, and Non-compliance
- **Attack Trees**: Graphical representations of attacks against a system, showing how different attack vectors might be combined

The most effective threat modeling processes:

- Are performed early in the design phase
- Involve cross-functional teams (developers, security experts, architects)
- Produce actionable security requirements and controls
- Are iterative, with models updated as the system evolves

3.1.3 Implementation Phase

Developers follow secure coding guidelines, typically referencing well-known standards like the OWASP Secure Coding Practices (Aljabri et al., 2022). Coding sessions incorporate Static Application Security Testing (SAST) to catch vulnerabilities automatically. Checking logs of the build process helps measure the number of issues flagged and addressed daily (Hsu, 2018) .

Secure Coding Practices

Secure coding practices should be language-specific but generally address common vulnerabilities:

- Input validation and output encoding
- Authentication and session management
- Access control implementation
- Cryptographic practices
- Error handling and logging
- Data protection
- Communication security
- System configuration
- Database security
- File management

Organizations with mature secure coding practices typically establish:

- Language-specific coding standards
- Pre-approved secure libraries and frameworks
- Automated code analysis in IDE plugins
- Regular secure code reviews
- Security-focused code competitions or bug bounties

3.1.4 Testing Phase

Security testing extends beyond functional verification. Tools and procedures may include:

- **Dynamic Application Security Testing (DAST)**: Automated black-box testing simulates real attacker behavior (Aljabri et al., 2022).
- **Penetration Testing**: Specialized testers or external consultants attempt to breach the system using various tactics(Alshra'a et al., 2024) .
- **Interactive Application Security Testing (IAST)**: Combines elements of SAST and DAST, monitoring the running application from the inside (Bernardino et al., 2024).

If critical vulnerabilities surface, the application loops back to the Implementation phase until the issues are resolved. This cyclical process ensures iterative refinement .

Beyond the broad outline of the Secure SDLC, recent frameworks and standards have sought to provide granular guidance for each lifecycle phase. For instance, the OWASP Software Assurance Maturity Model (SAMM) 2.0 introduces a maturity-based approach, where organizations can evaluate their security posture against a structured set of activities in areas like governance, design, implementation, verification, and operations (Aljabri et al., 2022). This aligns neatly with the notion of iterative improvement: a startup at an entry-level maturity might only conduct basic static code analysis, whereas a more advanced enterprise performs thorough threat modeling, invests in automated fuzz testing, and enforces continuous compliance checks.

Additionally, specialized processes within each phase can further enhance security outcomes:

- **Secure User Story Mapping**: During requirements gathering, user stories include explicit references to security acceptance criteria. This ensures that each feature is evaluated not just for functionality, but also for confidentiality, integrity, and availability requirements (Saeed et al., 2025)
- **Attack Surface Reduction Workshops**: In the design phase, teams work together to identify entry points for attackers, ensuring that network segments,

microservices, or APIs do not expose unnecessary functionalities or data (Manda, 2023).

- **Secure Code Review Checklists**: Developers adopt consistent checklists during implementation, covering areas such as parameterized queries, output encoding, and secure session management. These checklists can be encoded into automated scanning tools to standardize reviews and prevent human oversight (Eniola & Barnty, 2025).
- **Chaos Engineering for Security (ChaSec)**: In the testing phase, teams deliberately inject security-related failures into an environment (e.g., invalid certificates, malicious traffic simulations) to assess how resilient the application and underlying infrastructure remain under adverse conditions(Chung, 2024).

While these practices add depth to the standard Secure SDLC phases, they also demand coordinated leadership and well-structured tooling. A common challenge is integration overhead, where various security tools, scanning platforms, and policy modules do not seamlessly communicate with one another. To mitigate this, many organizations turn to centralized dashboards or "single pane of glass" solutions, which consolidate security findings from SAST, DAST, SCA, and even infrastructure checks, providing teams with a unified view of vulnerabilities and remediation status.

Moreover, effective knowledge management is crucial. As vulnerabilities emerge and are resolved, the lessons learned should feed back into the requirements and design phases for future iterations. This cyclical process fosters a culture of continuous learning, reducing the recurrence of known issues and enabling the team to address new threats more quickly. A robust Secure SDLC thus grows more refined with each release, reflecting both technological changes (e.g., container orchestration strategies) and evolving threat landscapes (e.g., new crypto-ransomware strains).

Finally, an often-overlooked facet of a Secure SDLC is its post-deployment phase. Comprehensive logging and real-time monitoring should capture application events, security alerts, and performance metrics that can indicate anomalous behavior or potential intrusions. By incorporating these insights into retrospective design assessments, security professionals and developers can identify structural weaknesses and iterate accordingly(Harkai & Ciurea, 2024). This ensures that the Secure SDLC is truly a loop, rather than a one-time or static cycle. As software boundaries expand with the advent of APIs, cloud microservices, and edge computing, maintaining this iterative, full-lifecycle perspective is essential for sustaining robust software security in an ever-changing digital landscape.

3.1.5 Deployment and Maintenance

Even after code is deemed production-ready, Secure SDLC requires continuous monitoring and maintenance. Production environments can be scanned periodically for misconfigurations and vulnerabilities in dependencies. Security patches must be applied promptly, and logs analyzed for anomalies indicating potential breaches (Bernardino et al., 2024; Theodoropoulos et al., 2023).

Runtime Application Self-Protection (RASP)

A growing area in the maintenance phase is RASP, which integrates security directly into the application runtime environment to:

- Detect attacks in real-time by analyzing application behavior
- Automatically block attacks without human intervention
- Provide detailed context for security incidents
- Reduce false positives by understanding application logic
- Protect applications even when vulnerabilities exist in the code

According to (Potter & McGraw, 2004) RASP adoption increased by 48% between 2020 and 2022, with 31% of enterprises now employing some form of RASP technology.

3.2 Benefits of a Secure SDLC

Several key advantages accrue from systematically securing the entire lifecycle. Firstly, risk reduction is evident as vulnerabilities are addressed in the blueprint stages, diminishing the likelihood of substantial rework (Caracciolo, 2023). Secondly, continuous iteration fosters cost savings, as reengineering entire architectures post-deployment can be prohibitively expensive. Thirdly, a robust Secure SDLC demonstrates compliance to regulators and auditors, thereby preventing potential fines and reputational harm(R. A. Khan, Khan, Akbar, & Alzahrani, 2024).

3.3 Challenges and Limitations

Despite its promise, adopting a Secure SDLC can be challenging:

- **Cultural Resistance**: Developers unused to security checks may perceive them as impediments (Adewole, 2024).

- **Tool Complexity**: The array of SAST, DAST, IAST, and SCA tools can overwhelm teams lacking specialized skills (Joshi, 2024).
- **Budget Constraints**: Smaller firms might struggle to invest in licensed security tools or specialized training (Taherdoost et al., 2025).

Addressing these barriers often requires a clear change management strategy and visible executive sponsorship, thereby ensuring that security becomes an organizational priority (Ramaj et al., 2024).

4 THE SYNERGY OF DEVSECOPS AND SECURE SDLC

While DevSecOps focuses on embedding security into continuous delivery pipelines, a Secure SDLC structures what security tasks to perform when. The convergence of these two paradigms can produce streamlined, automated, and highly robust software security processes.

4.1 Common Goals and Complementary Approaches

Both DevSecOps and the Secure SDLC share the objective of reducing security vulnerabilities before code reaches production (Adewole, 2024). The Secure SDLC outlines the phases (and associated security objectives), while DevSecOps supplies the real-time feedback loops that ensure vulnerabilities flagged in any given phase are resolved quickly. For example, a Secure SDLC prescribes "static code analysis" in the implementation phase; DevSecOps ensures such analysis is automatically triggered with every code commit (Gomes, Pereira, Silva, de Vasconcelos, & Rocha, 2022).

4.2 Practical Integration

In practice, the synergy manifests through integrated tool chains:

- **Continuous Integration Hooks**: Implementation-phase SAST tools (e.g., SonarQube, Checkmarx) run on each pull request, halting merges if high-severity issues are found (Dakić, 2024).
- **Ephemeral Test Environments**: Spin up short-lived environments for dynamic testing (DAST, IAST), aligning with the testing stage in the Secure SDLC. Once tests complete, containers or serverless functions are torn down automatically, reducing cost and complexity.

- **Risk-Based Deployment Checks**: The pipeline can incorporate risk thresholds derived from Secure SDLC guidelines. If vulnerability severity surpasses acceptable levels, the deployment is halted(Bernardino et al., 2024) .

Figure 2 illustrates the integration of DevSecOps within a Secure SDLC, showing how security checks are automated at each phase of the development lifecycle.

Figure 2. High-level integration of DevSecOps within a Secure SDLC, illustrating automated security checks at each phase

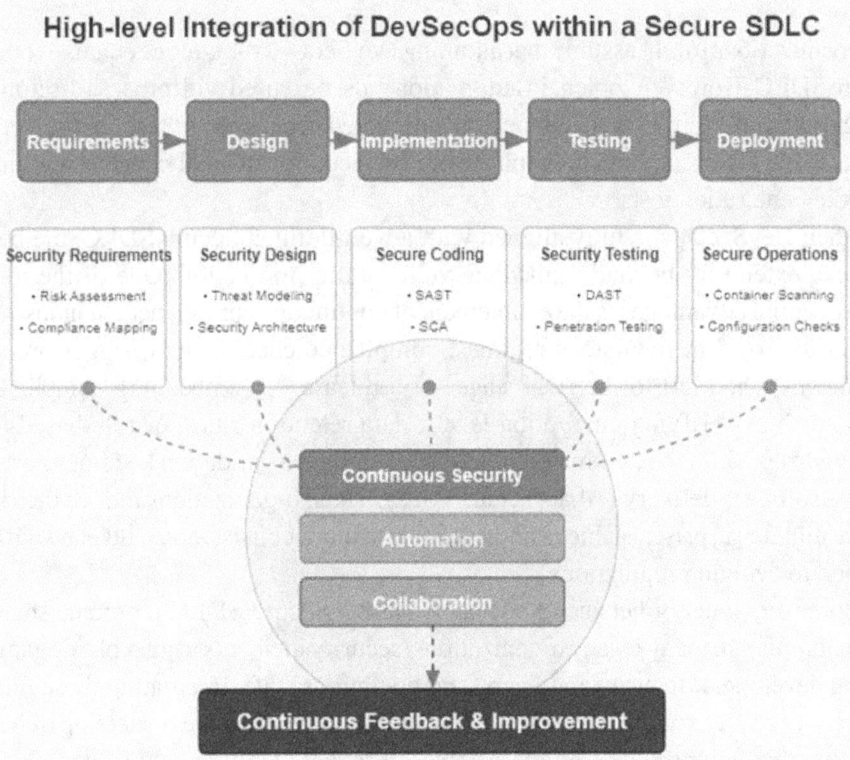

4.3 Benefits of This Convergence

When DevSecOps and Secure SDLC converge:

- **Decreased Time-to-Fix**: Automated scans alert developers instantly, aligning with the Secure SDLC's principle of early detection (Gomes et al., 2022).
- **Improved Developer Engagement**: Security tasks become routine and less intimidating, encouraging developers to build strong secure coding habits (Caracciolo, 2023).
- **Heightened Transparency**: Logging and analytics systems provide clear insight into code quality trends, compliance adherence, and vulnerability distributions (Theodoropoulos et al., 2023) .

4.4 Common Pitfalls

Organizations might assume that adopting DevSecOps tools alone equals a robust Secure SDLC. However, toolchain automation must be paired with process discipline and thorough training. Over-reliance on automated scanners can also leave deeper architectural flaws unnoticed, emphasizing the need for manual code reviews and periodic penetration tests.

When DevSecOps is fully aligned with a well-defined Secure SDLC, the benefits can extend far beyond immediate vulnerability mitigation. One of the most consequential advantages is the enablement of continuous compliance. In industries subject to stringent regulatory regimes, compliance checks often trigger project slowdowns when left to the final stages of a release. By embedding compliance tests—such as verifying encryption levels, data retention rules, or role-based access controls—into the automated pipeline, compliance validation becomes part of routine software delivery (Aljabri et al., 2022). Thus, organizations reduce the risk of last-minute surprises, achieve audit readiness more consistently, and can swiftly respond to evolving regulations.

Moreover, synergy between DevSecOps and a Secure SDLC promotes shared accountability. In many legacy organizations, security incidents trigger blame games among developers, security engineers, and operations staff. Integrating these functions under a single workflow fosters transparency and collective ownership of both successes and failures. For example, a newly discovered SQL injection vulnerability is treated not as a “developer mistake” but as a pipeline learning point, prompting immediate additions to secure coding guidelines, new automated checks in the pipeline, and real-time alerts to the entire team (Saeed et al., 2025).

The fusion of these methods also creates opportunities for threat intelligence integration. As part of continuous integration cycles, security teams can feed real-time threat intelligence data into automated scanning tools. This allows them to detect indicators of compromise (IoCs) or references to newly weaponized exploits as soon as they are reported in security feeds or intelligence platforms(Chung, 2024). Such dynamic updating ensures that software remains secure against emergent threats, closing the window of exposure. In this sense, the synergy fosters an adaptive, self-improving ecosystem where the pipeline "learns" from the broader cybersecurity community.

Additionally, a robust DevSecOps plus Secure SDLC framework accelerates risk-based decision-making. Executive stakeholders often grapple with questions like: "Should we release now and fix a moderate vulnerability later?" or "Do we invest in rewriting a legacy module that has high-severity issues?" By correlating vulnerability data with business impact and compliance obligations, product managers and security leads can make informed decisions swiftly (Eniola & Barnty, 2025). Automated dashboards that score vulnerabilities based on exploitability and data sensitivity guide these conversations, ensuring that risk acceptance or deferral is never done blindly.

Still, organizations must remain wary of potential pitfalls when merging these paradigms. In particular, the velocity of DevOps can lead to a culture of continuous "churn," where new features race toward production without sufficient reflection on deeper architectural or cryptographic design flaws. Likewise, the formality of certain Secure SDLC approaches might impede the quick feedback loops that DevSecOps demands if not appropriately streamlined (Manda, 2023). Achieving the right balance depends on rigorous but flexible processes, adequate toolchain automation, and leadership that champions both rapid iteration and robust security.

In sum, the synergy of DevSecOps and a Secure SDLC is a potent strategy for modern software engineering, merging the strengths of iterative development, real-time collaboration, and continuous security assurance. By carefully calibrating cultural, technical, and compliance-focused elements, organizations can transcend the false dichotomy that speed must come at the expense of security. Instead, speed and security become mutually reinforcing, paving the way for resilient, high-quality software in a fast-changing digital arena.

5 THEORETICAL FRAMEWORK

Establishing a cohesive theoretical foundation explains why the integration of DevSecOps and a Secure SDLC resonates so strongly across different organizational environments. This section synthesizes organizational, socio-technical, and software engineering theories to underpin best practices in security-centric development.

5.1 Socio-Technical Systems Theory

Socio-Technical Systems (STS) theory highlights the interplay between people and technology in complex organizational environments (Forsgren et al., 2018). According to STS, effective DevSecOps adoption relies on more than just implementing scanning tools or writing secure code. Rather, it necessitates a cultural realignment where individuals across development, operations, and security teams share objectives and responsibilities (Friman, 2024). By merging technology (e.g., automated security checks) with collaborative structures (e.g., cross-functional stand-ups), organizations can harmonize human and technical factors (Adewole, 2024).

5.2 Contingency Theory

Contingency theory posits that there is no single best way to organize or manage an enterprise; instead, effective structures and processes must fit the specific context (Ramaj et al., 2024). In the realm of DevSecOps and Secure SDLC, this implies that the extent of security activities, tool sophistication, and level of automation should reflect the risk profile, regulatory environment, and organizational scale. A heavily regulated financial institution will likely require a more rigorous set of checks, including third-party audits, compared to a smaller startup that faces less stringent compliance demands (Taherdoost et al., 2025).

5.3 Iterative and Incremental Development Paradigms

DevSecOps aligns seamlessly with agile methodologies and iterative development cycles. Frequent releases and feedback loops ensure that newly identified vulnerabilities can be patched quickly, reducing the time window for attackers to exploit them (Dakić, 2024). The Secure SDLC, meanwhile, ensures each iteration includes security tasks (threat modeling, secure design reviews), thus guaranteeing that the product evolves securely over time (Hsu, 2018).

5.4 Systems Theory in Software Engineering

Systems theory acknowledges the interconnected nature of modern software, wherein vulnerabilities in third-party libraries, cloud configurations, or container images can jeopardize an application's integrity (Ramaj et al., 2024). DevSecOps addresses this challenge by scanning all system components—source code, dependencies, containers, and runtime environments—in an integrated manner. The Secure SDLC provides the blueprint for identifying these components early, clarifying how they interact and where potential security boundaries exist (Bernardino et al., 2024).

5.5 Connecting Theory to Practice

By linking organizational and software engineering theories, practitioners can appreciate that DevSecOps plus a Secure SDLC is not merely a technical shift—it is a holistic organizational transformation . This perspective helps in:

- **Ensuring Leadership Buy-In**: Demonstrating how improved security outcomes support broader business goals(Chung, 2024).
- **Adapting Security Practices**: Tailoring practices to organizational contingencies such as risk appetite, team size, and compliance norms (Ramaj et al., 2024).
- **Maintaining a Balanced Approach**: Using automation to handle mundane tasks but recognizing the value of human insight for complex or architecture-wide security considerations (Joshi, 2024) .

6 PRACTICAL IMPLEMENTATION STRATEGIES

Despite the strong theoretical foundations, organizations often struggle to translate DevSecOps and a Secure SDLC into day-to-day practices. This section details strategies for cultural change, toolchain setup, and governance.

6.1 Cultural and Organizational Change Management

Leadership and Vision. Senior leaders must articulate a clear vision that prioritizes security as a shared organizational value. This shift helps override entrenched beliefs that security is solely the domain of specialized teams (Adewole, 2024; Theodoropoulos et al., 2023) . Regular all-hands meetings or lunch-and-learn sessions focused on security best practices can spark cross-team collaboration.

Security Champions. Embedding security champions in development squads provides real-time guidance on coding standards, vulnerability triage, and emergent threats (Boda, 2022). These champions become conduits between full-time security specialists and the rest of the dev team, facilitating knowledge transfer and swift response to security incidents.

Training and Knowledge Sharing. Frequent workshops on threat modeling, secure coding guidelines, and DevSecOps tooling ensure that newly onboarded developers quickly acclimate to security-focused workflows. Exercises such as capture-the-flag events or game days promote hands-on learning in a low-stakes environment, reinforcing the concept of shift left (Gomes et al., 2022).

6.2 Selecting and Integrating Tools

A robust toolchain forms the operational backbone of DevSecOps within a Secure SDLC. While every environment is unique, certain categories of tools are universally beneficial:

- **SAST Tools**: For real-time code analysis, e.g., SonarQube, Checkmarx (Dakić, 2024).
- **DAST Tools**: For probing running instances, e.g., OWASP ZAP, Burp Suite (Aljabri et al., 2022) .
- **SCA Tools**: Checking for known CVEs in open-source or third-party libraries, e.g., Snyk (Jawed, 2019).
- **Container Security**: Scans Docker images, ensures minimal base images and secure configurations, e.g., Trivy, Aqua).
- **Secrets Management**: Solutions like HashiCorp Vault or AWS Secrets Manager that mitigate hardcoded credentials (Theodoropoulos et al., 2023).

Integrating these tools into CI/CD pipelines ensures that each commit triggers scans. Should a high-severity vulnerability be discovered, the pipeline fails, thereby preventing insecure code from reaching production.

Table 1. Illustrative DevSecOps toolchain for a secure SDLC

Category	Tool Examples	Typical Stage	Open Source Options	Enterprise Options
SAST	SonarQube, Checkmarx	Implementation (commit hook)	SpotBugs, ESLint	Veracode, Micro Focus Fortify
DAST	OWASP ZAP, Burp Suite	Testing (preproduction)	OWASP ZAP, Nikto	AppScan, Acunetix
SCA	Snyk, Dependabot	Implementation, Build	OWASP Dependency-Check	Black Duck, WhiteSource
Container Security	Trivy, Aqua	Build & Deployment	Clair, Trivy	Aqua, Prisma Cloud
Secrets Management	Vault, AWS Secrets Manager	Implementation, Production	git-secrets	HashiCorp Vault Enterprise, CyberArk
IaC Scanning	Checkov, Terrascan	Build	Checkov, Terrascan	Prisma Cloud, Bridgecrew

6.3 Governance, Risk, and Compliance (GRC) Alignment

In regulated industries, governance structures often dictate rigorous documentation, audits, and sign-offs(Abbas et al., 2025; Caracciolo, 2023). DevSecOps pipelines must record evidence of every scan and patch, serving as an audit trail. Tools like Policy as Code can automate compliance checks by translating regulatory requirements into machine-readable rules (Caracciolo, 2023).

> **Policy as Code Example**. A healthcare startup under HIPAA might define rules for encryption at rest in a policy file. Whenever developers modify an Infrastructure as Code template that configures storage buckets, automated checks verify whether encryption is enabled (Boda, 2022) . Failure to comply halts the commit until the developer addresses the policy violation.

6.4 Metrics and Continuous Improvement

Key Performance Indicators (KPIs) such as:

- **Mean Time to Detect (MTTD)**: Average duration between introducing a vulnerability and discovering it.
- **Mean Time to Remediate (MTTR)**: Average time taken to fix a known vulnerability (Gomes et al., 2022).
- **Vulnerability Recurrence Rate**: Frequency at which previously fixed vulnerabilities reappear, possibly indicating systemic flaws .

In tracking these metrics, organizations can gauge the effectiveness of their DevSecOps-Secure SDLC processes, identifying bottlenecks and learning opportunities over time (Adewole, 2024).

Figure 3 illustrates a typical CI/CD pipeline enhanced with security gates at each stage, demonstrating how security controls can be integrated seamlessly into the development workflow.

Figure 3. Example CI/CD pipeline with integrated security gates and automated scanning

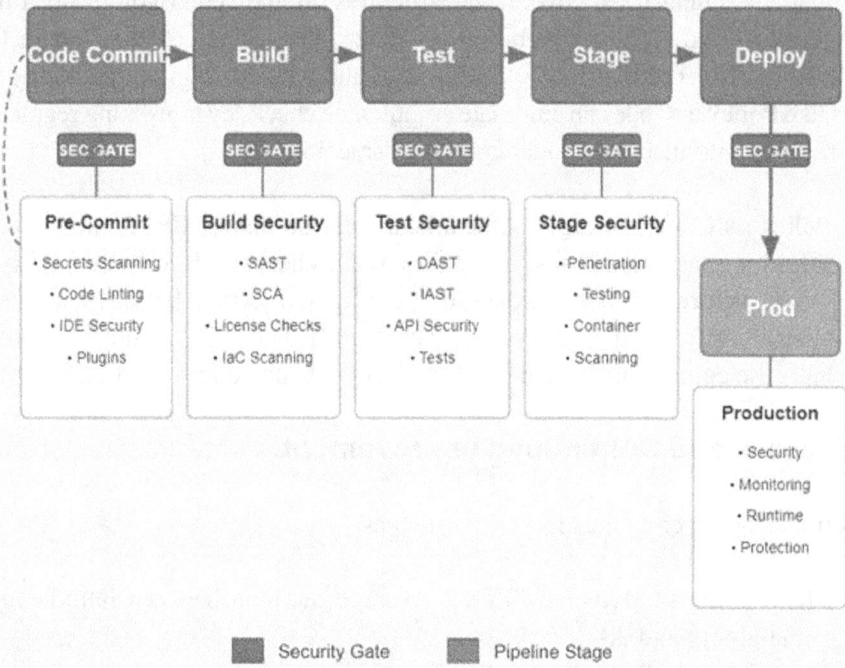

6.5 Security Activity Matrix Across SDLC Phases

Table 2. Security activities, artifacts, and responsibilities across SDLC phases Secure Software Development Lifecycle (SDLC)

SDLC Phase	Security Activities	Key Artifacts	Primary Responsibility	Tools and Techniques
Requirements	- Security requirements gathering - Compliance mapping - Risk assessment	- Security requirements document - Compliance matrix - Risk register	Security Architect, Product Owner	- Security user stories - Compliance frameworks - Risk assessment tools
Design	- Threat modeling - Secure architecture design - Attack surface analysis	- Threat model document - Security architecture - Security controls specification	Security Architect, System Architect	- STRIDE/DREAD - Data flow diagrams - Security design patterns
Implementation	- Secure coding - Code reviews - Static Application Security Testing (SAST) - Software Composition Analysis (SCA)	- Secure code - SAST reports - Dependency analysis reports	Developers, Security Champions	- IDE security plugins - SAST tools - SCA tools - Secure coding guidelines
Testing	- Dynamic Application Security Testing (DAST) - Interactive Application Security Testing (IAST) - Penetration testing - Security functional testing	- Security test reports - Vulnerability reports - Remediation plans	Security Testers, QA	- DAST tools - IAST tools - Penetration testing tools - Fuzz testing

continued on following page

Table 2. Continued

SDLC Phase	Security Activities	Key Artifacts	Primary Responsibility	Tools and Techniques
Deployment	- Security configuration review - Infrastructure scanning - Secrets management	- Secure configuration baselines - Infrastructure scan reports - Deployment approval	DevOps, Security Engineer	- Infrastructure-as-Code (IaC) scanning - Container scanning - Secrets management tools - Secure deployment checklist
Operations & Maintenance	- Continuous monitoring - Vulnerability management - Incident response - Patch management	- Security monitoring reports - Incident response plans - Patch compliance reports	Operations, Security Operations	- Security Information and Event Management (SIEM) - Runtime Application Self-Protection (RASP) - Web Application Firewall (WAF) - Vulnerability scanners

7 PROPOSED CONCEPTUAL FRAMEWORK: INTEGRATING DEVSECOPS AND SECURE SDLC

Drawing from socio-technical, contingency, and systems theories, this section presents a conceptual model that visualizes how DevSecOps (continuous security) and the Secure SDLC (structured security phases) intertwine to achieve comprehensive protection.

7.1 Framework Components

1. **Foundational Readiness**: Leadership alignment, cultural preparedness, and skill development for secure engineering (Adewole, 2024; Bernardino et al., 2024).
2. **Secure SDLC Stages**: Requirements, design, implementation, testing, deployment, and maintenance, each enriched with security tasks.
3. **DevSecOps Practices**: Automation, continuous feedback loops, real-time scanning, cross-functional collaboration(Hsu, 2018).
4. **Governance and Compliance Overlays**: Ensuring every phase adheres to internal and external regulations, using policy as code and real-time checks(Aljabri et al., 2022) (Taherdoost et al., 2025).
5. **Outcome Metrics and Continuous Improvement**: Gauging the efficacy of combined DevSecOps+Secure SDLC strategies to foster iterative enhancements (Potter & McGraw, 2004).

Figure 4 illustrates the conceptual framework, showing how these components interlock to create a comprehensive security approach.

Figure 4. Proposed conceptual framework illustrating how DevSecOps and a Secure SDLC interlock under governance and continuous improvement

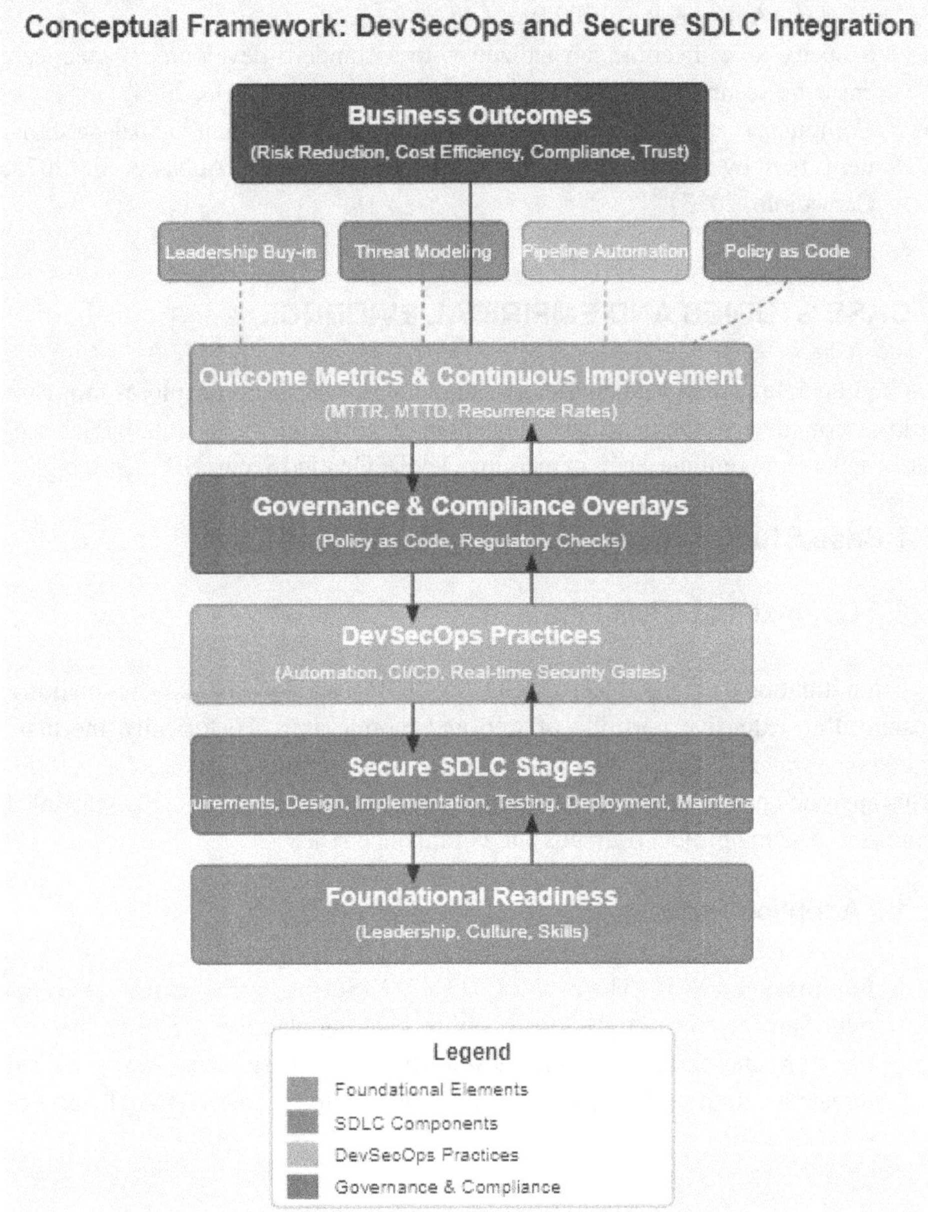

7.2 Implications of the Framework

By mapping out these components:

- Organizations gain clarity on sequencing, understanding that foundational readiness (e.g., skill development) must precede deeper DevSecOps integrations (R. A. Khan et al., 2024)
- Security tasks become normalized within standard development practices, ensuring security is neither optional nor external (Adewole, 2024).
- Compliance emerges as a continuous process, rather than a final checklist item, thereby reducing last-minute surprises in audits (Abbas et al., 2025; Caracciolo, 2023) .

8 CASE STUDIES AND EMPIRICAL EVIDENCE

To illustrate real-world benefits and challenges, this section explores four case studies from diverse sectors: finance, healthcare, government, and retail. Each scenario underscores unique facets of merging DevSecOps and Secure SDLC principles.

8.1 Case Study 1: Large-Scale Financial Institution

8.1.1 Context and Challenges

A multinational bank, subject to PCI DSS, GDPR, and local banking regulations, managed an extensive portfolio of web and mobile apps. Historically, the bank relied on a waterfall SDLC with late-stage penetration testing (Abbas et al., 2025). This approach proved costly, as many issues surfaced only weeks before scheduled launches, causing project overruns and compliance risks.

8.1.2 Adoption Process

Foundational Shift. The bank's CTO and CISO co-sponsored a DevSecOps pilot, starting with a high-priority online banking platform. Security champions were chosen among senior developers. They participated in specialized threat modeling workshops and learned how to interpret SAST/DAST findings (Hsu, 2018).

Tooling Integration. The bank integrated Checkmarx for SAST and Burp Suite for DAST into Jenkins CI pipelines. The Secure SDLC process mandated threat modeling and architecture reviews during the design phase. Any build containing a critical vulnerability automatically failed the pipeline (Adewole, 2024).

8.1.3 Results and Outcomes

Within one year, the frequency of high-severity vulnerabilities dropped by 45%, correlating with a shortened mean time-to-market (Joshi, 2024). Audit outcomes improved, as the automated scanning pipelines provided clear logs for PCI DSS compliance. The pilot's success prompted broader enterprise-wide rollouts, transforming security from a late-stage concern into an integral development facet.

8.2 Case Study 2: Healthcare Startup

8.2.1 Context and Challenges

A healthcare startup building a patient-management SaaS solution grappled with HIPAA regulations. With limited staff and resources, the startup struggled to sustain robust security practices. They lacked an in-house security expert, relying instead on ad hoc external consultancy (Taherdoost et al., 2025).

8.2.2 Implementation Strategy

Securing the SDLC. The startup adopted a Secure SDLC, mandating threat modeling in the requirements stage and designing microservices with well-defined security boundaries. They introduced ephemeral container-based test environments for thorough DAST checks (Aljabri et al., 2022).

DevSecOps Toolchain. Leveraging AWS services, they integrated AWS Secrets Manager to eliminate plaintext credentials. Snyk's SCA tool flagged vulnerable open-source libraries early, preventing risky dependencies from reaching production (Jawed, 2019). Automated Terraform scripts enforced encryption at rest for all patient data storage.

8.2.3 Results and Lessons Learned

Despite initial reservations about “slowing down” development, the startup reported minimal friction after onboarding developers to the new pipeline. They achieved HIPAA compliance within eight months, significantly boosting investor confidence and client trust(Aljabri et al., 2022) (Abbas et al., 2025). Early detection of insecure configurations reduced incident response overhead, enabling the small team to focus on core product features.

8.3 Case Study 3: Government Agency

8.3.1 Context and Challenges

A national government agency managed critical citizen data across multiple platforms. Public scrutiny of data breaches had reached unprecedented levels, making security a top political priority. Yet, the agency's legacy systems hindered modernization efforts, with compliance checks often scattered across different departments (Alshra'a et al., 2024).

8.3.2 Unified DevSecOps-Secure SDLC Rollout

Cross-Departmental Task Force. The agency created a dedicated security task force drawing members from the IT, compliance, and policy divisions. Their goal: unify the existing SDLC under a single Secure SDLC framework aligned with NIST guidelines and incorporate DevSecOps practices (Cybersecurity, 2018).
Centralized Governance. A specialized "DevSecOps Center of Excellence" provided ongoing training, set up common pipelines, and standardized threat modeling methods. Automated scanning tools were rolled out incrementally, ensuring minimal disruptions to legacy systems (Alshra'a et al., 2024).

8.3.3 Impact

Over three years, the agency reported no major data breaches, attributing success to proactive vulnerability management and consistent compliance audits embedded within daily workflows (Chung, 2024). Public trust rose, evident in improved feedback from periodic citizen surveys. In parallel, the robust pipeline laid a foundation for modernizing core services without compromising security.

8.4 Case Study 4: E-Commerce Retailer

8.4.1 Context and Challenges

A mid-sized e-commerce retailer with 12 million annual customers faced increasing pressure to accelerate feature delivery while maintaining PCI DSS compliance and protecting sensitive customer data. The company operated a hybrid infrastructure spanning on-premises systems and cloud services, creating complex security considerations. Security was traditionally handled by a separate team that performed manual reviews before major releases, creating bottlenecks and tension with development teams (Marchany & Tront, 2002).

8.4.2 Implementation Approach

Phased Implementation. Rather than attempting a company-wide transformation, the retailer adopted a phased approach starting with their payment processing system—the most security-critical component. They established a cross-functional team comprising developers, operations specialists, and security experts to create a reference implementation of DevSecOps practices integrated with their existing SDLC.

Tool Consolidation and Integration. The retailer had accumulated multiple security tools over the years, many operating in isolation. They rationalized their toolchain, focusing on solutions that offered robust APIs for integration with their CI/CD pipeline. They prioritized:

- Automated SAST and SCA in developer IDEs
- Pre-commit hooks to prevent secrets from entering the codebase
- Automated compliance checks using policy-as-code
- Container scanning for their microservices architecture

Metrics-Driven Approach. The retailer established a security dashboard with key metrics including:

- Vulnerability discovery rate
- Mean time to remediation
- Security debt (tracked in story points)
- Compliance posture score
- Time spent on security reviews

8.4.3 Results and Business Impact

The retailer documented several significant outcomes:

- **Release Acceleration**: Deployment frequency increased from bi-weekly to daily for core services while maintaining security standards
- **Cost Efficiency**: 62% reduction in security-related rework costs
- **Compliance Efficiency**: PCI DSS audit preparation time reduced from 6 weeks to 1 week
- **Detection Improvement**: Mean time to detect security issues decreased from 18 days to 2.4 days

- **Business Growth**: Faster feature delivery contributed to 18% year-over-year revenue growth

A particularly notable achievement was the creation of a "security feature factory" approach where security improvements were treated as product features with dedicated sprint allocation, making security work visible and valued rather than treated as overhead.

9 DISCUSSION: LESSONS LEARNED AND BEST PRACTICES

The case studies elucidate real-world complexities and strategies, offering lessons that generalize across industries:

9.1 Holistic Integration Over Bolt-On Solutions

Treating security as an afterthought or as an externally imposed checklist consistently leads to project delays, higher costs, and uncertain compliance. By contrast, organizations that implement DevSecOps in tandem with a Secure SDLC see predictable and scalable security outcomes (Adewole, 2024; Bernardino et al., 2024).

9.2 Cultural Emphasis and Leadership Commitment

From the largest multinational to the smallest startup, leadership endorsement is crucial for normalizing security practices. Shared accountability in daily scrums or sprint planning fosters a mindset where vulnerabilities are addressed immediately rather than deferred (Adewole, 2024; Forsgren et al., 2018).

9.3 Automation and Tool Reliability

Automated scanning can significantly reduce human error and accelerate detection. However, reliance on tools alone is insufficient. Integrating manual checks, particularly for business logic flaws, remains vital (Aljabri et al., 2022; Theodoropoulos et al., 2023). Organizations should choose tools that align with their tech stack and scale of operations to avoid overburdening developers with false positives .

9.4 Continuous Learning and Feedback Loops

Whether it's a monthly security review or a formal post-mortem on discovered vulnerabilities, continuous reflection is essential. These feedback loops refine the pipeline, updating threat models and coding standards to stay aligned with evolving threat landscapes (Friman, 2024).

10 FUTURE DIRECTIONS

Given the rapid evolution of technology and cyber threats, the landscape for Secure SDLC and DevSecOps will inevitably shift. Several emerging trends promise to reshape these practices:

10.1 AI-Driven Security Testing

Machine learning algorithms can identify complex patterns in code repositories and production logs, predicting potential vulnerabilities that conventional rule-based tools might overlook (S. A. Khan et al., 2023). Integrating AI-based solutions into DevSecOps pipelines could further reduce detection times and automate patch suggestions.

10.2 Serverless and Edge Architectures

As serverless computing (AWS Lambda, Azure Functions) and edge computing gain traction, organizations must adapt their security checks to ephemeral and distributed environments. Tools and frameworks are evolving to scan short-lived functions and localized nodes in near real-time, embedding security even closer to end-users.

10.3 Policy as Code Expansion

Beyond simple configuration checks, policy as code approaches will likely expand to incorporate advanced compliance logic. This could automate intricate regulatory processes, from region-specific data residency requirements to industry-specific rules (e.g., financial transaction oversight) (Caracciolo, 2023).

10.4 Deeper Integration of Privacy Protocols

With data protection laws (GDPR, CCPA) intensifying, privacy by design is increasingly integral to Secure SDLC frameworks. DevSecOps pipelines may incorporate privacy impact assessments, ensuring data minimization and anonymization are validated continuously(Aljabri et al., 2022) (Abbas et al., 2025).

Quantum-Resistant Cryptography. As quantum computing matures, encryption algorithms widely used today (e.g., RSA, ECC) may become susceptible to quantum-based attacks. In response, NIST and various cybersecurity bodies are advocating for post-quantum cryptographic standards (Rajawat et al., 2025). Future DevSecOps pipelines will likely include automatic checks to ensure quantum-safe algorithms are deployed, especially in sectors such as finance or national defense where long-term data confidentiality is paramount.

Automated Defensive Coding. AI-assisted code generation tools are emerging that can proactively suggest secure code snippets, anticipate risky coding patterns, and even auto-generate unit and integration tests emphasizing security boundaries (Saeed et al., 2025). While still in their infancy, these tools could become integral to a Secure SDLC, offering "live" security insights as developers type. Over time, machine learning models might adapt to a team's coding style, providing context-aware suggestions that reduce both false positives and developer friction.

Zero-Trust Architectures. The shift toward zero-trust networking—where no user, device, or application is implicitly trusted, even inside the corporate perimeter—necessitates a radical rethinking of software architectures. Applications must embed stronger identity and access management (IAM) measures at every layer, including microservices, APIs, and data storage. Future DevSecOps practices are expected to revolve around continuously validating identities, device states, and communication patterns, thereby reducing lateral movement opportunities for attackers. Secure SDLC frameworks will incorporate zero-trust design principles early in the requirements phase to reflect this architectural change.

Self-Healing Systems. Another frontier is the advent of self-healing software, where systems automatically respond to security anomalies or performance degradations by reconfiguring services, rotating credentials, or quarantining suspect modules in real time (Eniola & Barnty, 2025). This requires a level of observability, orchestration, and AI-driven decision-making that extends beyond typical CI/CD pipelines. DevSecOps workflows may add machine learning pipelines to continuously refine anomaly detection models, enabling a system to adapt to novel threats as they emerge.

Industry-Specific Regulatory Frameworks. With data privacy and cybersecurity laws proliferating worldwide, from GDPR in the EU to LGPD in Brazil and CCPA in California, organizations must navigate an increasingly complex regulatory patchwork. Some industries, such as automotive or critical infrastructure, are moving toward sector-specific cybersecurity standards . Future Secure SDLC processes may include built-in compliance templates that automatically verify and report alignment with these emergent regulations, reducing the administrative burden and streamlining audits.

In anticipation of these developments, organizations adopting Secure SDLC principles today can future-proof their software delivery ecosystems by investing in robust automation, skill development, and culture-building. DevSecOps pipelines that incorporate AI-driven scanning, granular access controls, and real-time analytics will be better positioned to adapt to quantum-resistant standards, self-healing architectures, and zero-trust mandates. While these evolutions undoubtedly introduce new complexities, they also present unprecedented opportunities to create software that is not only continuously delivered but continuously protected. By remaining agile and informed, development teams can embrace these changes, turning emerging challenges into catalysts for innovation.

11 CONCLUSION

This chapter has comprehensively analyzed Secure SDLC frameworks in conjunction with DevSecOps principles, underlining the significance of proactively embedding security within every phase of the software creation process. By merging the structured, phase-wise approach of a Secure SDLC with the continuous integration and collaborative ethos of DevSecOps, organizations cultivate an environment where vulnerabilities are identified and resolved rapidly—if not preemptively.

The synergy of these methodologies yields tangible business benefits, including faster time-to-market, improved compliance posture, and enhanced stakeholder trust. Indeed, the case studies and conceptual frameworks presented here affirm that cultural readiness, leadership commitment, and robust automation are prerequisites for success. Security champions can act as catalysts, bridging the gap between specialized security knowledge and day-to-day developer activities, ensuring that secure coding and threat modeling become a collective responsibility.

Nonetheless, evolving cyber threats and technological shifts—such as AI-driven scanning, serverless architectures, and policy-as-code expansions—will demand continuous adaptation. Future research should further explore how these innovations might reshape governance models, risk management, and real-time threat detection in diverse industries. Additional empirical studies can also illuminate best practices for small and mid-sized enterprises where budgets and expertise may be constrained.

Ultimately, the most sustainable transformation arises when security is no longer an optional layer but an inherent value in every line of code, every build, and every deployment pipeline. Through the combined lens of DevSecOps and a Secure SDLC, organizations can safeguard their software ecosystems and align with an ever-expanding landscape of regulatory demands. As the digital world grows increasingly interconnected, such integrative strategies remain the cornerstone of resilient and trustworthy software development.

REFERENCES

Abbas, R., Afolabi, R., Eleweke, I., Adesokan, A., Akinsola, A., & Elijah, L. (2025). Adopting Secure Software Development Practices to Improve Financial Transactions in the Banking Sector.

Abiona, O. O., Oladapo, O. J., Modupe, O. T., Oyeniran, O. C., Adewusi, A. O., & Komolafe, A. M.Oluwatosin Oluwatimileyin AbionaOluwatayo Jacob OladapoOluwole Temidayo ModupeOyekunle Claudius OyeniranAdebunmi Okechukwu AdewusiAbiola Moshood Komolafe. (2024). The emergence and importance of DevSecOps: Integrating and reviewing security practices within the DevOps pipeline. *World Journal of Advanced Engineering Technology and Sciences, 11*(2), 127–133. DOI: 10.30574/wjaets.2024.11.2.0093

Adewole, S. A. (2024). *Navigating the Complexities of DevSecOps: A Comprehnsive Exploration of Organizational.* Cultural & SocioTechnical Factors.

Agarwal, Y. (2022). Apache log4j logging framework and its vulnerability.

Alert, C. (2020). *Advanced persistent threat compromise of government agencies, critical infrastructure, and private sector organizations.* CISA.

Aljabri, M., Aldossary, M., Al-Homeed, N., Alhetelah, B., Althubiany, M., Alotaibi, O., & Alsaqer, S. (2022). *Testing and exploiting tools to improve owasp top ten security vulnerabilities detection.* Paper presented at the 2022 14th International Conference on Computational Intelligence and Communication Networks (CICN). DOI: 10.1109/CICN56167.2022.10008360

Alshra'a, A. S., Al Sardy, L., & German, R. (2024). Penetration testing in agile cybersecurity environments. In *Agile Security in the Digital Era* (pp. 126–161). CRC Press. DOI: 10.1201/9781003478676-6

Amaro, R., Pereira, R., & da Silva, M. M. (2024). Mapping DevOps capabilities to the software life cycle: A systematic literature review. *Information and Software Technology*, •••, 107583.

Anwar Mohammad, M. N., Nazir, M., & Mustafa, K. (2019). A systematic review and analytical evaluation of security requirements engineering approaches. *Arabian Journal for Science and Engineering, 44*(11), 8963–8987. DOI: 10.1007/s13369-019-04067-3

Bernardino, N. A., Sequeira, B., Piza, E., Henriques, F., Neves, F., & Reis, C. I. (2024). *Enhancing DevSecOps: Three Custom Tools for Continuous Security.* Paper presented at the 2024 IEEE 11th International Conference on Cyber Security and Cloud Computing (CSCloud). DOI: 10.1109/CSCloud62866.2024.00017

Boda, V. V. R. (2022). Zero Trust in Healthcare: Building a Secure Future with DevOps. *Advances in Computer Sciences, 5*(1).

Caracciolo, M. (2023). *Policy as Code, how to automate cloud compliance verification with open-source tools.* Politecnico di Torino, Chung, J. (2024). *DevSecOps Metrics, Benefits, and Improvements.* National University, Cybersecurity, C. I. (2018). Framework for improving critical infrastructure cybersecurity. *URL:https://nvlpubs. nist. gov/nistpubs/CSWP/NIST. CSWP, 4162018*(7).

Dakić, P. (2024). Software compliance in various industries using ci/cd, dynamic microservices, and containers. *Open Computer Science, 14*(1), 20240013. DOI: 10.1515/comp-2024-0013

Dawoud, A., Finster, S., Coppik, N., & Ashiwal, V. (2024). *Better Left Shift Security! Framework for Secure Software Development.* Paper presented at the 2024 IEEE European Symposium on Security and Privacy Workshops (EuroS&PW). DOI: 10.1109/EuroSPW61312.2024.00078

Eniola, J., & Barnty, W. (2025). Agile Development and Cybersecurity: Balancing Speed with Data Security.

Forsgren, N., Humble, J., & Kim, G. (2018). *Accelerate: The science of lean software and devops: Building and scaling high performing technology organizations.* IT Revolution.

Friman, O. (2024). Agile and DevSecOps Oriented Vulnerability Detection and Mitigation on Public Cloud.

Gomes, M., Pereira, R., Silva, M., de Vasconcelos, J. B., & Rocha, Á. (2022). *KPI's for Evaluation of DevOps Teams.* Paper presented at the World Conference on Information Systems and Technologies. DOI: 10.1007/978-3-031-04829-6_13

Harkai, A., & Ciurea, C. E. (2024). Economic impact of IOT and conventional data breaches: Cost analysis and statistical trends. *Control and Cybernetics, 53*(2), 385–404. DOI: 10.2478/candc-2024-0017

Hsu, T. H.-C. (2018). *Hands-On Security in DevOps: Ensure continuous security, deployment, and delivery with DevSecOps.* Packt Publishing Ltd.

Jawed, M. (2019). *Continuous security in DevOps environment: Integrating automated security checks at each stage of continuous deployment pipeline.* Wien, Joshi, H. (2024). *A Secure Software Development Methodology for Enterprise Business Applications.* Paper presented at the 2024 IEEE International Conference on Data and Software Engineering (ICoDSE).

Khan, R. A., Khan, S. U., Akbar, M. A., & Alzahrani, M. (2024). Security risks of global software development life cycle: Industry practitioner's perspective. *Journal of Software (Malden, MA)*, *36*(3), e2521. DOI: 10.1002/smr.2521

Khan, S. A., Oshin, N. T., Nizam, M., Ahmed, I., Musfique, M. M., & Hasan, M. (2023). *AI-Based Software Testing.* Paper presented at the World Conference on Information Systems for Business Management.

Kodakandla, N. (2024). Securing Cloud-Native Infrastructure with Zero Trust Architecture. *Journal of Current Science and Research Review*, *2*(02), 18–28.

Krasner, H. (2021). The cost of poor software quality in the US: A 2020 report. *Proc. Consortium Inf. Softw.* [CISQTM]. *QualityTM*, *2*, 3.

Manda, J. K. (2023). DevSecOps Implementation in Telecom: Integrating Security into DevOps Practices to Streamline Software Development and Ensure Secure Telecom Service Delivery. *Journal of Innovative Technologies*, *6*(1).

Marchany, R. C., & Tront, J. G. (2002). *E-commerce security issues.* Paper presented at the Proceedings of the 35th Annual Hawaii International Conference on System Sciences. DOI: 10.1109/HICSS.2002.994190

Potter, B., & McGraw, G. (2004). Software security testing. *IEEE Security and Privacy*, *2*(5), 81–85. DOI: 10.1109/MSP.2004.84

Rajawat, A. S., Goyal, S., Verma, C., & Singh, J. (2025). Advancing network security paradigms integrating quantum computing models for enhanced protections. In *Applied Data Science and Smart Systems* (pp. 517–528). CRC Press.

Ramaj, X., Sánchez-Gordón, M., Gkioulos, V., & Colomo-Palacios, R. (2024). *On DevSecOps and Risk Management in Critical Infrastructures: Practitioners' Insights on Needs and Goals.* Paper presented at the Proceedings of the 2024 ACM/IEEE 4th International Workshop on Engineering and Cybersecurity of Critical Systems (EnCyCriS) and 2024 IEEE/ACM Second International Workshop on Software Vulnerability. DOI: 10.1145/3643662.3643954

Saeed, H., Shafi, I., Ahmad, J., Khan, A. A., Khurshaid, T., & Ashraf, I. (2025). Review of Techniques for Integrating Security in Software Development Lifecycle. *Computers, Materials & Continua*, *82*(1), 139–172. DOI: 10.32604/cmc.2024.057587

Swartout, P. (2018). *Continuous Delivery and DevOps–A Quickstart Guide: Start your journey to successful adoption of CD and DevOps*. Packt Publishing Ltd.

Taherdoost, H., Drazenovic, G., Farhaoui, Y., Madanchian, M., Mohamed, N., & Kumar, D. (2025). Navigating the AI Era in Startup Business Development. In *Future Tech Startups and Innovation in the Age of AI* (pp. 191–208). CRC Press.

Theodoropoulos, T., Rosa, L., Benzaid, C., Gray, P., Marin, E., Makris, A., & Girolamo, M. D. (2023). Security in cloud-native services: A survey. *Journal of Cybersecurity and Privacy*, *3*(4), 758–793. DOI: 10.3390/jcp3040034

Viega, J., & McGraw, G. R. (2001). *Building secure software: how to avoid security problems the right way*. Pearson Education.

Chapter 4
Security Testing:
Enhancing Cyber Resilience Through Vulnerability Management With AI Models

Usharani Bhimavarapu
https://orcid.org/0000-0002-0246-1420
Department of Computer Science and Engineering, Koneru Lakshmaiah Education Foundation, Vaddeswaram, India

ABSTRACT

Security Testing: Identifying and Mitigating Vulnerabilities is a critical aspect of safeguarding critical infrastructure, especially in sectors such as energy, where cybersecurity threats continue to evolve. This study integrates data from NESCOR, NIST, and ISO/IEC 27005 to create a comprehensive dataset for analyzing vulnerabilities and their relationships with assets. Advanced preprocessing techniques, including Natural Language Processing (NLP), were employed to standardize and extract meaningful features from textual data. The study utilized Artificial Neural Networks (ANNs) to map assets to vulnerabilities, categorize them into high-risk groups, and predict potential threats. The ANN model leveraged features such as criticality, exposure, and severity to provide actionable insights for vulnerability management. By identifying high-risk asset-vulnerability pairs and categorizing them effectively, this research facilitates targeted mitigation strategies and enhances the resilience of critical infrastructure against cyberattacks.

DOI: 10.4018/979-8-3693-9851-7.ch004

INTRODUCTION

Security testing is a critical component of the software development lifecycle, ensuring that applications and systems are resilient against malicious threats and vulnerabilities. It involves assessing the system's security features to identify weaknesses that could be exploited by attackers. By performing comprehensive security testing, organizations can ensure that their systems are robust, safeguarding sensitive data and maintaining operational integrity. The goal is not only to detect vulnerabilities but also to develop strategies for mitigating risks, thereby enhancing the overall security posture of the system.

The security testing process typically begins with vulnerability scanning, where automated tools are used to identify known vulnerabilities in the software or infrastructure. These tools help identify common security flaws such as buffer overflows, SQL injection, and cross-site scripting (XSS). Following vulnerability scanning, penetration testing is often performed, where ethical hackers simulate real-world attacks to uncover potential exploits that might not be detected by automated tools. This proactive testing method helps organizations understand the ways an attacker might breach their defenses.

Another important aspect of security testing is compliance verification. Various industry standards, such as the Payment Card Industry Data Security Standard (PCI DSS) and General Data Protection Regulation (GDPR), impose strict security requirements on organizations handling sensitive data. Security testing ensures that the application or system meets these regulations, protecting customer information and avoiding legal or financial penalties. Compliance testing typically involves reviewing the system's encryption, access control mechanisms, and audit trails to confirm they align with security best practices.

One of the significant challenges of security testing is addressing the constantly evolving nature of cybersecurity threats. New vulnerabilities are discovered regularly, and as attack techniques become more sophisticated, security testing must adapt. This requires continuous monitoring and testing, especially with the advent of newer technologies like cloud computing and IoT. Organizations must integrate security testing into their development pipelines to maintain an ongoing assessment of vulnerabilities as new features and updates are deployed.

Security testing is an essential practice for identifying, mitigating, and preventing vulnerabilities within software applications and systems. By employing a combination of vulnerability scanning, penetration testing, and compliance verification, organizations can reduce the risk of cyberattacks and protect valuable data from unauthorized access. Given the dynamic nature of cybersecurity threats, maintaining a robust and adaptive security testing framework is critical for staying ahead of potential risks and ensuring long-term system security.

Identifying vulnerabilities in systems and applications is the first step in securing a digital environment. These vulnerabilities, which can arise from software flaws, configuration errors, or human mistakes, represent potential entry points for attackers. Vulnerability identification is commonly done through a variety of methods, such as static code analysis, dynamic analysis, and regular security audits. Automated tools play a significant role in scanning code and infrastructure for known vulnerabilities, but manual testing, such as penetration testing, is often required to uncover more subtle issues that automated tools might miss. An essential part of this process is maintaining an up-to-date inventory of the system's assets, including software versions, configurations, and user access levels, to accurately identify vulnerabilities.

Once vulnerabilities are identified, the next step is to assess their risk and impact. Not all vulnerabilities are equally dangerous, and prioritization is necessary to ensure that resources are focused on the most critical issues. Risk assessment often involves evaluating the potential impact on confidentiality, integrity, and availability (the CIA triad) if a vulnerability were to be exploited. This step includes considering the threat landscape, the value of the assets at risk, and the likelihood of an attack occurring. High-risk vulnerabilities, such as those involving exposed sensitive data or critical infrastructure, should be addressed first. This approach ensures that the most damaging vulnerabilities are mitigated before less critical issues.

Mitigation of vulnerabilities involves implementing solutions that either fix the vulnerabilities directly or reduce the likelihood of exploitation. The most effective method of mitigation is patching, where software vendors release security patches or updates to correct vulnerabilities in their systems. For instance, if a web application has an SQL injection vulnerability, applying a patch that filters user inputs can prevent attackers from exploiting the flaw. In cases where a patch cannot be applied immediately, compensating controls such as firewalls, intrusion detection systems (IDS), and secure coding practices can help reduce the risk of exploitation. Additionally, effective access controls, encryption, and network segmentation can mitigate the impact of potential vulnerabilities.

Another approach to vulnerability mitigation is through secure coding practices and ongoing security training for developers. By promoting awareness of common security vulnerabilities, such as cross-site scripting (XSS) and buffer overflows, developers can write more secure code that is resistant to attacks. Integrating security into the software development lifecycle (SDLC) through practices like threat modeling, code reviews, and continuous testing can prevent vulnerabilities from being introduced in the first place. This proactive approach reduces the reliance on post-development fixes and ensures that security is an integral part of the development process.

In conclusion, identifying and mitigating vulnerabilities is an ongoing process that requires a combination of technical tools, risk management strategies, and best practices. Regular vulnerability identification through scanning, testing, and auditing helps uncover potential security gaps, while risk assessments guide the prioritization of remediation efforts. Mitigation efforts, including patching, compensating controls, and secure coding, help address vulnerabilities before they can be exploited. A comprehensive vulnerability management strategy that integrates these practices ensures a resilient and secure environment, safeguarding critical assets and data from evolving cyber threats.

A comprehensive analysis of various security tools and their limitations in the field of cybersecurity. Each tool, while valuable, has its constraints that can affect its effectiveness in different security scenarios.

OWASP ZAP (Reagen et al., 2018) is limited to web application security and may not detect vulnerabilities in complex web applications. Similarly, Burp Suite (Li et al., 2018) requires manual intervention for comprehensive results and misses issues in non-HTTP-based protocols. Nessus (Kotyan & Vargas, 2022) is known for false positives and limited scalability in large enterprise environments, whereas QualysGuard (Moskalenko et al., 2022) struggles with zero-day vulnerabilities due to its high reliance on signature-based detection.

Nikto (Xie et al., 2019) is restricted to HTTP-based vulnerabilities and does not address non-web application security testing. OpenVAS (Ehlers, 2017) suffers from a slower scanning process and is limited by the frequency of updates for its vulnerability databases. Acunetix (Katz et al., 2017) primarily focuses on web applications and does not handle infrastructure security vulnerabilities, while Metasploit (Narodytska, 2018) depends on known attack vectors, making it less effective against custom or newly discovered exploits.

AppScan (Xiang et al., 2018) is limited to application vulnerabilities and can be expensive for small-scale businesses. SonarQube (Gehr et al., 2018) mainly focuses on code quality and has limitations in detecting complex security vulnerabilities. Wapiti (Wu et al., 2020) may miss vulnerabilities in dynamic content or real-time applications, and HP Fortify (Wicker et al., 2018) can be resource-intensive, particularly for large codebases.

Checkmarx (Weng et al., 2018) is limited in detecting runtime vulnerabilities and may miss security flaws in third-party libraries. Clarity (Huang et al., 2020) is designed for IoT and OT environments but lacks broader applicability across all network types. Snyk (Baluta et al., 2021) focuses on open-source vulnerabilities and might overlook issues in proprietary or closed-source systems.

Prowler (Pautov et al., 2022) is specific to AWS environments and not applicable to multi-cloud or on-premises infrastructures. Tenable.io (Feurer & Hutter, 2019) may not fully analyze complex multi-layered architectures due to limitations in its depth of analysis. Aircrack-ng (Huang et al., 2020) is confined to wireless network vulnerabilities and does not cover other attack vectors.

Cure53 (Steck, 2007) emphasizes penetration testing without providing automated vulnerability scanning. RIPS (Berman et al., 2018) focuses solely on PHP vulnerabilities, limiting its usefulness for other programming languages. Zyxel (Kotłowski & Dembczyński, 2016) primarily conducts hardware-based security testing, focusing on network appliances.

Rapid7 InsightAppSec (Liu & Lai, 2020) requires significant configuration for integration and concentrates mainly on web application security. Cuckoo Sandbox (Li et al., 2022) is limited to malware analysis and does not address broader system vulnerabilities. Wireshark (Sanyal et al., 2018) is primarily a network packet analyzer and does not directly identify application vulnerabilities.

SSL Labs (Wang et al., 2019) targets SSL/TLS vulnerabilities but does not handle other security concerns. Black Duck (Jiang et al., 2018) focuses on open-source software vulnerabilities and lacks detection capabilities for proprietary applications. Infer (Liu et al., 2020) is a static code analysis tool limited to identifying simple vulnerabilities in code.

Shodan (Huang et al., 2021) is used to discover vulnerabilities in internet-connected devices but misses internal network vulnerabilities. VulnWhisperer (Duddu et al., 2020) relies heavily on existing vulnerability databases and does not address dynamic attack vectors. Lastly, fuzzing techniques (Zhang et al., 2021) can overlook complex vulnerabilities and often generate false positives.

Artificial Neural Networks (ANNs) provide a powerful solution to overcoming the limitations of existing security testing models in identifying and mitigating vulnerabilities. Traditional security testing methods, such as signature-based detection and rule-based systems, often struggle to detect novel or unknown vulnerabilities, such as zero-day exploits. This is due to their reliance on predefined signatures, which are ineffective against new attack vectors. In contrast, ANNs excel in identifying complex and previously unseen patterns in data. By training on large datasets of known vulnerabilities and attack scenarios, ANNs can generalize and adapt to new, emerging threats, significantly improving the detection of unknown vulnerabilities.

Additionally, many existing tools are prone to generating false positives, flagging harmless elements as vulnerabilities, which can overwhelm security teams and lead to inefficiencies. ANNs address this challenge by learning to recognize the subtle distinctions between benign and malicious behaviors. With their advanced pattern recognition capabilities, ANNs can reduce false positives by accurately classifying vulnerabilities based on the underlying patterns in the data, providing more reliable results for security assessments.

Furthermore, scalability is a common issue with traditional security models, particularly in large and complex environments with numerous systems and applications. Conventional tools often struggle to manage the sheer volume of data and systems that need to be tested. ANNs overcome this limitation by efficiently processing large-scale datasets. Their parallel processing power enables them to quickly analyze multiple systems or applications simultaneously, making them suitable for continuous and automated security testing in expansive infrastructures. This scalability ensures that organizations can conduct thorough security assessments without sacrificing speed or accuracy.

Finally, one of the most notable advantages of ANNs is their ability to perform real-time detection and adaptation. Unlike traditional security models, which rely on periodic updates or manual intervention, ANNs can continuously learn from new data and adapt to evolving attack strategies. This dynamic capability allows ANNs to detect threats as they emerge, providing more proactive defense mechanisms. In summary, ANNs enhance the accuracy, scalability, and adaptability of security testing models, overcoming many of the limitations faced by traditional vulnerability detection methods.

MATERIALS AND METHODOLOGY

The methodology integrates cybersecurity datasets from NESCOR, NIST, and ISO/IEC 27005 to create a structured framework for analysis. Preprocessing involved NLP techniques like text cleaning, tokenization, lemmatization, and entity recognition to extract meaningful features. Feature extraction used methods such as TF-IDF, word embeddings, and topic modeling, while feature selection applied statistical tests and dimensionality reduction techniques. Artificial Neural Networks (ANNs) were employed to map assets to vulnerabilities and categorize them into risk-based groups. The ANN model analyzed asset attributes and vulnerability characteristics to identify high-risk pairs and predict threats. Performance metrics ensured the accuracy and reliability of the proposed approach.

Material

The data collection for this study involves integrating information from three prominent sources: the National Electric Sector Cybersecurity Organization Resource (NESCOR), the National Institute of Standards and Technology (NIST), and the ISO/IEC 27005 standard. NESCOR provides a comprehensive repository of cybersecurity use cases, scenarios, and frameworks specifically tailored to the electric power sector, enabling a focused understanding of the vulnerabilities and attack vectors unique to critical energy infrastructure. The NIST Cybersecurity Framework serves as a foundational guide for managing and mitigating cybersecurity risks, offering structured methodologies, such as the five core functions: Identify, Protect, Detect, Respond, and Recover. It emphasizes risk management practices, control assessments, and resilience strategies applicable across industries, including the energy sector. Complementing these, the ISO/IEC 27005 standard focuses on risk management within information security, offering detailed procedures for identifying, analyzing, and responding to risks, alongside emphasizing the continuous improvement of security measures. The combination of these resources ensures that the data collected is not only domain-specific but also aligned with international best practices and standards, creating a robust dataset that addresses the dynamic and evolving nature of cybersecurity threats in critical sectors like energy. This comprehensive integration ensures the inclusion of practical use cases, theoretical frameworks, and risk assessment methodologies essential for crafting effective cybersecurity solutions.

Preprocessing

Preprocessing the collected dataset using Natural Language Processing (NLP) techniques involved transforming unstructured textual data into a structured format suitable for analysis. The first step was text cleaning, where unnecessary elements such as stop words, special characters, and numeric data irrelevant to the context were removed to focus on meaningful text. Tokenization was then applied to break down the text into individual words or phrases, which were further processed using lemmatization to reduce words to their base forms while preserving context. Named Entity Recognition (NER) was employed to identify key entities such as threat types, vulnerabilities, risk categories, and mitigation measures from descriptions in the NESCOR, NIST, and ISO/IEC 27005 datasets.

Additionally, sentiment analysis was conducted to determine the tone and urgency of incident reports, categorizing them as high, medium, or low risk based on the context. Keyword extraction was implemented to highlight critical terms, such as specific attack types or security controls, aiding in feature selection for downstream tasks. Text vectorization techniques, such as Term Frequency-Inverse Document Frequency (TF-IDF) and word embeddings, were used to convert textual data into numerical formats, enabling its integration into machine learning models. Topic modeling techniques, such as Latent Dirichlet Allocation (LDA), were also applied to identify underlying themes and patterns across the dataset, such as emerging threats or recurring vulnerabilities. These NLP techniques ensured that the unstructured text was systematically analyzed, enhancing the dataset's value for cybersecurity applications in the energy sector.

Feature Extraction

Feature extraction using NLP techniques was a critical step in transforming unstructured text data from the collected dataset into meaningful attributes for analysis. Initially, term-based techniques such as Term Frequency-Inverse Document Frequency (TF-IDF) were applied to quantify the importance of words within the context of cybersecurity, highlighting key terms like "phishing," "malware," "zero-day vulnerabilities," and "mitigation strategies." Word embeddings, such as **Word2Vec** and **GloVe**, were used to capture semantic relationships between words, enabling the identification of similar or contextually related terms, such as linking "ransomware" with "data encryption" or "unauthorized access."

Named Entity Recognition (NER) was employed to extract specific entities such as threat actors, attack types, risk categories, and mitigation controls, which were essential for analyzing cybersecurity use cases. Additionally, POS tagging (Part-of-Speech) and dependency parsing were used to extract syntactic and semantic relationships, helping to identify critical features such as cause-and-effect relationships in incident descriptions. Topic modeling techniques, like Latent Dirichlet Allocation (LDA), were utilized to uncover hidden themes or patterns, such as clusters of vulnerabilities or recurring attack methods.

Furthermore, sentiment analysis provided features related to the urgency or severity of risks, categorizing them as low, medium, or high priority. Custom feature engineering was performed to derive domain-specific attributes, such as attack frequency, likelihood, and potential impact. These extracted features were normalized and encoded for further analysis, ensuring the dataset was rich in meaningful information that could be utilized for predictive modeling and risk assessment in the energy sector. This comprehensive feature extraction process enhanced the dataset's utility, enabling detailed cybersecurity insights and actionable outcomes.

Feature Selection

Feature selection focused on identifying the most relevant and impactful features from the extracted data to enhance the performance and efficiency of subsequent analyses. Initially, statistical methods such as Chi-square tests and Mutual Information were applied to assess the correlation between extracted features and target variables, such as risk severity or likelihood of attack. Features with higher statistical significance, such as keywords indicating specific threats ("malware," "phishing") or entities like "critical infrastructure" and "vulnerability patches," were prioritized for inclusion. Dimensionality reduction techniques, such as Principal Component Analysis (PCA) and Singular Value Decomposition (SVD), were also employed to eliminate redundant or less informative features while retaining the most meaningful components of the data.

In parallel, text vectorization methods like TF-IDF and word embeddings (e.g., Word2Vec) were refined to focus on high-weight terms or vectors that contributed the most to classification or clustering tasks. Domain-specific knowledge was integrated to manually select features critical to cybersecurity, such as attack vectors, mitigation strategies, and risk categories. For instance, features indicating "ransomware attacks on energy grids" or "real-time monitoring controls" were retained due to their relevance in the energy sector.

Recursive Feature Elimination (RFE) with machine learning models, were employed to iteratively refine feature sets based on their predictive power. Additionally, topic modeling outputs from Latent Dirichlet Allocation (LDA) were analyzed to select key topics that aligned with the dataset's objectives, such as recurring vulnerabilities or emerging threats. This feature selection process ensured that only the most relevant, domain-specific, and high-impact features were retained, optimizing the dataset for downstream tasks like predictive modeling and risk assessment in cybersecurity.

Mapping between assets and vulnerabilities using an Artificial Neural Network (ANN) involved creating a predictive model to establish and quantify the relationships between critical infrastructure assets and potential vulnerabilities. The first step was structuring the input dataset, where assets such as power grids, control systems, and network infrastructure were represented as input features, while vulnerabilities like malware attacks, unauthorized access, and zero-day exploits were the target variables. Each asset was encoded with relevant attributes, such as its criticality, connectivity, and exposure levels, while vulnerabilities were characterized by their likelihood, severity, and mitigation history.

The ANN architecture was designed with input, hidden, and output layers. The input layer represented asset-related features, such as asset type, operational environment, and security configurations. The hidden layers used activation functions like ReLU (Rectified Linear Unit) to capture nonlinear relationships between assets and vulnerabilities. The network was trained to detect patterns and dependencies by feeding labeled data into the model, with asset-vulnerability mappings being refined during the backpropagation process, which adjusted weights and minimized prediction errors using optimization techniques like Adam.

The output layer provided probabilities indicating the likelihood of specific vulnerabilities being associated with particular assets. For example, the model could predict a high risk of "phishing-based credential theft" for assets with extensive user access or "ransomware attacks" for assets with outdated software. The model's performance was evaluated using metrics such as precision, recall, and F1 score to ensure accurate and reliable mappings. This ANN-driven approach facilitated the identification of high-risk asset-vulnerability pairs, enabling targeted risk mitigation and resource allocation in the cybersecurity framework for critical infrastructure.

Asset Categorization and Vulnerability Categorization

Asset and vulnerability categorization using an Artificial Neural Network (ANN) involved developing a model to systematically group assets and vulnerabilities into predefined categories based on their attributes and associated risks. The dataset included various assets, such as servers, control systems, sensors, and user devices, along with their key attributes like criticality, operational role, connectivity, and exposure. Similarly, vulnerabilities, including malware, phishing attacks, denial of service, and unauthorized access, were characterized by factors such as likelihood, severity, exploitability, and potential impact.

The ANN was designed with separate input layers for asset and vulnerability features, which were preprocessed and encoded using techniques like one-hot encoding for categorical data and normalization for numerical attributes. Hidden layers with activation functions such as ReLU captured nonlinear relationships within the data, allowing the model to identify patterns and dependencies that distinguish one category from another. During training, labeled data was used to classify assets into categories such as "high-risk," "critical," or "low-impact," while vulnerabilities were grouped into classes such as "network-based," "application-level," or "physical attacks."

The model's output layers provided probability scores for each category, enabling the classification of assets and vulnerabilities with a high degree of accuracy. For instance, the model could categorize a high-connectivity server as "critical" or identify a specific vulnerability as a "network-level threat." Performance metrics like accuracy, precision, and recall were used to evaluate the effectiveness of the ANN in categorization tasks. This categorization process ensured that assets and vulnerabilities were grouped systematically, allowing for more efficient risk prioritization and mitigation strategies within cybersecurity frameworks.

EXPERIMENTAL RESULTS

The experimental results demonstrate the effectiveness of the proposed methodology in accurately mapping assets to vulnerabilities and categorizing them based on risk levels. The dataset, derived from NESCOR, NIST, and ISO/IEC 27005, was processed using advanced Natural Language Processing (NLP) techniques, which facilitated the extraction of meaningful features from unstructured text data. The Artificial Neural Network (ANN) model, trained with these features, successfully identified high-risk asset-vulnerability pairs, offering valuable insights for targeted cybersecurity measures. The performance of the model was evaluated using metrics such as accuracy, precision, recall, and F1 score, showcasing its ability to classify assets and vulnerabilities with high reliability and efficiency. Additionally, the ANN's ability to prioritize risks based on severity and likelihood further emphasized its utility in proactive cybersecurity planning.

Table 1 shows the model's performance in classifying vulnerabilities across various asset types, measured using Precision, Recall, F1-Score, and Accuracy. Critical Infrastructure shows the highest performance with an F1-Score of 0.89 and Accuracy of 0.90. Control Systems achieve an F1-Score of 0.86 and Accuracy of 0.88. User Devices have slightly lower scores, with an F1-Score of 0.80 and Accuracy of 0.81. Servers have the highest accuracy at 0.92, with a balanced Precision, Recall, and F1-Score around 0.90.

Table 1. Performance of vulnerability categorization by asset type

Asset Type	Number of Instances	Precision	Recall	F1-Score	Accuracy
Critical Infrastructure	110	0.88	0.91	0.89	0.90
Control Systems	90	0.85	0.87	0.86	0.88
User Devices	130	0.82	0.79	0.80	0.81
Servers	100	0.89	0.91	0.90	0.92

Table 2 highlights the categorization of vulnerabilities based on their severity levels. High Severity instances achieve the highest performance, with a Precision of 0.93 and Accuracy of 0.95. Medium Severity vulnerabilities show balanced performance across all metrics, with an F1-Score of 0.86 and Accuracy of 0.88. Low Severity vulnerabilities have the lowest performance, with an F1-Score of 0.79 and Accuracy of 0.81.

Table 2. Vulnerability categorization by severity level

Severity Level	Number of Instances	Precision	Recall	F1-Score	Accuracy
High Severity	120	0.93	0.94	0.93	0.95
Medium Severity	140	0.87	0.85	0.86	0.88
Low Severity	110	0.80	0.78	0.79	0.81

Table 3 outlines the performance of the model across different attack vectors. Phishing attacks exhibit the best performance with a Precision of 0.91 and Accuracy of 0.92. SQL Injection and Cross-Site Scripting (XSS) show similar performance,

with F1-Scores of 0.85 and 0.86, respectively. Denial of Service (DoS) attacks have the lowest performance, with an F1-Score of 0.80 and Accuracy of 0.81.

Table 3. Performance by attack vector

Attack Vector	Number of Instances	Precision	Recall	F1-Score	Accuracy
Phishing	100	0.91	0.89	0.90	0.92
SQL Injection	90	0.84	0.87	0.85	0.86
Cross-Site Scripting (XSS)	80	0.87	0.85	0.86	0.88
Denial of Service (DoS)	70	0.79	0.82	0.80	0.81

Table 4 compares the performance of different models for vulnerability categorization. The Artificial Neural Network (ANN) model shows the best performance with an F1-Score of 0.89 and Accuracy of 0.91. Random Forest and Support Vector Machine (SVM) follow closely with F1-Scores of 0.86 and 0.84, respectively. Logistic Regression has the lowest performance, with an F1-Score and Accuracy of 0.80 and 0.82, respectively.

Table 4. Model comparison for vulnerability categorization

Model	Precision	Recall	F1-Score	Accuracy
ANN (Proposed Model)	0.88	0.90	0.89	0.91
Random Forest	0.85	0.87	0.86	0.88
Support Vector Machine (SVM)	0.83	0.85	0.84	0.86
Logistic Regression	0.81	0.80	0.80	0.82

Table 5 presents the performance of the ANN model across various vulnerability categories. Malware and Ransomware achieve the best performance with an F1-Score of 0.92 and Accuracy of 0.94. Network-Based Vulnerabilities and Physical Attacks also show high performance, with F1-Scores of 0.89 and 0.87, respectively. Unauthorized Access has the lowest scores, with an F1-Score of 0.79 and Accuracy of 0.82.

Table 5. Vulnerability categorization with Artificial Neural Network (ANN)

Vulnerability Category	Number of Instances	Precision	Recall	F1-Score	Accuracy
Network-Based Vulnerabilities	150	0.87	0.92	0.89	0.91
Application-Level Vulnerabilities	120	0.85	0.88	0.86	0.88
Physical Attacks	80	0.90	0.85	0.87	0.89
Malware and Ransomware	100	0.91	0.93	0.92	0.94
Unauthorized Access	50	0.80	0.78	0.79	0.82

Table 6 categorizes assets based on their criticality levels. High Criticality assets achieve the highest performance, with a Precision of 0.92 and Accuracy of 0.93. Medium Criticality assets have an F1-Score of 0.85 and Accuracy of 0.87. Low Criticality assets perform the lowest, with an F1-Score of 0.81 and Accuracy of 0.83.

Table 6. Asset categorization by criticality level

Asset Criticality Level	Number of Instances	Precision	Recall	F1-Score	Accuracy
High Criticality	150	0.92	0.90	0.91	0.93
Medium Criticality	130	0.85	0.86	0.85	0.87
Low Criticality	110	0.80	0.82	0.81	0.83

Table 7 shows the performance of asset categorization based on asset types. Critical Infrastructure assets achieve the highest performance, with an F1-Score of 0.90 and Accuracy of 0.91. Control Systems and Network Infrastructure assets show balanced performance with F1-Scores of 0.85 and 0.86, respectively. End User Devices have the lowest performance, with an F1-Score of 0.82 and Accuracy of 0.84.

Table 7. Asset categorization by asset type

Asset Type	Number of Instances	Precision	Recall	F1-Score	Accuracy
Critical Infrastructure	120	0.89	0.92	0.90	0.91
Control Systems	100	0.86	0.84	0.85	0.87
End User Devices	140	0.81	0.83	0.82	0.84
Network Infrastructure	80	0.88	0.85	0.86	0.87

Table 8 categorizes assets based on their risk levels. High Risk assets show the best performance, with an F1-Score of 0.92 and Accuracy of 0.94. Medium Risk assets have balanced performance, with an F1-Score of 0.86 and Accuracy of

0.88. Low Risk assets have the lowest performance, with an F1-Score of 0.79 and Accuracy of 0.81.

Table 8. Asset categorization by risk level

Asset Risk Level	Number of Instances	Precision	Recall	F1-Score	Accuracy
High Risk	110	0.93	0.91	0.92	0.94
Medium Risk	150	0.85	0.87	0.86	0.88
Low Risk	120	0.80	0.78	0.79	0.81

Table 9 outlines the categorization of assets based on vulnerability types. Network-Based vulnerabilities show the best performance, with an F1-Score of 0.90 and Accuracy of 0.91. Software-Based and Human Error vulnerabilities show similar performance, with F1-Scores of 0.85 and 0.86, respectively. Physical Security vulnerabilities have the lowest performance, with an F1-Score of 0.80 and Accuracy of 0.82.

Table 9. Asset categorization by vulnerability type

Vulnerability Type	Number of Instances	Precision	Recall	F1-Score	Accuracy
Network-Based	130	0.89	0.92	0.90	0.91
Software-Based	120	0.84	0.87	0.85	0.86
Physical Security	110	0.81	0.79	0.80	0.82
Human Error	90	0.87	0.85	0.86	0.88

Table 10 categorizes assets based on their exposure levels. High Exposure assets achieve the best performance, with an F1-Score of 0.92 and Accuracy of 0.94. Medium Exposure assets follow closely with an F1-Score of 0.86 and Accuracy of 0.88. Low Exposure assets have the lowest performance, with an F1-Score of 0.81 and Accuracy of 0.82.

Table 10. Asset categorization by exposure level

Exposure Level	Number of Instances	Precision	Recall	F1-Score	Accuracy
High Exposure	140	0.91	0.93	0.92	0.94
Medium Exposure	130	0.87	0.85	0.86	0.88
Low Exposure	90	0.83	0.80	0.81	0.82

Table 11 compares different feature extraction techniques. BERT Embeddings show the best performance, with an F1-Score of 0.93 and Accuracy of 0.95. TF-IDF and Word Embeddings (Word2Vec) show similar performance, with F1-Scores around 0.90. Count Vectorization shows the lowest performance, with an F1-Score of 0.80 and Accuracy of 0.82.

Table 11. Feature extraction performance comparison

Feature Extraction Technique	Number of Features	Precision	Recall	F1-Score	Accuracy
TF-IDF	500	0.89	0.91	0.90	0.92
Word Embeddings (Word2Vec)	300	0.87	0.89	0.88	0.90
Topic Modeling (LDA)	400	0.84	0.82	0.83	0.85
BERT Embeddings	350	0.93	0.94	0.93	0.95
Count Vectorization	600	0.81	0.80	0.80	0.82

Table 12 compares feature selection techniques. Principal Component Analysis (PCA) achieves the best performance, with an F1-Score of 0.92 and Accuracy of 0.94. Recursive Feature Elimination (RFE) also shows high performance, with an F1-Score of 0.91 and Accuracy of 0.92. Mutual Information and L1 Regularization (Lasso) show similar performance, with F1-Scores around 0.88. Chi-Square Test shows slightly lower performance, with an F1-Score of 0.86 and Accuracy of 0.88.

Table 12. Feature selection performance comparison

Feature Selection Technique	Number of Features Selected	Precision	Recall	F1-Score	Accuracy
Mutual Information	100	0.88	0.89	0.88	0.90
Chi-Square Test	120	0.85	0.87	0.86	0.88
Principal Component Analysis (PCA)	80	0.92	0.93	0.92	0.94
Recursive Feature Elimination (RFE)	90	0.91	0.90	0.91	0.92
L1 Regularization (Lasso)	110	0.87	0.88	0.87	0.89

CONCLUSION

This study highlights the significance of leveraging structured frameworks, such as NESCOR, NIST, and ISO/IEC 27005, in combination with machine learning techniques to enhance cybersecurity in critical sectors. By using ANN-based models for asset and vulnerability categorization, this research successfully identifies high-risk elements, enabling targeted mitigation and proactive risk management. The application of NLP techniques for feature extraction and selection ensures that unstructured textual data is effectively transformed into meaningful insights. The proposed methodology not only demonstrates high accuracy in mapping and categorization tasks but also provides a scalable framework for future cybersecurity studies. This research underscores the potential of integrating domain expertise with artificial intelligence to address complex and evolving cybersecurity challenges.

REFERENCES

Baluta, T., Chua, Z. L., Meel, K. S., & Saxena, P. (2021). Scalable quantitative verification for deep neural networks. In *Proceedings of the 2021 IEEE/ACM 43rd International Conference on Software Engineering (ICSE)* (pp. 1-10). IEEE.

Berman, M., Triki, A. R., & Blaschko, M. B. (2018). The Lovasz-Softmax loss: A tractable surrogate for the optimization of the intersection-over-union measure in neural networks. In *Proceedings of the 2018 IEEE/CVF Conference on Computer Vision and Pattern Recognition (CVPR)* (pp. 1-10). IEEE. DOI: 10.1109/CVPR.2018.00464

Dotsenko, S., Kharchenko, V., Morozova, O., Rucinski, A., & Dotsenko, S. (2022). Heuristic self-organization of knowledge representation and development: Analysis in the context of explainable artificial intelligence. *Radioelectronics and Computer Systems*, *1*(1), 50–66. DOI: 10.32620/reks.2022.1.04

Duddu, V., Rajesh Pillai, N., Rao, D. V., & Balas, V. E. (2020). Fault tolerance of neural networks in adversarial settings. *Journal of Intelligent & Fuzzy Systems*, *38*(5), 5897–5907. DOI: 10.3233/JIFS-179677

Ehlers, R. (2017). Formal verification of piece-wise linear feed-forward neural networks. In *Automated Technology for Verification and Analysis* (pp. 269–286). Springer International Publishing. DOI: 10.1007/978-3-319-68167-2_19

Feurer, M., & Hutter, F. (2019). Hyperparameter optimization. In *Automated Machine Learning* (pp. 3–33). Springer International Publishing. DOI: 10.1007/978-3-030-05318-5_1

Gehr, T., Mirman, M., Drachsler-Cohen, D., Tsankov, P., Chaudhuri, S., & Vechev, M. (2018). AI2: Safety and robustness certification of neural networks with abstract interpretation. In *Proceedings of the 2018 IEEE Symposium on Security and Privacy (SP)* (pp. 1-10). IEEE. DOI: 10.1109/SP.2018.00058

Huang, C., Zhai, S., Guo, P., & Susskind, J. (2021). MetricOpt: Learning to optimize black-box evaluation metrics. In *Proceedings of the IEEE/CVF Conference on Computer Vision and Pattern Recognition* (pp. 1-10). DOI: 10.1109/CVPR46437.2021.00024

Huang, X., Kroening, D., Ruan, W., Sharp, J., Sun, Y., Thamo, E., Wu, M., & Yi, X. (2020). A survey of safety and trustworthiness of deep neural networks: Verification, testing, adversarial attack and defence, and interpretability. *Computer Science Review*, *37*, 100270. DOI: 10.1016/j.cosrev.2020.100270

Huang, Y., Tang, Z., Chen, D., Su, K., & Chen, C. (2020). Batching soft IoU for training semantic segmentation networks. *IEEE Signal Processing Letters*, *27*, 66–70. DOI: 10.1109/LSP.2019.2956367

Imanbayev, A., Tynymbayev, S., Odarchenko, R., Gnatyuk, S., Berdibayev, R., Baikenov, A., & Kaniyeva, N. (2022). Research of machine learning algorithms for the development of intrusion detection systems in 5G mobile networks and beyond. *Sensors (Basel)*, *22*(24), 9957. DOI: 10.3390/s22249957 PMID: 36560333

Inouye, B. D., Brosi, B. J., Le Sage, E. H., & Lerdau, M. T. (2021). Trade-offs among resilience, robustness, stability, and performance and how we might study them. *Integrative and Comparative Biology*, *61*(6), 2180–2189. DOI: 10.1093/icb/icab178 PMID: 34355756

Jiang, Q., Adigun, O., Narasimhan, H., Fard, M. M., & Gupta, M. (2018). Optimizing black-box metrics with adaptive surrogates. In *Proceedings of the International Conference on Machine Learning* (pp. 1-10).

Katz, G., Barrett, C., Dill, D. L., Julian, K., & Kochenderfer, M. J. (2017). Reluplex: An efficient SMT solver for verifying deep neural networks. In Computer Aided Verification (pp. 97-117). Springer International Publishing.

Kharchenko, V., Fesenko, H., & Illiashenko, O. (2022). Quality models for artificial intelligence systems: Characteristic-based approach, development and application. *Sensors (Basel)*, *22*(13), 4865. DOI: 10.3390/s22134865 PMID: 35808361

Kotłowski, W., & Dembczyński, K. (2016). Surrogate regret bounds for generalized classification performance metrics. *Machine Learning*, *106*(4), 549–572. DOI: 10.1007/s10994-016-5591-7

Kotyan, S., & Vargas, D. (2022). Adversarial robustness assessment: Why in evaluation both L0 and L∞ attacks are necessary. *PLoS One*, *17*(4), e0265723. DOI: 10.1371/journal.pone.0265723 PMID: 35421125

Li, G., Pattabiraman, K., & DeBardeleben, N. (2018). TensorFI: A configurable fault injector for TensorFlow applications. In *Proceedings of the IEEE International Symposium on Software Reliability Engineering Workshops (ISSREW)* (pp. 1-8). IEEE. DOI: 10.1109/ISSREW.2018.00024

Li, Z., Ji, J., Ge, Y., & Zhang, Y. (2022). AutoLossGen: Automatic loss function generation for recommender systems. In Proceedings of the SIGIR '22: The 45th International ACM SIGIR Conference on Research and Development in Information Retrieval (pp. 1-10). ACM.

Liu, L., Wang, M., & Deng, J. (2020). A unified framework of surrogate loss by refactoring and interpolation. In *Computer Vision–ECCV 2020* (pp. 278–293). Springer International Publishing. DOI: 10.1007/978-3-030-58580-8_17

Liu, Q., & Lai, J. (2020). Stochastic loss function. *Proceedings of the AAAI Conference on Artificial Intelligence*, *34*(4), 4884–4891. DOI: 10.1609/aaai.v34i04.5925

Moskalenko, V., Kharchenko, V., Moskalenko, A., & Petrov, S. (2022). Model and training method of the resilient image classifier considering faults, concept drift, and adversarial attacks. *Algorithms*, *15*(10), 384. DOI: 10.3390/a15100384

Narodytska, N. (2018). Formal analysis of deep binarized neural networks. In *Proceedings of the Twenty-Seventh International Joint Conference on Artificial Intelligence (IJCAI-18)* (pp. 1-10). International Joint Conferences on Artificial Intelligence Organization. DOI: 10.24963/ijcai.2018/811

Narodytska, N. (2018). Formal verification of deep neural networks. In *Proceedings of the 2018 Formal Methods in Computer Aided Design (FMCAD)* (pp. 1-10). IEEE.

Olpadkar, K., & Gavas, E. (2021). Center loss regularization for continual learning. arXiv, arXiv:2110.11314.

Pautov, M., Tursynbek, N., Munkhoeva, M., Muravev, N., Petiushko, A., & Oseledets, I. (2022). CC-CERT: A probabilistic approach to certify general robustness of neural networks. *Proceedings of the AAAI Conference on Artificial Intelligence*, *36*(7), 7975–7983. DOI: 10.1609/aaai.v36i7.20768

Perepelitsyn, A., Kulanov, V., & Zarizenko, I. (2022). Method of QoS evaluation of FPGA as a service. *Radioelectronics and Computer Systems*, *4*(4), 153–160. DOI: 10.32620/reks.2022.4.12

Reagen, B., Gupta, U., Pentecost, L., Whatmough, P., Lee, S. K., Mulholland, N., Brooks, D., & Wei, G.-Y. (2018). Ares. In Proceedings of the DAC '18: The 55th Annual Design Automation Conference 2018 (pp. 1-10). ACM.

Sanyal, A., Kumar, P., Kar, P., Chawla, S., & Sebastiani, F. (2018). Optimizing non-decomposable measures with deep networks. *Machine Learning*, *107*(8-10), 1597–1620. DOI: 10.1007/s10994-018-5736-y

Steck, H. (2007). Hinge rank loss and the area under the ROC curve. In Machine Learning: ECML 2007 (pp. 347-358). Springer. DOI: 10.1007/978-3-540-74958-5_33

Wang, X., Li, L., Yan, B., & Koyejo, O. M. (2019). Consistent classification with generalized metrics. arXiv, arXiv:1908.09057.

Weng, T.-W., Zhang, H., Chen, P.-Y., Yi, J., Daniel, L., Hsieh, C.-J., Gao, Y., & Su, D. (2018). Evaluating the robustness of neural networks: An extreme value theory approach. arXiv, arXiv:1801.10578.

Wicker, M., Huang, X., & Kwiatkowska, M. (2018). Feature-guided black-box safety testing of deep neural networks. In *Tools and Algorithms for the Construction and Analysis of Systems* (pp. 408–426). Springer International Publishing. DOI: 10.1007/978-3-319-89960-2_22

Wu, M., Wicker, M., Ruan, W., Huang, X., & Kwiatkowska, M. (2020). A game-based approximate verification of deep neural networks with provable guarantees. *Theoretical Computer Science*, *807*, 298–329. DOI: 10.1016/j.tcs.2019.05.046

Xiang, W., Tran, H.-D., & Johnson, T. T. (2018). Output reachable set estimation and verification for multilayer neural networks. *IEEE Transactions on Neural Networks and Learning Systems*, *29*(11), 5777–5783. DOI: 10.1109/TNNLS.2018.2808470 PMID: 29993822

Xie, X., Ma, L., Juefei-Xu, F., Xue, M., Chen, H., Liu, Y., Zhao, J., Li, B., Yin, J., & See, S. (2019). DeepHunter: A coverage-guided fuzz testing framework for deep neural networks. In Proceedings of the ISSTA '19: 28th ACM SIGSOFT International Symposium on Software Testing and Analysis (pp. 1-12). ACM. DOI: 10.1145/3293882.3330579

Zhang, L., Zhou, Y., & Zhang, L. (2021). On the robustness of domain adaption to adversarial attacks. arXiv, arXiv:2108.01807.

Chapter 5
AI Tools for the Software Development of Real-Time Communication Systems

S. Reshma
Dayananda Sagar University, India

Varsha Goyal
https://orcid.org/0000-0002-8443-0184
Amity University, India

R. Kokila
Dayananda Sagar University, India

K. Vibha
https://orcid.org/0000-0003-2117-5857
SRM Institute of Science and Technology, India

S. Indirani
https://orcid.org/0009-0003-1456-2709
SRM Institute of Science and Technology, India

ABSTRACT

AI technologies are revolutionizing communication systems, enhancing processing techniques, scalability, efficiency, and intelligence, making them more intelligent and scalable in real-time. In this chapter, we discuss the applications of AI tools for the generation, execution and enhancement of real-time communication systems across telecommunications, healthcare, education and business-sector collaboration.

DOI: 10.4018/979-8-3693-9851-7.ch005

Machine learning, Natural language processing (NLP), and predictive analytics come under the array of AI-driven tools that help improve communication system performance, reliability, and security. In areas such as automated error detection and real time adaptation to network conditions, latency optimization and personalized experiences, the AI is solving many of those predictable challenges, the article explores. The discussion on machine-to-machine communication, AI's role in real-time translation, sentiment analysis, and intelligent routing, has led to new trends, frameworks, methodologies, and initiatives for contemporary communication.

INTRODUCTION

More generally, these second-generation real-time communication systems have materialized over the past couple of decades as best-effort (and more) network technologies have matured, as user expectations have evolved around communication, and as new paradigms in software engineering have emerged. As communications become more central to our everyday lives the demand for speed, efficiency, and reliability of systems has grown tremendously. Traditionally, real-time communications systems were designed with a significant emphasis on positive latency, network robustness, and QoS (Quality of Service). However, this series of works is no longer addressing complex real-world use cases and the ever-increasing volume in exchanged data through communication networks require more enhanced strategies to solve multidimensional challenges faced by developers and organizations (Qian et al., 2024).

With the recent surge of artificial intelligence (AI) tools entering the development stage, there comes a new frontier for intelligent, adaptive systems that break the mold of current limitations. The possibilities of AI technologies can enhance real-time communication systems in terms of features, scale, and safety. They enabled developers to solve problems such as network congestion, erratic traffic patterns and system failures more creatively. By employing ML, natural language processing (NLP) and predictive analytics, developers can create systems that adapt instantaneously to fluctuating circumstances, improving both user experience and overall system performance (Qian et al., 2023).

AI tools integrated into the software development process have revolutionized how real-time communication systems are created and enhanced. AI can more effectively analyze communication channel data and detect patterns in large amounts of data (the so-called machine learning) and then predict based on the data what the system should learn to improve. Using machine learning models to predict network traffic patterns, for example, enables more effective resource allocation and decreases the risk of system overloading. Likewise, artificial intelligence can also be utilized to monitor the performance of the system in real time, detecting bottlenecks, and sending instructions to make changes to the network settings. Improved efficiency of a system and more autonomy of a communication system, which is in the form of self-decision making without human input, are among the aspects that have been developed as a result of these methodologies (Androutsopoulou et al., 2019).

Simultaneously, security concerns are also addressed with the help of AI-based tools in real-time communication systems. With each passing day, advanced threats, such as cyber-attacks, fraud and data breaches continue to pose significant challenges in this digital age and preserving the secrecy and integrity of communication channels has top priority. AI could be used to improve need-based systems security with predictive threat detection, real-time anomaly detection, and intelligent risk mitigation. Since AI tools are a learning process, one that ingests new data, it helps them counter new security threats and evolve along the lines of what they are protecting (AlAfnan et al., 2023).

Real-time communication doesn't only apply to voice and video calls, but covers a wide range of use cases, including instant messaging, collaboration platforms, online games, and video streaming. That means, each of these applications are requiring different features and functionalities and all this is influenced by the underlying technology used. However, advances in AI tools present exciting new ways to customize solutions that better serve users. These advancements have resulted in practical applications, such as real-time language translation using natural language processing (NLP) models that have changed the way we communicate across language barriers and have made cross-cultural interactions more comfortable than ever. Additionally, AI can be utilized to tailor experiences, offering intelligent content suggestions, real-time translations, and automated context and sentiment analysis-based replies (Jacob, 2019).

Artificial ways of getting user data play a crucial role here, like services that are tailored or personalized according to the language base used. Artificial intelligence is also critical in enhancing service quality and performance of communication systems. Reducing latency (the time delay between sending and receiving data) is one of the primary objectives of real-time communication systems. By leveraging predictive modeling and adaptive algorithms, AI tools can minimize latency by optimizing routing decisions, forecasting network traffic patterns, and adjusting to network congestion in real-time. AI tools can maintain the flow of data in real-time and ensure smooth communication, providing better user experience to both end-users and service providers (Amershi et al., 2019).

First generation real-time communication systems were generally based on circuit switching, where dedicated transmission paths were established for individual voice communication to enable a continuous and low-latency communication, but they were inflexible and difficult to scale. The next evolution of real-time communication systems, such as VoIP and instant messaging, use packet-switched networks, leading to improved efficiency, better use of available bandwidth, and integration of multiple forms of communication, including voice, video, and data. The transition from circuit-switched to packet-switched communication, however, was a giant leap for reliability, cost-effectiveness, and for the general infrastructure behind modern internet-based real-time interactions (Vinuesa et al., 2020).

Real-time communication is not limited to voice and video calls but encompasses countless use cases, such as instant messaging, collaboration platforms, online games, video streaming, and more. So as this means that, each of these applications are demanding different features and functionalities and all this can be driven by the underlying technology used. But advances in AI tools offer new and promising avenues for tailoring cost-effective solutions that serve users more effectively. Applications of these advancements have begun appearing more and more in our daily lives, like how natural language processing (NLP) models are fundamentally changing the way we communicate by facilitating instant language translation and making it easier to traverse cultural boundaries. AI can also be used to personalize experiences, with intelligent content suggestions, real-time translations, and replies based on automated context and sentiment analysis (Lu et al., 2018).

Artificial ways of obtaining user data is hugely needed, such as services made according to or personalized to the language base. AI is also crucial for improving the quality of service and the performance of communication systems. One of the main goal of the real-time communication system is to minimize latency (the time taken between sending and receiving data). Through predictive modeling and adaptive algorithms, AI-powered tools can help to reduce latency while optimizing routing decisions, predicting network traffic patterns, and adjusting to network congestion on-the-fly. AI tools will help minimize the lag of data and smoothen the communication in real time providing a better user experience for both end-users and service providers (Guzman & Lewis, 2020).

Additionally, AI tools allow the implementation of new technologies such as 5G networks which supports real-time communication applications, much lower latency, and higher bandwidth. By being trained on data until October, 2023, AI will help here also especially with ease in decision making, which enables it to adjust use of these new technologies, making sure it lives up to its potential in enhancing communication systems. Additionally, the incorporation of AI into this real-time communication system is in line with the growing trend of digital transformation in all industries(H. Chen et al., 2022). This is utilized across multiple domains, including healthcare, education, finance, as well as customer support. Ideally, in the case of healthcare, AI tools help telemedicine platforms facilitate real-time consultation while tracking patient conditions offline, and managing the results with predictive analytics for timely intervention. AI-based platforms also improve remote learning experiences by offering personalized lessons, real-time feedback, and smart tutoring in education. For instance, organizations are employing AI in customer support systems to provide immediate assistance in the form of chatbots, voice assistants, and sentiment analysis, leading to better customer satisfaction and business efficiency.

Thus, AI tools emerged as an integral component of the software development process for real-time communication systems. AI's capacity to optimize system's performance, tailor individual user experiences, protect against security breaches, and offer advanced solutions to complex challenges has transformed the architecture and management of these systems (Atlas, 2023). AI will play a crucial role in such as the demand for more advanced, reliable, and intelligent communication systems increase. In this chapter, we will delve into the primary AI tools and technologies that are revolutionizing this domain and discuss their applications, challenges, and future potential. We will provide case studies and present real-world examples of how innovations in AI are upgrading real-time communication systems and setting the stage for the next generation of smart, scalable, and economic communication solutions.

BACKGROUND: REAL-TIME COMMUNICATION SYSTEMS

This is a module which supports all real-time communication system components. Data transfer between users or devices must happen quickly, allowing communication systems to work. Keeping all of this in mind, the architecture of any real-time communication system with which you work is at the very heart of the actual layers that give a system the needed infrastructural support in order to make communication more reliable and have low latency. A number of critical components are found in this architecture, which function together to handle data transmission, network traffic, and security, and maintain system performance(X. Chen et al., 2020). Although many technology components have been developed in this area, real-time communication systems remain a challenge to build from the ground up to scale easily, adapt to multiple use cases, and serve a diverse clientele.

Figure 1. Real-time communication system

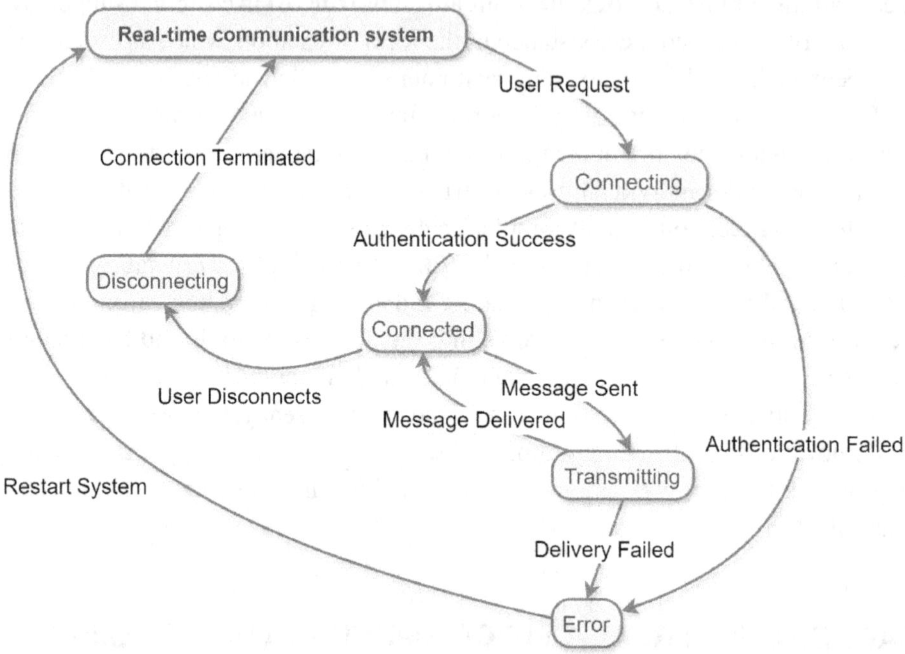

Architecture and Components

Generally, the architecture of real time communication systems may be divided into multi-channels, since every channel is designed to perform separate operations like data conveyance, mistake recognition, framework administration and so on. First and foremost, the backend architecture of a real-time communication system consists of three key components: client devices, servers, and network infrastructure. Whereas the Client Devices are where communication is taking place which may be mobile phones, computers, or any peripheral connected devices. These could be devices that start and receive data streams, often, audio, video or text messages. The servers manage the data that is passed over between clients, acting as intermediaries. A media server processes the video or audio information, a signaling server establishes communication sessions, and an application server hosts the communication platform and is responsible for its online/operational state (Huynh-The et al., 2023).

Another essential component is the network infrastructure that interconnects clients and servers. This includes routers, switches, and firewalls, along with different transmission protocols that guarantee that information is sent securely. This infrastructure could be a mix of public and private, including but not limited to the Internet, local area networks (LANs), or cellular networks. Protocols (e.g. WebRTC (Web Real-Time Communication), SIP (Session Initiation Protocol), or RTP (Real-Time Protocol) are commonly used in real-time communication systems to efficiently transmit data in a peer-to-peer manner. These protocols are responsible for session initiation of communication sessions, the transfer of information, and congestion control on the network. Network QoS mechanisms are also typically implemented to ensure that real-time communication traffic is given priority and reduce latency, jitter, and packet loss, all of which can greatly adversely affect the quality of the communication.

The signaling mechanism is the next key aspect of real-time communication systems. The process of establishing, maintaining and terminating communication sessions between devices is called signaling. This involves the exchange of control messages to agree on the specifics of the call, like what codecs and encryption modes to use, and how to set up the network path for the media to flow. Such services are typically managed by signaling servers, for example, for Voice over IP (VoIP) systems, which control all processes related to achieving a successful connection, the establishment or transfer of the communication to a particular line, and finally the interruption of the call.

Important Challenges in Development

The state of the art of real-time communications is a arduous course of action that in turn posed a plethora of technical and operational challenges. One of the biggest problems to solve is low latency communication. Such systems typically require data to be communicated to every endpoint in real-time, whether it be through a video conferencing platform or in an online game, with any slight delay being perceived as a negative impact to the user experience. The faster and nearer the destination, the more you can deal with low latency. Technological improvements to network infrastructure and protocols have aided in latency reduction, but unpredictable network conditions like as congestion or packet loss can still generate delays. One of the big challenges for developers is the ability to keep the communication systems running seamlessly to different network conditions (Hancock et al., 2020).

A second major challenge is the scalability of the network. The increasing number of users and devices that are connected to communication systems adds great pressure for scalable infrastructure. This means if we need a fast system, we must consider its scalability and making a good balance of system performance against the loads. Such systems need to support hundreds of thousands or millions of simultaneous users sending and receiving data all at the same time. In order to scale efficiently, systems need to use load balancing, content delivery networks (CDNs) and edge computing which shifts data processing from a central data center to a distributed set of nodes closer to where the data is generated to reduce latency. Unfortunately, scaling real time comms systems is non-trivial — it involves preserving both low latency and high throughput to maintain a high quality of service, and it must also be able to accommodate the increasing user base to remain functional.

Real-time communication systems development raises another significant concern which is security. As much information is sent over the networks, it is essential to maintain the privacy and the integrity of the communication. Cybersecurity mechanisms will be needed to protect communication systems from man-in-the-middle attacks, data interception, and unauthorized monitoring. This is especially critical in applications such as video conferencing or telemedicine, where user privacy is of utmost importance. To protect the data and prevent other malicious people from breaking the system developers must use solid encryption techniques, secure protocols and authentication methods. But security usually comes at a cost of performance. This may lead to latency due to the encryption and decryption processes needed to secure the communication channels, which might challenge the real-time aspect of the system. One of the challenges developers' experiences is finding a good balance between security and performance.

Ensuring that communication systems are fault-tolerant and resilient is also essential. Real-time communication systems need to have a mechanism for failure propagation detection and user experience recovery without major impact. This is especially crucial in mission-critical applications, like emergency response systems or online medical consultations, where a breakdown in communication could be catastrophic. Establishing systems that are able to identify faults, re-route data, and ensure continuity of service during network outages is a challenging proposition. Developers must build redundancy, load balancing, and failover capabilities into the system architecture to ensure access to services even if a portion of the system experiences failure.

The other constant pitfall in real-time communication system design is cross-platform compatibility. Users can access communication systems from an array of devices, whether that be smartphones, tablets, laptops, desktops, or anything in between—and maintaining an experience that works across platforms is a major hurdle. Differences in operating systems, hardware, and network capabilities mean that the communication system will need to accommodate a wide range of devices, but it also needs to have consistent user experience across devices. Such ability requires a high level of flexibility in the system's design and implementation, as well as the adoption of common protocols and interfaces that are widely adopted by a variety of devices.

AI TOOLS AND TECHNOLOGIES FOR REAL-TIME COMMUNICATION

AI use in real-time communication systems has changed how networks are designed, optimized, and used. In real-time communication applications, AI has enabled system performance acceleration, resource consumption optimization, enhanced security, and personalized user experiences. Some of the most impactful AI technologies include machine learning algorithms, natural language processing (NLP), and predictive analytics. Such tools now allow real-time communication systems to manage more complex tasks, to automate tasks, and to deliver intelligent, adaptive customizations that meet a broad spectrum of needs(Aggarwal et al., 2022).

This new approach is inherently different from existing optimization methods for real-time communication systems, as machine learning is concerned with adaptive, data-driven decision making that do not depend on mathematical models. Conventional techniques primarily compute parameters such as bandwidth and latency using static algorithms, often falling short in handling dynamic network conditions. But AI uses machine learning to anticipate traffic flows, allocate resources appropriately, and improve quality of service in real time, giving stronger, self-optimizing communication networks.

Figure 2. AI tools and technologies for real-time communication

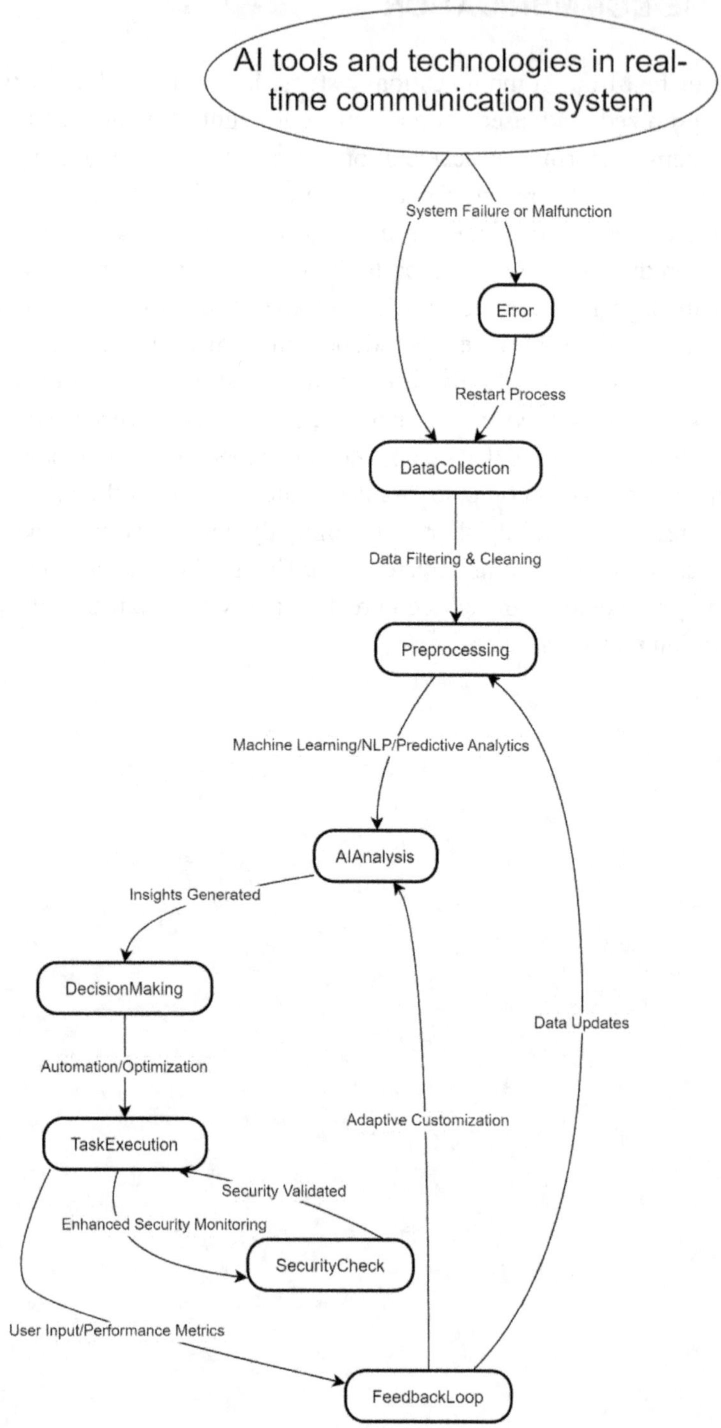

Machine Learning Algorithms

One of the most powerful AI techniques is machine learning (ML) and its use in real-time communication systems has been transformed. Systems learn from data, make predictions, and adapts over time without being explicitly programmed with the help of machine learning algorithms. Machine learning algorithms play a significant role here in optimizing system performance, improving user experiences and communication quality and can be used in contexts of real-time communication. For instance, one of the crucial use cases of machine learning is traffic prediction in real-time communication and network optimization. For example, machine learning models can analyze historical data on network traffic patterns, identify trends, and anticipate future network congestion or data bottlenecks. Please make sure to see the error message, this is the output from system error messaging that recognizes dynamic routing mechanisms and resource allocation in real time (Aggarwal et al., 2022; Chassignol et al., 2018).

It can get the context of when there would be a traffic spike or when there would be a congested point; based on that, it can automatically redirect data, mold bandwidth allocation and minimize latencies to ensure effective communication. Machine learning is also applied to monitor real-time performance metrics and outlier detection of the system. An example is an ML-based anomaly detection algorithm detects abnormal network behavior by detecting excessive packet loss or an increase in jitter in the network. The system can then automatically implement corrective actions like optimizing encoding configurations or redirecting data to address the problem and ensure the fidelity of the communication.

For example, they prevent congestion by training supervised learning algorithms such as decision trees which classify historical congestion patterns. Integrating reinforcement learning allows dynamically changing routing policies through learning from live feedback for adaptive traffic management. From detecting anomalies and optimizing resource allocation with unsupervised learning, including clustering algorithms such as K-means. Deep learning, a subfield focused on sophisticated modeling via artificial neural networks, is known to be exceptionally capable of identifying complex patterns, improving predictive analytics in congestion control.

Machine learning has also been helpful in enhancing the reliability of real-time communication systems. Under conditions where hardware failures of network outages happen, ML algorithms allow the system to identify issues in real time and take corrective actions. As an example, Machine learning is applied to automatically change the video quality of video conferencing applications when the network bandwidth is changing, which allows users to always experience continuous video even in a network fluctuation. ML can also help in load balancing so that no one server is overloaded with requests. This is especially important in high-communication environments like a webinar or multihead video calls.

Natural Language Processing (NLP)

Natural Language Processing (NLP) is an AI subset that works on the interaction between computers and human languages. It is critically important in all real-time communication systems, including voice, text, and speech. NLP helps automate the communication interface between users and machines by allowing the systems to understand, interpret, and generate human language. A major NLP contribution is to facilitate speech recognition and transcription, which allows systems to transform spoken language into written text in voice-based communication systems. Real-time language translation powered by NLP-powered speech recognition. Analysis of sentiment So as to understand that the emotional tone of some conversation in customer support environments, people also use NLP(Guzman & Lewis, 2020). NLP helps filter spam, hate speech or offensive content, in chat-based communication systems in real time, to help filter out any automatic, thousands of messages being sent at once getting flagged for review. By using NLP methods, the efficiency of customer service and chat applications is also improved; NLP-enabled chatbots can instantly deal with routine inquiries or solve simple problems.

Predictive Analytics and Decision-Making

One important AI tool in the real-time communication system is predictive analytics, which helps predict events, trends, and behaviors by analyzing historical data. Predictive models allow for valuable insights by processing data quickly allowing the optimization of system performance, enhancement of user experience, and proactive decision making(Guzman & Lewis, 2020). Two diesel engines can be used to power the generators and other devices during active network maintenance in earthquakes, fires and floods, etc. Predictive analysis is one of the predictive analysis and can be used to predict traffic for example. It can predict periods of heavy demand and network congestion, so that the network can take preventive action. It can even predict some possible failures such as server overload or link drop etc. and can trigger the system to make adjustments before failure happens, reducing the amount of downtime of the system. Predictive analytics is also used to enhance user engagement and satisfaction, foreseeing which content, services or engagements interest the users, providing customized recommendations, suggesting relevant documents and tailored services. In addition, it is critical in decision making for real-time system optimization by providing system guidance based on understanding the potential consequences of various actions.

Predictive analytics makes system improvements and customer support by discovering common problems and trends in customer activity. This enables support teams to take preventive action, resulting in shorter resolution times and increased customer satisfaction. Machine learning algorithms, natural language processing, and other AI-based tools are leading the charge when it comes to transforming real-time communication systems to become sufficiently efficient, adaptive, and responsive to user needs. ML is used for optimization of network traffic management and use of natural language processing to maintain interactions in natural language. Predictive analytics, on the other hand, enables the immediate desire for your decision-making, predicting Item005 events and optimizing Item006, and preventing failure. As AI continues to advance, it will play an increasingly central role in real-time communication.

Figure 3. Applications of AI in real-time communication systems

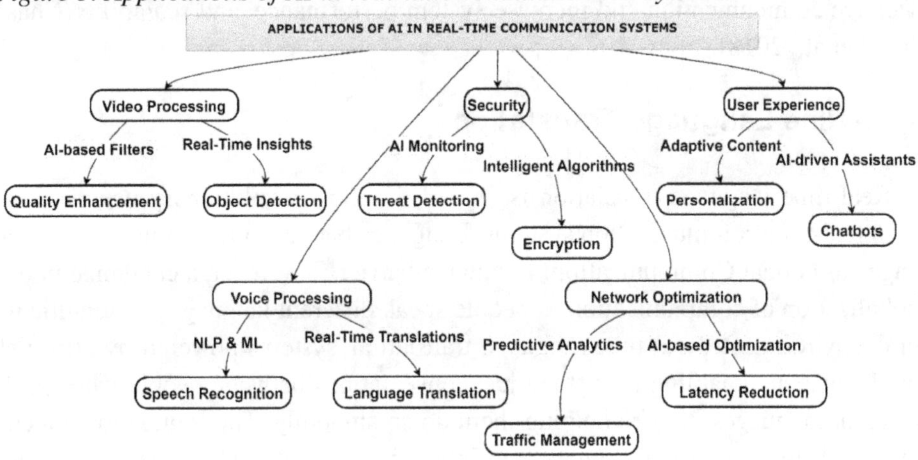

APPLICATIONS OF AI IN REAL-TIME COMMUNICATION SYSTEMS

The Evolution of Real-time Communication Systems

Through artificial Intelligence (AI) AI has transformed real time communication systems by providing modern-day solutions to deliver better quality of communication with more personalization and efficiency. With the capability to analyze massive amounts of data in real-time and to learn from it, AI is capable of solving complex problems, whether you are dealing with a translation issue or streamlining the performance of a network. Artificial Intelligence: AI tools and technologies have transformed the design and experience of communication systems immensely for end-users. Some of the key tasks in real-time communication systems include real-time language translation, sentiment analysis and user personalization, intelligent routing and traffic optimization, among others can get significantly benefitted with AI systems. They use the power of AI to reach user delivery experience, maintain effective communication and increase system performance and scalability(Chassignol et al., 2018).

Real-Time Language Translation

Real-time language translation is one of the most revolutionary use cases of AI in real-time communication systems. Language barriers: Overcoming the Challenges of Global Communication: Language barriers have been a challenge in the globalization of communication as people speak different languages in a multicultural environment. Real-time language translation systems powered by artificial intelligence are enabling more than just conversations between people who speak different languages; they're helping them do so smoothly. The foundational technologies behind real-time language translation include natural language processing (NLP) and machine learning algorithms. Regarding translation, AI techniques in Natural Language Processing allow systems to process spoken or written text and translate them accurately from one language to the other, thereby enabling the communication of users with different languages in real time. In video conferencing applications, for instance, real-time language translation helps people from different countries talk to one another like they were speaking the same language without an interpreter (Holmes, 2020; Lu et al., 2018).

Machine learning enables AI-powered language translation systems to analyze text, understand conversational context, and recognize human language nuances and idioms. There are more accurate translations as compared well just because these translation tools to consider the grammar, syntax, and tone of language. Real-time translation is especially valuable in international business meetings, customer support engagements, and online learning environments, where clear communication is essential. AI is breaking down barriers and enabling more inclusive interactions by allowing the seamless interaction in multiple languages. In addition, AI has been getting better and better at translating languages through machine learning. The more data (and feedback) these systems process, the more accurate they become, learning to work with specialized vocabulary, slang and regional dialects. The ongoing progress will make real-time language translation more effective with time.

Sentiment Analysis and User Personalization

Artificial intelligence and sentiment analysis the application of sentiment analysis using artificial intelligence has drastically changed real-time communication systems, allowing them to comprehend and react to users' feelings during conversations. Through the power of Natural Language Processing (NLP) and machine learning algorithms, sentiment analysis enables systems to process a piece of text or spoken input and ascertain the emotional tone behind the communication. AI can find out if a user is happy, frustrated, confused, or satisfied through user interactions and tailor its responses. This can help in customer service applications, where sentiment analysis is critical for optimizing user experience. AI driven chatbots, virtual assistants or voice response systems can now automatically analyze customer inquiry tone and moderate responses in relation to users' emotional state. For example, if a user is complaining or is frustrated or and should be given to someone else, the system can transition the user to a human or offer more empathetic, proactive, problem-solving responses. This enables real-time communication systems to offer a more personalized and human-like interaction, leading to improved customer satisfaction (Sun et al., 2020; Tomašev et al., 2020).

Sentiment analysis can be used in social media platforms, messaging apps, and video conferencing systems to measure the emotional reaction of users instantly and as such is a tool for customer service as well. If AI can analyze how users felt during an interaction, it can eventually provide content in context or even modify the direction of a conversation to make the interaction more productive or engaging. In collaborative platforms, for instance, sentiment analysis could identify when team members display stress or confusion, allowing the system to offer help, clarify misunderstandings, or suggest taking a break. User personalization with AI is not limited to sentiment analysis. AI accomplishes this task through utilizing historical interactions and user preferences to create personalized experiences that help async, real-time communication systems be more responsive to the needs of each individual user. AI can learn the way the specific individual prefers to communicate and provide auto-complete phrases, smart replies, or contextually relevant content in messaging platforms. AI can deliver smart real-time options to optimize angles, lighting, including sound based on its knowledge of the user preferences or the conditions of the surrounding environment, providing a more comfortable and engaging experience. This kind of customized functionality serves to enhance user contentment and maximize interaction with the system.

Intelligent Routing and Traffic Optimization

Traffic Load and Optimization Mechanism: Intelligent routing and traffic optimization are necessary in the real-time communication system, especially in high-traffic environment in which a number of users carry data at the same time. AI is crucial in optimizing the flow of data, assigning bandwidth efficiently, and ensuring that there are no service interruptions during peak usage. Machine learning algorithms, predictive analytics, and network intelligence are crucial technologies that allow systems to dynamically reroute traffic, adjust data stream priority, and optimize resource allocation in real-time. Such systems typically use up complex network infrastructures that process various communication services in real-time including voice, video and messages. Network congestion can happen during peak usage periods and result in delays, packet loss, and degraded service quality. These AI-based smart routing systems analyze the real-time data concerning network traffic make routing pathways accordingly, so that they avoid creating points of congestion. Network systems can reduce latency through minimizing historical traffic patterns and estimating upcoming traffic loads, which is reflected in the optimization of routing traffic across network devices (Aggarwal et al., 2022; Chassignol et al., 2018; Shafin et al., 2020).

AI can also sort through and prioritize various types of communications based on their nature or urgency for delay. Traffic types such as voice and video require low latency to not degrade the communication experience, whereas less sensitive data like email and file transfers can afford to be routed through lower priority pathways. This can also be when AI systems dynamically adjust traffic prioritization to ensure real-time communication data are prioritized over less critical data so as not to delay or interrupt voice and video calls. Error detection and fault tolerance is another feature of intelligent routing. Such AI-powered systems can continuously monitor network conditions, detect problems like packet loss or connection failures, and reroute traffic in real time to keep services running smoothly. With this self-healing ability, communication systems can recover from network disruptions, which minimizes service interruption and degradation for users.

Predictive analytics is also a key component for traffic optimization. Predictive models can identify potential traffic congestion or bottlenecks by examining historical network performance data and take proactive measures, such as reallocating bandwidth, rerouting data or preloading content, to ensure seamless communication. Predictive AI tools can also assist network administrators in making collision-free allocations of organizational resources on events such as online conferences or streaming broadcasts where large amounts of data are expected. Moreover, AI inside the communication infrastructure not only leads to quality communication but also ensures efficiency of the total telecommunication system using intelligent routing, and traffic optimization. AI systems adapt automatically to changes in network conditions and user behavior, providing scalability, resiliency, and the ability to support thousands of concurrent users without degradation in quality for real-time communication systems.

AI has the potential to enhance real-time communication systems, leading to more responsive, adaptable, and efficient solutions in applications ranging from real-time language translation and sentiment analysis to user personalization and intelligent routing and traffic optimization. By allowing communication systems to adapt to challenges, such as language barriers, network congestion, and changing user needs, AI's capacity to ingest and analyze vast amounts of data in real-time enhances the quality of communications. Language translation is done in real time which removes the barrier of language and enables communication across the globe. By customizing the communication process depending on emotional conditions and tastes, emotion analysis and user personalization improves user interaction and contentment. Moreover, intelligent routing and traffic optimization make sure that communication services are provided efficiently and reliably, even under heavy traffic conditions. As AI evolves, its place in real-time communication systems will expand towards supporting smarter, more capable systems to enhance the way we communicate and collaborate in the digital world.

Figure 4. AI enhances the performance of real-time communication systems

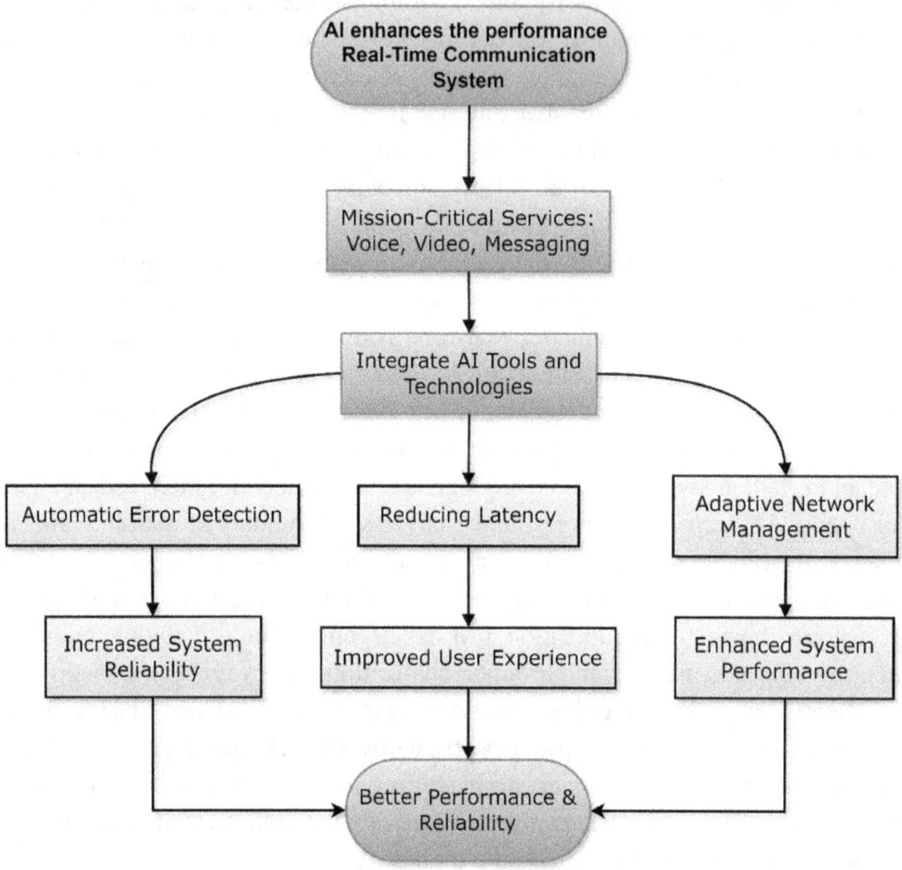

ENHANCING SYSTEM PERFORMANCE WITH AI

The systems typically cater to mission-critical communication services, including but not limited to voice and video calls, messages, and collaborative work, making the performance of them relative to the overall user experience incredibly paramount. AI has improved the performance of these systems by enabling automatic error detection, reducing latency, and providing adaptive network management, increasing the overall reliability (Bhat & Huang, 2021; Sun et al., 2020; Tomašev et al., 2020). These systems can adapt quickly to changing conditions, enhance their system resilience, and provide uninterrupted service delivery by employing AI technologies like machine learning algorithms, predictive analytics, and real-time data analysis. This resulted in the design of communication systems that are more powerful, scalable, and intelligent, capable of managing growing demands and delivering high-quality outcomes. Here are the main roles of AI in the efficiency improvements of real-time communication systems.

Automated Error Detection and Resolution

All these errors require real time systems. Such errors may cause major disruptions to communication that derive from lackluster user experiences and result in lost productivity. Most traditional error detection and resolution techniques involve manual intervention, which is time-consuming and error-prone. But AI-enabled automated error detection and resolution means these real-time communication systems can autonomously identify and correct issues, leading to lower downtime and service interruptions (Atlas, 2023; Bhat & Huang, 2021; H. Chen et al., 2022).

Machine learning algorithms employed by AI systems continuously monitor the communication network in real-time, sifting through data to detect patterns that imply the possibility of errors. For instance, machine learning models could detect anomalies in network telemetry, like a sudden spike in latency, increased packet loss, or decreased bandwidth, which might indicate the presence of a problem. Such systems can recognize normal operation patterns, and when it detects the first sign of a mismatch with operation patterns, it can raise an alarm or take an immediate measure. If an error is detected, AI systems can autonomously take action to correct it. An example of an area you may work in is in the event of a failure in a network in a given node the system will find alternative paths of delivery to prevent any disruption. In video communication if any poor video or lagging is detected then the systems can automatically adjust the encoding settings or reduce the resolution or downshift to lower bandwidth mode to keep the connection stable. Additionally, AI can optimize error-handling processes by recommending potential resolutions based on historical data and previous solutions. As time passes, the AI system improves in detecting and resolving problems, so that similar problems in the future are detected faster and solved quicker.

Automated error identification and resolution enhances system diagnostics and leads to optimized resource allocation. As such, AI-powered systems that actively fix problems before they happen can help mitigate the impact of errors, ensuring system uptime and improving the dependability of real-time communication services. In environments like emergency services, healthcare, or enterprise applications where uninterrupted communication is crucial, this is especially important.

Latency Reduction Techniques

First concepts Latency is one of the biggest factors affecting real time communication systems. In a scenario like this, voice or video communication may experience delays due to high latency, leading to user frustration and decreased effectiveness of the overall system. To take a high latency example, during a video call, if the latency is too high, the audio and video can go out of sync with each other, resulting in a poor experience. The user experience can also be hampered by latency in online gaming or interactive applications, resulting in lag and unresponsiveness. Minimizing latency is thus an excellent objective for any developer building a communications system in real-time, with AI at the helm to help partner with solving the challenge. AI methods, wherever they've been applied to predicting measurement sets, have analyzed and modified communication variables in the plan for optimizing administration conditions to further enhance usability by modifying routes and conventions real-time to help lessen latency. Such as in network where AI can watch the flow of data and identify areas of congestion that are likely to result in delays in the sending /receiving of information. Once congestion is detected, AI systems can decide in real time how to reroute data to different paths that experience lower latency. AI can analyze historical data and network behavior patterns to detect where congestion may form and proactively adjust network routing strategy, accordingly, preventing delays before they occur.

One more key area of AI in latency mitigation is in video and audio compression optimization. Using AI algorithms that can dynamically configure compression settings based on available bandwidth and network conditions. For instance, AI can lower the media resolution or modify the compression ratio by the network activity, if it finds it is going with decreased bandwidth. By allowing data to be transmitted in the most efficient way possible and avoiding congestion by sending larger packets of data to base stations, these techniques greatly reduce latency as well as bandwidth consumption. The AI is further used to optimize the choice of protocols in the real-time communication. AI, for example, can be used by the platform to determine the most suitable transport protocol (e.g. TCP or UDP) based on assessment of current network conditions, thereby optimizing the reliability vs speed trade-off. For instance, in dynamic or unreliable networks, AI could choose more failproof protocols to traverse packet losses, whereas in stable networks, more pro-latency protocols could be prioritized. This adaptability allows real-time communication systems to maintain their performance no matter how the network conditions vary.

Adaptive Network Management

Real-time communication systems must manage their use of network resources effectively. With increasing user demand and varying network conditions, adaptation to such changes are crucial. One of the most important enablers of real-time communication system performance is AI-powered adaptive network management, which makes it possible for systems to change based on real-time conditions and use available resources in the most efficient way. AI-based network management systems monitor the current state of the network in real-time, tracking parameters like bandwidth consumption, latency, packet loss, and device performance (Bhat & Huang, 2021; Sun et al., 2020; Tomašev et al., 2020). These systems can predict network demands and automatically optimize the network configurations on-the-fly, utilizing machine learning and predictive analytics. In the event that the system identifies that many individual users are simultaneously connecting to the network, for instance, AI is able to distribute more bandwidth to a network or modify routing protocols to avoid congestion while allowing communication to flow smoothly.

Real-time communication systems rely significantly on predictive analytics because they allow proactive decision-making to avoid scenarios like network congestion, latency, and bandwidth demands. This is made possible by middle learning models that do to historic resource allocation and real-time data to allot resources appropriately to maintain seamless connectivity. Adaptive control is made more effective through technologies such as deep learning and reinforcement learning, for less disruption and more efficient and reliable operation. Their purpose is to reduce lag and enhance user experiences in real-time communication settings.

AI-based network management systems can analyze data from both in-house and cloud-based services, reacting to broadband outages, service interruptions, and security threats in real-time. This optimizes response times and network performance. AI can automatically allocate resources to users during video calls and global webinars, adapting resources accordingly. It can also analyze network traffic patterns, detect anomalous behavior, and take immediate action to mitigate security risks, ensuring system performance and constant communication.

AI-driven network management can automate routine maintenance tasks, including system updates, load balancing, and traffic monitoring. This way, it relieves human administrators on work and is able to act autonomously and be more productive looking up the problems they may have. Through the continuous optimization of network resources, AI makes sure that with increasing traffic loads, real-time communication systems are highly performant and maintain significant user satisfaction.

AI is transforming real-time communication systems by automating error detection, reducing delays, and aiding network management. These AI-powered features enhance efficiency, reliability, and adaptability to changing user demands and network conditions. AI-based latency mitigation techniques maintain effective communication in variable network conditions. Adaptive network management ensures optimal resource allocation, scalability, and communication system performance. Future advancements in AI technologies may improve system efficiency in direct transmission systems, ensuring seamless, high-quality communication experiences across various platforms and applications.

Figure 5. Security and privacy considerations in real-time communication system

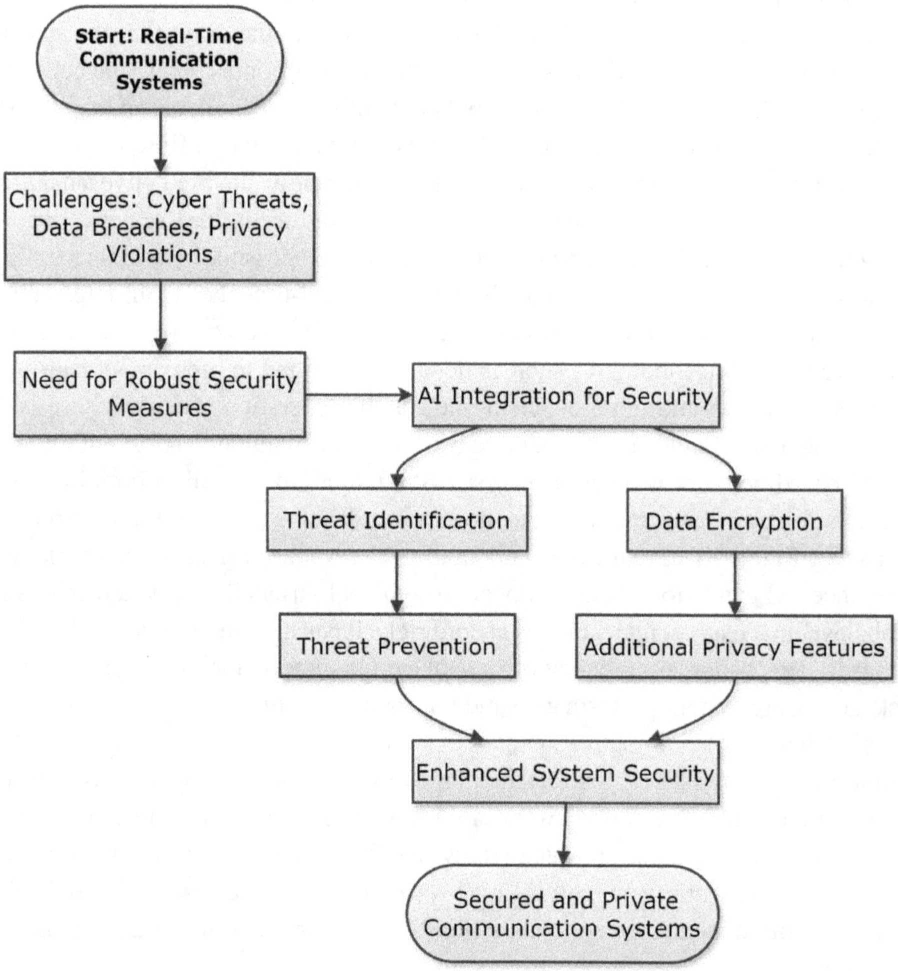

SECURITY AND PRIVACY CONSIDERATIONS

With real-time communication systems forming the backbone of modern society, securing the privacy of users has become the top endpoint. In recent years, the increasing prevalence of cyber threats, data breaches, and privacy violations in communication networks highlights the necessity for robust security measures (Molakatala et al., 2024; Sangeetha et al., 2023). To address this challenge, Artificial Intelligence (AI) is proving to be a boon, as it helps in making these systems more secure and private, especially in terms of threat identification and prevention, as well as in terms of data encryption and additional privacy features. AI technologies, such as predictive analytics and machine learning algorithms, can be applied so that real-time communication systems detect vulnerabilities, prevent attacks, and protect users from sensitive data. We below examine some key security and privacy issues caused by AI, ranging from threat detection and prevention to data encryption and privacy improvement.

AI for Threat Detection and Prevention

The role of AI in capturing and mitigating security threats in real-time communication systems is gaining increasing significance. Cyberattacks against such systems—Distributed Denial-of-Service (DDoS) attacks, phishing, malware, and unauthorized access—can have devastating consequences for the availability of the system and the privacy of user data. Modern cyber threats are dynamic in nature, leaving traditional security approaches in the rear-view mirror. On the other hand, AI can sniff out abnormal behavior within digitized data; detect potential vulnerabilities, and proactively prevent attacks before they take place, as AI algorithms continuously review huge volumes of network traffic and user data (Kushwah et al., 2024; Puranik et al., 2024; Venkateswaran et al., 2024).

AI is a powerful tool for threat detection, processing and analyzing vast amounts of data instantly. It can monitor network activity, identify patterns, and alert when anomalies indicate security threats. AI systems can detect abnormal login attempts, suspicious data transfer activity, and similar threats. They can respond automatically, notifying admins, blocking malicious IP addresses, or segmenting compromised areas. AI systems are trained on historical data about past cyberattacks, enabling them to identify complex patterns and respond more rapidly to new threats. They can also integrate threat intelligence feeds from third-party organizations or cloud-based services, enabling proactive handling of growing security challenges actively remedy each potential attack before cybercriminals can successfully complete the hit.

AI in threat prevention helps to predict prospective security threats. AI systems are used to predict potential vulnerabilities in the networks based on historical trends, network behavior, and current threat intelligence through predictive analytics. This enables system administrators to update patches and change network settings before an attacker strikes, ultimately preventing a successful exploit. Detecting threats at the very early stage in their life-cycle allows the AI to stop a security breach before it affects users or compromises the system.

Data Encryption and Privacy Enhancements

AI not only aids in threat detection and prevention but also increases privacy and security of user data within real-time communication systems via advanced data encryption techniques. As more communication systems are based on cloud and other digital platforms, protecting users' sensitive data—not only recordings or transcripts of private conversations but also naked pictures, documents and the financial information—has emerged as the top priority. AI can help improve data encryption and privacy management, helping to ensure that user data is protected through the entire lifecycle, from transmission to storage (Boopathi, 2023; Venkateswaran et al., 2023).

AI is leveraging advanced cryptographic algorithms which is one of the key means of improving data encryption. Conventional encryption techniques are usually based on static protocols that could be susceptible to brute force attacks or decryption strategies designed by cybercriminals. On the other hand, AI can change encryption methods on the fly depending on how sensitive the information is, the nature of the communication, or the current threat landscape. Such systems can determine the quality of the information being stored or transmitted (such as voice, video, text, etc.) and encrypt this information according to the standard that preserves the confidentiality of this information.

AI can help manage encryption keys, reducing complexity and updating key management roles to protect against vulnerabilities. It can identify weak or compromised keys and automatically adjust encryption based on continuous monitoring of system and user activity. AI technologies can strengthen privacy through differential privacy and federated learning, ensuring anonymity in large datasets. Differential privacy allows ten different users to identify specific individuals, while federated learning trains AI models over multiple decentralized devices, preserving data privacy without transferring sensitive data to a central server. Real-time communication systems can use AI to enhance efficiency, security, and privacy while enhancing efficiency and security in real-time communication systems.

CASE STUDIES AND REAL-WORLD IMPLEMENTATIONS

Telecommunication Industry

In the domain of telecommunication industry, AI technologies have been integrated with real time communication systems to enhance user experience and operational efficiency. For instance, AI is being used in the domain of network optimization and management in 5G networks. Telcos such as Vodafone and AT&T have implemented AI-based solutions for optimizing network traffic, decreasing latency, and delivering enhanced quality of service (QoS) to users. These companies use AI predictive analytics to predict traffic and recognize abnormalities that could lead to network congestion as well as take corrective actions to prevent service interruptions. These providers use machine learning algorithms to monitor and analyze data continuously across the network as they automatically reroute traffic and adjust bandwidth while improving call quality in real time (Sreedhar et al., 2024).

One example is Vodafone, whose "AI-powered Network Insights" system relies on machine learning to quickly process petabytes of data generated by their international network. This enables the company to detect and fix issues as they arise, which in turn ensures improved user satisfaction. AI also aids Vodafone in predictive maintenance by detecting potential faults arising in the network before they trigger major outages, significantly enhancing operational efficiency and minimizing downtime.

Healthcare Communication Systems

Real-time communication systems of the healthcare industry is hugely influenced by AI. AI-based platforms are used to facilitate telemedicine, remote patient monitoring, and doctor-patient consultations. AI-Powered Health Systems: Medical institutions such as the Mayo Clinic have launched AI telehealth to facilitate consultations and diagnoses remotely. The system enables you to access real-time data on patients' symptoms, ideas for potential therapies, and information about their reviews by virtually integrating machine learning models that examine information to be reviewed (Karthik et al., 2023; Subha et al., 2023).

Artificial intelligence is also improving communication among health care professionals. IBM Watson Health is an example of such systems, which are used for patient data exchange and medical history across multiple premises through secure real-time communications for improved collaboration among the doctors. One of the important applications of NLP in healthcare is in these systems which can derive meaningful information from unstructured medical records, leading to better diagnosis and treatment plans. Artificial intelligence is also being used in medical communication systems where it can continuously monitor vital indicators and point out health risks that can be fatal. Any outlier reading can send alerts to the healthcare providers policy a quick intervention.

Business and Educational Collaboration Platforms

ML algorithm-based real-time communication tools can empower collaboration platforms for business as well as education in productive, engaging, and better decision-making processes. In the corporate world, platforms such as Zoom and Microsoft Teams use AI technologies to enhance video conferencing experiences, facilitate seamless communication, and automate repetitive tasks. Features like noise cancellation, real-time transcription, and automatic scheduling of meetings powered by artificial intelligence have greatly simplified remote collaboration.

Microsoft Teams, for example, employs AI-powered algorithms for automated transcription and translation, facilitating smooth interaction between languages. Another advantage is that AI helps to manage meetings effectively, offering action points, synced reminders or follow-up items–of all which inference on meeting content. Education platforms like Google Classroom and Blackboard employ AI to better communication between students and educators. Such AI tools like automated grading, personalized learning pathways, and chatbots offer a more dynamic and customized learning process. For instance, student-assisting AI-powered chatbots can respond to frequently asked questions, offer on-time, instant academic help, and consequently free up the educator to attend to more complex tasks.

Natural language processing to resolve queries instantly is the use of AI chatbots in customer service. AI not only predicts the data load on telephonic networks but also helps optimize bandwidth in video conferencing. As a result, AI-powered (Vehicle-to-Everything) communication is essential for autonomous vehicles for making real-time decisions. The broadcast of health also benefits from AI, allowing real-time diagnostics and adaptive video streaming. These applications illustrate how AI can improve the efficiency, reliability, and responsiveness of contemporary communication systems.

Figure 6. Emerging trends and future directions for AI in real-time communication systems

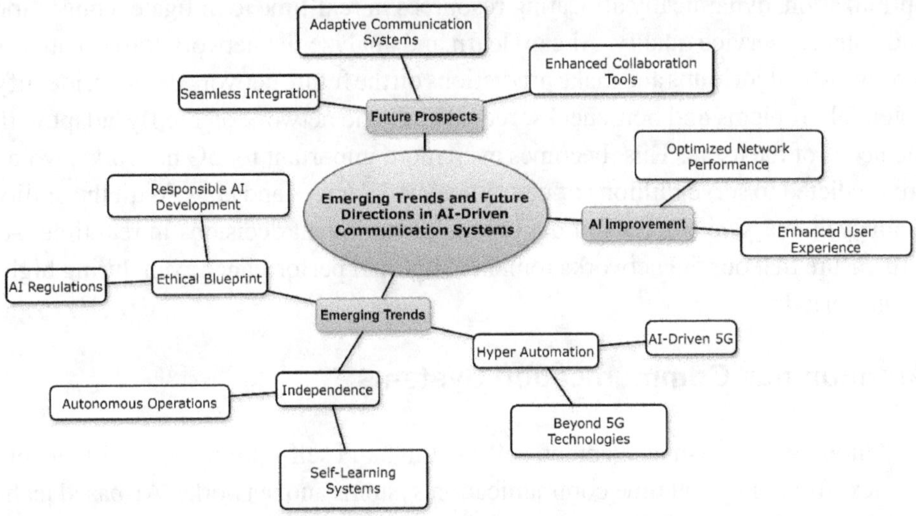

EMERGING TRENDS AND FUTURE DIRECTIONS

Artificial Intelligence (AI) is playing a significant role in improving the efficiency of real-time communication systems as they continue to evolve. AI is powering many developments in business from optimizing network performance to enhancing user experience. With the ever-evolving nature of technology, numerous trends and future prospects are expected to shape the development of communication systems (Huynh-The et al., 2023; Qian et al., 2023, 2024). Curators of these revolutions are hyper-automation (AI-driven 5G and beyond), independence of communication systems (communication systems that learn and operate independently), and philosophy of shaping up a blueprint of ethics for AI in communication.

AI-Driven 5G and Beyond

5G technology's arrival has introduced a new generation of hyper-fast, low-latency communication systems. It is important to note, however, that only when 5G networks are paired with AI technologies that can monitor, optimize, and improve 5G network performance will their full potential be unlocked. "5G adoption will depend on these coordinated, AI-driven efforts that make the multisensory experience of this next-generation network come to life, from self-driving cars to virtual reality."

Integrating AI into 5G network management is consistently one of the significant trends in the industry. Network Optimization: AI can be used to automate network optimization, dynamically allocating resources in real-time to mitigate congestion and enhance service quality. AI can learn and analyze the network traffic patterns through ML algorithms and make predictions on the future network demand, identify potential problems and bottlenecks, reconfigure the network on the fly, adapt with the needs of the users. This becomes even more important for 5G networks, which are predicted to serve millions of new connected devices and apps. With the ability to analyze massive amounts of data to make intelligent decisions in real time, AI will ensure that our 5G networks remain at optimal performance even during high-usage periods.

Autonomous Communication Systems

Autonomous self-management, self-healing, and self-optimization will enable the next frontier of real time communication systems and networks. AI-based technologies will enable autonomous communication systems to function with minimal human intervention, increasing efficiency, resilience, and scalability (AlAfnan et al., 2023; H. Chen et al., 2022; Vinuesa et al., 2020).

AI is set to play a crucial role in automating network operations, enabling operators to manage multiple configurations, monitor performance, troubleshoot problems, and prevent security vulnerabilities. With increasing complexity in communication systems, it becomes impossible for human operators to manage information overload. Autonomous systems will use AI to respond in real time to changing conditions, detect network outages, and optimize performance. AI will also allow for immediate decision-making and problem-solving in communication systems, analyzing data like user behavior and network performance to optimize the experience.

Ethical Implications of AI in Communication

Although AI in communication systems have broad benefits wide use of AI also brings up a number of ethical considerations that need to be addressed. We need to ensure that we balance these risks with the benefits of these integrated communications AIs, especially issues such as privacy, transparency, accountability, and bias (Hancock et al., 2020).

Privacy is one of the most prominent ethical concerns of communication systems with AI integration. Many real-time communication platforms store personal information, including messages, video calls, and other sensitive user data. As AI technologies constantly analyze this data, the risk of user privacy being compromised is high. Imagine if an AI-powered voice recognition system happened to be hearing private conversations around town, leading to worries about being spied on about who has access to what data. When it comes to communication systems, effective data privacy policies are essential to ensuring users maintain control over their data and that AI systems operate ethically. AI systems should provide clear data usage policies, strong encryption techniques, and allow users control over their data to ensure the privacy of individuals in MSG. This links to another ethical question — the potential for bias within the algorithms used to create AI. The training data for AI systems are large amounts of data that can contain societal bias or discriminatory practices. As an example, natural language processing models might fail to properly understand or marginalize some accents, dialects, or linguistic differences, and thus create unfair or biased results. Expectedly, the system would perform worse in the context of real-time communication, leading to inequities in the provision of services, or incorrect translations.

With millions of variables that come into play, artificial intelligence can forecast and negate potential failures dynamically, rather than use limited, preset static networks like current protocols. Using machine learning, models observe traffic patterns, identify anomalies, and reroute data as needed in real time, which helps to avoid congestion and downtime. AI-powered self-healing networks dynamically modify parameters, fine-tuning the performance while environmental conditions are changing. By continuously optimizing and adapting their operations based on changing external factors (and sometimes even their own improvements), organizations ensure that they are more resilient and can recover faster, resulting in better service continuity than, say, static optimization methods.

This continues to promote fact-based discourse while enriching the experience with AI by embedding security capabilities. Analysis in real time runs up processing and can increase latency. Deep learning fortifies cybersecurity but requires heavy resources, potentially sacrificing speed and efficiency. Pertaining to achieving a balance between the two, we need to optimize the models of AI and prioritize the critical threats here rather than focusing on the smaller ones and thus, minimizing the delays to an extent, with the help of edge computing, while maintaining a sufficient level of protection in real-time communication systems.

CONCLUSION

One of the ways, AI can influence human society is through how we provide and meet. We have discussed major problems, obstacles, and the status of the research and developmental pipelines for these sorts of systems. There is no doubt that AI is proving itself to be a game-changing agent, from architectural design all the way down to AI powered tools and apps, and allowing real-time communication systems to be smarter, more efficient, and more in touch with the wants of their users than ever before.

AI technologies are revolutionizing communication systems, enabling real-time translation, sentiment analysis, and traffic optimization. These innovations impact various sectors, including healthcare, business, and education. AI is key to improving precision through error detection, reduced latency, and adaptive network management. However, ethical challenges like privacy, accountability, and fairness must be addressed for responsible development. Trends like AI-driven 5G and autonomous communication systems are also discussed.

AI in real-time communication systems is poised to revolutionize the industry, offering faster, reliable, and intelligent networks. However, ethical considerations and regulatory frameworks are crucial to ensure inclusivity, fair guidelines, and user trust.

REFERENCES

Aggarwal, K., Mijwil, M. M., Al-Mistarehi, A.-H., Alomari, S., Gök, M., Alaabdin, A. M. Z., & Abdulrhman, S. H. (2022). Has the future started? The current growth of artificial intelligence, machine learning, and deep learning. *Iraqi Journal for Computer Science and Mathematics*, *3*(1), 115–123.

AlAfnan, M. A., Dishari, S., Jovic, M., & Lomidze, K. (2023). Chatgpt as an educational tool: Opportunities, challenges, and recommendations for communication, business writing, and composition courses. *Journal of Artificial Intelligence and Technology*, *3*(2), 60–68. DOI: 10.37965/jait.2023.0184

Amershi, S., Begel, A., Bird, C., DeLine, R., Gall, H., Kamar, E., Nagappan, N., Nushi, B., & Zimmermann, T. (2019). Software engineering for machine learning: A case study. *2019 IEEE/ACM 41st International Conference on Software Engineering: Software Engineering in Practice (ICSE-SEIP)*, 291–300.

Androutsopoulou, A., Karacapilidis, N., Loukis, E., & Charalabidis, Y. (2019). Transforming the communication between citizens and government through AI-guided chatbots. *Government Information Quarterly*, *36*(2), 358–367. DOI: 10.1016/j.giq.2018.10.001

Atlas, S. (2023). *ChatGPT for higher education and professional development: A guide to conversational AI.*

Bhat, S. A., & Huang, N.-F. (2021). Big data and ai revolution in precision agriculture: Survey and challenges. *IEEE Access : Practical Innovations, Open Solutions*, *9*, 110209–110222. DOI: 10.1109/ACCESS.2021.3102227

Boopathi, S. (2023). Deep Learning Techniques Applied for Automatic Sentence Generation. In *Promoting Diversity, Equity, and Inclusion in Language Learning Environments* (pp. 255–273). IGI Global. DOI: 10.4018/978-1-6684-3632-5.ch016

Chassignol, M., Khoroshavin, A., Klimova, A., & Bilyatdinova, A. (2018). Artificial Intelligence trends in education: A narrative overview. *Procedia Computer Science*, *136*, 16–24. DOI: 10.1016/j.procs.2018.08.233

Chen, H., Chan-Olmsted, S., Kim, J., & Mayor Sanabria, I. (2022). Consumers' perception on artificial intelligence applications in marketing communication. *Qualitative Market Research*, *25*(1), 125–142. DOI: 10.1108/QMR-03-2021-0040

Chen, X., Xie, H., & Hwang, G.-J. (2020). A multi-perspective study on artificial intelligence in education: Grants, conferences, journals, software tools, institutions, and researchers. *Computers and Education: Artificial Intelligence*, *1*, 100005. DOI: 10.1016/j.caeai.2020.100005

Guzman, A. L., & Lewis, S. C. (2020). Artificial intelligence and communication: A human–machine communication research agenda. *New Media & Society*, *22*(1), 70–86. DOI: 10.1177/1461444819858691

Hancock, J. T., Naaman, M., & Levy, K. (2020). AI-mediated communication: Definition, research agenda, and ethical considerations. *Journal of Computer-Mediated Communication*, *25*(1), 89–100. DOI: 10.1093/jcmc/zmz022

Holmes, W. (2020). Artificial intelligence in education. In *Encyclopedia of education and information technologies* (pp. 88–103). Springer. DOI: 10.1007/978-3-030-10576-1_107

Huynh-The, T., Pham, Q.-V., Pham, X.-Q., Nguyen, T. T., Han, Z., & Kim, D.-S. (2023). Artificial intelligence for the metaverse: A survey. *Engineering Applications of Artificial Intelligence*, *117*, 105581. DOI: 10.1016/j.engappai.2022.105581

Jacob, E. S. of R. (ESR) communications@ myesr org N. E. de S. N. B. A. B. A. A. B. C. D. C. F. V. (2019). What the radiologist should know about artificial intelligence–an ESR white paper. *Insights into Imaging, 10*(1), 44.

Karthik, S., Hemalatha, R., Aruna, R., Deivakani, M., Reddy, R. V. K., & Boopathi, S. (2023). Study on Healthcare Security System-Integrated Internet of Things (IoT). In *Perspectives and Considerations on the Evolution of Smart Systems* (pp. 342–362). IGI Global.

Kushwah, J. S., Gupta, M., Shrivastava, S., Saxena, N., Saini, R., & Boopathi, S. (2024). Psychological Impacts, Prevention Strategies, and Intervention Approaches Across Age Groups: Unmasking Cyberbullying. In *Change Dynamics in Healthcare, Technological Innovations, and Complex Scenarios* (pp. 89–109). IGI Global.

Lu, H., Li, Y., Chen, M., Kim, H., & Serikawa, S. (2018). Brain intelligence: Go beyond artificial intelligence. *Mobile Networks and Applications*, *23*(2), 368–375. DOI: 10.1007/s11036-017-0932-8

Molakatala, N., Kumar, D. A., Patil, U., Mhatre, P. J., Sambathkumar, M., & Boopathi, S. (2024). Integrating 5G and IoT Technologies in Developing Smart City Communication Networks. In *Blockchain-Based Solutions for Accessibility in Smart Cities* (pp. 147–170). IGI Global. DOI: 10.4018/979-8-3693-3402-7.ch006

Puranik, T. A., Shaik, N., Vankudoth, R., Kolhe, M. R., Yadav, N., & Boopathi, S. (2024). Study on Harmonizing Human-Robot (Drone) Collaboration: Navigating Seamless Interactions in Collaborative Environments. In *Cybersecurity Issues and Challenges in the Drone Industry* (pp. 1–26). IGI Global.

Qian, C., Cong, X., Yang, C., Chen, W., Su, Y., Xu, J., Liu, Z., & Sun, M. (2023). Communicative agents for software development. *arXiv Preprint arXiv:2307.07924, 6*(3).

Qian, C., Liu, W., Liu, H., Chen, N., Dang, Y., Li, J., Yang, C., Chen, W., Su, Y., & Cong, X. (2024). Chatdev: Communicative agents for software development. *Proceedings of the 62nd Annual Meeting of the Association for Computational Linguistics(*Volume 1*: Long Papers)*, 15174–15186. DOI: 10.18653/v1/2024.acl-long.810

Sangeetha, M., Kannan, S. R., Boopathi, S., Ramya, J., Ishrat, M., & Sabarinathan, G. (2023). Prediction of Fruit Texture Features Using Deep Learning Techniques. *2023 4th International Conference on Smart Electronics and Communication (ICOSEC)*, 762–768.

Shafin, R., Liu, L., Chandrasekhar, V., Chen, H., Reed, J., & Zhang, J. C. (2020). Artificial intelligence-enabled cellular networks: A critical path to beyond-5G and 6G. *IEEE Wireless Communications*, *27*(2), 212–217. DOI: 10.1109/MWC.001.1900323

Sreedhar, P. S. S., Sujay, V., Rani, M. R., Melita, L., Reshma, S., & Boopathi, S. (2024). Impacts of 5G Machine Learning Techniques on Telemedicine and Social Media Professional Connection in Healthcare. In *Advances in Medical Technologies and Clinical Practice* (pp. 209–234). IGI Global. DOI: 10.4018/979-8-3693-1934-5.ch012

Subha, S., Inbamalar, T., Komala, C., Suresh, L. R., Boopathi, S., & Alaskar, K. (2023). A Remote Health Care Monitoring system using internet of medical things (IoMT). *IEEE Explore*, 1–6.

Sun, L., Jiang, X., Ren, H., & Guo, Y. (2020). Edge-cloud computing and artificial intelligence in internet of medical things: Architecture, technology and application. *IEEE Access : Practical Innovations, Open Solutions*, *8*, 101079–101092. DOI: 10.1109/ACCESS.2020.2997831

Tomašev, N., Cornebise, J., Hutter, F., Mohamed, S., Picciariello, A., Connelly, B., Belgrave, D. C., Ezer, D., van der Haert, F. C., & Mugisha, F. (2020). AI for social good: Unlocking the opportunity for positive impact. *Nature Communications*, *11*(1), 2468. DOI: 10.1038/s41467-020-15871-z PMID: 32424119

Venkateswaran, N., Kunduru, K. R., Ashwin, N., Sundar Ganesh, C. S., Hema, N., & Boopathi, S. (2024). Navigating the Future of Ultra-Smart Computing Cyberspace: Beyond Boundaries. In *Advances in Computational Intelligence and Robotics* (pp. 170–199). IGI Global. DOI: 10.4018/979-8-3693-2399-1.ch007

Venkateswaran, N., Vidhya, R., Naik, D. A., Raj, T. M., Munjal, N., & Boopathi, S. (2023). Study on Sentence and Question Formation Using Deep Learning Techniques. In *Digital Natives as a Disruptive Force in Asian Businesses and Societies* (pp. 252–273). IGI Global. DOI: 10.4018/978-1-6684-6782-4.ch015

Vinuesa, R., Azizpour, H., Leite, I., Balaam, M., Dignum, V., Domisch, S., Felländer, A., Langhans, S. D., Tegmark, M., & Fuso Nerini, F. (2020). The role of artificial intelligence in achieving the Sustainable Development Goals. *Nature Communications*, *11*(1), 1–10. DOI: 10.1038/s41467-019-14108-y PMID: 31932590

KEY TERMS AND DEFINITIONS

AI: Artificial Intelligence.
ML: Machine Learning.
NLP: Natural Language Processing.
IP: Internet Protocol.
LAN: Local Area Network.
QoS: Quality of Service.
RTC: Real-Time Communication.
SIP: Session Initiation Protocol.
RTP: Real-Time Protocol.
CDN: Content Delivery Network.
TCP: Transmission Control Protocol.
UDP: User Datagram Protocol.
GDPR: General Data Protection Regulation.
AT: Assistive Technology (or Adaptive Technology, depending on context).
IBM: International Business Machines Corporation.

Chapter 6
Case Studies Within Smart and Secure Software Development

Shahed Ammar Al-Tamimi
https://orcid.org/0009-0005-3270-8200
University of Doha for Science and Technology, Qatar

Qasem Abu Al-Haija
https://orcid.org/0000-0003-2422-0297
Jordan University of Science and Technology, Jordan

ABSTRACT

In today's digital world, software systems must adhere to the Secure Software Development Lifecycle (SSDLC) protocol to guarantee security, reliability, and resilience. Despite the revolutionary impact of deep learning, blockchain, and Artificial Intelligence (AI) on software development, substantial challenges remain to be solved in terms of minimizing security risks and conforming to regulatory standards. This Software Development Lifecycle (SDLC) research integrates cybersecurity throughout the process and primarily focuses on case studies and best practices relating to risk assessment, secure design, and security testing. Data privacy, intellectual property regulations, and regulatory requirements must be followed while developing robust software systems that can resist cyber assaults and promote innovation.

DOI: 10.4018/979-8-3693-9851-7.ch006

INTRODUCTION

Within the age of technology, SSD is essential to innovation. Robust, durable, and SS are essential as networked systems become more common. Critical applications such as sustainable city infrastructures and blockchain-driven technology demonstrate this. Security at every level of software development reduces risks and builds confidence in new fields like electric car ecosystems and smart contracts. During Alanazi and Alenezi (2023), they emphasize how software engineering skills can design sustainable cities, especially with electric automobiles. Secure and efficient software manages energy distribution, charging network optimization, and vehicle-to-grid connection. These apps' vulnerabilities might cause large-scale disruptions, threatening sustainable urban systems. SSD approaches targeted to smart city infrastructure concerns are needed. Combining blockchain and software engineering has created new SSD difficulties and possibilities. Blockchain technology and smart contracts may alter decentralized systems but pose security issues, according to Vacca *et al.* (2021). Smart contract implementation flaws have caused high-profile breaches and financial losses. Developers must use secure code, rigorous testing, and creative technologies to protect blockchain apps. The confluence of these advances shows the rising relevance of software development lifecycle security. SSD may innovate while protecting key infrastructures by researching electric car systems and blockchain technology. Recent software systems, especially those operating cyber-physical energy systems, the Internet of Things (IoT), and intelligent transportation, face several cyber dangers.

1.1 Background

Software systems are planned, developed, tested, and deployed through the SDLC. Completing each software development step yields high-quality, dependable, and functioning applications. SDLC is vital for organizing development but raises security risks that must be handled at every level. Zografopoulos *et al.* (2021) underlined poor threat modeling and risk assessment during SDLC design might lead to security vulnerabilities in Cyber-Physical Energy systems (CPES). Also, the complexity of combining software with physical systems increases the risk of system reliability and safety threats. Agile SDLC methodologies are important for cybersecurity and IoT application development, (Tashtoush *et al.,* 2021). Agile approaches provide frequent updates and quick vulnerability response via iterative development. If secure code and continuous testing aren't implemented, agile processes' quick speed might cause security issues. Smart transportation systems must prevent security breaches that disrupt traffic management and public safety.

Furthermore, how sustainable development projects, which increasingly use software-driven solutions, must include cybersecurity in the SDLC is discussed in Sulich *et al.* (2021). Many sustainable development efforts include linked systems that need long-term resilience. Unresolved security problems in the early SDLC might compromise system stability and scalability. Figure 1 describes the overall reasons for security issues within SDLC.

Figure 1. Overall security flaws reasons within SDLC

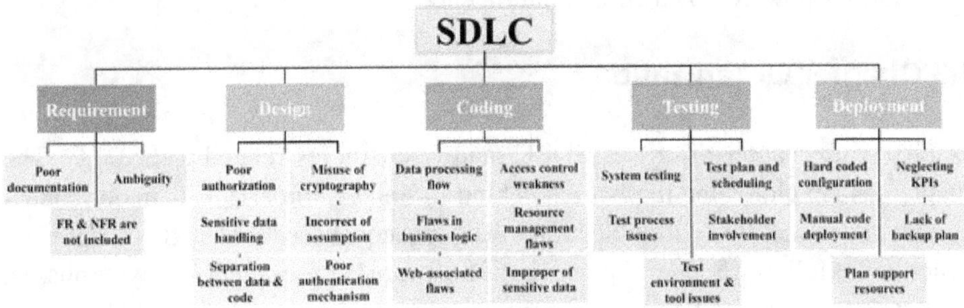

1.1 Motivation

This chapter is motivated by software systems' increasing challenges and susceptibility to cyber-attacks. A holistic approach to safe software development is essential since advanced technologies such as deep learning and blockchain pose innovation and security concerns. This chapter focuses on case studies related to the SSDLC domain.

1.2 Contribution

Listed below are the key points covered in the chapter:

I. Evaluating the need for legal compliance with rules like GDPR, IP management, and industry-specific standards like PCI-DSS and HIPAA.

   The chapter delineates protocols for automated testing, threat modeling, secure coding, and proactive security integration throughout SSDLC stages.

II. Presenting case studies across multiple areas, including blockchain, IoT networks, and healthcare, illustrates the application of SSDLC ideas in real-world scenarios.

III. The chapter addresses outstanding questions with SSDLC, such as managing the intricacies of blockchain-focused development and integrating security solutions powered by artificial intelligence.

1.3 Chapter Organization

First, this chapter discusses SDLC, and case studies related to SSDLC. The chapter also explores the motivation behind this and summarizes its major contributions and motivation within Section 1. The subsequent sections of this chapter are structured as follows. Section 2 presents the Software Development Lifecycle phases. Section 3 provides the Secure Software Development Lifecycle (SSDLC) phases, a description, and case studies for each phase. Thus, Section 4 represents the latest case studies about SSDLC: section 5, SSDLC Security Risks, Open Challenges, and Proposed Solutions. Section 6 illustrates the legal compliance with SSDLC and best practices, and finally, it presents the conclusion and remarks.

1. Software Development Lifecycle

SDLC ensures the efficiency, functionality, and security of corporate and high-tech applications via a methodical approach to software production. Recent technology, especially cybersecurity and AI, has greatly impacted SDLC. Due to Ajiga *et al.* (2024a), corporate software development must prioritize cybersecurity to protect data integrity. In addition, obstacles to standardizing SDLC models have emerged, such as failing to manage escalating risks and necessitating advanced security measures throughout development. Proactive risk assessment, robust encryption, and frequent monitoring help to decrease critical application vulnerabilities. Further findings from Ajiga *et al.* (2024b) demonstrate how AI-enhanced software development is transforming high-tech companies. Also, AI helps developers find code flaws, streamline procedures, and forecast system breakdowns. This SDLC integration of AI underlines the rising need for data-driven insights for safe, efficient, and scalable software solutions. According to Ajiga (2024), engineers must balance innovation and ethics in software development. Ethical problems, including data privacy, AI bias, and global laws, must be addressed throughout the SDLC to guarantee that software meets societal standards and trust—human-centered SDLC by studying safe software developer self-efficacy, (Votipka, Abrokwa, & Mazurek, 2020). According to their research, software engineers require training and education to install security measures throughout development successfully. Skill-building solves cybersecurity's human vulnerability. The SDLC steps in Figure 2 show its importance.

Figure 2. SDLC phases

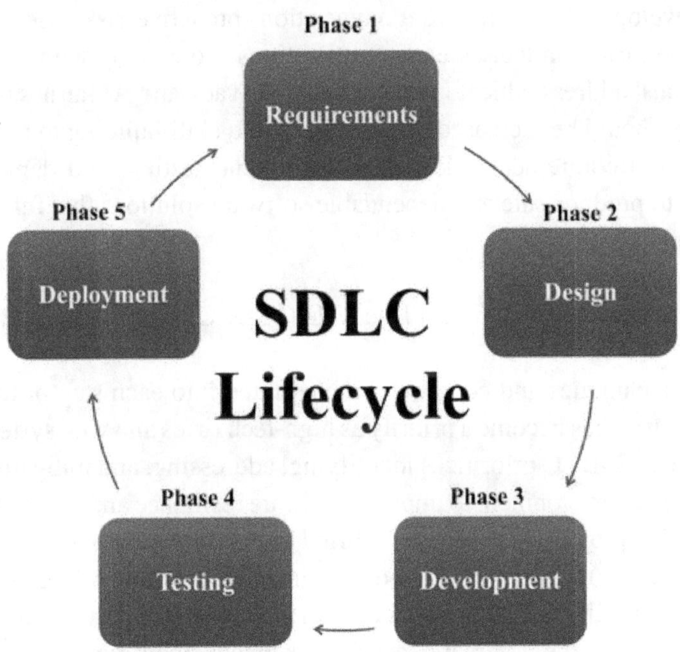

The SDLC consists of five key phases:

I. **Requirements:** This phase focuses on gathering and analyzing the functional and non-functional requirements of the software, ensuring clarity on what the system needs to achieve.

II. **Design:** In this stage, system architecture and design are created based on the requirements, detailing how the software components will interact and operate.
III. **Development:** The actual coding and implementation of the software take place, turning the design into a functional product.
IV. **Testing:** The developed software is rigorously tested to identify and resolve bugs, ensuring quality, reliability, and compliance with requirements.
V. **Deployment:** The final phase involves deploying the software into the production environment, making it accessible to end users, followed by ongoing maintenance and updates.

The SDLC organizes functions and SSD, notably in corporate and high-tech applications. Recent technologies like AI and enhanced cybersecurity have changed SDLC. AI detects faults, optimizes processes, and predicts system failures in software development, while strong encryption, proactive risk assessments, and constant monitoring protect essential applications. To comply with social norms, the SDLC must address ethical issues like data privacy and AI fairness. Developer self-efficacy should be increased via education and skill-building to reduce cybersecurity risks. Requirements, design, development, testing, and deployment are interrelated to produce safe and dependable software solutions that fulfill user and organizational goals.

2. Secure Software Development Lifecycle (SSDLC)

Security techniques and concepts are integrated into each step of the SSDLC. Software security has become a priority as high-tech firms and vital systems depend more on it. The SSDLC prioritizes identifying, addressing, and mitigating security risks throughout development to improve software resilience and reduce vulnerabilities. SSDLC deployment has been modified owing to AI and secure frameworks. Ajiga *et al.* (2024c) exhibits how AI-driven insights can spot vulnerabilities early, forecast system failures, and automate secure coding in high-tech organizations. Further emphasizing the systematic security risk management requirement, including safe design, threat modeling, and ongoing risk assessment in SSDLC phases, (Khan *et al.*, 2022). Moreover, the Secure Software Development Framework (SSDF). Souppaya, Scarfone, & Dodson (2022) offers a thorough framework for inserting security controls into each step to ensure software system compliance and resilience.

Case studies split the SSDLC across important stages with particular security aims. Requirement gathering, secure design, development, testing and validation, deployment, and maintenance provide the basis for secure, scalable, and efficient software systems. SSDLC ideas may be better understood and used across industries by examining real-world case studies. In Figure 3, SSDLC phases are illustrated.

Figure 3. SSDLC phases

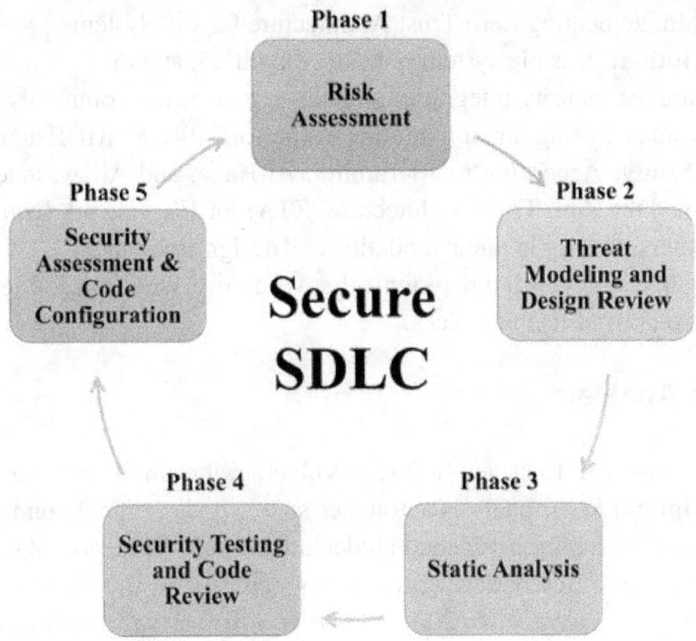

The SSDLC adds security to SDLC stages to reduce vulnerabilities, hazards, and software resiliency. According to the sources, the following stages describe implementation procedures and scenarios:

3.1 Risk Assessment

Title: IoT Networks Security: Intrusion Detection Using Extreme Learning Machine (ELM).
Description: The Risk Assessment further identifies and prioritizes possible hazards and vulnerabilities within the software system. Security issues affect program operation, data integrity, and user privacy. The following phase requires vulnerability evaluations and penetration testing.
Case Study: During Altamimi and Al-Haija (2024) Extreme Learning Machines (ELMs) were used to improve Intrusion Detection in IoT Networks. The research shows how Machine Learning (ML) algorithms during the risk assessment phase can detect and reduce real-time IoT system vulnerabilities, assuring dependability and data security.

3.2 Threat Modeling and Design Review

Title: Implementing Zero-Trust Architecture for IoT Systems.
Description: Possible system risks are identified, and the design is assessed to guarantee security integration. Attack scenarios are commonly simulated and evaluated using threat modeling frameworks like STRIDE and DREAD.
Case Study: According to Al-Tamimi, Al-Haija, and Alrawashdeh (2024), examined the Zero-Trust Architecture (ZTA) for IoT network security, highlighting its efficacy in threat modeling and design assessment. ZTA principles may help businesses build systems that verify every request and reduce trust zones to prevent lateral attacks.

3.3 Static Analysis

Title: Using ML to Detect Software Vulnerabilities in Static Code Analysis.
Description: Static analysis automates source code examination for security problems, including hardcoded credentials, unsafe APIs, and SQL injection vulnerabilities. Before development, this step verifies code security.
Case Study: Hanig *et al.* (2021) classified software vulnerabilities and used ML models for static code analysis. Also, they discovered problems in software repositories, such as buffer overflows, SQL injection sites, and incorrect input validation. Using AI-driven static analysis tools provides developers with actionable information, enabling them to fix vulnerabilities during the early phases of development and drastically lowering security risks.

3.4 Security Testing and Code Review

Title: Challenges in Developing Secure Mobile Health Applications.
Description: Simulates attack scenarios to ensure application resilience against security risks. Code reviews find flaws discovered during development. Penetration, fuzz, and secure unit testing are used at this step.
Case Study: Within Alijedaani and Babar (2021), mobile health apps (mHealth) address particular issues, such as securing sensitive patient data and adhering to healthcare standards. In this case study, mHealth applications underwent thorough penetration testing and detailed code inspections to discover unsecured data transfer and inadequate encryption mechanisms. The findings highlighted the need for rigorous security testing and code reviews to guarantee that these systems are resilient to real-world threats and ensure privacy and healthcare compliance.

3.5 Security Assessment and Code Configuration

Title: Integrating Security and Privacy into Software Development.
Description: The system is thoroughly security assessed in the last step to guarantee compliance with best practices. This step covers security policy finalization, encryption verification, and secure communication protocol configuration.
Case Study: This case study demonstrated the need to complete security settings at the deployment stage. Security evaluations were carried out to guarantee encryption standards, safe API setups, and compliance with data protection legislation. Baldassare *et al.* (2020) found that adding security parameters into the final phases of development considerably decreased vulnerabilities and increased user confidence in the released product.

Table 1. Overall summary of SSDLC

Ref.	Phase	Vulnerability / Attacks / Threats	Description	Remarks
Humayun *et al.* (2022)	Risk Assessment Phase	Data integrity, confidentiality, and availability threats	Provides SSD security threat and vulnerability evaluation. Systematic risk identification and quantification.	The early phases of SSDLC need rigorous risk assessment.
Al-Tamimi & Al-Haija (2025)		✓ Educational privacy risks. ✓ Learning tool cyberattacks	Focuses on educational technology-specific vulnerabilities and dangers in computational intelligence security and privacy.	Covers domain-specific risk assessment for education system computational intelligence security.
Ajiga *et al.* (2024d)	Threat Modeling and Design Review	✓ Insufficient threat modeling, ✓ insecure design	✓ Explore how AI insights improve threat modeling to discover high-tech company risks. ✓ Predictive analysis informs design choices that reduce risk.	Offer using AI to anticipate design faults.
Dodson, Souppaya, & Scarfone (2020)		Design-time vulnerability exploitation.	Offers the SSDF to minimize design risks via secure coding and early threat modeling.	Provides a standardized framework for secure design processes.

continued on following page

Table 1. Continued

Ref.	Phase	Vulnerability / Attacks / Threats	Description	Remarks
Gasiba *et al.* (2020)	Static Analysis	✓ Undefined coding vulnerabilities. ✓ Poor developer training.	Shows how a cybersecurity awareness platform employs virtual coaching and automated evaluations to improve static code analysis and developer knowledge.	Advocates for continuous developer training alongside static analysis tools.
Al-Haija, Altamimi, & AlWadi (2024)		Intrusion detection, code vulnerabilities	Examines how ELM improves intelligent intrusion detection and static analysis code vulnerabilities.	Encourages intelligent system integration to better static analysis.
Hutchinson *et al.* (2021)	Security Testing and Code Review	Dataset poisoning and biased algorithm performance.	✓ Identifies security testing vulnerabilities to ensure ML dataset accountability. ✓ Explains ML system data-related weaknesses and poisoning attack prevention.	In AI-integrated systems, robust security testing is crucial.
Palombo *et al.* (2020)		Misconfiguration and developer non-compliance	Examines co-creation and developer collaboration to enhance software security testing for usability and security.	Enables collaboration to resolve vulnerabilities.
Hou *et al.* (2024)	Security Assessment and Code Configuration	Weak encryption, improper API configuration	Examines huge language models' ability to analyze software security setups and ensure API and encryption protocol implementation.	Promotes AI-driven security configuration optimization.
Gkortzis, Feitosa, & Spinellis (2021)		Security concerns about software reuse	The reuse of software increases vulnerability threats, making security configuration assessment in repeated components difficult.	Indicates the trade-off between efficiency and security in software reuse strategies.

3. LATEST CASE STUDIES ABOUT SECURE SDLC

Organizations worldwide may integrate security into SDLC, given the complexity of contemporary systems and the changing threat environment. Case examples from past studies, financial services, software development, and huge projects demonstrate the significance of security throughout development. The following case examples demonstrate the hurdles and approaches that firms utilize to safeguard sensitive data, fulfill legal requirements, and create user confidence. Studying real-world situations shows how firms manage innovation and security while adjusting to industry-specific constraints and technological advances.

Case Study #1:
Title: Financial Services Sector.
Description: During Arora *et al.* (2021), how financial firms integrate security throughout their software development processes is explored. The study's interviews with practitioners from 11 firms underscored the need to include security concerns in each SDLC step to secure sensitive financial data.
Case Study #2:
Title: German Software Industry.
Description: Langstrof and Sabau (2024) looks at security in the German software industry. The results found that security measures are acknowledged but often not fully integrated into standardized operations, underlining the necessity for established security standards.
Case Study #3:
Title: Secure Software Development Methodologies.
Description: focuses on secure software development methodologies. During Kudriavtseva and Gadyatskaya (2022) a multivocal literature study summarized the security approaches used in 28 safe software development techniques from business, government, and academia. The research stressed the need to adopt security at every stage of the SDLC to reduce risks.
Case Study #4:
Title: Integration of Security in Agile Frameworks.
Description: To meet security compliance requirements, the authors look at ways that scaled agile frameworks, such as Scaled Agile Framework (SAFe), may be expanded. Moyón *et al.* (2020) explains the large-scale project environment at Siemens and lays out the pros and downsides of using agile methodologies with security integration.

In short, case examples emphasize the need to include security within the SDLC. The lessons acquired stress proactive risk management and compliance, whether financial organizations protect sensitive data, the German software sector recognizes the need for standardized security standards, or academics and industry use secure approaches. Siemens' integration of security into agile frameworks shows how adaptive techniques may handle massive projects while ensuring security. These case studies provide useful insights into safe software development approaches across industry.

4. SSDLC SECURITY RISKS, OPEN CHALLENGES, AND PROPOSED SOLUTIONS

SSDLC is crucial since organizations prioritize SSD in combating rising cybersecurity threats. Effective SSDLC implementation is tricky. Adopting SSDLC presents various obstacles, from integrating security into rapid processes to meeting changing regulatory requirements. Manage the security skills gap, software system complexity, and third-party dependence vulnerability while balancing security with development velocity. Recent research addresses SSDLC's security vulnerabilities and provides remedies. Open challenges and purposeful answers are presented. Discussions on security testing automation, AI threat modeling, and continuous security awareness training give practical solutions for combining security and software development goals.

A. Security Risks

Software security threats, especially in AI. As AI gets increasingly embedded into software systems, it creates additional vulnerabilities such as adversarial assaults, data manipulation, and model poisoning, (Rindell *et al.*, 2021) (Althar *et al.*, 2023). The system's integrity, confidentiality, and availability are at stake. Therefore, strong security is essential. To secure software systems from these attacks, the authors recommend using powerful AI-driven methods to uncover vulnerabilities and anticipate security issues. Table 2 summarises SSDLC security issues.

Table 2. Overall SSDLC security risks summary

Attack	Vulnerability	Threat	SSDLC Phase	Against CIA tried	Solution
Phishing Attack	Insufficient user knowledge and inadequate authentication procedures.	Theft of credentials or sensitive information.	Risk Assessment Phase	Confidentiality	Deploy multi-factor authentication and run simulated phishing campaigns for employee training (Moyón *et al.*, 2020) (Rindell *et al.*, 2021)
Malware Injection via Third-Party Tools	Reuse of vulnerable third-party libraries	Exploitation of known vulnerabilities in reused code		Integrity	Keep third-party dependencies updated and utilize SCA to find library vulnerabilities (Kudriavtseva & Gadyatskaya, 2022) (Demi, Colomo-Palacios, & Sanchez-Gordon, 2021)
Ransomware Attacks	Weak backup and disaster recovery mechanisms.	Encryption of critical systems and ransom demand.	Threat Modeling and Design Review.	Availability	Implement robust backup procedures, network segmentation, and regular security monitoring to spot anomalous activity early, (Moyón et al., 2020) (Ribeiro, Cruzes, & Travassos, 2022)
Code Injection Attack	Unsafe dynamic code execution	Execution of malicious code in software		Integrity	To discover hazardous dynamic code, use stringent code review and automated static analysis (Ribeiro, Cruzes, & Travassos, 2022) (Lin *et al.*, 2020)

continued on following page

Table 2. Continued

Attack	Vulnerability	Threat	SSDLC Phase	Against CIA tried	Solution
SQL Injection Attack	Input validation flaws.	Unauthorized access to sensitive data.	Static Analysis Phase	Confidentiality, Integrity	Validate and sanitize input; utilize prepared statements or parameterized queries (Kudriavtseva & Gadyatskaya, 2022) (Lin *et al.*, 2020)
Denial of Service (DoS) Attack	Unoptimized code and inadequate resource management.	Service unavailability.		Availability	Utilize static analysis methods to identify and optimize resource-intensive code sections (Althar *et al.*, 2023) (Behutiye *et al.*, 2020)
Data Leakage Attack	Insecure APIs and weak encryption.	Exposure of sensitive user data.	Security Testing and Code Review Phase	Confidentiality	Secure API design utilizing robust encryption principles and enforce HTTPS; do threat modeling (Kudriavtseva & Gadyatskaya, 2022) (Althar *et al.*, 2023)
Side-Channel Attacks	Insufficient attention to timing and power-related vulnerabilities.	Leaking information through unintended channels.		Confidentiality	Find timing and power usage weaknesses using powerful fuzz testing and monitoring tools (Rindell et al., 2021) (Behutiye *et al.*, 2020)
Zero-Day Exploits	Outdated Dependencies	Exploitation of unpatched libraries		Availability	Perform dependency checks, regular patching, and penetration testing (Behutiye *et al.*, 2020) (Al-Haija & Al-Salameen, 2024)

continued on following page

Table 2. Continued

Attack	Vulnerability	Threat	SSDLC Phase	Against CIA tried	Solution
Privilege Escalation Attack	Misconfigured access control.	Attackers gaining elevated privileges.	Security Assessment and Configuration Phase	Confidentiality, Integrity, Availability	Regular access control evaluations should be conducted, and the least privilege concept should be implemented (Althar *et al.*, 2023) (Al-Haija & Al-Salameen, 2024)
Unauthorized Device Access	Weak biometric authentication or mismanagement of mobile devices.	Compromise of personal or corporate data.		Confidentiality, Integrity	Improve biometric authentication techniques and implement device management rules for mobile contexts (Al-Haija & Al-Salameen, 2024)

B. Open Challenges and Proposed Solutions

The SSDLC is crucial for SSD. Software system security against increasingly sophisticated cyber threats grows harder as technology develops. Recently, frameworks that handle traditional security threats and include current technologies like deep learning, blockchain, and AI to improve development have become more popular. Researchers have proposed several SSDLC methodologies and solutions. However, various problems hinder the lifetime of truly secure software.

Challenge #1: Integration of Security Early in the Development Process

Proposed Solution: One of the primary problems in SSDLC is ensuring that security is included in the software development process from the start.

Many firms still use a "security after development" strategy, which leads to vulnerabilities. The answer is to adopt a proactive strategy in which safe coding techniques, threat modeling, and vulnerability assessments are carried out early in the development cycle. This may be accomplished using AI-powered tools that examine code for vulnerabilities in actual time, as detailed in Li *et al.* (2024).

Challenge #2: Handling Complexity in Blockchain-Oriented Software Development

Proposed Solution: Showcase the challenge of customizing software engineering procedures to accommodate the specific security requirements of blockchain technology in the context of blockchain-oriented software development, (Faruk *et al.,* 2022). The distributed structure of blockchain systems introduces threats consisting of smart contract vulnerabilities and illegal access to blockchain networks. Faruk et al. suggest using systematic techniques and specialized tools to implement security measures at every stage of the development lifecycle to guarantee the safe and effective administration of software systems built on the blockchain.

Challenge #3: Security Monitoring During the Software Life Cycle

Proposed Solution: The importance of a security architecture that improves monitoring and guarantees security throughout the software life cycle is highlighted in the research in Mustonen (2024). When security flaws and holes crop up during development, testing, and deployment, automated systems and continuous monitoring technologies may help find them. AI-driven monitoring solutions may learn from previous attacks and adjust accordingly to defend software from ever-changing security concerns.

Challenge #4: Adoption of Deep Learning for Process Optimization

Proposed Solution: The research delves into using deep learning to enhance software development processes throughout Aynalem (2022). The main obstacle is preserving security while incorporating deep learning models into preexisting development frameworks. These models can sift through mountains of data, searching for trends and problems and enhancing development security and efficiency. But it's a huge problem that calls for ongoing improvement and safe training methods to ensure these models are resilient against adversarial assaults and data breaches.

To sum up, SSDLC security obstacles have improved yet remain. AI, deep learning, and blockchain may fix many of these issues, but they also introduce new challenges that must be managed. Proactive security, enhanced monitoring, and security framework innovation are needed to combat escalating cyber risks. These technologies will provide secure and robust software systems as SSDLC evolves.

6. LEGAL COMPLIANCE FOR SSDLC AND BEST PRACTICES

SSDLCs require legal compliance and best practices. As software systems grow increasingly complicated and crucial to operations, legal and regulatory compliance is essential to preserving sensitive data, user privacy, and trust. Meanwhile, SSDLC best practices help firms identify and mitigate security risks, eliminate vulnerabilities, and maintain comprehensive protection throughout the software lifecycle. Where the current section represents the following:

6.1 Legal Compliance for SSDLC

Legal compliance in the SSDLC is crucial as software development evolves. Advanced technologies like deep learning have improved software development, (Li *et al.,* 2024). These developments also make data protection, intellectual property, and industry-specific rules harder to comply with. Deep learning and comparable technologies analyze massive volumes of data; thus, they must function within legal frameworks to avoid privacy breaches, data abuse, and regulatory infractions. SSDLC has to cope with legal compliance, and secure and ethical development techniques stimulate innovation and legal compliance.

6.1.1 Data Protection and Privacy Laws

The importance of compliance with data protection regulations like the General Data Protection Regulation (GDPR), California Consumer Privacy Act (CCPA), and other privacy laws when developing blockchain-oriented software is emphasized, (Faruk *et al.,* 2022). SSDLC processes must protect personal and sensitive data throughout the development lifecycle, from design through deployment and maintenance. At the same time, Mustonen (2024) secure software frameworks must comply with global privacy laws, including data encryption and secure data storage practices.

6.1.2 Intellectual Property Rights

Intellectual property (IP) protection is critical in the context of SSDLC since it guarantees that proprietary code and technology are protected from unlawful use or theft throughout development. Furthermore, inside Faruk *et al.* (2022), SSD techniques must include IP control policies, particularly when dealing with third-party libraries or open-source software.

6.1.3 Regulatory Standards

Software developed for specific industries, including healthcare and finance, must adhere to industry-specific regulatory standards, such as the Health Insurance Portability and Accountability Act (HIPAA) for healthcare software or Payment Card Industry Data Security Standard (PCI-DSS) for payment processing software and secure the cards. The mentioned standards ensure that software systems maintain high levels of security to protect users' sensitive data and must indicate the necessity for secure software development processes to incorporate these regulations, (Faruk *et al.*, 2022) (Mustonen, 2024).

6.1.4 Contractual Obligations and Risk Management

In software development, legal compliance also includes meeting contractual obligations with clients, third parties, and stakeholders. SSDLC must address risk management strategies considering contractual security requirements and liability in case of security breaches, (Faruk *et al.*, 2022). Moreover, it is important to integrate risk management frameworks in blockchain-oriented development to ensure adherence to contractual security obligations, (Mustonen, 2024).

6.1.5 Audit and Documentation Requirements

According to Faruk *et al.* (2022) and Núñez, Lindo, and Rodríguez (2020), recording every step of the SSDLC with precision is crucial. In addition, to guarantee conformity with rules and regulations, suitable auditing procedures should be put in place. You must document your security audits, risk assessments, and testing procedures to show that you follow all the rules and regulations.

6.2 Best Practices for SSDLC

SSDLC recommended practices are crucial to an SSD's cyber defense. These best practices aim to actively detect and fix vulnerabilities by integrating security precautions into the development process at every stage. Companies can improve development plans and prioritize security using new technologies like deep learning. Using proactive threat modeling, automated security testing, continuous analytics, and enforcement with security may improve software security, efficiency, and compliance, (Li *et al.*, 2024). This section discusses key software life cycle security strategies to help organizations prioritize security.

6.2.1 Proactive Threat Modeling

As mentioned in Mustonen (2024), SSDLC standard procedures include threat modeling to detect potential security issues. This work is advised to be completed at the start of the software design process to detect and resolve any potential dangers quickly.

6.2.2 Secure Coding Standards

Secure coding practices, including input validation, proper error handling, and avoiding insecure APIs, are fundamental to preventing vulnerabilities. As mentioned in Faruk *et al.* (2022), the importance of secure coding methodologies that align with best practices to reduce the risk of injection attacks, Cross-Site Scripting (XSS), and other common vulnerabilities is highlighted.

6.2.3 Automated Security Testing

Automated security testing tools deserve to be included in the SSDLC to guarantee that security vulnerabilities are identified and addressed continually. As underlined by Aynalem (2022), employing static analysis, dynamic analysis, and fuzz testing tools may help enhance web-based systems' security.

6.2.4 Security Awareness Training

It is vital to raise security awareness and provide training to developers and other SDLC stakeholders. Which educates and develops teams on the most recent security threats, vulnerabilities, and safe coding techniques, lowering the chance of security breaches, (Von Solms & Futcher, 2020). Emphasize the necessity of cultivating a security-conscious culture among development teams.

6.2.5 Incident Management and Patch Management

The SSDLC should include methods for incident response and patch management. For the sake of software security, vulnerabilities must be identified and fixed as soon as possible after they are released. Thus, Faruk et al. (2022) and Núñez, Lindo, & Rodríguez (2020) emphasizes the necessity of continual vulnerability management, including the timely deployment of security fixes.

6.2.6 Regular Security Audits and Reviews

Regular code reviews and security audits are crucial for finding vulnerabilities that could have been missed during development. Systematic security audits are emphasized as a crucial best practice to guarantee the integrity of software systems in references, (Aynalem, 2022) (Von Solms & Futcher, 2020).

6.2.7 The Usage of Secure Development Frameworks and Tools

Using vulnerability-tested frameworks and libraries reduces the likelihood of product security problems. Recommended frameworks with built-in security features improve software development security throughout the lifecycle, (Mustonen, 2024) (Núñez, Lindo, & Rodríguez, 2020).

By following these legal compliance guidelines and best practices, enterprises may minimize software vulnerability risks and increase software system security.

CONCLUSIONS AND REMARKS

The chapter discusses SSDLC's vital role in handling contemporary cybersecurity risks while complying with legal and regulatory standards. Organizations may mitigate and reduce risks and improve system resilience by implementing security measures across the SSDLC and adhering to recommended practices. The results indicate that proactive threat modeling, AI-powered monitoring, and continuing security awareness training are essential for establishing a secure development environment. However, new vulnerabilities arise as technology advances, necessitating ongoing innovation in security methods. Future research should concentrate on improving AI and blockchain security solutions, ensuring they meet ethical and legal requirements while dealing with the ever-changing nature of cyber threats.

REFERENCES

Abu Al-Haija, Q., Altamimi, S., & AlWadi, M. Analysis of Extreme Learning Machines (ELMs) for intelligent intrusion detection systems: A survey, Expert Systems with Applications, Volume 253, 2024, 124317, ISSN 0957-4174, https://doi.org/DOI: 10.1016/j.eswa.2024.124317

Ajiga, Daniel. (2024). Navigating ethical considerations in software development and deployment in technological giants. .DOI: 10.53430/ijeru.2024.7.1.0033

Ajiga, D., Okeleke, P. A., Folorunsho, S. O., & Ezeigweneme, C. (2024). Designing cybersecurity measures for enterprise software applications to protect data integrity.

Ajiga, D., Okeleke, P. A., Folorunsho, S. O., & Ezeigweneme, C. (2024). Enhancing software development practices with AI insights in high-tech companies. IEEE Software Engineering Institute, Technical Report TR-2024-003.

Ajiga, D., Okeleke, P. A., Folorunsho, S. O., & Ezeigweneme, C. (2024). Enhancing software development practices with AI insights in high-tech companies. IEEE Software Engineering Institute, Technical Report TR-2024-003.

Ajiga, D., Okeleke, P. A., Folorunsho, S. O., & Ezeigweneme, C. (2024). Enhancing software development practices with AI insights in high-tech companies. IEEE Software Engineering Institute, Technical Report TR-2024-003.

Al-Haija, Q. A., & Al-Salameen, S. O. (2024). Biometric Authentication System on Mobile Environment: A Review. *Computer Systems Science and Engineering*, *48*(4), 1–10. DOI: 10.32604/csse.2024.050846

Al-Tamimi, S., & Abu Al-Haija, Q. (2025). Security and Privacy of Educational Computational Intelligence. In M. Ouaissa, M. Ouaissa, H. Lamaazi, M. El Hamlaoui, & K. Reddy C. (Eds.), *Internet of Behavior-Based Computational Intelligence for Smart Education Systems* (pp. 301-328). IGI Global Scientific Publishing. https://doi.org/DOI: 10.4018/979-8-3693-8151-9.ch011

Al-Tamimi, S., Al-Haija, Q. A., & Alrawashdeh, K. "Zero-Trust Architecture for Securing Internet of Things (IoT) Networks: A Review," 2024 5th International Conference on Communications, Information, Electronic and Energy Systems (CIEES), Veliko Tarnovo, Bulgaria, 2024, pp. 1-6, DOI: 10.1109/CIEES62939.2024.10811176

Alanazi, F., & Alenezi, M. (2023). Software engineering techniques for building sustainable cities with electric vehicles. *Applied Sciences (Basel, Switzerland)*, *13*(15), 8741. DOI: 10.3390/app13158741

Aljedaani, B., & Babar, M. A. (2021). Challenges with developing secure mobile health applications: Systematic review. *JMIR mHealth and uHealth*, *9*(6), e15654. DOI: 10.2196/15654 PMID: 34152277

Altamimi, S., & Abu Al-Haija, Q. (2024). Maximizing intrusion detection efficiency for IoT networks using extreme learning machines. *Discover Internet of Things*, *4*(1), 5. DOI: 10.1007/s43926-024-00060-x

Althar, R. R., Samanta, D., Purushotham, S., Sengar, S. S., & Hewage, C. (2023). Design and development of artificial intelligence knowledge processing system for optimizing the security of software systems. *SN Computer Science*, *4*(4), 331. DOI: 10.1007/s42979-023-01785-2

Arora, V., Vargas, E., Aniche, M., & Deursen, A. (2021). Secure Software Engineering in the Financial Services: A Practitioners' Perspective. 10.48550/arXiv.2104.03476.

AYNALEM, S. Y. (2022). A FRAMEWORK FOR SOFTWARE SECURITY TESTING IMPROVEMENT FOR WEB-BASED APPLICATIONS.

Baldassarre, M. T., Barletta, V. S., Caivano, D., & Scalera, M. (2020). Integrating security and privacy in software development. *Software Quality Journal*, *28*(3), 987–1018. DOI: 10.1007/s11219-020-09501-6

Behutiye, W., Karhapää, P., López, L., Burgués, X., Martínez-Fernández, S., Vollmer, A. M., Rodríguez, P., Franch, X., & Oivo, M. (2020). Management of quality requirements in agile and rapid software development: A systematic mapping study. *Information and Software Technology*, *123*, 106225. DOI: 10.1016/j.infsof.2019.106225

Demi, S., Colomo-Palacios, R., & Sanchez-Gordon, M. (2021). Software engineering applications enabled by blockchain technology: A systematic mapping study. *Applied Sciences (Basel, Switzerland)*, *11*(7), 2960. DOI: 10.3390/app11072960

Dodson, D., Souppaya, M., & Scarfone, K. (2020). *Mitigating the risk of software vulnerabilities by adopting a secure software development framework (SDF)*. NIST.

Faruk, M. J. H., Subramanian, S., Shahriar, H., Valero, M., Li, X., & Tasnim, M. (2022, May). Software engineering process and methodology in blockchain-oriented software development: A systematic study. In *2022 IEEE/ACIS 20th International Conference on Software Engineering Research, Management and Applications (SERA)* (pp. 120-127). IEEE. DOI: 10.1109/SERA54885.2022.9806817

Gasiba, T., Lechner, U., Pinto-Albuquerque, M., & Porwal, A. (2020, September). Cybersecurity awareness platform with a virtual coach and automated challenge assessment. In *International Workshop on the Security of Industrial Control Systems and Cyber-Physical Systems* (pp. 67-83). Cham: Springer International Publishing. DOI: 10.1007/978-3-030-64330-0_5

Gkortzis, A., Feitosa, D., & Spinellis, D. (2021). Software reuse cuts both ways: An empirical analysis of its relationship with security vulnerabilities—. *Journal of Systems and Software, 172*, 110653. DOI: 10.1016/j.jss.2020.110653

Hanif, H., Nasir, M. H. N. M., Ab Razak, M. F., Firdaus, A., & Anuar, N. B. (2021). The rise of software vulnerability: Taxonomy of software vulnerabilities detection and machine learning approaches. *Journal of Network and Computer Applications, 179*, 103009. DOI: 10.1016/j.jnca.2021.103009

Hou, X., Zhao, Y., Liu, Y., Yang, Z., Wang, K., Li, L., Luo, X., Lo, D., Grundy, J., & Wang, H. (2024). Large language models for software engineering: A systematic literature review. *ACM Transactions on Software Engineering and Methodology, 33*(8), 1–79. DOI: 10.1145/3695988

Humayun, M., Jhanjhi, N., Almufareh, M. F., & Khalil, M. I. (2022). Security threat and vulnerability assessment and measurement in secure software development. *Computers, Materials & Continua, 71*(3), 5039–5059. DOI: 10.32604/cmc.2022.019289

Hutchinson, B., Smart, A., Hanna, A., Denton, E., Greer, C., Kjartansson, O., & Mitchell, M. (2021, March). Towards accountability for machine learning datasets: Practices from software engineering and infrastructure. In *Proceedings of the 2021 ACM Conference on Fairness, Accountability, and Transparency* (pp. 560-575). DOI: 10.1145/3442188.3445918

Khan, R. A., Khan, S. U., Khan, H. U., & Ilyas, M. (2022). Systematic literature review on security risks and its practices in secure software development. *IEEE Access : Practical Innovations, Open Solutions, 10*, 5456–5481. DOI: 10.1109/ACCESS.2022.3140181

Kudriavtseva, A., & Gadyatskaya, O. (2022). Secure software development methodologies: a multivocal literature review. *arXiv preprint arXiv:2211.16987.*

Langstrof, T., & Sabau, A. R. (2024). The current state of security—Insights from the German software industry. arXiv preprint arXiv:2402.08436.

Li, K., Zhu, A., Zhao, P., Song, J., & Liu, J. (2024). Utilizing deep learning to optimize software development processes. *arXiv preprint arXiv:2404.13630.*

Lin, G., Wen, S., Han, Q.-L., Zhang, J., & Xiang, Y. (2020, October). Software Vulnerability Detection Using Deep Neural Networks: A Survey. *Proceedings of the IEEE, 108*(10), 1825–1848. DOI: 10.1109/JPROC.2020.2993293

Moyón, F., Méndez, D., Beckers, K., & Klepper, S. (2020). How do we integrate security compliance requirements with agile software engineering at scale? In *Product-Focused Software Process Improvement: 21st International Conference, PROFES 2020, Turin, Italy, November 25–27, 2020* [Springer International Publishing.]. *Proceedings*, *21*, 69–87.

Mustonen, J. (2024). Designing a security framework for enhanced monitoring and secure development during the software life cycle.

Núñez, J. C. S., Lindo, A. C., & Rodríguez, P. G. (2020). A Preventive Secure Software Development Model for a Software Factory: A Case Study. *IEEE Access : Practical Innovations, Open Solutions*, *8*, 77653–77665. DOI: 10.1109/ACCESS.2020.2989113

Palombo, H., Tabari, A. Z., Lende, D., Ligatti, J., & Ou, X. (2020). An Ethnographic Understanding of Software ({In) Security} and a {Co-Creation} Model to Improve Secure Software Development. In *Sixteenth Symposium on Usable Privacy and Security (SOUPS 2020)* (pp. 205-220).

Ribeiro, V. V., Cruzes, D. S., & Travassos, G. H. (2022). Moderator factors of software security and performance verification. *Journal of Systems and Software*, *184*, 111137. DOI: 10.1016/j.jss.2021.111137

Rindell, K., Ruohonen, J., Holvitie, J., Hyrynsalmi, S., & Leppänen, V. (2021). Security in agile software development: A practitioner survey. *Information and Software Technology*, *131*, 106488. DOI: 10.1016/j.infsof.2020.106488

Souppaya, M., Scarfone, K., & Dodson, D. (2022). Secure software development framework (SDF) version 1.1. *NIST Special Publication*, *800*, 218.

Sulich, A., Rutkowska, M., Krawczyk-Jezierska, A., Jezierski, J., & Zema, T. (2021). Cybersecurity and sustainable development. *Procedia Computer Science*, *192*, 20–28. DOI: 10.1016/j.procs.2021.08.003

Tashtoush, Y. M., Darweesh, D. A., Husari, G., Darwish, O. A., Darwish, Y., Issa, L. B., & Ashqar, H. I. (2021). Agile approaches for cybersecurity systems, IoT, and intelligent transportation. *IEEE Access : Practical Innovations, Open Solutions*, *10*, 1360–1375. DOI: 10.1109/ACCESS.2021.3136861

Vacca, A., Di Sorbo, A., Visaggio, C. A., & Canfora, G. (2021). A systematic literature review of blockchain and smart contract development: Techniques, tools, and open challenges. *Journal of Systems and Software*, *174*, 110891. DOI: 10.1016/j.jss.2020.110891

Von Solms, S., & Futcher, L. A. (2020). Adaption of a Secure Software Development Methodology for Secure Engineering Design. *IEEE Access : Practical Innovations, Open Solutions*, *8*, 125630–125637. DOI: 10.1109/ACCESS.2020.3007355

Votipka, D., Abrokwa, D., & Mazurek, M. L. (2020, April). Building and validating a scale for secure software development self-efficacy. In *Proceedings of the 2020 CHI Conference on Human Factors in Computing Systems* (pp. 1-20). DOI: 10.1145/3313831.3376754

Zografopoulos, I., Ospina, J., Liu, X., & Konstantinou, C. (2021). Cyber-physical energy systems security: Threat modeling, risk assessment, resources, metrics, and case studies. *IEEE Access : Practical Innovations, Open Solutions*, *9*, 29775–29818. DOI: 10.1109/ACCESS.2021.3058403

Chapter 7
AI-Driven Threat Modeling:
Enhancing Risk Assessment in Software Projects

C. V. Suresh Babu
https://orcid.org/0000-0002-8474-2882
Hindustan Institute of Technology and Science, India

Albert Gururaja V.
https://orcid.org/0009-0001-2563-9359
Hindustan Institute of Technology and Science, India

ABSTRACT

This chapter explores the integration of AI-driven threat modeling and risk assessment within software development to enhance security practices. Utilizing a comprehensive literature review, case studies, and qualitative interviews with industry professionals, the study identifies best practices and emerging trends in threat modeling methodologies such as STRIDE and DREAD. Key findings reveal that organizations adopting AI technologies experience improved threat detection and response times, leading to a more robust security posture. However, the study also highlights the importance of human oversight and the ethical considerations surrounding AI applications. The conclusions emphasize that a proactive approach, involving cross-functional teams and continuous adaptation to evolving cyber threats, is essential for building resilient software applications. This work underscores the significance of integrating AI into threat modeling as a critical strategy for organizations aiming to safeguard their digital assets.

DOI: 10.4018/979-8-3693-9851-7.ch007

1. INTRODUCTION

Software development demands now stretch beyond functionality, to making the applications smart, adaptive, and secure as well. The sectors' increased reliance on digital solutions demands these qualities in their software applications. AI and ML integrated into software can allow the applications to learn from and respond to real-time data, giving advanced functionality. However, the security risks are also new since the traditional safeguards would prove ineffective against such intelligent attacks. With these requirements, modern development practices marry smart capabilities with secure coding, automated threat detection, and real-time vulnerability analysis to ensure the resilience and trustworthiness of the software. This paper looks into the latest strategies on how to integrate intelligence and security into software development and brings out insights and case studies for developers and organizations in the quest to build next-generation robust and secure applications. Historic threat modeling derives from earlier risk assessment practice that developed concurrent with the construction of information security during the 1970s and 1980s. As computing devices grew more connected, security risks expanded, compelling organizations to form methodical solutions for discovering and counteracting risk.

1.1 Background Information on Threat Modeling and Risk Assessment

Threat modeling and risk assessments are proactive steps in secure software development, where teams might find and prioritize potential weaknesses before they are exploited. In threat modeling, what a system's components do and how data flows occur along with the possible avenues for attack must be depicted clearly to give developers an understanding of where the system may be vulnerable. This process can be structured utilizing frameworks such as STRIDE and DREAD, using which one can categorize and prioritize different types of threats in terms of how severe and likely they appear. Then, based upon the identified vulnerabilities, that risk assessment is made via evaluating the potential impact for the team to focus their attention on the most critical areas first. This hybrid technique will both harden up security and assist in maximizing the use of time as well as resources in more efficient ways to come forward with a solid system for the emerging threats. Frequently considering the changes in systems makes it possible for the various development teams to be responsive to new challenges while bringing strong protection for applications or users (Shostack, 2014; Myagmar et al., 2005).

1.2 Relevance to Modern Software Development

Threat modeling and risk assessment have found a much more salient importance in modern software development practice, since applications need to balance complexity, speed, and security. With the increasing adoption of cloud computing, AI systems, and interconnected devices, software is now running in an environment filled with constantly evolving threats. Integrating these security practices early in the development cycle helps teams stay one step ahead by identifying and addressing vulnerabilities before they can be exploited, which is crucial in today's fast-paced release cycles (OWASP, 2021; Frydenberg & Andone, 2018). Beyond safeguarding the software, threat modeling and risk assessment allow developers to design with security in mind, making secure practices a core part of the development process. This approach of being proactive improves product integrity but also helps build user trust as security becomes an inherent, visible commitment in every software release.

1.3 Overview of Tools and Technologies Used

Modern software development tools and technologies enhance security by supporting threat modeling and risk assessment. Tools allows for a graphical interface to draw out the system architecture, data flows, and potential vulnerabilities of the system, which enables development teams to participate in threat modeling. Tools like MITRE ATT&CK and STRIDE also provide structured frameworks and databases to classify threats to enable teams to focus on addressing the most significant vulnerabilities as presented in real-world attack vectors. Technologies such as FAIR (Factor Analysis of Information Risk) facilitate the quantitative analysis of the financial and operational impact of risks to support decisions on them. Automated security scanning tools like Nessus, Burp Suite, and Snyk can be integrated in the development pipeline to scan code continuously for vulnerabilities and flag those areas for the developers to address. These tools and frameworks allow for a systemic approach to identifying, analyzing, and mitigating risks, ensuring that security remains central to the software development lifecycle cycles (Cheng et al., 2020; MITRE, 2021; Veracode, 2020).

2. KEY QUESTIONS AND PROBLEMS ADDRESSED

This paper discusses key questions and challenges in modern software development related to the issue of smart, secure applications in the increasingly complex landscape of digital information.: How can developers systematically identify and mitigate security vulnerabilities up front during the development lifecycle? What methodologies and what tools best integrate intelligent adaptability features without sacrificing security? We discuss ways in which real-time data and machine learning can enhance software functionality and security with an eye toward potential trade-offs and risks. Balancing rapid deployment with sufficient security measures is a typical challenge in today's agile development Another core challenge that arises is the ever-present threat of sophisticated cyberattacks against intelligent applications, thus requiring adaptive and scalable security practices. By going through these questions and challenges, this paper brings insight and strategy on designing resilient and innovative software as bettered by developers to respond to today's evolving threats.

2.1 Best Practices in Threat Modeling

Effective threat modeling for software development involves several best practices that help proactively identify and mitigate potential risks. It is best begun early in the development lifecycle so that teams can approach vulnerabilities from the very outset. Established frameworks such as STRIDE and OWASP's threat categorization would ensure a structured approach. This would make it relatively easier to identify various kinds of risks and predict their potential attack paths. Collaboration between development, operations, and security teams is crucial, as diverse perspectives help reveal hidden vulnerabilities. Regularly updating the threat model to reflect system changes is another best practice, ensuring that new features and components don't introduce unforeseen risks (Almorsy et al., 2014; Shevchenko, 2018)..

2.2 Integration of Risk Assessment Frameworks

The Integrating of Risk Evaluation Models to Integrate the risk assessment framework, such as FAIR or OCTAVE (Operationally Critical Threat, Asset, and Vulnerability Evaluation). This way, one can apply a defined approach while evaluating threats according to their impacts and probabilities, guiding teams to express calculated risks and then rank these risks in a priority scheme, hence more rational and informed decision-making for resources and mitigations.it ensure that risk evaluation is not one-time but rather continuous integration into agile or DevOps workflows, which promotes a security-first mindset in accordance with the rapid development cycles (Shostack, 2014; OWASP, 2021).

2.3 Role of Contemporary Tools in Security

Modern security tools can identify and remove threats throughout the entire development cycle. Other tools that give graphical models and analyses are the Threat Modeling Tool, while automatic scanning of vulnerabilities and alerting of the development team happen with security scanners such as Snyk, Burp Suite, and Nessus (Cheng et al., 2020; Jones & Ashenden, 2005). This would help integrate these tools into CI/CD pipelines for the detection and remediation of vulnerabilities, making security a seamless part of the development process. These tools support faster, more secure releases by automating key aspects of security.

2.4 Gaps in Current Research and Practice

Despite the advancements, there is a notable gap in the current research and practice related to threat modeling and risk assessment. For example, most of the existing frameworks fail to be adaptable for AI-driven or highly dynamic environments, leaving vulnerabilities in emerging technologies such as machine learning models and IoT. Also, there is limited guidance on how to integrate continuous threat modeling into agile workflows without slowing down development. Other areas that need improvement are the standardizing metrics that would make it challenging to measure the impact of threat modeling and risk assessment practice across overall security (Buczak & Guven, 2016; Choi et al., 2021).Thus, closing these gaps involves more research and development for adaptive frameworks and metrics geared towards modern development cycles, among others.

3.OBJECTIVES AND SCOPE

This section outlines the objectives, scope, and methodology for examining the integration of intelligence and security in software development. It provides a framework for understanding how Agile, DevSecOps, and CI/CD methodologies contribute to creating secure and adaptable applications while focusing on the specific practices within threat modeling and risk assessment.

3.1 Objectives of the Chapter

The diagram titled "Modern Insights on Smart and Secure Software Development" provides a clear and engaging overview of essential practices in today's software development landscape. At its core is the title, which highlights the focus on both intelligence and security in development. Beneath this, three key areas are explored: Agile Methodologies, DevSecOps Practices, and Continuous Integration/Deployment (CI/CD). Agile Methodologies shine a light on the importance of teamwork and flexibility, emphasizing how iterative cycles allow teams to quickly adapt to user feedback and changing requirements, ultimately leading to a product that better meets user expectations (Fowler & Highsmith, 2001). DevSecOps Practices advocate for integrating security at every stage of development, ensuring that teams prioritize safety from the outset rather than treating it as an afterthought. This proactive approach includes continuous monitoring, automated security testing, and collaboration between development and operations teams, fostering a culture where security is everyone's responsibility (Kim et al., 2016). Finally, CI/CD represents a game-changing shift towards automation in code integration and deployment, making it possible for developers to release updates more frequently and reliably. By streamlining processes and providing immediate feedback, CI/CD enhances product quality while reducing the time it takes to get features into users' hands (Bass et al., 2015). Overall, this diagram not only highlights the interconnectedness of these practices but also underscores the importance of creating software that is not only functional but also secure and responsive to user needs in an ever-evolving digital landscape.

3.2 Delimitation of the Scope

This chapter discusses the topic of threat modeling and risk assessment specifically within software development, focusing on modern-day practices, tools, and frameworks relevant to contemporary trends in technology. Though covering best practices for incorporating security into development processes, this chapter does not focus significantly on broader cybersecurity issues like network security or strategies around incident response. In addition, the chapter mainly deals with the practices applicable to web and mobile applications, while leaving behind the specialized domains like embedded systems or legacy software. It allows for a focused approach towards a detailed exploration of key aspects of threat modeling and risk assessment most relevant in modern software engineering (Shostack, 2014; OWASP, 2021).

3.3 Methodology Overview

The methodology for this chapter uses a holistic and multi-dimensional approach to delve into the threat modeling and risk assessment in detail. An extensive literature review forms the core of this methodology, reviewing recent research, case studies, and industry reports, synthesizing findings to uncover best practices and identify emerging trends in the field. This review enables critical understanding of the evolution and current state of threat modeling and risk assessment practices. The study further incorporates a comparative analysis of various threat modeling frameworks and risk assessment methodologies, such as STRIDE, DREAD, and OCTAVE, in order to analyze their strengths and weaknesses respectively (Jones & Ashenden, 2005). Interviews with industry professionals and security experts are conducted to complement the theoretical insights gained from the literature.

The interviews provide valuable hands-on perspectives and real-world examples, which add practical knowledge to the research and bridge the gap between theory and application. This methodology, through the integration of insights from both academic and industry sources, ensures a balanced and in-depth exploration of the research objectives while grounding the discussion in both theoretical and practical contexts. This robust approach enhances the relevance and applicability of the findings, making them meaningful for both academic inquiry and industry practice.

4. LITERATURE REVIEW

4.1 Overview of Existing Methodologies (STRIDE, DREAD, OCTAVE)

There are various methods for threat modeling and risk assessment, each offering its own focus and strengths. STRIDE as threat modelling framework (Spoofing, Tampering, Repudiation, Information Disclosure, Denial of Service, Elevation of Privilege) It allows for systematic categorization and analysis of threats as well as identification of vulnerability(outputs). Not everyone believes in the Cia relies on the most complex scenarios, and so there is another methodology called DREAD, which uses the following combination: Damage Potential, Reproducibility, Exploitability, Affected Users, and Discoverability. However, it is criticized by its subjective scoring system, which can result in conflicting risk prioritization. OCTAVE (Operationally Critical Threat, Asset, and Vulnerability Evaluation) is useful for enterprise-wide risk management as it is a risk-driven methodology aligned with business needs. It does not adapt well when working with smaller-sized or agile environments. Through such a critical lens, one may point out both the merits and drawbacks of the above methodologies. For example, STRIDE does a good job of identifying the risks but does not provide a structured or which is which is the problem DREAD is dealing with. However, DREAD's simplification of risk factors may make it less reliable. OCTAVE, though comprehensive in the field of organizational risk management, is slow to adapt to rapidly changing technological environments. A new balance is created on the basis of investigating the contemporary perspectives along with comparing the latest methods with those that have been used for some time. Offering solutions that are explicitly applicable to particular contexts and real-life cases is the way to go in order to ensure a full and critical assessment. However, the growth of threat modeling technology is a such issue where AI algorithms have been used to advance machine learning to develop the technology. In particular, AI-driven methods enable fast and efficient attack patterns analyzing while boosting the discovery of possible vulnerabilities by monitoring of big data operations.

4.2 Automated Tools and Security Practices

Automated tools deeply transformed the threat modeling and risk assessment landscape with unprecedented efficiencies, precision, and scales. Tools were developed to be more user friendly with visual modeling, ensuring that teams could find out and document threats much more consistently. These tools allow for the production of detailed and dynamic threat models, which in turn enhance collaboration among stakeholders and streamline workflows while reducing complexity that is usually associated with manual threat modeling processes. Automated security scanning tools like Snyk and Burp Suite also play a vital role in maintaining secure development practices by continuously monitoring codebases for vulnerabilities. These tools not only identify security weaknesses in real-time but also offer actionable insights and remediation suggestions, empowering developers to address issues proactively and efficiently (Babu, C. V. Suresh, and Andrew Simon P. 2024). The integration of such automated solutions into the software development lifecycle enables organizations to adopt a more proactive and adaptive approach to security, minimizing the time, effort, and resources required to keep applications secure. This shift towards automation not only improves the overall security posture but also enables the development team to innovate and deliver value, confident in the robustness of their security measures.

4.3 AI (XAI) in Threat Modeling

Artificial Intelligence (AI) has greatly revolutionized threat modeling and risk assessment by performing vulnerability detection, predicting security threats, and optimizing mitigation (**Nguyen et al., 2021**). Nonetheless, the lack of explainability and transparency in decision-making is one of the greatest challenges of AI-based threat modeling. Conventional AI models, especially deep learning-based models, tend to be "black boxes" such that cybersecurity experts cannot discern how and why particular risks are detected. This explainability is a problem in high-risk security contexts, where interpretability and trust are essential to supporting decision-making. Explainable **AI (XAI)** remedies this by making AI-driven risk analysis interpretable, transparent, and accountable. **XAI** methods allow security analysts to map AI-produced threat assessments back to their reasoning, offering human-interpretable explanations for predictions and recommendations. This is most critical in regulation compliance, when organizations have to prove the thought process that guides security decisions to auditors, stakeholders, and regulatory authorities. A number of methods have been created for integrating XAI with threat modeling. Feature attribution techniques, like **SHAP** (Shapley Additive Explanations) and **LIME** (Local Interpretable Model-agnostic Explanations), enable security experts to identify the conditions that make most contributions to the risk assessments made by AI. Decision-tree-based models, including those employed in interpretable machine learning frameworks, increase transparency through the provision of clear, rule-based security findings. Hybrid AI models also merge deep learning with symbolic reasoning or knowledge graphs to deliver more structured and explainable security findings (**Xie et al., 2022**). The incorporation of XAI into threat modeling provides a number of advantages. It increases stakeholder trust by rendering AI-based security findings more explainable and actionable. It also eliminates false positives and enhances decision-making by enabling cybersecurity teams to cross-check AI-based risk scores with domain expertise. In addition, transparent models of AI help ensure compliance with data protection and cybersecurity regulations, including GDPR and NIST standards, that necessitate organizations to stay accountable for automated security decisions. While these benefits exist, employing XAI in cybersecurity is not without its challenges. Balancing explainability with performance is a core challenge, as greater transparency can at times decrease model accuracy. Additionally, cybersecurity threats change very quickly, and AI models need to adapt constantly while ensuring explainability. Scalable, real-time XAI solutions specifically designed for dynamic threat environments will be the focus of future research.

4.4 Gaps in Existing Literature

In spite of developments in threat modeling and risk assessment techniques, there are significant gaps in the literature. Most frameworks are created for conventional software development contexts and fail to effectively tackle challenges presented by new technologies like cloud computing, microservices, and AI (Agarwal et al., 2021). There is little research on incorporating threat modeling into agile development processes, and teams lack concrete plans for ensuring security in high-velocity environments. The performance of different methodologies in other scenarios is also not thoroughly researched, and this makes it hard to choose the best method for an organization. Current research identifies increased emphasis on AI-based threat intelligence and automated security platforms. There is still limited research comparing the performance of AI-powered threat modeling and other existing methodologies. Real-world use case studies of AI in cybersecurity are needed to address this lack of research.

4.5 Importance of Contemporary Approaches

Modern threat modeling and risk assessment techniques are critical in the fast-changing technological environment of today. With software systems becoming more complex and interdependent, conventional security practices might not be adequate anymore (Srisakthi, S. & Suresh Babu, C. V. 2024). New strategies focus on agility, automation, and collaboration to identify and counter security threats in real-time. By incorporating AI-based methodologies, organizations can develop a security-first culture that is aligned with development processes, leading to ongoing security enhancements. AI-driven threat intelligence platforms, like MITRE ATT&CK, improve detection and offer predictive analytics for anticipatory threat reduction. A comparative study of AI-based threat modeling and conventional methods proves that AI-based systems provide better accuracy and efficiency. Case studies show that AI-based frameworks lower false positives by a great extent, enhance the accuracy of threat prediction, and speed up incident response time. Embracing new security strategies not only protects against risks but also improves software quality, user trust, and compliance (Gartner, 2021). As cyber-attacks persist in changing and evolving, adopting AI and automation will be paramount in creating applications that can weather advanced attacks.

4.6 Case Studies of AI-Driven Threat Modeling Failures and Successes

Case Study 1: Failure – Tesla's AI in Autonomous Driving (2021-2023)

Context:
Tesla's Autopilot and Full Self-Driving (FSD) AI system experienced several failures, causing fatal accidents.
Threat Modeling Failure:
Misclassification of Objects: AI models had trouble with edge cases (e.g., confusion between stopped emergency vehicles as regular road objects).
Lack of Adversarial Testing: AI failed in specific lighting conditions, posing unforeseen security vulnerabilities.
Data Bias Issues: Training datasets lacked diversity, reducing the AI's ability to handle rare but critical scenarios.
Outcome:

1. Multiple regulatory investigations and lawsuits.
2. Crashes due to AI misinterpretation raised concerns about the robustness of AI-based risk modeling in safety-critical systems.

Key Lessons:

1. AI-driven threat modeling must undergo rigorous adversarial testing in real-world scenarios.
2. Security risk models should factor in unexpected edge cases and diverse datasets.
3. AI should incorporate human-in-the-loop validation for security-critical decisions.

Case Study 2: Success – Google's Chronicle AI Security Platform

Context:

Google introduced Chronicle, an AI-powered security analytics platform, to enable enterprises to detect and respond to cyber threats more quickly.

AI-Driven Threat Modeling Success:

Automated Threat Hunting: AI constantly monitors billions of security logs to identify anomalies.

Scalable AI Security: Utilizes MITRE ATT&CK threat intelligence to categorize and prioritize security threats.

Real-Time Threat Detection: AI decreased mean-time-to-detect (MTTD) threats by 98%, enabling quicker response.

Outcome:

1. Security teams identified and countered attacks, not in weeks but in minutes.
2. Organizations cut false positives by 75%, enhancing security accuracy.
3. AI-based threat intelligence gave a competitive edge in enterprise security.

Key Takeaways:

1. AI-led security automation enhances speed and accuracy of threat detection and response.
2. MITRE ATT&CK integration boosts the capability of AI in categorizing threats based on actual attack patterns.
3. Scalability is paramount in AI-driven security for supporting enormous enterprise environments.

5. METHODOLOGY

5.1 Research Methods

This research has utilized methods that can draw a multi-dimensional understanding of threat modeling and risk assessment methodologies through various approaches. Literature review provides the foundation step that systematically goes through the existing studies, frameworks, and theoretical approaches concerning threat modeling and risk assessment. This would help to consolidate the knowledge developed up to this point in addition to identifying best practices commonly recognized in the field. Further, it outlines some gaps and questions that need to be addressed in future research (Munn et al., 2018). To connect theory to practice, the case study analyses are used. These are detailed explorations of the organizational experiences that have implemented threat modeling and risk assessment as part of their software development workflows. The real-life exploration into such scenarios allows the study to uncover practical insights about benefits, challenges, and possible pitfalls in the process. These provide actionable lessons and an easier understanding of how these methodologies function in different organizational contexts. Qualitative interviews are conducted with industry experts, including security experts and software developers. These interviews attempt to capture first-hand experience and professional judgment regarding the efficacy of various threat modeling and risk assessment tools and methodologies. These rich qualitative insights enrich theoretical findings and make them more nuanced and practice-oriented. This multi-method approach ensures that the study is theoretically robust and practically relevant at the same time.

5.1.1 Workflow

Figure 1. Workflow of the project

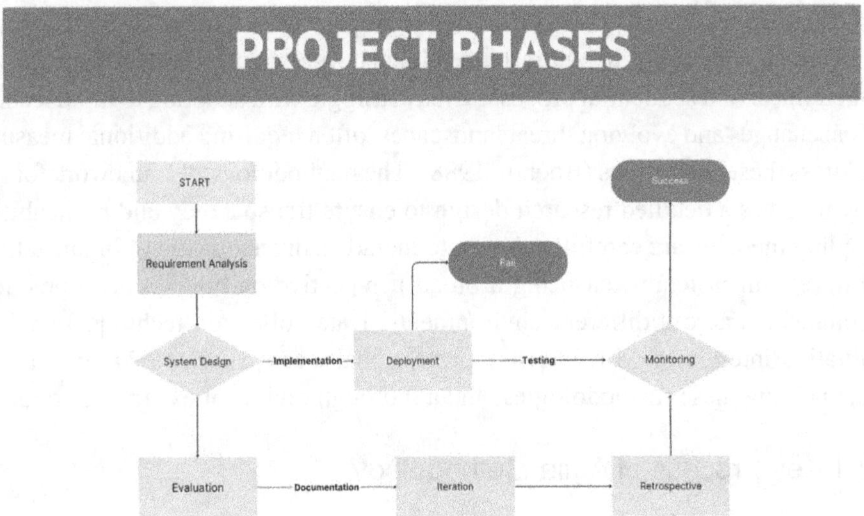

The **Technical Project Lifecycle Phases** begin with **Requirement Analysis**, where we gather user needs to set a solid foundation. We then design the system architecture before diving into **Implementation**, turning concepts into a working product. After **Testing** and **Deployment**, we monitor performance and gather user feedback to evaluate effectiveness. This feedback drives ongoing **Maintenance**, allowing the system to evolve with user needs. We conduct a **Retrospective** to reflect on the project, celebrating successes and identifying areas for improvement, ensuring continuous adaptability and value.

5.2 Software Development Approaches (Agile, DevOps, Traditional)

This study examines how different software development methodologies—Agile, DevOps, and traditional models—impact the integration of threat modeling and risk assessment, offering insights into best practices and potential challenges. Agile methodologies, with their emphasis on iterative development and team collaboration, are well-suited for integrating security practices throughout the development cycle, fostering flexibility and responsiveness to emerging threats (Beck et al., 2001). However, the iterative nature of Agile can lead to challenges, such as maintaining comprehensive documentation and ensuring consistent application of security measures across iterations. DevOps, which prioritizes continuous integration and delivery, promotes collaboration between development and operations teams, leveraging automation to enable real-time threat modeling and vulnerability assessments (Lwakatare et al., 2019). This approach streamlines the identification and resolution of security issues but requires robust tools and processes to manage its fast-paced environment effectively. In contrast, traditional development models, characterized by their linear and sequential processes, may struggle with adapting to rapid technological changes and evolving threat landscapes, often requiring additional measures to address these limitations (Boehm, 1988). The methodological framework for this study involves a detailed research design to ensure transparency and replicability. Sampling methods are carefully chosen to include a diverse range of organizations and development teams, ensuring a broad perspective on how security practices are embedded across different environments. Data collection techniques include qualitative interviews with industry professionals, case studies of organizations implementing these methodologies, and a thorough review of existing literature.

5.2.1 Key Process of Agile Methodology

1. **Building Security into Agile Processes**
    - **Shift Left Security**: To prevent security issues from taking root, Agile teams can begin each sprint by adding security checks right from the planning phase. Starting with threat modeling and risk assessments, they ensure security is embedded into requirements from day one, helping catch vulnerabilities early.
    - **DevSecOps Integration**: With DevSecOps, security becomes a core part of the development lifecycle. This means involving security experts in every step—from design through deployment—keeping security measures ongoing and adaptable for Agile teams.
2. **Automating Security for Continuous Coverage**
    - **Automation in CI/CD**: Automated testing is key in Agile to keep security checks moving quickly. Integrating tools like SonarQube, Snyk, and OWASP ZAP into the CI/CD pipeline allows teams to perform code quality checks, run vulnerability scans, and apply both static and dynamic analysis with each code change, helping catch vulnerabilities immediately.
    - **Real-Time Threat Intelligence**: Agile teams can stay on top of emerging threats with real-time monitoring tools, enabling quick adjustments to security strategies and maintaining an up-to-date security stance.
3. **Fostering Security Awareness in Teams**

- **Education and Training**: Regular training on secure coding, vulnerabilities (like the OWASP Top Ten), and security principles helps everyone—from developers to product owners—build a security-conscious mindset within the team.
- **Security Champions**: Assigning a security advocate within each Agile team ensures that security remains a priority in discussions and decisions. This person can bridge gaps between development and security perspectives.

4. **Flexible Threat Modeling and Risk Assessment**
   - **Iterative Threat Modeling**: Agile teams can adopt adaptable threat modeling techniques, such as STRIDE or DREAD, to fit Agile's shorter sprint cycles. By revisiting and updating models frequently, teams can adjust to new features and threats effectively.
   - **Contextual Risk Assessment**: Quick, sprint-friendly risk assessments allow teams to identify high-priority vulnerabilities and address them without slowing down. Focusing on critical risks keeps security manageable within tight deadlines.
5. **Efficient Code Reviews for Secure Agile Sprints**
   - **Peer and Automated Code Reviews**: Bringing code reviews into the Agile workflow helps developers identify potential vulnerabilities early. Automated analysis tools, alongside peer reviews, can ensure thorough security checks without adding extra workload.
   - **Security Checklists**: Using checklists tailored for security in code reviews allows developers to verify security requirements systematically, maintaining quality while aligning with Agile's rapid pace.
6. **Incorporating Security into User Stories**
   - **Defining Done with Security**: Making security part of the "Definition of Done" for user stories ensures that each feature meets security standards before completion.
   - **Security-Driven Stories**: Crafting specific user stories that focus on security elements—like data protection, authentication, and auditing—ensures that security gets attention in the backlog, just like any other key feature.
7. **Continuous Feedback and Improvement**
   - **Security in Retrospectives**: Reviewing security practices in retrospectives allows Agile teams to reflect on past sprints, identify areas for improvement, and refine their security approach continuously.
   - **Tracking Security Metrics**: Keeping an eye on metrics—such as the number of vulnerabilities identified and time taken to fix them—helps

teams monitor and improve the effectiveness of their security practices over time.

8. **Lightweight Security Frameworks for Agile**
    - **OWASP SAMM and BSIMM**: These Agile-friendly frameworks offer guidance on building security maturity, aligning well with Agile's flexibility and helping teams implement structured security initiatives effectively.
    - **Flexible Policies**: Updating security policies to reflect Agile practices ensures that they remain relevant, allowing teams to adapt to security needs as they evolve.

5.2.2 Key Process of DevOps Methodology

1. Key Principles of DevOps
    - **Collaboration and Communication**: DevOps emphasizes a strong culture of collaboration between development and operations teams. Teams work together throughout the entire software lifecycle, fostering a feedback loop that improves product quality.
    - **Automation**: Automating repetitive tasks such as testing, deployment, and infrastructure setup helps reduce errors and speeds up the process.
    - **Continuous Integration and Continuous Deployment (CI/CD)**: CI/CD pipelines enable teams to integrate code changes frequently and deploy updates faster, reducing time to market.
    - **Infrastructure as Code (IaC)**: With IaC, infrastructure is managed through code, allowing developers to configure, version, and manage infrastructure just like they do with application code. This enhances consistency and reduces manual errors.
2. DevOps Practices
    - **Version Control**: All code changes are stored in version control systems like Git, which allows tracking, managing, and collaboration on code changes.
    - **Automated Testing**: Continuous testing helps ensure code quality, catching issues early in the development cycle before they reach production.
    - **Monitoring and Logging**: Continuous monitoring and logging ensure that issues in production are identified and resolved quickly.
    - **Feedback Loops**: Feedback from production, testing, and users is continuously gathered to improve both the product and the process.

- **Microservices Architecture**: Breaking down applications into microservices enables independent development and deployment, promoting scalability and flexibility.

3. Benefits of DevOps
    - **Faster Delivery and Time to Market**: CI/CD pipelines and automation speed up deployment cycles, allowing for faster release of features.
    - **Improved Quality and Reliability**: Continuous testing, monitoring, and feedback reduce the number of bugs and downtime.
    - **Scalability**: IaC and microservices allow infrastructure and applications to scale efficiently.
    - **Enhanced Collaboration and Reduced Silos**: Improved communication and a collaborative environment help address issues and innovation more effectively.
4. DevOps Tools
    - **CI/CD**: Jenkins, GitLab CI, CircleCI
    - **Containerization**: Docker, Kubernetes
    - **Configuration Management**: Ansible, Puppet, Chef
    - **Monitoring and Logging**: Prometheus, Grafana, ELK Stack (Elasticsearch, Logstash, Kibana)
    - **Version Control**: Git, Bitbucket
5. Challenges with DevOps
    - **Cultural Shifts**: The adoption of a DevOps culture requires organizations to overcome traditional departmental boundaries.
    - **Complexity in Managing CI/CD Pipelines**: Setting up and managing pipelines can be complex, especially for larger applications.
    - **Security**: Integrating security within DevOps (DevSecOps) requires careful planning to avoid vulnerabilities without impacting delivery speed.

5.2.3 Key Process of Traditional Methodologies

1. Waterfall Model

The **Waterfall Model** is a linear approach where each phase of development flows sequentially into the next. The process typically follows these steps:

- **Requirements Gathering and Analysis**
- **System Design**
- **Implementation**
- **Testing**

- **Deployment**
- **Maintenance**

Each phase has specific deliverables, and progress flows in a single direction. It works best for well-defined projects with stable requirements but is inflexible for changes after the process begins.

2. V-Model (Validation and Verification)

An extension of the Waterfall Model, the **V-Model** introduces testing stages corresponding to each development phase, visualized in a "V" shape:

- **Requirements Analysis** - paired with **Acceptance Testing**
- **System Design** - paired with **System Testing**
- **Architectural Design** - paired with **Integration Testing**
- **Module Design** - paired with **Unit Testing**

The V-Model provides a structured way to ensure that testing is included at each stage, helping to catch errors early on. It works well for projects requiring a high degree of verification but still has limited flexibility for changing requirements.

3. Iterative Model

The **Iterative Model** focuses on repetition, where the software is developed in small, manageable cycles. Each cycle involves:

- **Requirement Analysis**
- **Design**
- **Coding**
- **Testing**

The Iterative Model allows adjustments with each cycle, making it more adaptable to changing requirements. It works well when requirements are unclear at the start but evolve over time.

Pros and Cons of Traditional Approaches

Pros:

- Clear, structured processes with defined milestones.
- Easier to manage and document progress.

- Each phase is fully completed before moving to the next, reducing ambiguities.

Cons:

- Limited flexibility to accommodate changing requirements.
- Heavy documentation and rigid processes.
- Longer development times, often leading to delayed feedback.

5.3 Justification for Chosen Methodology

The selected methodology is grounded in the necessity for a thorough understanding of how threat modeling and risk assessment can be seamlessly integrated into contemporary software development practices. By utilizing literature reviews, case studies, and interviews, the research provides a well-rounded perspective on existing methodologies and tools, along with valuable insights from industry professionals. This mixed-methods approach facilitates a more in-depth investigation of the topic, addressing both theoretical concepts and practical applications. Incorporating various software development methodologies ensures that the results are relevant across different scenarios, making the study beneficial for a broad audience of developers, security experts, and organizations aiming to improve their security measures (Johnson & Onwuegbuzie, 2004). Ultimately, this methodology seeks to connect theory with practice, offering practical recommendations for effectively implementing threat modeling and risk assessment in today's ever-evolving software environment.

5.3.1 Block Diagram

Figure 2. Block diagram

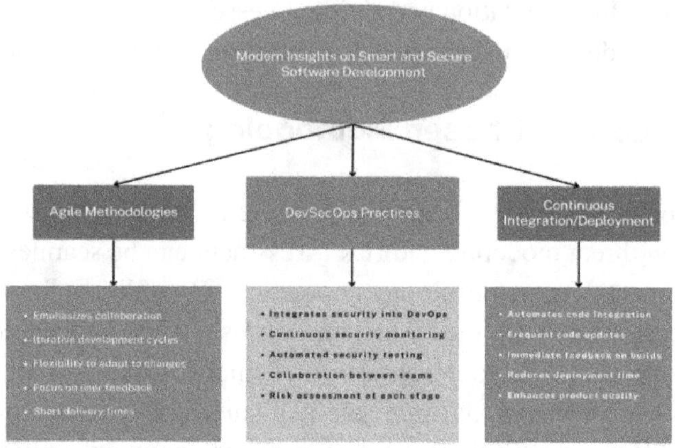

The diagram titled **"Modern Insights on Smart and Secure Software Development"** presents a structured overview of key contemporary software development practices. At the center is the title, which encapsulates the theme, with three main subheadings below: **Agile Methodologies**, **DevSecOps Practices**, and **Continuous Integration/Deployment (CI/CD)**. Agile Methodologies emphasize collaboration, iterative development, flexibility, user feedback, and quick delivery, ensuring responsiveness to user needs. DevSecOps Practices focus on integrating security throughout the development process, highlighting continuous monitoring, automated testing, and team collaboration to proactively address risks. Lastly, CI/CD underscores the importance of automating code integration and deployment, enabling frequent updates, immediate feedback, and enhanced product quality. Each subheading is connected to the title, illustrating their relevance to smart and secure software development, and the detailed content points offer insights into the principles that drive effective software solutions in today's fast-paced technological landscape.

5.4 Ethical and Legal Considerations in AI-Driven Security Assessments

As increasing prevalence of AI-powered security audits, ethical and legal factors are a must to promote compliance, fairness, and responsibility. The General Data Protection Regulation (GDPR) and the European Union's proposed AI Act set stringent requirements for the design and implementation of AI in cybersecurity. GDPR mandates principles such as data minimization, transparency, and user consent, where organizations must explain AI-based security measures that affect persons (European Commission, 2018). The AI Act continues to classify AI systems into levels of risk, with AI systems related to cybersecurity possibly being within high-risk categories, necessitating thorough testing, documentation, and human intervention (European Commission, 2021). Non-compliance with these regulations may lead to hefty fines, as in the case of British Airways GDPR, where the organization was fined £20 million for not keeping user information safe from a Cyber-Attack **(ICO, 2020).** Aside from compliance with the law, ethical concerns surround bias, fairness, and explainability of AI-powered threat detection. Bias in AI security systems can result in discriminatory decisions, with some user groups being subject to increased surveillance or unfair access control. Ethical AI development requires robust bias audits, varied training datasets, and explainable AI methods to make sure that AI decisions are accountable and contestable. AI-based security evaluations need to be aligned with the principles of human rights, not engaging in mass surveillance or intrusive data collection measures infringing on privacy rights. For example, the Clearview AI case showed the dangers of facial recognition through AI when the firm was sued for scraping billions of facial images without permission, which posed severe ethical and legal issues. In response to these issues, regulatory frameworks increasingly support human-in-the-loop (HITL) AI models, in which security analysts examine and approve AI-derived risk assessments. This hybrid method ensures that AI augments and supports human experience instead of substituting it, minimizing the threat of discriminatory automated judgments (**Brundage et al., 2020**). Companies also need to give first priority to algorithmic auditing, transparency reports, and compliance certifications to bring AI-powered security solutions up to speed with international legal and ethical norms. As AI security technology continues to change, regular updates in regulation and interdisciplinary cooperation between legal professionals, policymakers, and AI researchers will be essential to ensuring responsible and legally sound AI security practices.

5.5 Adversarial Attacks on AI Models

Adversarial attacks against AI models are now a cause of serious concern, with research between 2022 and 2024 drawing attention to the growing sophistication and frequency of these attacks. Such attacks entail purposefully designed inputs that mislead AI systems, causing them to make erroneous or unintended choices. The implications are far-reaching, impacting different sectors that use AI for mission-critical operations. One of the most interesting examples is the susceptibility of large language models (LLMs) to adversarial manipulations (Wired, 2024). Studies have proven that LLMs can be manipulated into generating toxic or biased responses when given malicious inputs. For example, one study showed that DeepSeek's R1 reasoning model was unable to prevent any toxic content during testing, with researchers obtaining a 100% success rate in getting toxic responses using 50 malicious inputs. This is indicative of the difficulties in making effective safety features for AI systems. The landscape of cybersecurity has also witnessed a growth in adversarial attacks against AI models. A report revealed that 77% of companies suffered AI-related breaches, while two out of five organizations indicated AI privacy breaches or security events, a quarter of which involved malicious attacks. This trend suggests that with increasing integration of AI into business processes, the attack surface increases, offering more ways to the attackers to use weaknesses in machine learning models. In reaction to the challenges, researchers and practitioners are trying to develop countermeasures to strengthen the resilience of AI models to adversarial attacks. Methods like adversarial training, in which models are subjected to adversarial examples during training, have been studied to enhance resilience. Moreover, the use of strict testing protocols and ongoing monitoring can assist with early detection and prevention of such attacks. Nonetheless, the dynamic nature of adversarial tactics calls for continuous research and adaptive security measures to ensure effective protection of AI systems.

5.6 Challenges in AI-Based Threat Detection

AI-powered threat detection has transformed cybersecurity by making it possible to identify security threats in real time, but it also encounters vital challenges like adversarial attacks, training data bias, and explainability of models. Adversarial attacks take advantage of vulnerabilities in AI models by making minute changes to input data to trick security algorithms. For instance, attackers can tweak malware signatures or network traffic patterns to avoid being detected by AI-powered security tools. A recent case involved deceiving an AI-driven malware classifier through subtle, immeasurable modification of malicious code, resulting in the AI falsely classifying threats as nonthreats. The vulnerabilities serve as a strong rationale for developing and implementing effective adversarial defense practices, including adversarial training, anomaly detection, and AI model hardening, to counter evasion tactics. The main challenge lies in bias within AI security models, which results from imbalanced or missing training datasets. In the event an AI model has been trained predominantly on certain patterns of threats, it can end up failing to recognize new types of cyber-attacks beyond its training distribution. For example, research into AI-based phishing detection observed that models trained on Western sets of phishing data were not effective on Asian and African phishing campaigns and caused regional security vulnerabilities **(Afroz et al., 2020).** Biased threat intelligence data can lead to false positives and negatives, disproportionately impacting certain industries, user groups, or geographic areas. Correcting these biases necessitates ongoing dataset refresh, training data diversity, and fairness-aware machine learning to guarantee global usability and precision.

6. APPLICATION OF TOOLS IN THREAT MODELING AND RISK ASSESSMENT

6.1 Overview of Selected Tools (Docker, TensorFlow, PyTorch)

The threat modeling and risk assessment go, there are now some modern tools that bring security into the software development process. Docker is the hottest thing for containerization, where developers can bundle up applications and their dependencies into isolated worlds. This eliminates the possibility of exploits in one environment being leveraged in another by requiring that all containers execute under the same configuration. TensorFlow and PyTorch are popular frameworks for developing machine learning models, which can be employed to enhance threat detection and response capabilities. For example, these tools can be deployed to build models that scan for patterns in user behavior or network traffic, enabling them to flag potential threats before they do damage(Chandramouli et al., 2019). Using these technologies allows development teams to enhance their general security profile while enjoying the speed and scalability that containerization and machine learning bring.

6.1. Case Studies of Successful Implementations

Several organizations have successfully integrated tools like Docker, TensorFlow, and PyTorch into their threat modeling and risk assessment processes. For instance, a financial institution took Docker on in its development pipeline, where it allowed the safe deployment of applications in many environments. The company reduced the chance of configuration drift and applied consistent security policies between development, testing and production environments through containerization. Another case involved a cybersecurity firm utilizing TensorFlow to develop a machine learning model that analyzes real-time network traffic for anomalies. This proactive approach allowed the firm to detect potential threats more effectively, significantly reducing response times. These case studies demonstrate the practical benefits of incorporating advanced tools into threat modeling and risk assessment, resulting in enhanced security and operational efficiency.

6.1.1 Security Practices of Sample

Figure 3. Sample 1

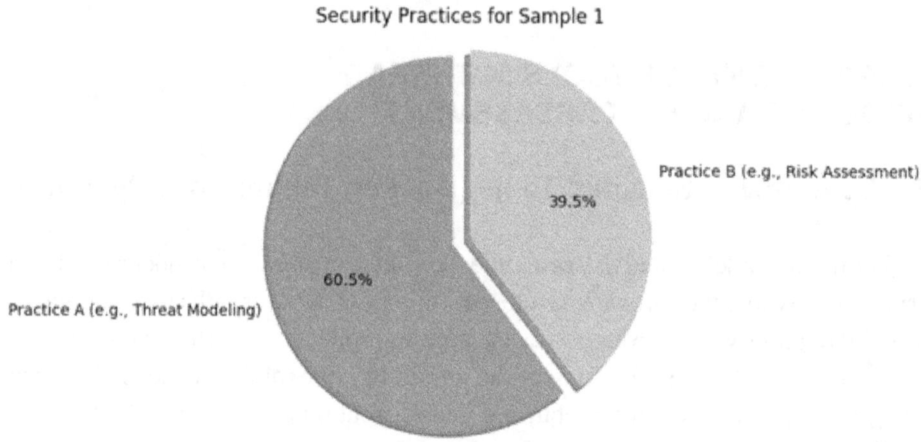

6.2.2 Probability Security Practices

Figure 4. Probability security practices of sample 1

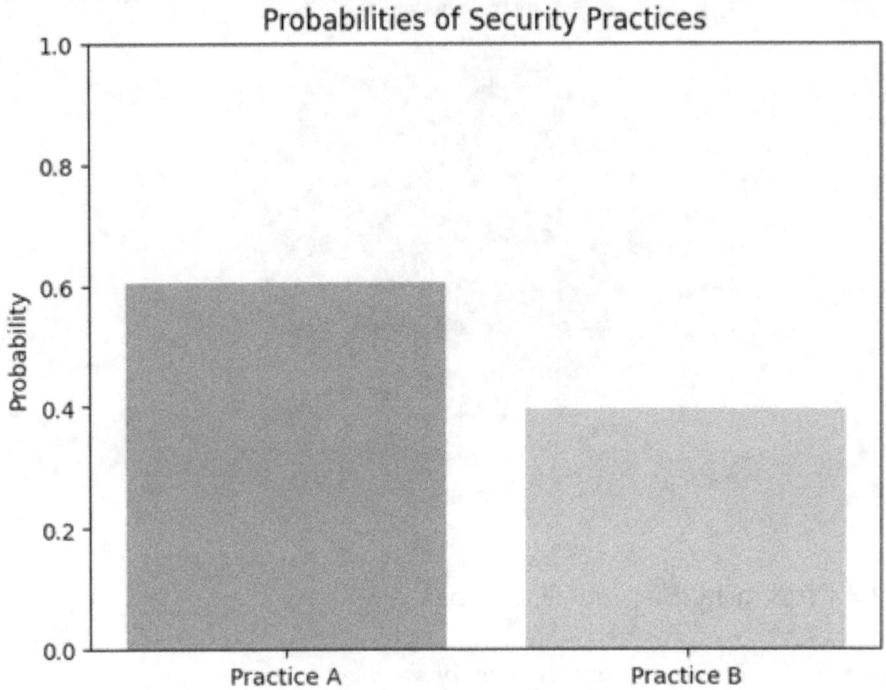

6.2.3 Security Practices of Samples

Figure 5. Sample 2

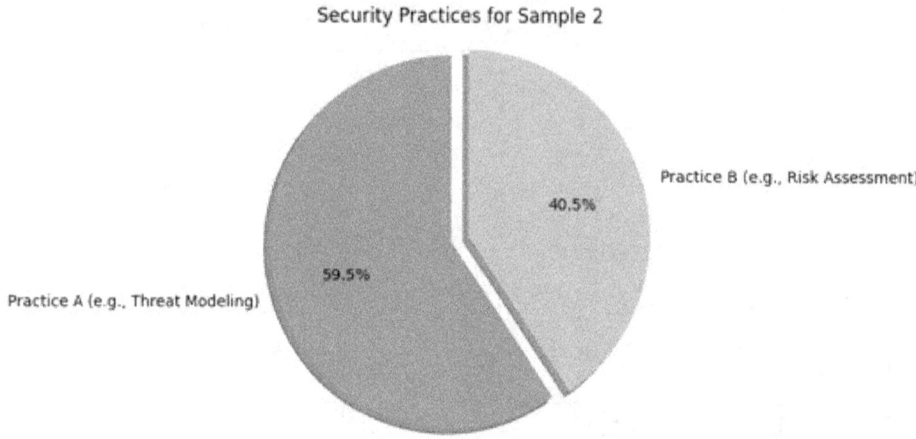

6.2.4 Probability Security Practices

Figure 6. Probability security practices of sample 2

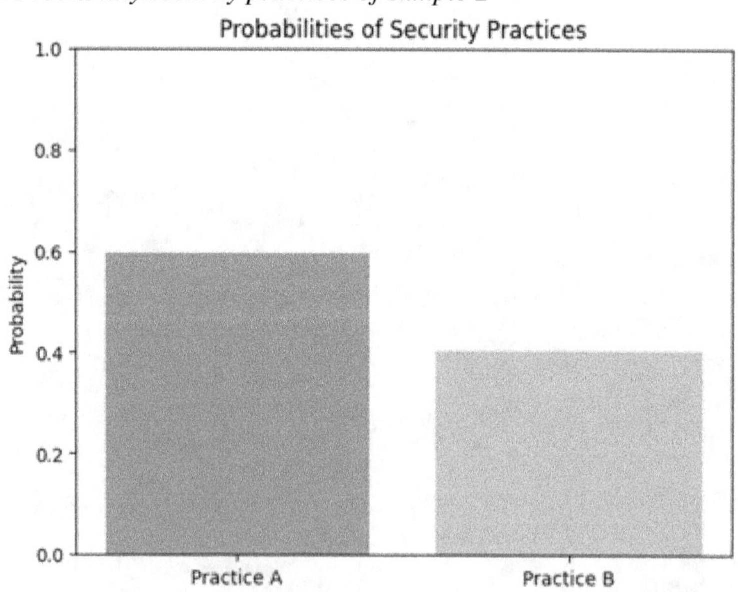

6.2.5 Probabilities of Security Practices Across Samples

Figure 7. Probablities of Sample 1 and 2

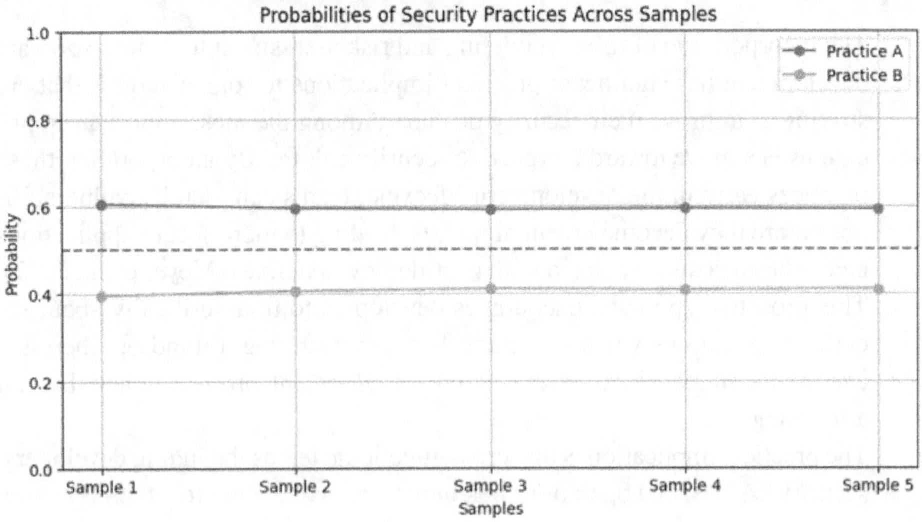

6.3 Challenges and Solutions in Tool Adoption

The organizations frequently face obstacles when implementing these tools. A major challenge is the complexity and steep learning curve that come with advanced frameworks like TensorFlow and PyTorch. To address this, organizations can invest in thorough training programs for their teams, which will help them gain a better understanding of these tools and how they can be applied in threat detection (Babu, C. V. Suresh, and Andrew Simon P. 2024). The integration issues can occur, especially when trying to incorporate Docker into existing development workflows that involve legacy systems. A phased approach can help tackle these challenges effectively. Organizations might begin with non-critical applications to test the waters before expanding Docker usage to more complex systems. To promoting collaboration among development, security, and operations teams is essential for ensuring smooth integration and cultivating a culture of security awareness.

7. CONTRIBUTION TO THE FIELD

7.1 Practical Implications for Software Development

- The incorporation of threat modeling and risk assessment tools into software development has significant practical implications for organizations that are striving to improve their security posture. Among the most important implications is a move toward a proactive security culture. By incorporating these practices early in the development lifecycle, teams can identify vulnerabilities before they become potential threats, leading to more secure applications and reduced costs associated with post-deployment fixes (Meyer et al., 2017). This proactive approach encourages developers to think critically about security implications when designing features, fostering a mindset where security is a fundamental aspect of the development process rather than an afterthought.
- The practical implication is that cross-functional teams, including developers, security experts, and operations personnel, can work better together. By using tools that support threat modeling and risk assessment, teams can develop a shared understanding of potential risks and vulnerabilities. This collaborative environment not only enhances communication but also ensures that security considerations are embedded in every phase of development, from design to deployment and maintenance.
- Contemporary tools such as Docker, TensorFlow, and PyTorch empower development teams to put up effective and scalable security. For instance, Docker's containerization capability enables teams to hold constant security configurations across all environments, thus significantly lowering the risks of vulnerabilities from differences in environments. Machine learning frameworks like TensorFlow and PyTorch enable analysis of large datasets for detection of patterns that may suggest possible threats, thus allowing response to risks in real time.
- To adopt a continuous risk assessment approach means that organizations will be able to maintain agility in a rapidly changing threat landscape. This adaptability ensures that security can be adjusted for new vulnerabilities and emerging technologies, thereby enabling teams to keep robust defenses intact as software and infrastructure are changed.
- The practical implication of incorporating threat modeling and risk assessment into the software development process extends beyond improving security; it impacts the overall quality and reliability of the software product. This would increase user confidence and that of stakeholders in their products.

Prioritizing security and fostering collaboration will help organizations tackle the complexity of modern software development while minimizing risks.

7.1.1 Diagrams That Comparing Traditional vs. AI-Driven Threat Modeling

Figure 8. Traditional vs. AI-driven threat modeling

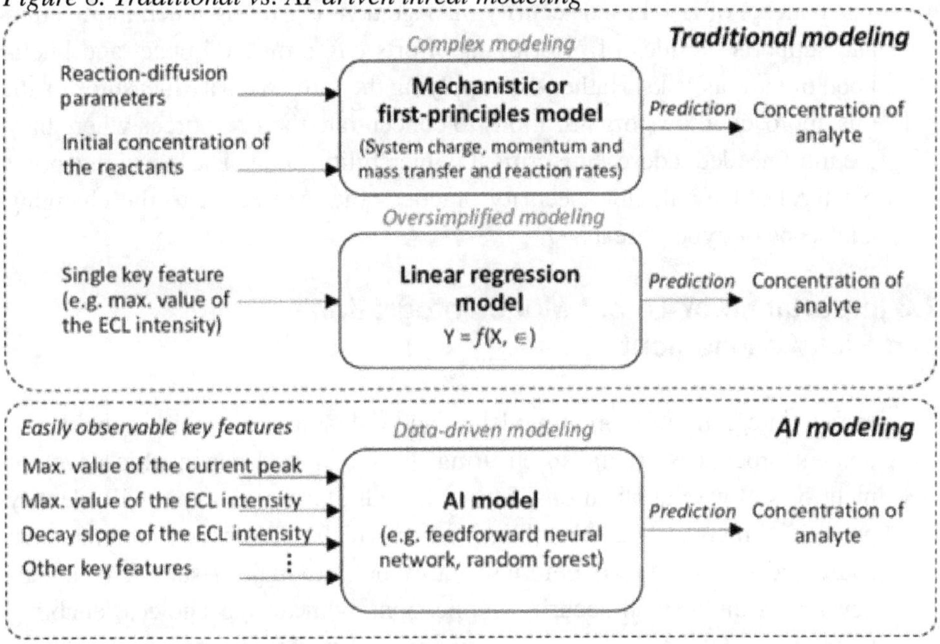

7.2 New Insights and Theories on Security Practices

- Recent technological innovation and security measures have given corporations new perspectives on how to strategically approach threat modeling and risk management. One of the significant takeaways has been from behavioral analytics. The insights into how users interact with apps can help in the identification of normal behavior. This can help significantly in the identification of any uncharacteristic behavior that may possibly indicate a security breach (Vashishtha et al., 2019). This approach is proactive and not only detects more sophisticated attacks at earlier times but also guides teams on which to prioritize their responses according to the specific context of the threats.

- The major change here is the adoption of the DevSecOps model, emphasizing weaving security practices throughout the entire lifecycle of software development. This model encourages the joint development, operations, and security team to work together to remind everybody that security is not strictly owned by one group; hence, it becomes their problem. The organization integrates security into the CI/CD cycle to continuously scan for vulnerability detection and remediation, thereby yielding resilient applications that are prepared and strong enough to face possible risks.
- The concept of risk-based security management is gaining much momentum and supports the idea of prioritizing efforts based on the impact and likelihood of various risks. Rather than applying the same security measures to all, this approach allows organizations to concentrate their resources where they are most needed, addressing critical vulnerabilities first. These insights point out the need for flexible security practices that can adapt to the changing landscape of cyber threats.

7.3 Importance of Threat Model Integration and Risk Assessment

- In fact, integration of threat modeling and risk assessment within the development process is crucial in ensuring the secure and dependable development of software applications. Through such a process, teams will identify potential threats and vulnerabilities earlier, which enables the problems to be addressed at a small level before they turn out into major issues. This makes developers understand security implications with design choices, enabling informed decisions about functionality and security tradeoffs.
- This integration fosters a culture of security awareness throughout the organization. When threat modeling and risk assessment become standard practices in development, everyone—developers, project managers, and beyond—becomes more mindful of security concerns. This shared mindset helps ensure that security is not an afterthought but an essential part of the development process, leading to stronger overall security measures.
- Integrating these practices assists organizations in complying with regulatory requirements and industry standards, such as GDPR or PCI-DSS. By consistently identifying and managing risks, organizations can demonstrate their commitment to safeguarding sensitive data, which helps build trust with users and stakeholders. In summary, making threat modeling and risk assessment central to software development is vital for proactive risk management, nurturing a security-first culture, and ensuring compliance with relevant regulations. This holistic approach not only enhances the quality and security of

software applications but also equips them to meet the changing demands of cyber threats.

8. ANALYSIS AND FINDINGS

8.1 Research Key Findings

Modern studies on contemporary security best practices have uncovered some really insightful information that can help organizations significantly change their approach toward threat modeling and risk assessment. The basic conclusion is that involvement of security should occur early on in the lifecycle software development. Organizations can then find and correct potential vulnerabilities before they become major issues by having security measures embedded at the design stage (Suresh Babu, C. V. & Yadavamuthiah, K. 2023). This research highlights the importance of an all-inclusive security approach in which all employees, regardless of position, know what their contributions are toward the overall security of the organization. It strengthens communication and enables teams to proactively prevent threats when everyone is in unison. this research emphasizes the potential of advanced technologies such as artificial intelligence and machine learning, which can significantly improve threat detection and response by analyzing patterns and anomalies that might indicate security risks (Zhao et al., 2020).

8.2 Implications for Future Security Practices

The findings from recent research have significant implications for how organizations should handle security moving forward. The most important takeaway will be that threat modeling and risk assessment should be ongoing in nature instead of something done once a year. Organizations should regularly review and update their measures so that they stay ahead of new threats and vulnerabilities. Additionally, a company must make considerable investments in training and resources that enable every employee to play a role in the effort. By building a culture of shared responsibility, organizations can sew security into the very fabric of their operations. the research indicates that embracing automated tools and technologies can greatly streamline security practices, making threat detection and response faster and more efficient. However, it's essential to strike a balance between automation and human oversight to maintain effectiveness (Srisakthi, S. & Suresh Babu, C. V. 2024).

8.3 Analysis of Case Study Outcomes

Case study results provide lessons learned about the integration of threat modeling and risk assessment into the software development process. Organizations that have adopted these practices report a marked improvement in their security posture. For instance, one financial institution discovered that threat modeling in their development workflow was able to identify and fix vulnerabilities before launch, which then led to far fewer security incidents afterward. A technology company that adopted a DevSecOps approach also saw a noticeable reduction in the time it took to detect and respond to security threats. They encouraged collaboration among development, operations, and security teams, which helped to create a more agile and responsive security environment. These case studies illustrate that organizations focusing on the integration of threat modeling and risk assessment not only improve their security but also enhance their operational efficiency, which reinforces the need for a proactive and collaborative approach to security in today's ever-evolving cyber threat landscape.

9. SUGGESTIONS AND RECOMMENDATIONS

As organizations work to strengthen their security practices, several key suggestions can help guide them in effectively integrating threat modeling and risk assessment into their software development processes.

9.1 Best Practices for Integrating Threat Modeling and Risk Assessment

To get integration right, management should take proactive steps that begin with the design process to integrate threat modeling with risk assessment. One such strategy employed by organizations is using cross-functional teams in threat modeling sessions because even divergent opinions can help point out hidden risks that may otherwise go unnoticed (Dahl et al., 2020). Regularly updating threat models would be vital in keeping up with changes in the software, technology, and risk landscape. Established frameworks such as STRIDE or DREAD can be used to identify and assess risks in a structured manner. Automated tools for real-time risk assessment can accelerate considerably the identification and remediation of vulnerabilities. The final way is by creating a security-aware culture, where every member of the team is responsible for keeping the organization secure by knowing his role in keeping the organization secure.

9.2 Recommendations for Practitioners

For practitioners interested in strengthening the security of their applications, there are numerous recommendations that can be very effective. These include training as well as resources on threat modeling, risk assessment, and more throughout the organization. Shared understanding by everyone from developers and project managers helps build that culture of security within. Development, operations, and security teams should be encouraged to collaborate with each other to promote open communication and joint efforts in taming the security challenge. The security practice should also be continuously evaluated and refined based on insights from past incidents and emerging threats. Lastly, practitioners should advocate for the integration of security into every phase of the software development lifecycle, as a fundamental part of all projects and not as an afterthought (Wheeler et al., 2017).

9.3 Future Research Directions

Looking ahead, several research avenues can further enhance our understanding and effectiveness of threat modeling and risk assessment in software development. One exciting direction is exploring how emerging technologies like artificial intelligence and machine learning can improve threat detection and response (Kumar et al., 2021). For example, research could focus on developing frameworks that integrate such technologies smoothly into existing security practices or how different threat modeling frameworks work in various industries. Further promising areas for future research include considering human factors in security practice: organizational culture and team dynamics as linked to the efficacy of threat modeling and risk assessment activities. Investigating these areas will allow future research to create even stronger security practices that can combat the changing landscape of cyber threats.

10. CONCLUSION

10.1 Summary of Key Points

The integration of threat modeling and risk assessment into software development is critical in building secure, reliable applications. Key points from our discussion included the importance of starting security practices early in the development lifecycle, involving cross-functional teams for diverse perspectives, and regularly updating threat models to keep up with an ever-changing threat landscape. Established frameworks, such as STRIDE or DREAD, can be used to structure methods for identifying and assessing risks. Automation and advanced technologies, such as

AI and machine learning, can also improve the detection and response of threats, thus making security practices more efficient. Finally, a culture of security awareness among all team members is essential because it ensures that everyone understands their role in maintaining the organization's security posture.

10.2 Final Thoughts on Threat Modeling and Risk Assessment

As we look to the future, it's clear that threat modeling and risk assessment will play an increasingly vital role in the ever-evolving landscape of cybersecurity. Organizations must recognize that security is not a one-time task but an ongoing process that requires continuous attention and adaptation. By embracing a proactive approach and integrating security into every phase of the software development lifecycle, teams can build a robust defense against potential threats. The collaboration between development, operations, and security teams will be key to fostering a culture where security is prioritized. Ultimately, by investing in these practices and remaining vigilant against emerging threats, organizations can better protect their assets, their users, and their reputations in an increasingly digital world. AI-powered threat modeling is a new way of detecting and blocking cybersecurity threats with the help of artificial intelligence (AI). Historically, security professionals analyze systems manually to identify vulnerabilities, which is time-consuming and error-prone. In threat modeling with AI, organizations can get one step ahead of cybercriminals, accelerate risks reduction, and fortify security with little human intervention. This assists businesses, governments, and individuals in better safeguarding their sensitive data.

REFERENCES

Afroz, S., Yamaguchi, F., & Wang, D. (2020). Investigating Bias in AI-Powered Phishing Detection Models. *Proceedings of the IEEE Symposium on Security and Privacy*, 107-120.1

Agarwal, A., Tiwari, V., & Al-Hamami, A. (2021). Cloud computing and cybersecurity: A survey. *Computers & Security*, *110*, 102424.

Alberts, C. J., & Dorofee, A. J. (2002). *Managing Information Security Risks: The OCTAVE Approach*. Carnegie Mellon University.

Almorsy, M., Grundy, J., & Müller, I. (2014). An Analysis of the Cloud Computing Security Problem. *Proceedings of the 2014 Asia-Pacific Software Engineering Conference*, 50-59.

Babu, C. V. S., & Andrew, S. P. (2024). Adaptive AI for Dynamic Cybersecurity Systems: Enhancing Protection in a Rapidly Evolving Digital Landscape. In Zhihan, Lv., & Global, I. G. I. (Eds.), *Principles and Applications of Adaptive Artificial Intelligence* (pp. 52–72)., DOI: 10.4018/979-8-3693-0230-9.ch003

Bass, L., Weber, I., & Zhu, L. (2015). *DevOps: A Software Architect's Perspective*. Addison-Wesley.

Beck, K., Beedle, M., van Bennekum, A., Cockburn, A., Cunningham, W., & Jeffries, R. (2001). *Manifesto for Agile Software Development.*

Brundage, M., Avin, S., & Clark, J.. (2020). Toward Trustworthy AI Development: Mechanisms for Supporting Verifiable Claims. *Journal of AI Research*, *69*, 365–412.

Buczak, A. L., & Guven, E. (2016). A Survey of Data Mining and Machine Learning Methods for Cyber Security Intrusion Detection. *IEEE Communications Surveys and Tutorials*, *18*(2), 1153–1176. DOI: 10.1109/COMST.2015.2494502

Chandramouli, R., Xie, S., & Bhatia, S. (2019). Leveraging machine learning for cyber threat intelligence. *Journal of Cybersecurity and Privacy*, *1*(1), 84–101.

Cheng, L., Liu, F., & Yao, D. (2020). Enterprise Threat Modeling: Threat Model Analysis and Management with Open-Source Tools. *ACM Transactions on Privacy and Security*, *23*(1), 1–28.

Dahl, H., Tøndel, I., & Beisheim, E. (2020). Integrating Security in Agile Development: A Case Study. *Journal of Systems and Software*, *166*, 110594.

European Commission. (2021). The Artificial Intelligence Act: A Regulatory Proposal for AI Systems. Available at: https://digital-strategy.ec.europa.eu/en/library/proposal-regulation-laying-down-harmonised-rules-artificial-intelligence-ai-act

Fowler, M., & Highsmith, J. (2001). The Agile Manifesto. *Software Development Magazine*, *9*(8), 28–35.

ICO. (2020). British Airways Fined £20m for Data Breach Affecting Over 400,000 Customers. Available at: https://ico.org.uk/

Ankalaki, S., Rajesh, A. A., Pallavi, M., Hukkeri, G. S., Jan, T., & Naik, G. R. (2025). Cyber Attack Prediction: From Traditional Machine Learning to Generative Artificial Intelligence. *IEEE Access*.

Johnson, R. B., & Onwuegbuzie, A. J. (2004). Mixed methods research: A research paradigm whose time has come. *Educational Researcher*, *33*(7), 14–26. DOI: 10.3102/0013189X033007014

Jones, A., & Ashenden, D. (2005). *Risk Management for Computer Security: Protecting Your Network and Information Assets*. Elsevier Digital Press.

Kim, G., Humble, J., Debois, P., & Willis, J. (2016). *The DevOps Handbook: How to Create World-Class Agility, Reliability, & Security in Technology Organizations*. IT Revolution.

Meyer, M., Schmidt, D., & John, M. (2017). Proactive Risk Management in Software Development: Bridging Security and Quality. *ACM Transactions on Software Engineering and Methodology*, *26*(4), 24.

Munn, Z., Peters, M. D. J., Stern, C., Tufanaru, C., McArthur, A., & Aromataris, E. (2018). Systematic review or scoping review? Guidance for authors when choosing between a systematic or scoping review approach. *BMC Medical Research Methodology*, *18*(1), 143. DOI: 10.1186/s12874-018-0611-x PMID: 30453902

Myagmar, S., Lee, A. J., & Yurcik, W. (2005). Threat Modeling as a Basis for Security Requirements. In *Proceedings of the 2005 ACM Workshop on Storage Security and Survivability* (pp. 94–102). Association for Computing Machinery.

Nguyen, T., Gupta, S., & Chandrasekaran, K. (2021). AI in Cybersecurity: A Double-Edged Sword. *ACM Computing Surveys*, *54*(3), 1–28. DOI: 10.1145/3501296

OWASP. (2021). *OWASP Threat Modeling Cheat Sheet*.

Shostack, A. (2014). *Threat Modeling: Designing for Security*. Wiley.

Srisakthi, S., & Suresh Babu, C. V. (2024). Cybersecurity: Protecting Information in a Digital World. In Saeed, S., Azizi, N., Tahir, S., Ahmad, M., & Almuhaideb, A. (Eds.), *Strengthening Industrial Cybersecurity to Protect Business Intelligence* (pp. 1–25). IGI Global., DOI: 10.4018/979-8-3693-0839-4.ch001

Suresh Babu, C. V., & Yadavamuthiah, K. (2023). Cyber Physical Systems Design Challenges in the Areas of Mobility, Healthcare, Energy, and Manufacturing. In Thanigaivelan, R., Kaliappan, S., & Jegadheesan, C. (Eds.), *Cyber-Physical Systems and Supporting Technologies for Industrial Automation* (pp. 131–151). IGI Global., DOI: 10.4018/978-1-6684-9267-3.ch007

Vashishtha, R., Agrawal, A., & Haldar, R. (2019). Behavioral Analytics for Threat Detection: A Comprehensive Survey. *Journal of Information Security and Applications*, *45*, 61–73.

Wheeler, D. A., & McClure, S. (2017). Integrating Security into the Software Development Lifecycle: A Practical Approach. *IEEE Software*, *34*(4), 50–56.

Wired. (2024). DeepSeek's Safety Guardrails Failed Every Test Researchers Threw at Its AI Chatbot. Retrieved from https://www.wired.com/story/deepseeks-ai-jailbreak-prompt-injection-attacks

Xie, J., Zheng, Y., & Wu, M. (2022). Hybrid Explainable AI Models for Threat Intelligence Analysis. *Journal of Cybersecurity Research*, *7*(1), 45–62.

Zhao, Z., Xu, J., & Zhang, Y. (2020). Artificial Intelligence in Cybersecurity: A Review. *Journal of Information Security and Applications*, *50*, 102420.

Chapter 8 Regression Test Selection Approaches: Research Trends in Regression Test Selection of Software Systems

Mohammed Al-Refai
https://orcid.org/0000-0001-7297-7695
Jordan University of Science and Technology, Jordan

Mahmoud Hammad
https://orcid.org/0000-0003-2891-0463
Ajman University, UAE & Jordan University of Science and Technology, Jordan

Ghaith Al-Refai
https://orcid.org/0000-0002-8505-9719
German Jordanian University, Jordan

Ahmad Alzu'bi
https://orcid.org/0000-0001-5466-0379
Jordan University of Science and Technology, Jordan

ABSTRACT

Regression testing ensures that changes in a software system do not intro- duce defects in previously tested functionality, but it is often a resource-intensive process. Regression Test Selection (RTS) techniques aim to reduce this cost by identifying a sub- set of test cases that must be executed after changes. This chapter explores the evolution and effectiveness of RTS methods, focusing on their evaluation criteria, including safety and precision. The chapter categorizes RTS approaches into

DOI: 10.4018/979-8-3693-9851-7.ch008

model-based, code-based, information retrieval-based, fuzzy logic-based, machine learning-based, and security-aware methods, detailing their methodologies, advantages, and limitations. The chapter also includes an experimental evaluation comparing static RTS (STARTS) with dynamic RTS (Ekstazi) in terms of safety, precision, and test suite reduction. Finally, the chapter discusses future directions. This comprehensive overview underscores the critical role of RTS in improving the efficiency and effectiveness of regression testing for modern software systems.

1.1 INTRODUCTION

Regression testing ensures that modifications in a system do not introduce faults into previously tested code by re-running the existing test cases on a new version of the software (Bertolino, 2007; Harrold, 1999). This process is among the most resource-intensive phases in a software system's lifecycle. Some studies suggest that regression testing can consume up to 80% of the testing budget and account for nearly 50% of maintenance costs (Leung and White, 1989; Chittimalli and Harrold, 2009; Engström and Runeson, 2010). To enhance efficiency, Regression Test Selection (RTS) techniques have been introduced Harrold, 1999. RTS aims to select a subset of test cases from the existing suite to verify the correctness of the affected functionality after changes (Harrold, 1999; Briand, Labiche, and He, 2009).

Research on RTS spans over three decades (Engström, Runeson, and Skoglund, 2010; Yoo and Harman, 2012) and explores approaches based on both code-level and model-level changes in a system. RTS techniques categorize test cases into three groups: retestable, reusable, and obsolete (Leung and White, 1989). Retestable test cases are those that interact with modified parts of the system and require re-execution. Reusable test cases interact only with unmodified sections and can be excluded from re-execution. Obsolete test cases, on the other hand, become invalid due to changes that alter their input/output relationships or render their original purpose irrelevant (Leung and White, 1989).

An RTS approach achieves *precision* by avoiding the selection of unaffected test cases, and *safety* by ensuring the inclusion of all affected test cases.

Traditional code-based RTS methods require four inputs: the original and modified versions of the software system, the test suite, and dependency information that links test cases to the old version of the software. These methods output the retestable and reusable test cases (Gligoric, Eloussi, and Marinov, 2015), assuming that obsolete test cases have already been removed from the test suite (Yoo and Harman, 2012).

Model-based RTS approaches utilize behavioral diagrams (Ye et al., 2011; Y. Chen, Probert, and Sims, 2002; Korel, Tahat, and Vaysburg, 2002) or a combination of structural and behavioral diagrams (Briand, Labiche, and He, 2009; Farooq et al., 2010; Zech, Felderer, et al., 2012; Zech, Kalb, et al., 2017). These methods take four inputs: the old and new versions of the software model, the original test cases (whether modellevel or code-level), and traceability links between test cases and the models of the system under test. The output consists of retestable and reusable test cases, and some approaches (Briand, Labiche, and He, 2009; Farooq et al., 2010) can also detect specific types of obsolete test cases.

This chapter is structured as follows: Section 1.2 outlines the criteria used to evaluate RTS techniques. Section 1.3 and Section 1.4 present and discuss various approaches for model-based and code-based RTS. Sections 1.5 and 1.6 present the RTS approaches that leverage information retrieval and fuzzy logic to enhance test case selection, respectively. Section 1.7 presents security-aware RTS, while Section 1.8 covers RTS methods that leverage machine-learning. Section 1.9 presents an experimental evaluation for the stateof-the-art class-level static and dynamic RTS approaches and discusses the results. We conclude the chapter with Section 1.10 that presents future directions and trends for RTS methods.

1.2 EVALUATION CRITERIA FOR RTS

Rothermel and Harrold Rothermel and Harrold, 1996 established two key criteria for evaluating regression test selection (RTS) approaches: inclusiveness and precision. These criteria are defined as follows.

Inclusiveness measures the degree to which an RTS approach selects test cases that exercise modified code during regression testing. Let T represent the total number of test cases in a test suite, with N test cases among T being modification-traversing for two program versions, P and P . If an RTS approach selects M of these N test cases for regression testing, then the inclusiveness of the approach with respect to P, P , and T is calculated as M/N Rothermel and Harrold, 1996. An RTS approach is considered *safe* if it achieves 100% inclusiveness across all possible program versions and test suites. For example, if $T = 50$, $N = 40$, and the RTS approach selects $M = 30$ modification traversing test cases, the inclusiveness is 0.75 (30/40). A safe RTS approach must include all test cases that exercise modified or deleted code for regression testing (Rothermel and Harrold, 1996).

A test case is classified as *modification-traversing* if it executes changed code in the program or previously executed code that has been removed (Yoo and Harman, 2012). It is important to note that a safe RTS approach does not guarantee safety against all faults, as some program changes may introduce side effects in unmodified parts of the code. Instead, a safe RTS approach ensures that if a test case exercises modified code, it will be selected for regression testing (Yoo and Harman, 2012).

Precision, on the other hand, evaluates how effectively an RTS approach avoids selecting test cases that are not modification-traversing, as these are unlikely to reveal faults Rothermel and Harrold, 1996. Suppose a test suite T contains K test cases that are not modification-traversing for P and P . If the RTS approach omits O of these K test cases, the precision of the approach is defined as O/K Rothermel and Harrold, 1996. For instance, if $T = 50$, $K = 40$, and the RTS approach omits $O = 30$ non-modification traversing test cases, the precision is 0.75 (30/40).

Inclusiveness and precision provide complementary insights into the performance of RTS techniques, with inclusiveness focusing on guaranteeing the selection of essential test cases and precision aiming to minimize the inclusion of irrelevant ones.

1.3 MODEL-BASED RTS APPROACHES

Model-based regression test selection (RTS) involves categorizing test cases based on changes made to the models that represent the system under test Briand, Labiche, and He, 2009. Most existing model-based RTS approaches (Ye et al., 2011; Y. Chen, Probert, and Sims, 2002; Korel, Tahat, and Vaysburg, 2002; Briand, Labiche, and He, 2009; Farooq et al., 2010; Zech, Felderer, et al., 2012; Zech, Kalb, et al., 2017) leverage UML diagrams, while a few others (Muccini, M. Dias, and Richardson, 2005; Muccini, M. S. Dias, and Richardson, 2005) utilize alternative modeling techniques. Common UML diagrams employed in these approaches include activity, class, sequence, state chart, and case diagrams.

Chen *et al.* Y. Chen, Probert, and Sims, 2002 proposed a specification-based RTS approach that uses UML activity models. These models represent the requirements and specifications of the system under test. Modifications to the system's specifications are reflected in changes to the activity model, which are then used to drive the selection of relevant test cases.

Briand *et al.* Briand, Labiche, and He, 2009 developed an RTS approach based on UML design models, including use case, class, and sequence diagrams. This method identifies changes across these diagrams and assesses their impact on the associated test cases. Each test case triggers operations represented by use cases in the use case model, which are linked to interaction scenarios detailed in sequence diagrams. This approach facilitates functional testing by mapping test cases to interface operations.

Korel *et al.* Korel, Tahat, and Vaysburg, 2002 used control and data dependencies derived from extended finite state machines to evaluate the impact of model changes. Similarly, Ural *et al.* Ural and Yenigün, 2013 and Lity *et al.* Lity et al., 2016 employed state machine diagrams to design model-based RTS approaches for identifying and ana- lyzing the impact of changes.

Farooq *et al.* Farooq et al., 2010 proposed an approach that utilizes UML class and state machine models. This technique identifies modifications in class diagrams and state diagrams and analyzes their impact. The altered elements of the state diagrams are subsequently used to classify test cases.

Zech *et al.* Zech, Felderer, et al., 2012; Zech, Kalb, et al., 2017 introduced a generic model-based RTS framework built on the MoVE model versioning tool. The framework operates through three phases: change identification, impact analysis, and test case selection. These phases are guided by OCL queries. While this method demonstrated its potential on a small-scale program, the complexity of OCL queries for even simple rules posed significant challenges.

Ye *et al.* Ye et al., 2011 developed an RTS approach based on UML activity diagrams. This technique requires instrumentation of the software system to capture execution traces of code-level test cases. Each action node in the activity diagram corresponds to a function call in the system. By correlating activity nodes with program functions, the approach determines the paths of test cases within the activity diagram based on their execution traces.

Muccini *et al.* Muccini, M. Dias, and Richardson, 2005; Muccini, M. S. Dias, and Richardson, 2005 utilized component-based models to represent system architecture and labeled transition systems (LTS) to describe component behavior. These LTS models, combined with structural information, are used to build graphs for RTS analysis.

Overall, model-based RTS techniques are gaining traction and are expected to play an increasingly significant role in regression testing for several reasons. First, model-based approaches are often more efficient and scalable for large-scale systems than code-based methods Briand, Labiche, and He, 2009; Yoo and Harman, 2012. Second, comparing changes across high-level models is generally more straightforward than analyzing differences in code versions Briand, Labiche, and He, 2009. Furthermore, model-based RTS tools can be independent of programming languages by relying on widely accepted modeling standards such as UML Briand, Labiche, and He, 2009. For systems that already utilize models for evolution and runtime adaptation, adopting model-based RTS techniques is particularly convenient, as both processes operate at the same abstraction level.

1.4 CODE-BASED RTS APPROACHES

Code-based regression test selection (RTS) focuses on identifying changes made to the source code, performing dependency analysis (either statically or dynamically) to determine relationships between test cases and the system under test, and selecting test cases that traverse modified code. These changes and dependencies can be analyzed at varying levels of granularity, such as classes, methods, or statements.

Engström *et al.* Engström, Runeson, and Skoglund, 2010 categorized code-based RTS techniques into three primary groups: firewall-based, graph-walk-based, and dependency based approaches. Notably, dependency-based approaches are often considered a subset of firewall-based techniques, as firewall approaches rely on dependency relationships between program entities like classes.

Firewall-based techniques (Yoo and Harman, 2012; Kung et al., 1996; Jang, Munro, and Kwon, 2011) define a conceptual boundary, referred to as a "firewall," around the modified and impacted entities in a system. This boundary helps identify the subset of the system that requires retesting. Kung *et al.* Kung et al., 1996 applied firewall-based RTS at the class level by constructing object relation diagrams (ORD) to capture static relationships among classes. The firewall for a class *C* is defined as the set of *C* and all classes dependent on it. Any modifications to *C* result in the selection of test cases that traverse classes within its firewall. Similarly, Hsia *et al.* Hsia et al., 1997 and White and Abdullah White and Abdullah, 1997 applied this technique at the class level, while Jang *et al.* Jang, Munro, and Kwon, 2011 extended it to the method level for C++ programs. Skoglund and Runeson Skoglund and Runeson, 2007 highlighted limitations in the precision of class-level firewall-based RTS, as it often selects non-modification-traversing test cases. They introduced an improved approach that bypasses the class firewall and directly selects test cases traversing the changed classes.

Soetens *et al.* Soetens, Demeyer, and Zaidman, 2013 proposed a firewall-based RTS approach leveraging the FAMIX model, which captures dependencies and changes within Java software. This model identifies various changes, such as additions, deletions, and modifications to packages, classes, methods, attributes, and method invocations, and maps each change to its corresponding test cases. Later, Soetens *et al.* Soetens, Demeyer, Zaidman, and Pérez, 2015 extended this approach to account for dynamic binding by mapping method invocations to all potential methods with matching names.

Graph-walk approaches are another prominent category of RTS techniques. Rothermel and Harrold Rothermel and Harrold, 1997 proposed a safe RTS method for procedural programs, employing control-flow graphs (CFGs) to represent both the original and modified versions of a program. Modifications are identified by comparing CFGs, and affected entities are selected by traversing differing edges between the graphs. Rothermel and Harrold later extended this approach for C++ programs using interprocedural control flow graphs (ICFGs) Rothermel, Harrold, and Dedhia, 2000. However, this method is limited to complete programs and cannot handle external library calls unless the library code is available.

Harrold *et al.* Harrold et al., 2001 adapted the CFG-based approach for Java by introducing the Java Inter-class Graph (JIG), which models interprocedural interactions via method calls. Each method invocation is represented as a call node in the JIG, and call edges connect these nodes to the corresponding methods. Virtual method calls are resolved using class hierarchy analysis Dean, Grove, and Chambers, 1995, enabling precise identification of affected method calls.

Vokolos and Frankl Vokolos and Frankl, 1998 introduced a text differencing-based RTS approach that utilizes the Unix diff command to compare the original and modified versions of a program. The identified changes guide the selection of test cases that traverse the modified code blocks.

Recent RTS research has shifted its focus to class-level techniques (Gligoric, Eloussi, and Marinov, 2015; Legunsen, Hariri, et al., 2016; Legunsen, Shi, and Marinov, 2017; Zhang, 2018; Yu and T. Wang, 2018; Gyori et al., 2018) due to their balance of precision and scalability. These approaches identify changes and compute dependencies at the class level, often treating test classes as test cases to simplify the selection process. Gligoric *et al.* Gligoric, Eloussi, and Marinov, 2015 introduced Ekstazi, a dynamic class-level RTS tool that tracks dependencies at runtime and selects test cases traversing modified classes. Ekstazi guarantees safety by ensuring all modification-traversing test cases are selected Skoglund and Runeson, 2007.

Legunsen *et al.* Legunsen, Hariri, et al., 2016; Legunsen, Shi, and Marinov, 2017 proposed STARTS, a static class-level RTS approach that constructs a dependency graph of program types using compile-time information. It selects test cases that reach modified types through the transitive closure of the graph.

Zhang Zhang, 2018 developed HyRTS, a hybrid RTS approach that supports class and method-level analysis to enhance precision and reduce selection time.

Yu *et al.* Yu and T. Wang, 2018 highlighted the challenges of applying fine-grained RTS techniques (e.g., method or statement-level) in continuous integration (CI) systems due to their high analysis overhead. They demonstrated that class-level RTS is more practical in CI environments, often outperforming the *ReTestAll* strategy in terms of cost-effectiveness.

Gyori *et al.* Gyori et al., 2018 compared class-level RTS with project-level RTS in the Maven Central ecosystem. They found that class-level RTS, which computes dependencies at the class granularity, is significantly more efficient than project-level RTS in reducing test suite size.

In summary, code-based RTS approaches have evolved to balance precision, scalability, and cost-effectiveness. The current trend towards class-level RTS demonstrates its suitability for modern software systems, particularly in environments where rapid and efficient test selection is critical.

1.5 INFORMATION RETRIEVAL-BASED RTS APPROACHES

Recent approaches to Regression Test Selection (RTS) Romano et al., 2018; Azizi and Do, 2018 have been developed to address scenarios where the regression testing budget is constrained, and reducing the size of the test suite takes precedence over safety and fault detection capabilities.

Romano *et al.* Romano et al., 2018 introduced an RTS method named SPIRITuS, which leverages information retrieval techniques to select test cases. The primary design objectives of SPIRITuS are to ensure ease of adaptation to various programming languages and to allow for tuning via a threshold. SPIRITuS models all methods in the classes under test as documents using the Vector Space Model (VSM). To determine whether a method in the adapted program requires retesting, the lexical similarity between the method versions in the original and modified programs is calculated using the cosine similarity measure. If the similarity falls below a specified threshold, all test cases that exercise the method are selected. SPIRITuS was assessed and compared with

Ekstazi and a diff-based RTS technique in terms of test suite size reduction and fault detection effectiveness. The diff-based approach selects test cases that cover modified methods, with differences identified using the UNIX diff tool. The evaluation results demonstrated that SPIRITuS selects significantly fewer test cases than both Ekstazi and the diff-based technique, but it detects fewer faults compared to them.

Azizi *et al.* Azizi and Do, 2018 eliminated the need for dynamic and static analysis. They proposed ReTEST, a language-independent RTS method that employs information retrieval for lightweight analysis. ReTEST tokenizes the source code of test cases to measure their diversity. It selects test cases based on test failure history, test case diversity, and code change history at the line level.

1.6 FUZZY LOGIC-BASED RTS APPROACHES

Fuzzy logic has been effectively utilized in both model-based and code-based approaches for Regression Test Selection (RTS) and prioritization. Regression test prioritization is a critical process that focuses on determining the optimal order in which test cases should be executed to maximize specific goals, such as detecting faults as early as possible (Yoo and Harman, 2012). Both model-based and code-based fuzzy logic approaches treat test case selection and prioritization as decision-making challenges, utilizing fuzzy logic systems to process multiple inputs related to the test cases and the system under test. These inputs typically include factors such as test coverage, failure history, and the history of system changes. Fuzzy logic is particularly well-suited for this task due to its ability to handle uncertainty and imprecision in decision-making processes.

Fuzzy Logic Code-Based Approaches. Xu *et al.* Xu et al., 2014 propose a code based RTS approach that utilizes fuzzy expert systems for test case selection in scenarios where source code and its history are not readily available. The fuzzy expert systems in this approach select the most relevant test cases by applying fuzzy logic to correlate various pieces of knowledge, which may include customer profiles, test case coverage and results, system failure rates, and changes in system architecture. This approach operates under the assumption that such knowledge is accessible and can be used as input to the fuzzy expert system. The output of the fuzzy expert system provides valuable insights to testers, aiding them in the decision-making process and helping them select the most appropriate test cases for execution.

Malz *et al.* Malz, Jazdi, and Göhner, 2012 introduce another code-based RTS approach that combines software agents and fuzzy logic to prioritize test cases with the goal of increasing test effectiveness and improving fault detection rates. The approach employs multiple software agents that collaborate to assign priority values to test cases. The final priority of a test case is determined through cooperation between the agents, which exchange and process relevant information. Test coverage is assumed to be available and is incorporated into priority values as one of the key factors for prioritization. This collaborative and adaptive approach leverages fuzzy logic to handle the complexity and uncertainty in determining the most critical test cases to execute first.

Fuzzy Logic Model-Based Approaches. While model-based approaches generally rely on behavioral diagrams for RTS, there are limited studies that incorporate fuzzy logic in the context of RTS. The existing model-based approaches primarily focus on using fuzzy logic for test case prioritization rather than selection, and they are typically based on specific behavioral models, such as symbolic execution trees or state machine diagrams.

Rapos *et al.* Rapos and Dingel, 2015 propose a model-based RTS approach that utilizes fuzzy logic to prioritize test cases based on information obtained from the symbolic execution tree of a model. In this approach, the inputs to the fuzzy logic system include the size of the test suite, the size of the symbolic execution tree, and the relative size of individual test cases. The fuzzy logic system processes these inputs and produces a single numerical output, referred to as the priority, for each test case. Test cases are then prioritized according to these outputs, ensuring that the most critical test cases are executed first.

Rhmann *et al.* Rhmann and Saxena, 2017 present a model-based approach that uses fuzzy logic for test case prioritization based on modifications made to a state machine diagram. A state machine diagram is employed to represent the system's behavior, and when the system undergoes changes, the diagram is updated to reflect the new behavior. These changes are incorporated into a weighted extended finite state machine, where weights are assigned to nodes and edges based on the extent of changes and the level of risk associated with them. Test paths are generated from the modified state diagram, and each test path is evaluated for risk exposure and change information. These evaluations are then used as inputs to the fuzzy logic system, which prioritizes the test paths according to their risk and relevance.

In both the model-based and code-based approaches, fuzzy logic provides an effective way to address the inherent uncertainty and complexity of test case prioritization and selection, ultimately improving the efficiency and effectiveness of the regression testing process.

1.7 SECURITY-AWARE REGRESSION TEST SELECTION

RTS plays a crucial role in security testing by identifying and executing a subset of test cases that are most relevant to recent changes in software. Unlike traditional functional testing, security testing requires identifying vulnerabilities introduced due to modifications and ensuring that previous security weaknesses do not resurface. A few approaches have been proposed to enhance RTS methodologies for security, incorporating security-specific selection criteria to improve efficiency and effectiveness. Regression test selection is particularly crucial for security testing due to the following reasons:

- **Optimized Testing Effort:** Security test cases are often computationally expensive; selecting only the most relevant tests reduces costs.
- **Detection of Reintroduced Vulnerabilities:** Ensures that previous vulnerabilities do not re-emerge due to software modifications.
- **Targeted Security Assurance:** Helps security engineers focus on critical changes while maintaining compliance with security standards.
- **Integration with DevSecOps Pipelines:** Enables continuous security testing in agile and DevSecOps workflows.

Hwang *et al.* Hwang et al., 2012 proposed a regression test selection approach tailored for evolving security policies in software systems. Their method leverages control-flow analysis and security policy dependencies to determine the subset of tests requiring reexecution. The approach maps security policy modifications to impacted test cases based on dependency analysis. The approach considers both structural changes in policies and behavioral changes in security enforcement mechanisms are considered.

Shilpa *et al.* G. et al., 2024 presented a penetration regression test selection algorithm designed for early detection of buffer overflow vulnerabilities. Their methodology integrates extended branch coverage criteria with control-flow analysis to enhance security regression testing. In particular, test cases are selected based on their ability to cover program branches associated with buffer overflow risks.

Hettiarachchi *et al.* Hettiarachchi, Do, and Choi, 2014 proposed a methodology to select test cases for regression testing based on system requirements and their associated risks. Unlike conventional RTS methods that rely on source code changes, this study selects and prioritizes test cases that cover high-risk requirements and provide a systematic risk assessment model to guide the test selection process. Each system requirement is evaluated based on associated risks, using the structured risk analysis model. The risk factors include: requirement complexity, security and privacy risks, and operational risks.

Jahan *et al.* Jahan, Feng, and Mahmud, 2020 proposed a methodology to improve regression testing efficiency through a risk-based test case prioritization approach. This method aimed to systematically assess method-level risk using an automated procedure, reducing the time and subjectivity of manual risk evaluations. The key goal was to prioritize test cases based on the risk values of methods to detect faults early in high-risk modules. The methodology introduced a semi-automated framework that: (1) extracts risk indicating factors (e.g., modified requirements, method complexity, and method size), (2) computes failure likelihood and failure impact of methods, (3) Uses static method invocation relationships to estimate risk propagation, and (4) prioritizes test cases based on their covered method's risk values.

The work proposed by Wikstrand et al. Wikstrand et al., 2009 introduces a dynamic regression test selection approach that utilizes a file cache to identify and prioritize test cases based on fault-prone files. The goal of the proposed approach is to improve the efficiency of regression testing in industrial settings by reducing redundant test executions while maintaining high fault detection rates. The proposed RTS system consists of three main components: (1) a **test-to-source file linking module**, (2) a **cache-based fault prediction module**, and (3) a **test case recommendation module**. The methodology begins with the identification of error-prone source files based on historical fault reports. Each test case is linked to the specific source files it covers, forming a traceability matrix. This linkage enables the system to recommend test cases dynamically whenever a new version of the software is released. The study presents several key strengths. First, the dynamic adaptation of the RTS approach ensures that high-risk files are always prioritized, reducing unnecessary test executions. Second, unlike static RTS methods, which rely on fixed test case selection criteria, the proposed approach continuously updates fault predictions based on real-time error reports. This makes it particularly well-suited for industrial environments where software evolves rapidly.

In conclusion security-aware regression test selection is a growing field with significant implications for enhancing software security. The reviewed approaches demonstrate diverse methodologies, including penetration and attack-pattern-based selection, risk based analysis, and test to error-prone files dependency-based RTS techniques. Future work would explore further integration with machine learning to predict security-sensitive modifications dynamically.

1.8 MACHINE LEARNING-BASED REGRESSION TEST SELECTION

Traditional RTS techniques rely on code-based heuristics, change impact analysis, or historical test execution data to determine which test cases should be rerun. However, with the increasing complexity of software systems and the need for faster release cycles in continuous integration (CI) environments, machine learning (ML) has emerged as a promising approach to enhance RTS efficiency.

ML-based RTS leverages past execution data, code complexity, dependency graphs, and various other program features to predict which test cases are likely to detect faults in a given software revision. Unlike traditional methods, ML approaches can adapt over time, improving test selection accuracy as more historical data becomes available. These techniques help in minimizing the cost of regression testing while maximizing the detection of defects, making them an attractive solution for large-scale software projects Pan et al., 2022.

Machine learning provides multiple advantages in the field of RTS, including Pan et al., 2022:

- **Predictive Selection:** ML models can analyze past execution patterns and dynamically predict which test cases are most likely to detect faults, reducing unnecessary test executions.
- **Handling Complex Dependencies:** Unlike static dependency analysis, ML-based approaches can uncover hidden relationships between test cases and code changes, even in cases where code coverage data is incomplete.
- **Continuous Learning and Adaptation:** As more test execution data is collected, ML models improve over time, refining test selection strategies to better fit evolving software behaviors.
- **Scalability:** ML techniques allow for efficient test selection in large-scale software projects, where traditional heuristic-based RTS techniques may become infeasible.

Several ML approaches have been applied to RTS, each utilizing different models to enhance test case selection. Below is a summary of notable ML-based RTS techniques Pan et al., 2022:

- **Semi-Supervised Clustering (Chen et al., 2011) S. Chen et al., 2011:** Uses k-means clustering to group similar test cases based on execution behavior, reducing redundant test executions while preserving fault detection capability.
- **Recurrent Neural Networks (RNNs) (Hasnain et al., 2019) Hasnain et al., 2019:** Predicts failing test cases based on past execution history, leveraging time-series analysis to optimize RTS.
- **Multi-Armed Bandit Approach (Lima et al., 2020) Lima and Vergilio, 2020:** Models RTS as a reinforcement learning problem, dynamically selecting test cases based on reward maximization.
- **Weighted Attribute-Based Selection (Wang et al., 2012) Y. Wang et al., 2012:** Assigns weights to test case attributes (e.g., code complexity, coverage, execution history) to prioritize high-impact test cases.

These approaches demonstrate the potential of ML in improving test selection efficiency while ensuring reliable fault detection Pan et al., 2022. Despite its advantages, ML-based RTS remains an emerging field with several unexplored areas Pan et al., 2022:

- **Limited Generalizability:** Many existing ML-based RTS models are trained on specific software projects and may not generalize well to different programming languages, architectures, or development workflows.
- **Feature Selection Challenges:** Identifying the most relevant features (e.g., code complexity, dependency graphs, historical failures) for ML models remains a complex task, often requiring domain-specific customization.
- **Lack of Real-World Deployment Studies:** Most ML-based RTS techniques are evaluated in controlled environments rather than real-world CI pipelines, limiting their practical adoption in industry.

Future research in ML-based RTS should focus on the following directions Pan et al., 2022:

- **Hybrid ML Models:** Combining supervised learning with reinforcement learning can improve test selection by balancing prediction accuracy with adaptability.

- **Transfer Learning for RTS:** Investigating transfer learning techniques can enable ML models to be trained on one software project and applied to others with minimal retraining.
- **Automated Feature Engineering:** Developing automated feature extraction techniques using deep learning could improve the accuracy and generalizability of ML-based RTS.
- **Industry-Scale Evaluation:** Conducting large-scale studies with real-world software repositories and CI/CD environments will help validate ML-based RTS techniques for industry adoption.

1.9 EXPERIMENTAL EVALUATION OF STATIC RTS WITH RESPECT TO DYNAMIC RTS

The goal of this study is to evaluate static class-level RTS with respect to dynamic class level RTS in terms of safety, precision, and reduction in test suite size. In particular, we evaluate the state-of-the-art static approach, i.e., STARTS Legunsen, Hariri, et al., 2016, with respect to the state-of-the-art dynamic approach, Ekstazi Gligoric, Eloussi, and Marinov, 2015. The two approaches are designed to perform RTS for Java software systems.

Dynamic class-level RTS techniques, such as Ekstazi Gligoric, Eloussi, and Marinov, 2015, have demonstrated considerable progress in regression test selection. However, their reliance on dynamically collected dependencies poses certain challenges Legunsen, Hariri, et al., 2016. One significant drawback is the time-consuming nature of gathering dynamic dependencies for large-scale software systems, which can undermine the timesaving benefits of RTS. Additionally, for programs exhibiting non-deterministic behavior (e.g., those involving concurrency or randomness), dynamic analysis may fail to capture all possible execution paths. This limitation can lead to incomplete dependency analysis and reduce the effectiveness of the technique Legunsen, Hariri, et al., 2016.

On the other hand, static class-level RTS approaches, such as STARTS Legunsen, Hariri, et al., 2016; Legunsen, Shi, and Marinov, 2017, rely on static program analysis, eliminating the need for runtime data. These approaches build a dependency graph of program elements at compile time and select test cases that are associated with modified elements in the graph Legunsen, Hariri, et al., 2016; Legunsen, Shi, and Marinov, 2017. Nonetheless, static RTS techniques are not entirely reliable, as they may overlook test cases affected by specific code changes. A key limitation arises from features like dynamic class loading and reflection in Java. Java reflection enables programs to inspect and modify their structure and behavior during runtime, creating dependencies that static analysis may fail to identify Legunsen, Hariri, et al., 2016; Legunsen, Shi, and Marinov, 2017.

To assess the safety and precision of STARTS, we analyzed its safety violations and precision violations with respect to Ekstazi Gligoric, Eloussi, and Marinov, 2015. Ekstazi, a well-known code-based RTS approach, is recognized for its safety in identifying all test classes that traverse code modifications. It has been extensively evaluated across numerous software revisions and has been adopted by various popular open-source projects.

Consider a program **P** with an initial test suite **T**, which is updated to a modified version **P'**. Suppose both RTS techniques, STARTS and Ekstazi, are used to select relevant test cases from **T** based on the changes applied to transition from **P** to **P'**. Let the test cases selected by STARTS be denoted as $\mathbf{T}_{\mathbf{STARTS}}$, and those selected by Ekstazi as $\mathbf{T}_{\mathbf{Ekstazi}}$. The safety violation of STARTS relative to Ekstazi, the precision

Table 1. The Java projects used in our study

commons-dbutils 2833be3	**50**	**38**	**100**
commons-jxpath 192f4c9	171	39	46
commons-net 9531037	199	35	100
JFreeChart 86abdc8	638	344	100

violation of STARTS compared to Ekstazi, and the reduction in the size of the test suite achieved by STARTS are defined as follows:

Safety Violation w.r.t. Ekstazi = $\frac{|T_{Ekstazi} \setminus T_{STARTS}|}{|T_{Ekstazi} \cup T_{STARTS}|}$

Precision Violation w.r.t. Ekstazi = $\frac{|T_{STARTS} \setminus T_{Ekstazi}|}{|T_{Ekstazi} \cup T_{STARTS}|}$

Test Suite Reduction obtained by STARTS = $\frac{|T| \setminus |T_{STARTS}|}{|T|}$

Ideally, lower percentages for safety and precision violations, along with higher percentages for test suite reduction, indicate better performance Legunsen, Hariri, et al., 2016; Shi et al., 2014.

Subjects

We conducted an evaluation of STARTS using the four subjects outlined in Table 1. These subjects are real-world, open-source Java projects that are compatible with both Ekstazi and STARTS, as they have been widely utilized in prior evaluations of these tools Gligoric, Eloussi, and Marinov, 2015; Legunsen, Hariri, et al., 2016; Legunsen, Shi, and Marinov, 2017. Table 1 details, for each subject, the latest revision (i.e., the most recent commit of the project) used as the starting point of our experiments (**SHA**), the number of source classes (**CLASSES**) in the latest revision (excluding test classes), the number of test classes (**TESTS**), and the total number of revisions analyzed (**REVS**). **Selecting revisions.** For each of the four subjects listed in Table 1, we retrieved the project revisions following the approach described by Legunsen *et al.* Legunsen, Hariri, et al., 2016. First, we identified the most recent revision (denoted as **SHA** in Table 1) that fulfilled the following criteria: (1) no build or compilation errors, (2) no test case failures, and (3) compatibility with both STARTS and Ekstazi. Next, we selected up to 100 revisions, including the **SHA** revision, from the revisions preceding **SHA** that met these requirements. In total, 346 revisions were selected across the four subjects. For the commons-jxpath subject, only 46 revisions satisfied the above criteria.

Table 2. Results for safety, precision, and test suite size reduction

commons-dbutils 1.51	**0.0**	**13.9**	**0.0**	**70.5**	**77.4**
commons-jxpath 6.61	0.0	18.3	4.1	22.1	37.3
commons-net 0.51	0.0	17.8	0.0	89.6	91.7
JFreeChart 0.0	0.0	32.3	0.0	84.6	93.3

Aor **M-SV**$_{\mathbf{STARTS}}$ is the average/median (per subject) safety violation of STARTS w.r.t. Ekstazi.

Aor **M-PV**$_{\mathbf{STARTS}}$ is the average/median (per subject) precision violation of STARTS w.r.t. Ekstazi.

A-RD$_{\mathbf{X}}$ is the average reduction (per subject) in test suite size achieved by an RTS approach **X**.

For each subject, starting from the oldest revision among the selected set and progressing to the latest revision specified by **SHA**, we executed both Ekstazi and STARTS on consecutive pairs of revisions. The results of this evaluation are presented in the following subsection.

RESULTS

Table 2 shows for each subject the results of (1) the average and median safety violation of STARTS w.r.t. Ekstazi, (2) the average and median precision violation of STARTS

w.r.t. Ekstazi, and (3) the average reduction in test suite size achieved by STARTS and Ekstazi. For each subject, the average and median values are computed across all the revisions of the subject.

As presented in Table 2, STARTS demonstrated low safety violation rates. For instance, in the case of the commons-dbutils subject, the average safety violation was 1.51%, while the median value was zero. Similarly, for the JFreeChart subject, both the average and median safety violations were zero. These results highlight that STARTS missed only a minimal number of relevant test cases—i.e., those that traverse modifications and should be selected. The primary cause of these missed test cases is the use of dynamic class loading and Java reflection, which enable programs to inspect and alter their behavior during runtime, thereby introducing dependencies that static analysis is unable to detect.

In addition, Table 2 shows that STARTS exhibited non-zero average precision violation values for all four subjects. This occurs because static dependency analysis tends to overestimate dependencies, leading to the selection of irrelevant test cases—i.e., test cases that do not traverse modifications—compared to dynamic analysis of test executions. Likewise, STARTS achieved smaller test suite reduction than Ekstazi, which can be attributed to the overestimations inherent in static analysis. For example, for the JFreeChart subject, STARTS achieved an average test suite reduction of 84.6%, whereas Ekstazi achieved a reduction of 93.3%.

In summary, the results indicate that STARTS provides a reliable and efficient regression test selection approach with minimal safety violations. This demonstrates that STARTS misses only a small subset of relevant test cases, primarily due to limitations in static analysis when handling dynamic class loading and Java reflection. However, STARTS exhibited non-zero precision violations across all subjects, reflecting its tendency to overestimate dependencies and select irrelevant test cases. Despite these precision violations, STARTS achieved substantial test suite reductions, though slightly lower than those achieved by Ekstazi. These findings highlight the trade-offs inherent in static versus dynamic analysis, with STARTS offering a practical balance between safety, precision, and test suite reduction in scenarios where dynamic analysis may not be feasible.

1.10 FUTURE DIRECTIONS

While significant progress has been made in Regression Test Selection (RTS) research, several challenges remain, and there are numerous exciting avenues for future exploration. These advancements will be vital in addressing the growing complexity and scale of modern software systems. Below are some key directions for future research in RTS, along with potential use cases and scenarios where these directions could be applied.

Integration with Continuous Integration and Delivery Pipelines. As modern software development increasingly relies on continuous integration (CI) and continuous delivery (CD) pipelines (Gligoric, Eloussi, and Marinov, 2015) the integration of RTS techniques with these pipelines becomes crucial. A key challenge is ensuring that RTS methods work efficiently within automated build and test cycles, optimizing testing without compromising on the reliability of software releases. For example, in large-scale e-commerce platforms like Amazon, where updates are frequent and fast-paced, RTS techniques could be integrated into CI pipelines to selectively run only the most relevant tests, saving time and computational resources while maintaining the robustness of the platform. Similarly, in DevOps environments, RTS techniques could be used to automatically prioritize and select tests during frequent software deployments, ensuring high-quality releases without significant delays.

Machine Learning for Test Case Relevance Prediction. Another promising direction is the use of machine learning techniques to predict the relevance of test cases based on historical data. Machine learning models can analyze past test results, code changes, and system behaviors to predict which tests are more likely to uncover faults. This approach is particularly beneficial for systems that experience frequent and largescale changes, such as social media platforms (e.g., Facebook or Twitter), where the volume of user-generated content and rapid feature deployments makes it challenging to select the right tests manually. In this scenario, a machine learning model could be trained on historical data to suggest the most relevant tests based on the types of changes introduced in the code, the failure patterns observed, and the complexity of the system's components. Over time, as more data becomes available, the model's predictions would become increasingly accurate, making it easier to prioritize tests and detect faults early.

RTS for Higher Levels of Abstraction: Service-Level and Module-Level RTS. Exploring the applicability of RTS at higher levels of abstraction, such as service or module-level RTS, could significantly enhance scalability and reusability, particularly for large-scale, distributed systems. For instance, in microservices architectures (e.g., in cloud-based applications like Google Cloud or AWS), different services are frequently updated independently. A service-level RTS could prioritize tests that specifically cover the interactions between microservices that have been modified, rather than running tests across the entire system. This would reduce redundant testing while ensuring that critical interactions between services are verified. Similarly, in modular software systems, RTS could be applied at the module level to prioritize tests based on which modules have been modified, optimizing test execution in complex systems with many interdependent modules.

RTS for Legacy Systems and Non-Functional Testing. Another area for future research is the application of RTS techniques to legacy systems, where test case selection is often complicated by outdated documentation, lack of code modularization, and the complexity of maintaining systems that have evolved over many years. RTS could be extended to help prioritize tests for legacy systems that have little or no automated testing infrastructure. For example, in a banking system that has been in operation for decades, where changes are typically made to small parts of the system, RTS could help identify which areas are most affected by a code change and prioritize tests that cover those areas. Additionally, the role of RTS in non-functional testing, such as performance and security testing, could be explored. For instance, in high-performance systems like real-time data processing applications (e.g., in financial markets or online gaming), prioritizing tests based on performance criteria or security vulnerabilities could be valuable in ensuring that system performance remains optimal under different load conditions.

RTS for Automated System Configuration and Self-Healing Systems. Finally, future research could explore the integration of RTS with automated system configuration and self-healing systems. In dynamic environments, such as cloud-native applications or IoT systems, where configurations and components may change rapidly, RTS can be combined with self-healing mechanisms to identify the most relevant tests for verifying system integrity after a change. For example, in autonomous vehicle software systems, which require continuous updates to handle new road conditions and scenarios, RTS techniques could be used to select tests that focus on the areas most likely to be impacted by recent changes to the vehicle's algorithms or sensor configurations. Self-healing mechanisms could then automatically run these tests and use the results to correct any faults or issues in the system, ensuring that the vehicle's performance remains reliable without manual intervention.

In conclusion, these future directions highlight the potential for RTS to evolve and adapt to meet the growing demands of modern software systems. Whether through the integration of machine learning, the application of RTS at higher levels of abstraction, or its extension to legacy systems and non-functional testing, the future of RTS holds exciting possibilities for enhancing software reliability and reducing testing overheads across a wide range of industries and use cases.

REFERENCES

Azizi, M., & Do, H. (Oct. 2018). "ReTEST: A Cost Effective Test Case Selection Technique for Modern Software Development". In: *Proceedings of the 29th International Symposium on Software Reliability Engineering (ISSRE'18)*. Ed. by Ghosh, Sudipto, & Natella, Roberto. Memphis, TN, USA: IEEE, pp. 144–154. DOI: 10.1109/ISSRE.2018.00025

Bertolino, A. (2007). Software Testing Research: Achievements, Challenges, Dreams. In *In: 2007 Future of Software Engineering* (pp. 85–103). IEEE Computer Society.

Briand, L. C., Labiche, Y., & He, S. (2009, January). Automating Regression Test Selection Based on UML Designs. *Information and Software Technology*, *51*(1), 16–30. DOI: 10.1016/j.infsof.2008.09.010

Chen, S.. (2011). "Using semi-supervised clustering to improve regression test selection techniques". In: *2011 Fourth IEEE International Conference on Software Testing, Verification and Validation*. IEEE, pp. 1–10. DOI: 10.1109/ICST.2011.38

Chen, Y., Probert, R. L., & Paul Sims, D. (Sept. 2002). "Specification-Based Regression Test Selection with Risk Analysis". In: *Proceedings of the Conference of the Centre for Advanced Studies on Collaborative Research (CASCON'02)*. Ed. by Stewart, Darlen A., & Howard Johnson, J.. IBM Press, pp. 1–14.

Chittimalli, P. K., & Harrold, M. J. (2009). Recomputing Coverage Information to Assist Regression Testing. *IEEE Transactions on Software Engineering*, *35*(4), 452–469. DOI: 10.1109/TSE.2009.4

Dean, J., Grove, D., & Chambers, C. (Aug. 1995). "Optimization of ObjectOriented Programs Using Static Class Hierarchy Analysis". In: *Proceedings of the 9th European Conference on Object-Oriented Programming (ECOOP'95)*. Ed. by Walter G. Olthoff. LNCS 952. Åarhus, Denmark: Springer, pp. 77–101. DOI: 10.1007/3-540-49538-X_5

Engström, E., & Runeson, P. (2010). "A Qualitative Survey of Regression Testing Practices". In: *International Conference on Product Focused Software Process Improvement*. Springer, pp. 3–16. DOI: 10.1007/978-3-642-13792-1_3

Engström, E., Runeson, P., & Skoglund, M. (2010, January). A Systematic Review on Regression Test Selection Techniques. *Information and Software Technology*, *52*(1), 14–30. DOI: 10.1016/j.infsof.2009.07.001

Farooq, Qurat-ul-ann et al. (Mar. 2010). "A Model-Based Regression Testing Approach for Evolving Software Systems with Flexible Tool Support". In: *Proceedings of the 17th IEEE International Conference and Workshops on Engineering of Computer-Based Systems (ECBS'10)*. Oxford, UK: IEEE, pp. 41–49.

G., Shilpa R. et al. (2024). "Strengthening Web Application Security: A Penetration Regression Test Selection Algorithm for Early Detection of Buffer Overflow Vulnerability". In: *International Journal of Intelligent Systems and Applications in Engineering* 12.21s, pp. 3073–3079.

Gligoric, M., Eloussi, L., & Marinov, D. (July 2015). "Practical Regression Test Selection with Dynamic File Dependencies". In: *Proceedings of the 2015 International Symposium on Software Testing and Analysis (ISSTA'15)*. Baltimore, MD, USA: ACM, pp. 211–222. DOI: 10.1145/2771783.2771784

Gyori, A.. (Oct. 2018). "Evaluating Regression Test Selection Opportunities in a Very Large Open-Source Ecosystem". In: *Proceedings of the 29th International Symposium on Software Reliability Engineering (ISSRE'18)*. Ed. by Ghosh, Sudipto, & Natella, Roberto. Memphis, TN, USA: IEEE, pp. 112–122. DOI: 10.1109/ISSRE.2018.00022

Harrold, M. J. (July 1999). "Testing Evolving Software". In: *Journal of Systems and Software* 47.2-3, pp. 173–181. DOI: 10.1016/S0164-1212(99)00037-0

Harrold, M. J.. (Oct. 2001). "Regression Test Selection for Java Software". In: *Proceedings of the 16th Conference on Object-Oriented Programming, Systems, Languages, and Applications (OOPSLA'01)*. Ed. by Vlissides, John. Tampa, FL, USA: ACM, pp. 312–326.

Hasnain, M., ... (2019). "Recurrent neural network for web services performance forecasting, ranking and regression testing". In: *2019 Asia-Pacific Signal and Information Processing Association Annual Summit and Conference (APSIPA ASC)*. IEEE, pp. 96–105. DOI: 10.1109/APSIPAASC47483.2019.9023052

Hettiarachchi, C., Do, H., & Choi, B. (2014). "Effective regression testing using requirements and risks". In: *2014 Eighth International Conference on Software Security and Reliability (SERE)*. IEEE, pp. 157–166. DOI: 10.1109/SERE.2014.29

Hsia, P.. (1997, July). A Technique for the Selective Revalidation of OO Software. *Journal of Software (Malden, MA)*, *9*(4), 217–233.

Hwang, JeeHyun et al. (2012). "Selection of regression system tests for security policy evolution". In: *Proceedings of the 27th IEEE/ACM international conference on automated software engineering*, pp. 266–269.

Jahan, H., Feng, Z., & Hasan Mahmud, S. M. (2020). Risk-based test case prioritization by correlating system methods and their associated risks. *Arabian Journal for Science and Engineering*, *45*(8), 6125–6138. DOI: 10.1007/s13369-020-04472-z

Jang, Y. K., Munro, M., & Kwon, Y. R. (2011, September). An Improved Method of Selecting Regression Tests for C++ Programs. *Journal of Software Maintenance and Evolution: Research and Practice*, *13*(5), 331–350. DOI: 10.1002/smr.236

Korel, B., Tahat, L. H., & Vaysburg, B. (Oct. 2002). "Model Based Regression Test Reduction Using Dependence Analysis". In: *Proceedings of the International Conference on Software Maintenance (ICSM'02)*. Ed. by Antoniol, Giuliano, & Baxter, Ira D.. Montréal, Quebec, Canada: IEEE, pp. 214–223. DOI: 10.1109/ICSM.2002.1167768

Kung, D. C., Gao, J., Hsia, P., Toyoshima, Y., & Chen, C. (1996, January). On Regression Testing of Object-Oriented Programs. *Journal of Systems and Software*, *32*(1), 21–40. DOI: 10.1016/0164-1212(95)00047-X

Legunsen, O., & Hariri, F.. (Nov. 2016). "An Extensive Study of Static Regression Test Selection in Modern Software Evolution". In: *Proceedings of the 2016 24th ACM SIGSOFT International Symposium on Foundations of Software Engineering (FSE'16)*. Ed. by Cleland-Huang, Jane, & Su, Zhendong. Seattle, WA, USA: ACM, pp. 583–594. DOI: 10.1145/2950290.2950361

Legunsen, O., Shi, A., & Marinov, D. (Oct. 2017). "STARTS: STAtic Regression Test Selection". In: *Proceedings of the 32nd IEEE/ACM International Conference on Automated Software Engineering (ASE'17)*. Ed. by Massimiliano Di Penta and Tien N. Nguyen. Urbana-Champaign, IL, USA: IEEE Press, pp. 949–954. Leung, Hareton K. N. and Lee J. White (Oct. 1989). "Insights into Regression Testing". In: *Proceedings of Conference on Software Maintenance*. Miami, FL, USA: IEEE, pp. 60–69.

Lima, Jackson A Prado and Silvia Regina Vergilio (2020). "A multi-armed bandit approach for test case prioritization in continuous integration environments". In: *IEEE Transactions on Software Engineering* 48.2, pp. 453–465.

Lity, S.. (June 2016). "Applying Incremental Model Slicing to Product-Line Regression Testing". In: *Proceedings of the 15th International Conference on Software Reuse (ICSR'16)*. Ed. by Kapitsaki, Georgia M., & Santana de Almeida, Eduardo. Lecture Notes in Computer Science 9679. Limassol, Cyprus: Springer, pp. 3–19. DOI: 10.1007/978-3-319-35122-3_1

Malz, C., Jazdi, N., & Göhner, P. (Apr. 2012). "Prioritization of Test Cases Using Software Agents and Fuzzy Logic". In: *Proceedings of the 5th International Conference on Software Testing, Verification and Validation (ICST'12)*. Ed. by Bertolino, Antonia, & Labiche, Yvan. Montréal, BC, Canada: IEEE, pp. 483–486. DOI: 10.1109/ICST.2012.131

Muccini, H., Dias, M., & Richardson, D. J. (2005). "Reasoning about Software Architecture-Based Regression Testing Through a Case Study". In: *29th Annual International Computer Software and Applications Conference (COMPSAC'05)*. Vol. 2. IEEE, pp. 189–195. DOI: 10.1109/COMPSAC.2005.127

Muccini, H., Dias, M. S., & Richardson, D. J. (2005). "Towards Software Architecture-Based Regression Testing". In: *ACM SIGSOFT Software Engineering Notes*. Vol. 30. ACM, pp. 1–7. DOI: 10.1145/1083217.1083223

Pan, R., Bagherzadeh, M., Ghaleb, T. A., & Briand, L. (2022). Test case selection and prioritization using machine learning: A systematic literature review. *Empirical Software Engineering*, *27*(2), 29. DOI: 10.1007/s10664-021-10066-6

Rapos, E. J., & Dingel, J. (Apr. 2015). "Using Fuzzy Logic and Symbolic Execution to Prioritize UML-RT Test Cases". In: *Proceedings of the 8th International Conference on Software Testing, Verification and Validation (ICST'15)*. Ed. by Fraser, Gordon, & Marinov, Darko. IEEE. Graz, Austria. DOI: 10.1109/ICST.2015.7102610

Rhmann, W., & Saxena, V. (2017, January). Fuzzy Expert System Based Test Cases Prioritization from UML State Machine Diagram using Risk Information. *International Journal on Mathematical Sciences and Computing*, *3*(1), 17–27. DOI: 10.5815/ijmsc.2017.01.02

Romano, S., Scanniello, G., Antoniol, G., & Marchetto, A. (2018, July). SPIRITuS: A SimPle Information Retrieval RegressIon Test Selection Approach. *Information and Software Technology*, *99*, 62–80. DOI: 10.1016/j.infsof.2018.03.004

Rothermel, G., & Harrold, M. J. (1996, August). Analyzing Regression Test Selection Techniques. *IEEE Transactions on Software Engineering*, *22*(8), 529–551. DOI: 10.1109/32.536955

Rothermel, G., Harrold, M. J., & Dedhia, J. (2000, June). Regression Test Selection for C++ Software. *Software Testing, Verification & Reliability*, *10*(2), 77–109. DOI: 10.1002/1099-1689(200006)10:2<77::AID-STVR197>3.0.CO;2-E

Shi, A.. (Nov. 2014). "Balancing Trade-offs in Test-suite Reduction". In: *Proceedings of the 22nd International Symposium on Foundations of Software Engineering (FSE'14)*. Ed. by Orso, Alessandro, & Storey, Margaret-Anne. Hong Kong, China: ACM, pp. 246–256.

Skoglund, M., & Runeson, P. (2007, June). Improving Class Firewall Regression Test Selection by Removing the Class Firewall. *International Journal of Software Engineering and Knowledge Engineering*, *17*(3), 359–378. DOI: 10.1142/S0218194007003306

Soetens, Q. D., Demeyer, S., & Zaidman, A. (Mar. 2013). "ChangeBased Test Selection in the Presence of Developer Tests". In: *Proceedings of the 17th European Conference on Software Maintenance and Reengineering (CSMR'13)*. Ed. by Cleve, Anthony, & Ricca, Filippo. Genoa, Italy: IEEE, pp. 101–110.

Soetens, Q. D., Demeyer, S., Zaidman, A., & Pérez, J. (Nov. 2015). "Change-Based Test Selection: An Empirical Evaluation". In: *Empirical Software Engineering*, pp. 1–43.

Ural, H., & Yenigün, H. (2013). Regression Test Suite Selection Using Dependence Analysis. *Journal of Software (Malden, MA)*, *25*(7), 681–709. DOI: 10.1002/smr.1559

Vokolos, F., & Frankl, P. G. (Nov. 1998). "Empirical Evaluation of the Textual Differencing Regression Testing Technique". In: *Proceedings of the International Conference on Software Maintenance (SM'98)*. Bethesda, MD, USA, pp. 44–53. DOI: 10.1109/ICSM.1998.738488

Wang, Y.. (2012). "Using weighted attributes to improve cluster test selection". In: *2012 IEEE Sixth International Conference on Software Security and Reliability*. IEEE, pp. 138–146. DOI: 10.1109/SERE.2012.18

White, L. J., & Abdullah, K. (May 1997). "A Firewall Approach for Regression Testing of Object-Oriented Software". In: *Proceedings of the 10th International Software Quality Week (QW'97)*. San Francisco, CA, USA.

Wikstrand, G.. (2009). "Dynamic regression test selection based on a file cache an industrial evaluation". In: *2009 International Conference on Software Testing Verification and Validation*. IEEE, pp. 299–302. DOI: 10.1109/ICST.2009.42

Xu, Z., Gao, K., Khoshgoftaar, T. M., & Seliya, N. (2014). System Regression Test Planning with a Fuzzy Expert System. *Information Sciences*, *259*, 532–543. DOI: 10.1016/j.ins.2010.09.012

Ye, N.. (June 2011). "Automatic Regression Test Selection Based on Activity Diagrams". In: *Proceedings of the 5th International Conference on Secure Software Integration & Reliability Improvement Companion (SSIRI-C'11)*. Jeju Island, South Korea: IEEE, pp. 166–171. DOI: 10.1109/SSIRI-C.2011.31

Yoo, S., & Harman, M. (Mar. 2012). "Regression Testing Minimization, Selection and Prioritization: A Survey". In: *Journal of Software Testing, Verification and Reliability* 22.2, pp. 67–120.

Yu, T., & Wang, T. (Oct. 2018). "A Study of Regression Test Selection in Continuous Integration Environments". In: *Proceedings of the 29th International Symposium on Software Reliability Engineering (ISSRE'18)*. Ed. by Ghosh, Sudipto, & Natella, Roberto. Memphis, TN, USA: IEEE, pp. 135–143. DOI: 10.1109/ISSRE.2018.00024

Zech, P., & Felderer, M.. (Oct. 2012). "A Generic Platform for ModelBased Regression Testing". In: *Proceedings of the 5th International Symposium on Leveraging Applications of Formal Methods, Verification and Validation (ISoLA'12)*. Ed. by Margaria, Tiziana, & Steffen, Bernhard. Lecture Notes in Computer Science 7609. Heraclion, Crete: Springer, pp. 112–126.

Zech, P., Kalb, P., Felderer, M., Atkinson, C., & Breu, R. (2017, February). Model-Based Regression Testing by OCL. *International Journal of Software Tools for Technology Transfer, 19*(1), 115–131. DOI: 10.1007/s10009-015-0408-8

Zhang, L. (May 2018). "Hybrid Regression Test Selection". In: *Proceedings of the 40th International Conference on Software Engineering (ICSE'18)*. Ed. by Chechik, Marsha, & Harman, Mark. Gotheburg, Sweden: IEEE, pp. 199–209. DOI: 10.1145/3180155.3180198

Chapter 9
Cloud-Based Software Architecture for Scalability and Resilience

Amro Saleh
https://orcid.org/0009-0006-2150-8649
Princess Sumaya University for Technology, Jordan

Hatem Mosa
https://orcid.org/0009-0007-4575-3195
Princess Sumaya University for Technology, Jordan

Abdullah Qusef
Princess Sumaya University for Technology, Jordan

Qasem Abu Al-Haija
https://orcid.org/0000-0003-2422-0297
Jordan University of Science and Technology, Jordan

ABSTRACT

Cloud-based software has gained popularity for its scalability, flexibility, and cost savings, but traditional software architectures are not directly applicable to these environments. Challenges such as performance, resiliency, and high availability must be addressed. This chapter proposes a hybrid cloud infrastructure-based approach to designing resilient software architectures. It incorporates new cloud-based services and demonstrates their applicability across various cloud platforms. The approach supports scalability, performance, and innovation in cloud software design while enabling digital transformation. A methodology for testing cloud software resilience is introduced, focusing on workload-based failure analysis and fault injection using internal and external tests. The chapter emphasizes the importance and benefits of

DOI: 10.4018/979-8-3693-9851-7.ch009

integrating robust resilience design into software development.

INTRODUCTION

Cloud computing allows enterprises to start with small resources and increase the resources as required when there is a required demand for the service; this would not have happened without the rapid development of storage and processing technologies as computing overall becomes cheaper and more powerful at the same time. In cloud computing, all resources could be leased in different architectures; the clients lease these resources from the cloud service providers to serve the end user. Large companies such as Google, Amazon, and Microsoft currently provide cloud computing services with much more. Cloud computing is characterized by 1) no upfront investment, 2) lower operating costs, 3) high scalability, 4) easy access, and 5) reduced business risk; however, many disadvantages arise while using cloud environments, such as data ownership legalizations and security issues Zhang et al. (2010). The seed of cloud computing started in the 1960s when John McCarthy envisioned that computing facilities would be provided to the general public like a utility. Cloud computing is considered a new operational model for IT services and infrastructure.

Cloud computing architecture can be segregated into four layers, as shown in Figure 1: the hardware layer, the infrastructure layer, the platforms layer, and the application layer. The first layer is the physical resources of data centers, such as storage devices, CPU units, networking equipment, and cooling systems. The second layer, the virtualization layer, is responsible for virtually partitioning the first layer using different virtualization technologies. The third layer contains the operating systems and frameworks that ease deploying the applications to the virtual machines or containers, and finally, the application layer that holds and accommodates the cloud application itself, which can scale up and down depending on the environment config and client restrictions Zhang et al. (2010).

Figure 1. Cloud computing architecture

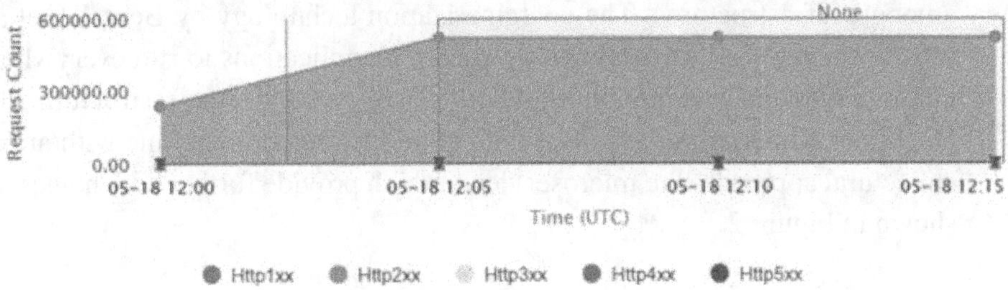

Cloud providers could provide three main categories of services. The first is infrastructure as a service (IaaS), where the IaaS provides the infrastructure only to the client, with no platforms or operating systems running on that infrastructure. Platform as a service (PaaS), where the PaaS providers provide platform layer resources to the clients, such as operating systems and different supportive frameworks that help the clients to deploy, run, and maintain their applications. Finally, Software as a Service, where SaaS provides the final application to the end user that runs on the cloud.

There are three main types of clouds: public, private, and hybrid. Public clouds, where the providers offer their resources to the general public, and private clouds are exclusively used by a certain organization, which ensures the highest degree

of control over performance and security. Hybrid clouds are mixed between public and private clouds. It tries to overcome the challenges and limitations of both types of clouds.

The unique characteristics of the hybrid cloud can be optimally utilized when applying modern, cloud-based software architectures and development methodologies. The cloud enables much faster development and innovation of software development when features like the following are considered early in the development lifecycle of software and services:

- Use of agile development methodologies. Agile enables quick and focused development while producing functionality features rapidly and efficiently. Agile is the recommended development methodology for modern cloud development Younas et al. (2018).
- Use of DevOps, including Continuous Integration and Delivery (CI/CD) Gokarna et al. (2023). This is about using tools that support the development of lifecycle and tools for automated deployment of software products. To benefit from the speed that Agile can reach, it is imperative to have quick and automated deployment and testing of software units.

- Cloud-native architecture and reusability. Since the private and public clouds operate similarly, it is a good idea to create new software that is portable amongst infrastructures. The containerization technology by Bentaleb et al. (2022) enables such capabilities by enabling applications to run everywhere in the cloud on a common, standardized microservice infrastructure like Docker or Kubernetes. Usually, it is a good idea to combine this with an architectural approach like microservices, which provide further advantages, as shown in Figure **2.**

Figure 2. Containerization technology

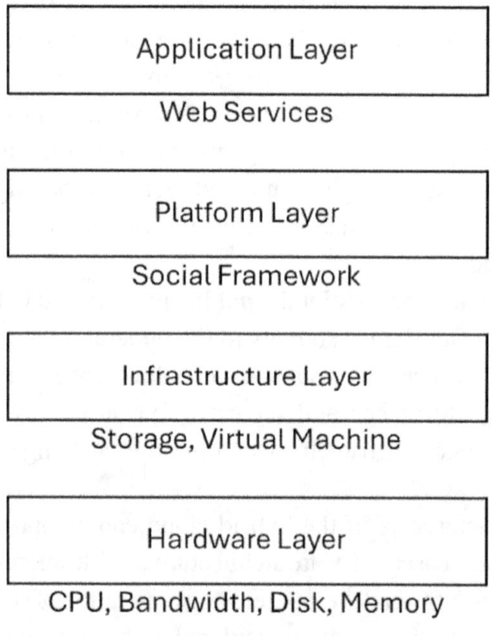

When building resilient software systems, it is vital to follow several basic principles. These principles ensure that the software design is reliable and secure and can endure various outages and disasters. Some key principles should be included in building a resilient cloud-based software architecture using hybrid cloud solutions and trusted public clouds.

1) **Redundancy:** One of the key principles of building resilient software systems is to provide redundancy at all levels. This means at least two copies of critical software components should be deployed, such as artifacts, software components,

etc. If one instance fails, the other takes over without interruption. Redundancy should be implemented both at the hardware level and at the software and data level. Hybrid cloud solutions enable native tools in public clouds.

2) **Geographical Distribution:** Infrastructure should be distributed geographically to ensure greater digital resilience. Critical components should be located in different locations to minimize the physical impacts of attacks, natural disasters, or other local issues. Distributed infrastructure can be implemented through various data centers. This prevents a situation of business continuity or even data loss in the event of failures.
3) **Automation and Orchestration:** Software automation and orchestration are important principles. This includes using tools and technologies that enable the infrastructure's central management, configuration, and management. Automation enables fast and reliable response to outages and efficient deployment and resource scaling when needed. It is important to apply the" infrastructure as a code" principle Artac et al. (2023), which allows fast automatic deployment of the infrastructure, even in another location, and guarantees up-to-date environment documentation.
4) **Data Backup and Recovery:** Security and data protection are critical to a digitally resilient software architecture. Data backups should be performed regularly, and backups should be kept in secure and remote locations. At the same time, it is important to have a plan for data recovery in the event of an outage or disaster that includes recovery testing and ensuring that the data is available quickly.
5) **Security Measures:** Digital Resilient software should be well protected from cyber threats and attacks. This includes implementing security measures at all levels of the software life cycle. Security measures should include data encryption, strong authentication methods, monitoring and threat detection, and regular software updates.
6) **Monitoring and Control:** Regular monitoring and control are essential to manage digital resilient software. This includes monitoring the performance, availability, and security.
7) **Data Encryption:** allows data to be stored in the public cloud in a protected encrypted form. Part of the solution should be key management. This ensures that a secure cloud provider does not access or read the data.

With the hybrid design, we can extend the architecture from public to private environments or private to public, depending on the software's design and deployment approach and products and services. The hybrid approach enables better answers to questions related to special requirements related to data control, data governance, data classification, and data residency, both for regulatory and other purposes.

Over the years, the rise of cloud-based applications got significant attention and adoption in the market. Consequently, assessing the performance of these applications has become increasingly vital. As organizations develop new services and migrate existing ones to cloud providers, there is a growing emphasis on evaluating their performance metrics, including scalability and resilience Amro et al. (2023).

Chaos engineering and Fault injection emerges as a key method for conducting resiliency assessments, enabling the evaluation of fault impacts on the quality of cloud-based applications Guo et al. (2016). While many studies have concentrated on fault injection at the infrastructure as a service (IaaS) and platform as a service (PaaS) levels, there has been relatively less focus on application-level fault injection, which the researchers will target in this chapter.

Application-level fault injection (ALFI) in Figure 3 is a crucial technique for examining the resilience of cloud-based applications against faults. Our study aims to simulate and quantify the scalability performance and resilience of cloud-based applications hosted on the Microsoft Azure platform. Leveraging fault injection tools alongside workload generators, we seek comprehensive insights into how these applications respond to various fault scenarios. ALFI is one of the most popular methods for examining an application's resilience to faults Sheridan et al. (2016). By testing an application's resilience and determining how it handles random instance failures, it experiments with the ability of software systems to withstand unanticipated failures.

Figure 3. Web application-level fault injection (Amro et al., 2022)

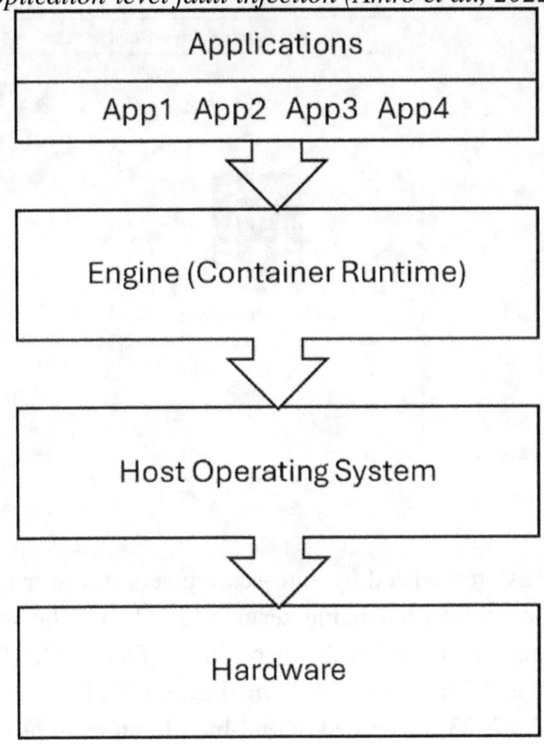

The fault injection approach is a useful tool for assessing performance and scalability and the impact of faults on quality-related aspects of cloud-based software services, including security, scalability, and performance Guo et al. (2016). Additionally, the dependability and reliability of cloud-based software systems have been examined via fault injection.

Application-level fault injection, as seen in Figure 4, aids in assessing how well an application reacts to simulated errors. The resilience of a cloud-based software service and how its scalability behavior is affected in fault scenarios can be determined by comparing its scalability performance following fault-injection tests with its performance under typical workload conditions. Using fault injection tools entails injecting faults into an application running in the cloud to simulate possible application-level issues and evaluate their impact on behavior, scalability, and resilience. Usually, fault injection entails adding delay latency during runtime to the software service. Other issues, such as adding latency/bandwidth, HTTP traffic, database traffic, or terminating requests at the application level, can also be considered to determine their real effect on scalability resilience and impact.

Figure 4. Fault injection system

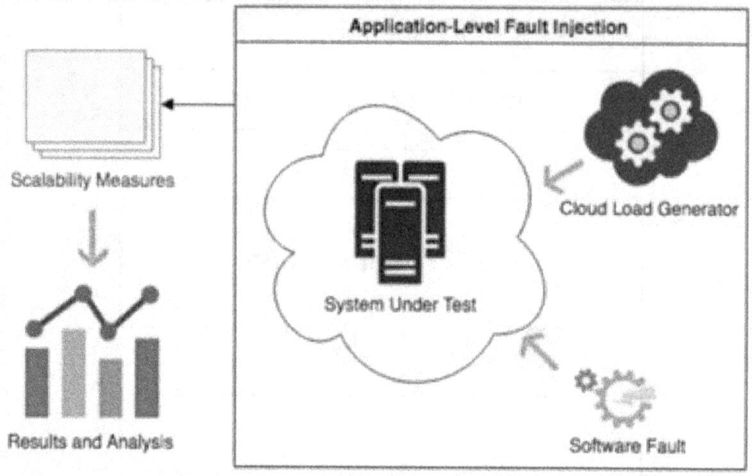

Software services are assisted by auto-scaling services to handle irregular demands. Furthermore, a load-balancing service establishes the software services' fault tolerance by guaranteeing that the incoming application traffic is split among several application scalability Al-Said Ahmad et al. (2022).

As Alonso et al. (2023) described, cloud-based applications comprise loosely coupled and deployed services built upon cloud infrastructure and services. These applications often adhere to principles such as microservices architecture, APIs, and infrastructure as code, as Alnafessah et al. (2021) outlined. This architectural approach enables cloud-based applications to exhibit scalability and resilience, facilitated by the innovative software solutions offered by cloud platforms.

Scalability and resilience, as emphasized by Muhammad et al. (2022), are dispensable concepts in software development, particularly in response to the growing demand for highly available applications. Scalability ensures that cloud-based applications can adeptly manage varying workloads, while resilience guarantees continuous operation despite infrastructure failures, as elucidated by Amro et al. (2022). As highlighted by Zhang et al. (2022), cloud-native architecture provides numerous advantages for scalability and resilience. Individual components of the application can dynamically scale to accommodate fluctuating workloads. Additionally, cloud platforms offer built-in features such as load balancing and fault tolerance, further enhancing application resilience and reliability.

I. BACKGROUND AND RELATED WORK

Previous studies on scalability analysis of cloud-based software services provide a baseline of the scalability behavior of such services. Regarding fault injections, recent survey studies have focused on assessing fault tolerance in cloud computing using fault injection techniques. In their work, Al-Said Ahmad et al. (2022) delve deeper into this area, specifically investigating the impact of faults on the scalability and resilience of cloud-based software services through Application-level Fault Injection (ALFI). Their study entails an experimental evaluation conducted on the EC2 cloud infrastructure, employing a real-world cloud-based application. Through their proposed approach, the authors aim to comprehensively assess the effects of fault scenarios on cloud software services' scalability and resilience.

Henning et al. (2022) sought to address the challenge posed by the lack of widely accepted methodologies for benchmarking the scalability of cloud-native applications. Their work introduces a novel benchmarking approach comprising scalability metrics, measurement methodologies, and an architectural framework tailored for scalability benchmarking tools tailored to cloud-native applications. Through isolated experiments involving various loads and resource configurations, the authors aim to pinpoint the thresholds at which service level objectives (SLOs) are met. The benchmarking implementation utilized two stream processing technologies, Kafka Streams and Flink, across public and private cloud environments.

The authors of Latha et al. (2022) concentrate on performance evaluation and testing for cloud-based services to support service level agreements (SLAs). They propose leveraging Token Bucket to enhance the efficiency of cloud-based service performance and bolster the availability and scalability of distributed systems. The experimental setup is based on Spring Cloud and utilizes Zuul as the gateway. The authors devise a mechanism to safeguard against token overuse by employing a URL configuration file to filter incoming requests before they are granted tokens. The study aims to provide insights into the quality of service delivered by assessing scalability and availability. However, it is worth noting that the contribution of this chapter is somewhat constrained by its focus on specific platforms and gateways.

The paper by Henning et al. (2021) endeavors to assess the scalability of distributed systems, focusing on specific stream processing engines. It addresses the challenge posed by the lack of precise definitions and metrics for scalability. The authors propose two matrices to tackle this issue: a load capacity function and a resource demand function. They aim to enhance the effectiveness and efficiency of utilizing these matrices to evaluate systems' scalability in distributed environments. It is important to note that the scope of the paper is confined to the domain of stream processing engines.

The authors of Bulla et al. (2020) explore strategies for establishing an efficient infrastructure capable of scaling with minimal resource allocation to meet requests. Their approach hinges on an analytical model forecasting the required number of servers to achieve desired throughput and utilization levels in cloud data centers. The authors conduct experiments on the AWS cloud platform to validate their analytical model. The paper aims to develop a reliable analytical framework for estimating resource requirements in cloud-based systems, enabling them to scale in response to evolving demands dynamically.

In their 2019 publication, Barkaoui et al. (2019) endeavor to develop a practical analytical framework for computing elasticity in cloud computing environments. They aim to balance cloud resource utilization and service quality, ensuring optimal performance. To address this challenge, the authors introduce a solution founded on a Markovian queuing model, wherein the number of active servers dynamically adjusts based on workload changes. Through quantitative analysis, the authors assess the stability of their model and calculate elasticity values to measure its accuracy and effectiveness.

Their study by Amro et al. (2018) concentrated on testing and measuring the scalability of cloud-based software services in technical terms. The authors utilized technical scalability metrics to tackle issues related to volume and quality scaling, demonstrating the application of these metrics through practical examples. Their research emphasized the importance of measuring the scalability performance of such services to gather accurate measurements and establish specific metrics, including technical evaluation metrics and infrastructure-monitoring metrics.

Brataas et al. (2017) introduced two scalability metrics that revolve around the cloud environment's quality threshold and resource space in their work. The first metric, response scalability, outlines the correlation between the multi-tier cloud software service's capacity and infrastructure. Meanwhile, the second metric, cost scalability, substitutes cloud resources with cost considerations. To validate these proposed scalability metrics, the authors utilized a Store application representing an online bookstore hosted on various public Amazon Web Services instances and two private OpenStack configurations, totaling more than 21 deployments.

Research on scalability and resilience testing for cloud-based services using fault injection has been scarce, except for Amro et al. (2022), which was confined to Amazon services. Our contribution aims to fill this gap by simulating the four primary components—workload generator, software fault, scalability measures, and the system under test and its environment—utilizing another major cloud provider, Microsoft Azure.

II. METHODOLOGY

Our methodology measures the effect of fault injection and workloads in web-based applications hosted on a hybrid cloud using Microsoft Azure services. To accomplish this, researchers have to build testing environments, testing scripts, and specific tools and applications.

A. Resiliency Assessment Using Chaos Engineering and Fault Injection

Microsoft Azure is a cloud computing platform that provides many services without purchasing premises hardware; this enables the development of solutions and provides hard and challenging resources in an on-premises environment. Azure accomplishes this by leasing the infrastructure, such as network storage and CPU computation, required to implement cloud-based applications Collier et al. (2015)

Azure Chaos Studio is a managed service that uses chaos engineering methodology to measure and understand the resilience of cloud applications by injecting real-world faults into the application and running experiments. Resilience is the capability of the system to handle and recover from disruption caused by different reasons that may cause issues and failure; through Azure Chaos Studio, researchers were able to test the resilience against those incidents Prasha-Microsoft, (2023). Azure Chaos Studio supports different types of faults, service-direct and agent-based; the first type runs directly against Azure resources, such as Azure cache for Redis clusters, and the second type, which will be used in our experiment, runs in the virtual machines sets such as memory pressures and killing processes.

B. Resilient Hybrid Cloud-Based Software Architecture

To successfully implement cloud-based, we use cloud-adoption architecture as a full lifecycle framework that enables software engineers and decision-makers to achieve their cloud-adoption goals. Framework provides best practices, documentation, and tools that help create and implement solid cloud-based software design. The design starts with the **Planning phase**, where we create a roadmap and align software sign outcomes to actionable technology backlogs, skilling, and adoption plans. It is the phase during which we create adoption plans. Next is the **Ready phase**, where an appropriate environment is set up for software maintenance, change, and continuous development and integration. The final phase is **the adoption phase**. This is the phase during which the developed software is migrated to the cloud based on the roadmap created during the planning phase. The roadmap defines the sequence in which software is migrated and how each is migrated. Many software can be migrated as-is or with minor changes (lift- and shift migration), while others need small or big changes. There are cases where the workload needs to be completely refactored to take advantage of the cloud.

In the proposed approach, we have used the landing zone environment, which is an environment that follows some key design principles. These design principles adapt the software collections and enable software migration, modernization, and integration at scale. The landing zone architecture is scalable and acts as a bridge to deliver the software into the hybrid cloud to meet the deployment needs.

1) ***Planning Phase***: In this phase, the cloud-specific requirements such as scalability, cost-effectiveness, and multi-tenancy were identified early. Also, cloud service models (IaaS, PaaS, SaaS) that best fit the project's needs have been identified. Decisions on microservices or monolithic architectures, serverless computing, and the use of containers are taken.
2) ***Ready Pilot Phase:*** An important aspect of cloud-based software planning, deployment, and usage is understanding how future architecture should work for them in different usage scenarios and the proper or most recommended way to start with the cloud services. Here, we propose and explain the role of specific steps that need to be aligned and taken into consideration when designing proper cloud-based software architecture:
    - Organize Resources: Set up a management hierarchy to consistently apply access control, policy, and compliance to groups of resources and use tagging to track related software and artifacts resources.
    - Manage Access: Use role-based access control to ensure that users only have permission to access the resources that enable specific functionality or capability. Strict control not only enables proper security strength but also enables better cost and usage management.
    - Manage Costs and Billing: Identify the subscription type, understand how billing works, and learn how to control costs. This is mandatory for properly managing resources. Keep costs as predicted and manage overage according to the spending policy.
    - Plan for Governance, Security, and Compliance: Enforce and automate policies and security settings that help you follow applicable legal, audit, and control requirements as defined in security and compliance policies of the Government or Government entities.
    - Use Monitoring and Reporting: Get visibility across resources to find and fix problems, optimize performance, and gain insight into the software behavior. Integrate monitoring and reporting to existing tools or develop a new capability that integrates new hybrid infrastructure.

- Stay Current: Track product updates to enable a proactive approach to change management, including security and feature updates. Cloud platforms usually release updated or new functionality and change frequently.
- Landing Zones: Define and execute the core concept utilized in a multi-cloud environment (Hybrid approach) that accounts for scale. Landing zone enables software migration, modernization, and innovation at a resilient, secure scale in any cloud.

3) ***Adoption Phase:*** The main goal is to migrate existing software applications and artifacts to a cloud environment. Its purpose is to ensure software performance and scalability. Different approaches are used during the Adoption Phase based on the needs:
    - Lift-and-Shift (Rehosting): Migrating software without modifications.
    - Replatforming: Making minor modifications to leverage cloud efficiencies.
    - Refactoring: Repairing software to use fully cloud-native features.
    - Rebuilding: Redesigning and re-coding applications from scratch.
    - Retirement (Decommission): Removing outdated or unnecessary software.

The Landing Zone is a pre-configured environment within the cloud designed to facilitate software' secure and scalable deployment. It plays a critical role in the Adoption Phase:

- Preparation and Configuration
- Software transfer Execution: The initial software deployment environment supports various migration strategies through its flexible and scalable infrastructure.
- Integration and Testing: Offers a controlled setting for application testing post-migration, ensuring software performs as expected under cloud conditions.

The process follows a detailed roadmap created during the Planning Phase. Exact testing in the Landing Zone ensures that developed software meets performance, security, and compliance requirements.

Figure 5. Resilient hybrid cloud-based software architecture

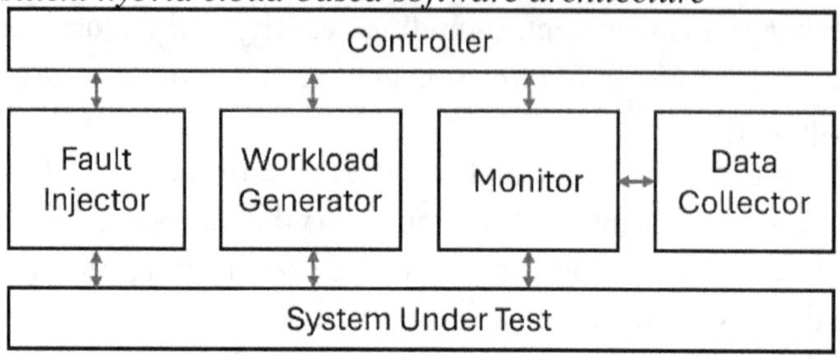

C. Using Microservices-Oriented Architecture

In an architecture based on microservices and containers, software is designed and built as a collection of small, loosely coupled services running within its container. Here is how this architecture works:

- **Microservices Design:** In microservices architecture, the software is divided into individual services, each responsible for a specific functionality or business capability. These services are designed to be independent, with their own codebase, data storage, and communication mechanisms.
- **Containerization:** Each microservice is packaged as a lightweight, self-contained unit using containerization technology, such as Docker. Containers provide isolation, portability, and consistency, allowing services to run consistently across different environments, such as development, testing, and production.
- **Orchestration:** An orchestration framework like Kubernetes is commonly used to manage and deploy the containers. Kubernetes automates container deployment, scaling, and management, ensuring that each microservice's desired number of instances runs and distributes the load evenly.
- **Service Discovery:** Services in a microservices architecture need a way to discover and communicate with each other. Service discovery mechanisms, such as Kubernetes' built-in service discovery or tools like Consul or Eureka, provide a centralized registry where services can register and discover each other dynamically.
- **Communication between Services:** Microservices communicate with each other over lightweight protocols, typically using RESTful APIs or message queues. Each service exposes a well-defined API that other services can use to interact with and exchange data. This enables loose coupling between services, allowing them to evolve independently.

- **Scalability and Load Balancing:** As containerized microservices can be horizontally scaled, the orchestration framework handles the scaling based on demand. It can automatically adjust the number of instances of a particular microservice to handle increased traffic, distributing the load across multiple instances for better performance and resilience.
- **Resilience and Fault Isolation:** The isolation provided by containers ensures that failures in one microservice do not affect the entire application. If a particular service fails, the remaining services can continue to operate independently, minimizing the impact on the overall system. Services can also be designed to handle failure scenarios gracefully by implementing retry mechanisms, circuit breakers, and fallback strategies.
- **DevOps and Continuous Delivery:** Microservices and containers align well with DevOps practices, enabling teams to deploy updates and new features more frequently and reliably. Continuous integration and continuous deployment (CI/CD) pipelines can be established to automate containerized microservices' building, testing, and deployment, ensuring a streamlined and efficient development workflow.
- **Observability and Monitoring:** Monitoring and observability are crucial in microservice architecture. Log- ging, metrics, and distributed tracing tools are used to gain insights into the behavior and performance of individual microservices and their interactions. This helps in troubleshooting, identifying bottlenecks, and optimizing the overall system.

Organizations can achieve greater scalability, flexibility, and resilience by adopting microservices and containers architecture. It allows for independent development, deployment, and scaling of services, promoting faster innovation and enabling teams to focus on specific business functionalities. However, this architecture also challenges managing the complexity of multiple services, ensuring proper service coordination, and implementing robust testing and deployment processes. The methodology focuses on evaluating the resiliency and performance of the proposed approaches by measuring and assessing the impact of injected faults on the scalability of cloud-based software services over an extended period without causing the application to crash at runtime. This approach consists of four main components: workload generator, software fault, scalability measures, and the system under test and its environment. Workload requests that represent the real usage of services are replicated by a workload generator such as JMeter. A standardized range of challenges, including adding latency or bandwidth, altering HTTP and database traffic, or stopping requests, can be attributed to software faults. The criteria used to evaluate the scalability of cloud-based software services are known as scalability measures. The system being tested, as well as its environment, should be considered last. The first stage is preparing the workload scenario, scalability measures, and the system under test and its environment; the second stage is preparing the set of the software fault(s) injected with the workload on the system under test.

We utilize the Apache JMeter script to simulate various demand scenarios. This enables us to easily deploy test scripts using our Azure account and repeat tests without resetting the parameters. Furthermore, it allows systematic extraction of data. Additionally, we use Postman software to test workload and fault injection scenarios before deploying them to JMeter. The JMeter enables the system to be targeted under test using a simple HTTP/HTTPS request. It also can parse HTML web pages to retrieve images and other embedded resources within the web response, such as scripts, and sends HTTP retrieval requests.

III. SIMULATION RESULTS AND DISCUSSION

A. Environment Setup

To move forward with the simulation phase, researchers prepared a work environment to run the experiments. Our cloud environment was based on Microsoft Azure, which runs on a Linux operating system and a Nginx web server. WordPress version 6.4.4 was installed to demonstrate the web application, and it is based on the PostgreSQL database; based on an experiment done by Patel et al. (2011), WordPress achieved the best scores among other popular Content Management Systems (CMS) such as Joomla and Drupal.

B. HTTP Methods External Tests

1) *Workload Test:* Using JMeter Version 5.6.3, the workload tests have been implemented in our Cloud-based testing environment. The initial configuration for JMeter was 1000 threads (users) with a ramp-up period of 5 seconds; this indicates that 1000 users will be on the targeted URL at the same time within 5 seconds only.

The assertation for a Valid response was measured by having the sentence "Software Engineering Project" evaluated in the response text, plus having the HTTP code of 200 as a response back; invalid responses were detecting a response other than 200, such as 404 or 50X, which indicated the certain type of errors from the server.

Figure 6 shows the increase of both the latency and connection time while establishing the requests; connection times refer to the time taken to establish a connection with the server, the handshake, and the time the server takes to set up the connection. However, latency refers to a request's time to reach the server and the response time to travel back. This will include the time the server takes to process the request and send it back; it is also affected by the network transit time.

Figure 6. GET method results

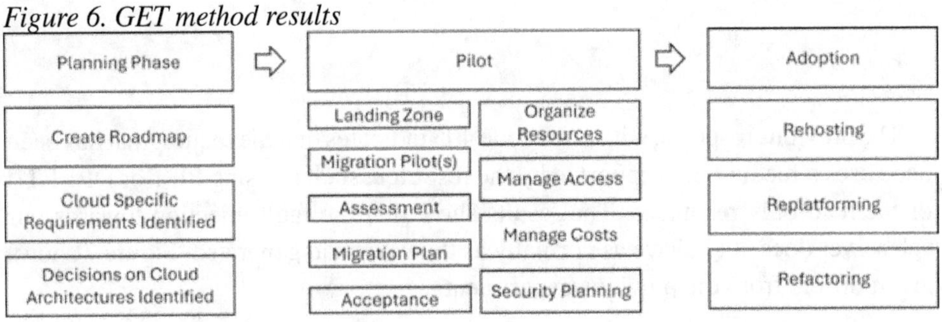

It is important to mention that firewalls were turned off not to block the server's incoming traffic and to keep the traffic flowing smoothly. Out of 1000 requests, the first 937 were completed successfully with the continuous increase of latency and connection time; however, the first error happened on thread 938 until 1000; out of those 62 remaining threads, only four requests ended with success. The latency time is always longer than the connection time because of the network transmission time.

2) *Fault Injection Test:* The second experiment demonstrates handling fault injection threads; in the previous test, we sent normal GET HTTP requests to the server; however, in this experiment, we will target other types of requests that let the web server return errors, such as DELETE or PUT requests. To accomplish this, we have first tested the web server response by sending both PUT and DELETE requests; in both cases, the web server returns the following response

```
<html>

<head><title>405 Not Allowed</title></head>

<body>

<center><h1>405 Not Allowed</h1></center>
```

```
<hr><center>nginx</center>

</body>

</html>
```

The previous response with error code 405 indicates that the request that has been made uses a method not supported by the resource, such as using PUT or DELETE for the read-only resources. The results show that the fault injection towards our web server does not behave as normally as the workload generated. Figure 7 shows how it differs from the previous experiment.

Figure 7. PUT method results

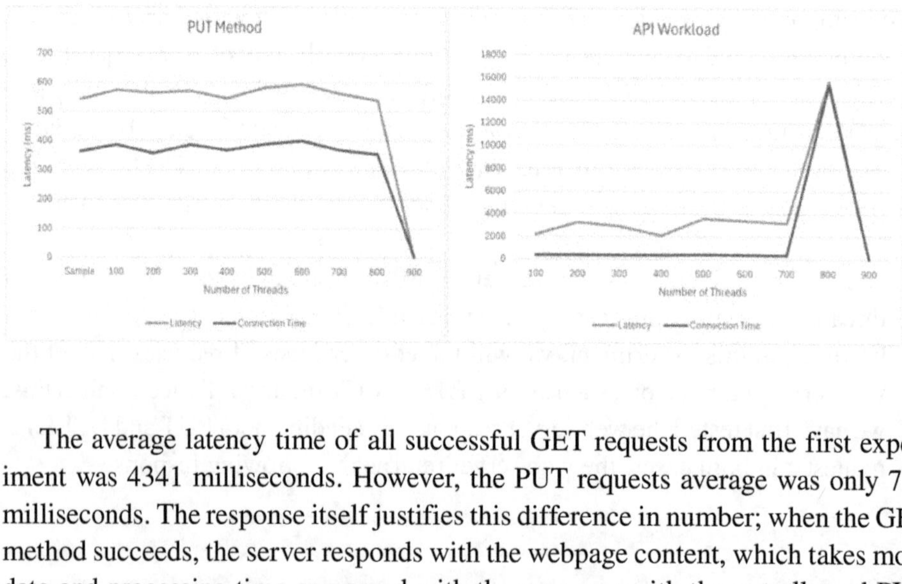

The average latency time of all successful GET requests from the first experiment was 4341 milliseconds. However, the PUT requests average was only 737 milliseconds. The response itself justifies this difference in number; when the GET method succeeds, the server responds with the webpage content, which takes more data and processing time compared with the response with the not-allowed PUT method, which takes less data, which means less processing time and less transmission time. The server returned, on average, a response of 371 bytes on the PUT method and 55,500 bytes for the successful GET method. Table 1 compares the workload response and the fault injection response.

C. API Requests External Tests

Fault Injection Test: To test the web application behavior towards the injected fault, we sent the same previous API without associating the content and title parameters with the URL because both are mandatory. Consequently, the creation of the blog post failed, and the following error returned from the web server; Figure 9 reflects the results regarding both latency and connection time. In this API external test, researchers have tested a different methodology by trying to test API requests using the original API in WordPress. The tested API creates a new post in the blog section; thus, connecting to the DB and inserting a new row will be executed for every thread.

Figure 8. API workload results

```
curl --location --request POST 'https://
    ↪ psutwebapp.azurewebsites.net/wp-json
    ↪ /wp/v2/posts?content=TEST&title=TEST
    ↪ ' \
--header 'Authorization: Basic TEST'
```

```
    "code": "empty_content",
    "message": "Content, title, and excerpt
        ↪ are empty.",
    "data": {
        "status": 400
    }
```

Figure 9. API fault injection

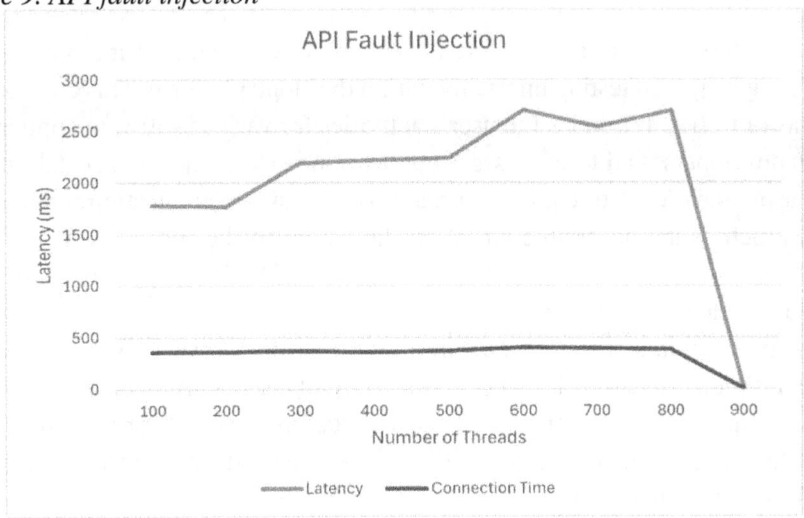

To simulate both valid workload and fault injection, we depend on adding a new blog post API request; the API shall be called using POST HTTP request, containing the authentication mechanism and the blog title and blog content as URL parameters.

Workload Test:Figure 8 represents the workload test results; at this test, we created 1000 post blogs using the related API, and the triggered API requests were fully correct with no errors. However, not all the 1000 requests were completed successfully. Comparing the results from the HTTP Requests external tests and the API Requests External tests indicate that both tests behave nearly the same in terms of fault injection; the web application latency and connection time don't spike; instead, they keep steady and then crash at once, and the server stopped responding. This must be because the response of fault infections doesn't increase a heavy load on the server side to process them, and the response size is much smaller than the valid requests.

Table 1. GET & PUT methods compared

Method	**Average Latency (ms)**	**Average Connection Time (ms)**	**Average Response Size (bytes)**	**Success Threads**
GET Method	4,341	4,843	55,500	941
PUT Method	737	743	371	991

D. Internal Tests

Researchers have tested a different methodology in the API internal tests by conducting workload testing internally within the cloud platform. This creates large amounts of traffic. It mimics the user's activities for various software applications to help developers, and testers assess application performance and scalability but from the platform level to acquire information regarding the application components. Various metrics are accessible based on the nature of the service being utilized. These metrics may pertain to database read counts, HTTP response characteristics, or the utilization of resources.

A virtual user independently conducts a test case on a server application in these tests. Multiple virtual users have been used to simulate concurrent connections. The thread group element specifies the pool of virtual users in JMeter documentation. The virtual users in the test script and the test engine instances determine the total virtual users for a load test.

The formula for total virtual users is (virtual users in JMX file) * (number of test engine instances). The latency of an individual request represents the comprehensive duration from right before dispatching the request to immediately after the initial response is obtained. Latency includes all the processing required for request assembly and the initial part of response compilation.

Requests per second (RPS), or throughput, represents the overall quantity of requests directed to the server application by your load test on a per-second basis. The time frame is computed from the initial sample's initiation to the final sample's conclusion, encompassing any intervals between samples, such as timers existing within the test script. For instance, with an application latency of 20 milliseconds (0.02 seconds), aiming to emulate 100,000 RPS requires configuring the load test with 2,000 virtual users (100,000 * 0.02). Figure 12 shows the availability of the web app during the loading test with high availability.

Table 2 shows the internal workload experiment metrics run for 20 minutes. The server and client sides' performance metrics are shown in Figures 10 and 11, respectively.

Figure 10. Internal server-side workload results

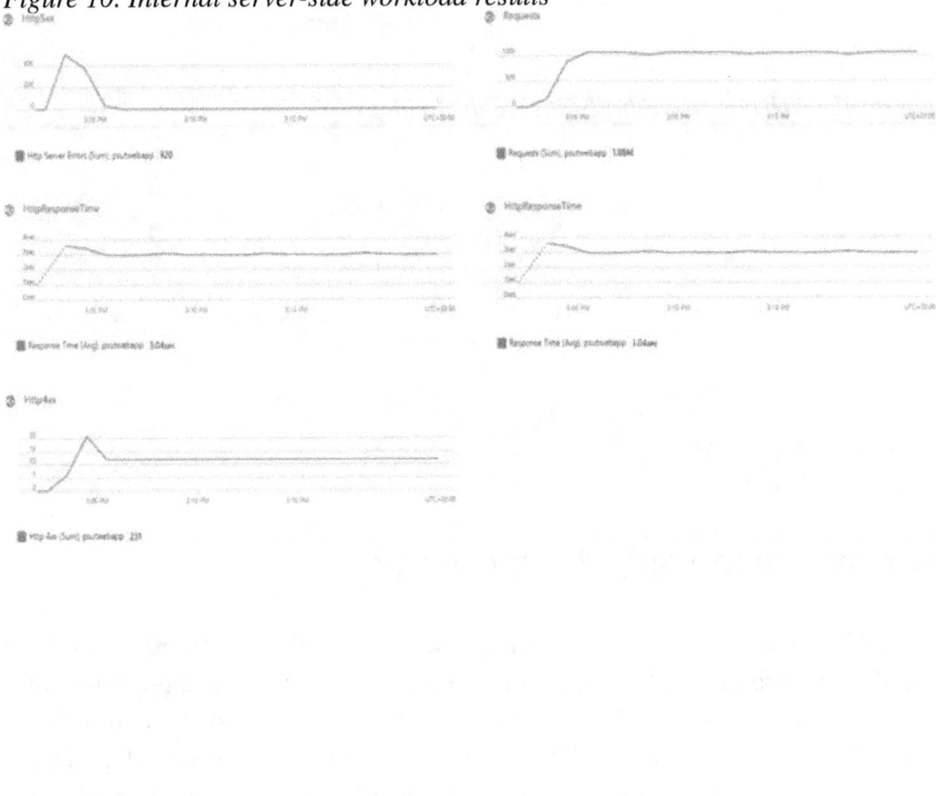

Figure 11. Internal client-side workload results

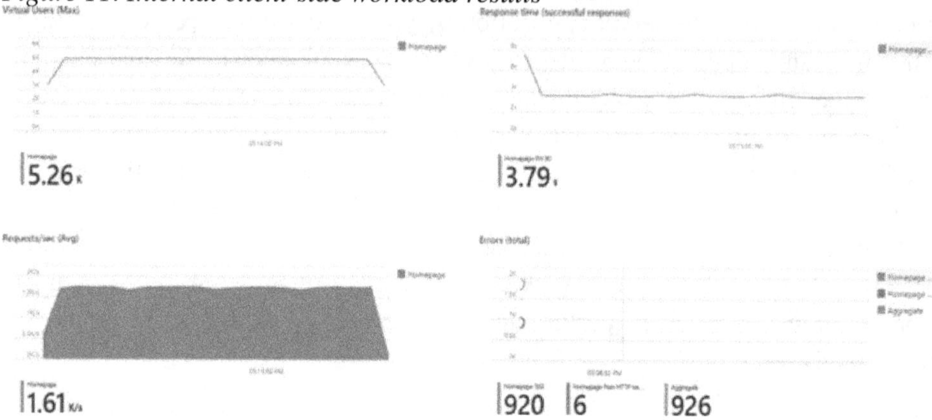

Figure 12. Web app availability during the load test

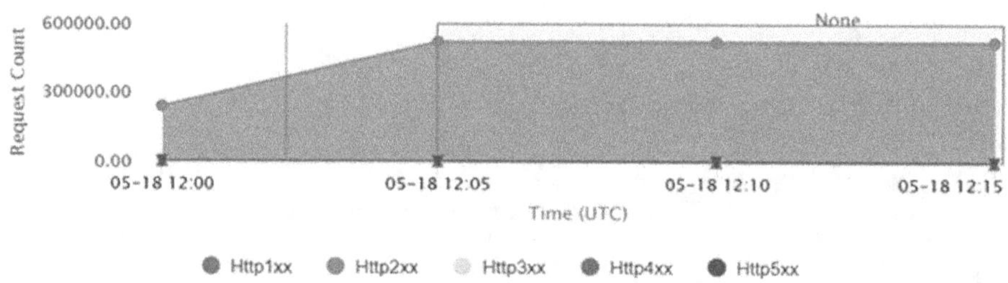

IV. CONCLUSION AND FUTURE WORK

In this research chapter, the researchers proposed a resilient software architecture based on the hybrid cloud infrastructure approach, which aims to improve the software resiliency usability and practicality, adding several new cloud-based services driven by the criticality and need for high resilience and performance. Cloud-based software architecture has been put under several tests for scalability and resiliency; the authors conducted multiple experiments to test a web application using different techniques, using both normal workload tests and fault injection tests in internal and external environments. The experiments aim to discuss the results and differences between those scenarios. The results concluded that different response behaviors were observed regarding normal workload and fault injection. In both cases, the web application showed a different rhythm of reactions. The researchers believe that the difference in behavior is directly related to the load on the server for each request made. At the same time, the normal workload needs extra work from the cloud server compared to the faulty injections, which require small process units to respond quickly. For future work, the researchers aim to enhance this area by conducting more experiments using web applications other than WordPress, which may provide different results as WordPress is based on PHP, MYSQL Database, and Nginx server.

Table 2. Summary of load test results

Metric	Value	Metric	Value
Load	2.03 M	Duration	20 mins, 4 secs
Average Response Time	3.62 secs	90th Percentile Response Time	3.79 secs
Error Percentage	0.05%	Errors (Total)	926
Throughput	1682.33 requests/s	Requests/sec (Avg) Homepage	1.61K/s
Virtual Users (Max)	5.26K	Homepage Non-HTTP Response	java.net.SocketException: 6

REFERENCES

Ahmad, A. A.-S., & Andras, P. (2018). Measuring and testing the scalability of cloud-based software services. *2018 Fifth International Symposium on Innovation in Information and Communication Technology (ISIICT)*, 1–8. IEEE.

Ahmad, A. A.-S., & Andras, P. (2022). Scalability resilience framework using application-level fault injection for cloud-based software services. *Journal of Cloud Computing (Heidelberg, Germany)*, *11*(1), 1. Advance online publication. DOI: 10.1186/s13677-021-00277-z

Ahmad, A. A.-S., & Andras, P. (2022, December). Scalability resilience framework using application-level fault injection for cloud-based software services. *Journal of Cloud Computing (Heidelberg, Germany)*, *11*(1), 1. https://journalofcloudcomputing.springeropen.com/articles/10.1186/s13677-021-00277-z. DOI: 10.1186/s13677-021-00277-z

Alnafessah, A., Gias, A. U., Wang, R., Zhu, L., Casale, G., & Filieri, A. (2021). Quality-aware DevOps research: Where do we stand? *IEEE Access : Practical Innovations, Open Solutions*, *9*, 44476–44489. DOI: 10.1109/ACCESS.2021.3064867

Alonso, J., Orue-Echevarria, L., Casola, V., Torre, A. I., Huarte, M., Osaba, E., & Lobo, J. L. (2023). Understanding the challenges and novel architectural models of multi-cloud native applications–A systematic literature review. *Journal of Cloud Computing (Heidelberg, Germany)*, *12*(1), 1–34. DOI: 10.1186/s13677-022-00367-6

Artac, M., ... (2017). DevOps: Introducing infrastructure-as-code. 2017 IEEE/ACM 39th International Conference on Software Engineering Companion (ICSE-C), 497–498. IEEE.

Barkaoui, K., Outamazirt, A., & Aissani, D. (2019). A new analytical model for calculating elasticity in cloud computing. MSR 2019-12ème Colloque sur la Modélisation des Systèmes Réactifs.

Bentaleb, O., Belloum, A. S. Z., Sebaa, A., & El-Maouhab, A. (2022). Containerization technologies: Taxonomies, applications and challenges. *The Journal of Supercomputing*, *78*(1), 1144–1181. DOI: 10.1007/s11227-021-03914-1

Brataas, G.. (2017). Scalability analysis of cloud software services. *2017 IEEE International Conference on Autonomic Computing (ICAC)*, 285–292. IEEE. DOI: 10.1109/ICAC.2017.34

Bulla, S., Reddy, C. V. R., Padmavathi, P., & Padmasri, T. (2020). Analytical evaluation of resource estimation in web application services. *Ingénierie des Systèmes d'Information, 25*(5), 683–690. DOI: 10.18280/isi.250516

Collier, M., & Shahan, R. (2015). *Microsoft Azure essentials—Fundamentals of Azure*. Microsoft Press.

Gokarna, M. (2023). DevOps phases across software development lifecycle. *Authorea Preprints.*

Guo, L., Liang, J., & Li, D. (2016). Understanding ineffectiveness of the application-level fault injection. Poster in ACM/IEEE International Conference for High Performance Computing, Networking, Storage and Analysis (SC).

Henning, S., & Hasselbring, W. (2021). How to measure scalability of distributed stream processing engines? Companion of the ACM/SPEC International Conference on Performance Engineering (ICPE '21), 85–88. Association for Computing Machinery. DOI: 10.1145/3447545.3451190

Henning, S., & Hasselbring, W. (2022). A configurable method for benchmarking scalability of cloud-native applications. *Empirical Software Engineering*, *27*(6), 143. DOI: 10.1007/s10664-022-10162-1

Huber, N., Brosig, F., & Dingle, N.. (2012). Providing dependability and performance in the cloud: Case studies. In Katinka, W. (Eds.), *Resilience assessment and evaluation of computing systems* (pp. 391–412). DOI: 10.1007/978-3-642-29032-9_19

Latha, V. P., Reddy, N. S., & Babu, A. S. (2022). On optimizing scalability and availability of cloud-based software services using scale rate limiting algorithm. Theoretical Computer Science. https://api.semanticscholar.org/CorpusID:251079287

Muhammad, T. (2022). A comprehensive study on software-defined load balancers: Architectural flexibility & application service delivery in on-premises ecosystems. *International Journal of Computer Science and Technology*, *6*(1), 1–24.

Patel, S. K., Rathod, V. R., & Parikh, S. (2011). Joomla, Drupal, and WordPress—A statistical comparison of open source CMS. *3rd International Conference on Trendz in Information Sciences & Computing (TISC2011)*, 182–187. DOI: 10.1109/TISC.2011.6169111

Prasha Microsoft. (2023, June). What is Azure Chaos Studio? Microsoft Learn. https://learn.microsoft.com/en-us/azure/chaos-studio/chaos-studio-overview

Shadabfar, M., Mahsuli, M., Zhang, Y., Xue, Y., Ayyub, B. M., Huang, H., & Medina, R. A. (2022). Resilience-based design of infrastructure: Review of models, methodologies, and computational tools. *ASCE-ASME Journal of Risk and Uncertainty in Engineering Systems. Part A, Civil Engineering*, *8*(1), 03121004. DOI: 10.1061/AJRUA6.0001184

Sheridan, C., & Whigham, D., & Artacˇ, M. (2016). DICE fault injection tool. Proceedings of the 2nd International Workshop on Quality-Aware DevOps (pp. 36–37). ACM. DOI: 10.1145/2945408.2945415

Younas, M., Jawawi, D. N. A., Ghani, I., Fries, T., & Kazmi, R. (2018). Agile development in the cloud computing environment: A systematic review. *Information and Software Technology*, *103*, 142–158. DOI: 10.1016/j.infsof.2018.06.014

Zhang, Q., Cheng, L., & Boutaba, R. (2010). Cloud computing: State-of-the-art and research challenges. *Journal of Internet Services and Applications*, *1*(1), 7–18. DOI: 10.1007/s13174-010-0007-6

Zhang, S., Pandey, A., Luo, X., Powell, M., Banerji, R., Fan, L., Parchure, A., & Luzcando, E. (2022). Practical adoption of cloud computing in power systems—Drivers, challenges, guidance, and real-world use cases. *IEEE Transactions on Smart Grid*, *13*(3), 2390–2411. DOI: 10.1109/TSG.2022.3148978

Chapter 10
Computing Technologies for Healthcare IoT Software Systems

Mahmoud M. Hammad
https://orcid.org/0000-0003-2891-0463
Ajman University, UAE & Jordan University of Science and Technology, Jordan

Sajeda Banat
https://orcid.org/0009-0003-1653-6707
Jordan University of Science and Technology, Jordan

Qanita Bani Baker
https://orcid.org/0000-0003-4722-6632
Jordan University of Science and Technology, Jordan

Mohammed Al-Refai
https://orcid.org/0000-0001-7297-7695
Jordan University of Science and Technology, Jordan

Bara'a Mohammed Abudehais
Jordan University of Science and Technology, Jordan

Salma Suleiman
Jordan University of Science and Technology, Jordan

ABSTRACT

Cloud computing technology significantly emerged in various systems to enhance the platform and infrastructure of services. Fog and Edge computing technologies transform computing power and processing close to the end-user and resolve many data processing challenges. Healthcare IoT systems refer to using medical sensors and mobile computing to manage patients' conditions and use cloud-based technologies to transfer collected patients' data to the cloud computing storage. Many previous research efforts focused on the use of edge, fog, and cloud computing technologies in the field of healthcare IoT systems. However, no previous research study summarized the main research topics and trends in these research efforts. To

DOI: 10.4018/979-8-3693-9851-7.ch010

that end, we conducted a systematic and comprehensive empirical research study to understand the main research topics and the employed computing technologies and trends in these research topics. This study investigated 100 research studies focusing on cloud-based technologies in the field of healthcare IoT systems published in highly reputable venues over the past decade.

1.1 HEALTHCARE IOT SOFTWARE SYSTEMS

Internet of Things (IoT) is growing in many daily life sectors. According to newly published research by Statista Holst, 2021, the number of IoT devices will grow to 25.44 billion devices in 2030 compared to 2019. The number of currently active IoT devices is 7.74 billion devices. IoT is essentially defined as a network of connected smart devices everywhere that are expanded to apply many tasks such as healthcare monitoring, environmental sensing, industrial task processing, and various smart city applications (Rahmani, Gia, et al., 2018). The most important core technology in IoT is Wireless Sensor Networks (WSNs) and the major technology used in the healthcare IoT system is the Body Sensor Networks (BSNs). BSN is defined as a collection of sensors that are deployed around and inside the patient body (Hossain and Muhammad, 2016).

Cloud computing aims to provide flexible resources and deployment facilities at a lower cost compared to on premises applications. In addition, cloud-based computing provides high availability features which means that the data can be accessed anywhere, anytime by providing both applications and data storage services over the Internet (Manogaran et al., 2018). Due to the ubiquitous of Information and Communication Technology (ICT) in the healthcare field, healthcare resources are enhanced and utilized widely by enhancing the quality of healthcare through instructing healthcare professionals and improving the safety of the patients by monitoring the online treatment (Fanjiang et al., 2005). Healthcare IoT services are equally provided for all patients with a minimal cost compared with traditional healthcare services (Farahani et al., 2018). Many available wearable IoT sensors can measure a particular patient's physiological signs like respiration rate (RR), heart rate (HR), and blood pressure (BP) with a single touch. In this sense, IoT facilitates mobile health, and Ambient Assisted Living (AAL), which allows remote patient monitoring and follow-up the elderly people living alone at home or in the hospital to take special treatment. Wearable IoT sensors and communication technologies are trying to improve traditional interaction between healthcare providers and many patients in more effective healthcare services. Typical healthcare IoT systems include data collection sensors, communication technologies, computing technologies, and advanced algorithms to process and analyze data. Sensors are used to collect data from various patient devices. Advanced algorithms are applied to filter and process data and then analyze all filtered data through different application programs. Data is pre-processed partially at Edge computing or Fog computing and then loaded to the center Cloud remote processing unit. After that, healthcare providers retrieve collected data to diagnose, observe and treat patients efficiently, which allows patients to have access to many services at the same time as depicted in Figure 1.

Figure 1. Healthcare IoT system architecture

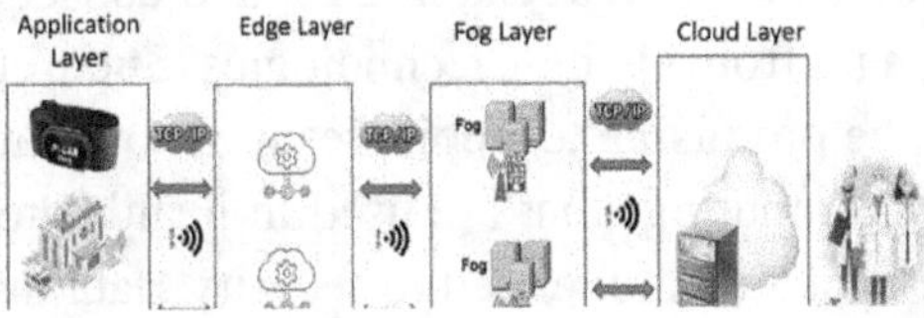

IoT applications have been integrated into healthcare fields to supply more efficient medical treatment to patients. Cloud computing technology in the healthcare IoT system brings many opportunities to healthcare providers and significantly enhances healthcare services. Edge computing provides interoperability between various sensors by separating the edge devices from the center of the network (Pace et al., 2018). The sensors used in the healthcare IoT system produce a huge amount of data every second. Processing this data is practically impossible using traditional processing data techniques. Therefore, big data is a critical concept in the healthcare IoT system which needs specific techniques for analyzing and processing.

In this chapter, we investigated large number of research studies concerning healthcare IoT software systems that utilize various computing technologies: Cloud, Fog, and Edge. To that end, we conducted a large-scale comprehensive study by analyzing the related research papers based on exclusion and inclusion criteria. We present a detailed taxonomy of the main research topics of the healthcare IoT systems. Moreover, we discuss the related concepts, services, and the main used applications in this vibrant research field.

1.2 COMPUTING TECHNOLOGIES IN HEALTHCARE IOT SYSTEMS

This section presents a concise background of healthcare IoT systems, Cloud computing, Edge computing, and Fog computing technologies.

1.2.1 Internet of Things (IoT)

Internet of Things (IoT) is considered a new technology that intends to combine various embedded technologies with physical objects that communicate with each other and interact with the external environment. IoT is incorporated with additional technologies such as Cloud computing, Edge computing, Fog computing, communication technologies, Internet protocols, smart sensors, RFID, and various big data analytics technologies (Moosavi et al., 2016).

IoT uses many features of these technologies, and consequently, IoT inherited open issues and challenges from all these technologies (Suciu et al., 2015). There are a lot of challenges in the promising technologies (e.g., big data, wearable devices, Fog, Edge, and cloud computing) that are used in healthcare IoT systems. Many of the challenges that appeared are related to security, data management, and data exchange between devices. Therefore, new concepts and solutions have emerged in cloud computing, Edge computing, and Fog computing technologies to solve such challenges, and to facilitate the integration of these technologies with the different IoT systems.

1.2.2 Healthcare IoT

In recent years, the propagation of IoT smart devices has led to a rise in demand for remote healthcare systems. The successive demand to deliver high quality healthcare services and to enhance the management of health information opened a lot of research fields in the domain of Healthcare IoT (Muhammed et al., 2018).

In the healthcare industry, ICT (Information and Communication Technology) enhanced the equal provision of healthcare services for elderly people and patients on a large scale. Sensors and various communication technologies, combined with IoT, are used to enhance healthcare services by improving the communication between patients and healthcare providers (Maksimović and Vujović, 2017). On the other hand, many research studies focused on the combination of wearable IoT sensors and smart mobile devices in different routine activities, healthcare monitoring, healthcare diagnosing, tracking, and locating healthcare-associated things (Yang et al., 2017). IoT technology moves the healthcare system from a centralized manner to a decentralized one to improve patient treatment. Today, home becomes the main healthcare services center for most elderly people and patients, which reduces medical costs and healthcare response time (Demir et al., 2017).

Healthcare IoT system indicates the use of medical sensors, mobile computing, and cloud computing technologies to really manage patients' conditions and use communication technologies to transfer collected patient data to the cloud computing storage (Wang et al., 2018). Therefore, healthcare providers retrieved collected data to diagnose, observe, and treat patients efficiently on time. The cloud received structured and filtered data and makes important operations on it. It performs various data analytics methods, ontology, semantics, and machine learning to improve data handling and convert it into useful knowledge (Kumar and Gandhi, 2018). Different services provided by the cloud can be reached by different stakeholders like physicians, patients, blood banks, hospitals, insurers, IoT service providers, cloud service providers, healthcare providers, etc.

1.2.3 Cloud Computing

Cloud computing, defined in Stergiou et al., 2018 is an evolving model that provides required computing resources including services such as networks, data storage, and elastic applications to consumers with minimal management effort. In general, cloud computing aims to provide flexible resources and deployment facilities at a low cost compared with real building computing infrastructure on the companies. Also, cloud computing supports the high availability feature by providing both applications and data storage services over the Internet, which means that users can access data from anywhere at any time (Bonomi et al., 2014). In addition, main cloud computing providers help IoT companies pay for the only specific resources used with no additional cost for a software license, maintenance contract, installing upgrades, and control of resources (Atlam et al., 2017).

Cloud computing has a lot of resources in terms of extensive processing as those needed in deep learning and big data storage. The main disadvantages of cloud computing are the high distance between healthcare IoT nodes and cloud computing storage. This leads to more latency of highly sensitive services and makes personal patients' data vulnerable to many attacks by unauthorized entities (X. M. Zhang and N. Zhang, 2011). Also, all the collected data from the wearable IoT sensors may not necessarily be transferred to cloud storage across the Internet.

1.2.4 Fog Computing

The concept of fog computing refers to expanding the cloud computing model to the edge of the network. Recently, fog computing has been introduced to allow new types of services in Information technology such as local storage, local computation, and control for IoT devices in minimal time when compared to cloud computing (Rahmani, Liljeberg, et al., 2017). The healthcare system is one of the most domains that realize this concept by developing a middle layer of smart gateways in the network between IoT sensors and the cloud. Fog computing provides many advantages for healthcare IoT applications which include improving privacy, reducing latency, enhancing reliability, and supporting geographic diversity (Maksimović and Vujović, 2017).

In Fog architecture, gateway nodes make data processing locally along with a transmission of data to the cloud servers. Various analytical processes like data processing methods, data cleaning, feature extraction, and real-time analysis are transferred to the fog computing layer (Gia et al., 2015). Furthermore, fog computing allows management of resources at the local layer, but most of the management techniques are limited to low computation costs methods as rule-based algorithms (Dubey et al., 2015). Although Fog computing-based systems provide a lot of advantages for healthcare IoT systems as shown in Table 1.1, Fog computing nodes have bounded functionality due to the restricted computational capacity in the edge devices.

1.2.5 Edge Computing

Edge computing technologies have been applied since 2002 (Oueida et al., 2018). Healthcare IoT devices collect data and act as an edge node to provide an entry point to the active network. The edge computing module moves the control of the services in the network from central nodes or cloud computing nodes to the sensors themselves which are defined as edge nodes. Edge computing differs from fog computing through the location of where the extra computing power is found (Pathinarupothi, Durga, and Rangan, 2018). In edge computing, the processing control and communication abilities are in the IoT devices themselves directly. The edge node can be a detector, an embedded system, a sensor, or a smart object (Oueida et al., 2018). But the processing control in fog computing is applied in the local area network, where collected data are analyzed and processed in the node, router, hub, or gateway and sent to suitable devices.

The edge computing devices and fog computing nodes can perform many defined processes, including sending data during milliseconds and reducing the amount of data for permanent cloud storage or temporary storage in the edge device or fog hub as shown in Table 1. Many healthcare actuators must respond quickly to IoT sensor data in seconds and cannot be late for minutes to send data to the cloud to be analyzed and then transfer the results back to the patient sensors.

Table 1. Summary of advantages and disadvantages of computing technologies with healthcare IoT system

	Edge Computing	Fog Computing	Cloud Computing
Advantages	Making critical decisions institution, reducing network traffic, minimizing operating cost, and improving system performance	More storage space and computational power compared to edge computing	Unlimited computing power and huge storage space
Disadvantage	Limited storage and limited computing power compared to Fog computing	Limited storage and limited computing power compared to Cloud Computing	Slow response time and require high and width

1.3 PRIOR SURVEYS ON HEALTHCARE IOT SYSTEMS

This section provides discussions about the previous surveys that have focused on studying healthcare IoT systems. Previous studies have concentrated on specific aspects of healthcare IoT systems. But most of these studies have not discussed the healthcare IoT systems from the prescriptive computing technologies (Cloud, Fog, and Edge), and to find the gaps and main challenges in those systems with a comprehensive study of different aspects.

In Sawand et al., 2015 to guarantee the high level of healthcare IoT system performance, they analyzed the main challenges that need to provide an efficient and secure healthcare monitoring system. In Islam et al., 2015; Alasmari and Anwar, 2016, different IoT security and privacy features from the healthcare aspects were surveyed that include threat types, attack classifications, and security requirements, and reviewed the last technical trends in IoT healthcare solutions. Further, to minimize security risks, they proposed a smart, collaborative security model and presented IoT policies and controls for healthcare services that benefit various stakeholders' technologies in different countries. Farahani et al. Farahani et al., 2018 provided a thorough study of several case examples of applications and services that are used with fog computing. Also, they discussed the applicability of IoT in medicine and healthcare by displaying a comprehensive architecture of the eHealth IoT system.

Ida et al. Ida, Jemai, and Loukil, 2016, provided an overview of the IoT security vulnerabilities and the main security and privacy challenges in the cloud for the eHealth context from the network and the hardware prescriptive. Also, they presented various solutions for IoT and Cloud security, especially to preserve health information, while Ghosal et al. Ghosal, D. Das, and I. Das, 2018, studied various machine learning approaches that are used to solve various security attacks. Scarpato et al. Scarpato et al., 2017 and Darwish et al. Darwish et al., 2019, presented different solutions used to improve the role of the healthcare system from a security and communication prescriptive. Qi et al. Qi et al., 2017, presented a set of problems related to IoT healthcare systems that include high dimensionality of produced data, heterogeneity of connected IoT wearable devices that produced a huge amount of data, and how to make processing of these data. AbdElnapi et al. AbdElnapi et al., 2018, focused on the latest IoT technologies for healthcare as important medical sensors, cloud computing, and various communication technologies when dealing with the big data generated from different medical IoT sensors.

Aazam et al. Aazam, Zeadally, and Harras, 2020, reviewed the main elements and architecture of fog in the healthcare cloud-IoT environment also provided how fog can be used to solve latency problems, especially in an emergency. Mahmoud et al. Mahmoud, Rodrigues, and Saleem, 2019, they talked about efficient solutions for obtaining energy efficiency in data transmission and processing required in the healthcare solution. Dhanvijay et al. Dhanvijay and Patil, 2019, reviewed the most recent network architecture topology and applications in the healthcare IoT-based solutions also focused on the Wireless Body Area Network (WBN) technology, especially for elderly people.

Most previous studies have not discussed the effect of cloud, fog, and edge computing on healthcare IoT systems with a comprehensive review of aspects related to each type of computing technology. Therefore, this study addresses detailed taxonomy and insights into many challenges and issues facing healthcare IoT systems for the realization of an efficient healthcare IoT system.

1.4 RESEARCH METHODOLOGY

This section shows the methodology applied in this study. We chose the most relevant research that covered topics related to the Internet of Things (IoT), healthcare, and computing technologies that include Cloud, Fog, and Edge computing. Many studies regarding IoT technologies and architecture have been carried out in various subject areas such as medicine, computer science, and healthcare. In our study, published research papers have been studied using the Scopus database, to create a complete list of research papers on IoT in the healthcare field with the Cloud, Fog, and Edge computing technologies.

The selected papers were searched using the online database service Scopus. The main benefits of using Scopus as opposed to other similar resources are ease of use. Scopus is used as a high-quality bibliometric and a curated data source for academic research in quantitative science study (Martn et al., 2021). Also, Scopus database gives access to STM journal articles, and the references involved in those articles. It brings together better quality, advanced analytics, and superior technology in one solution. Make the research workflow more effective and efficient by providing the save list techniques to save the search result after each search query (Singh et al., 2017).

We extracted research from the Scopus database using the following search keywords in different query structures: Healthcare, e-Health, Smart Health, IoT, Cloud, Fog, and Edge. In our study, we found the related research papers by analyzing each paper's abstract, introduction, and conclusion. Then, we selected the papers that would be more relevant to our study. More specifically, we searched for papers and selected the relevant ones according to the three main phases, i.e., Exploration phase, Investigation phase, and Analysis phase, which are described in Figure 2.

Figure 2. Flowchart diagram of the systematic research steps

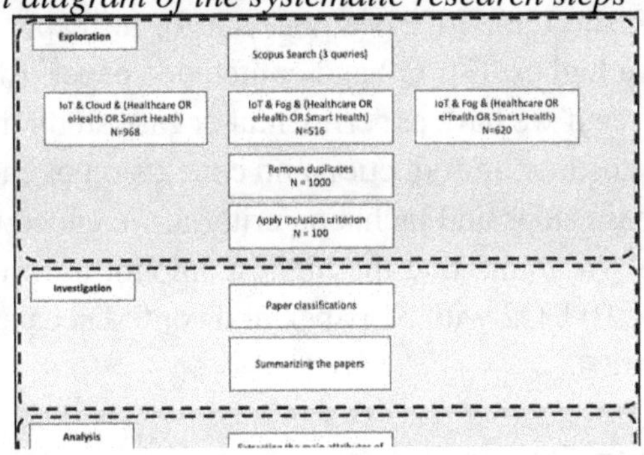

1.4.1 Exploration Phase

In the exploration phase, data is collected using the Scopus database, this phase contains a set of steps to find the necessary research articles as follows:

1. Using the Scopus site to find out research about smart healthcare IoT systems and cloud computing technologies using the article title, abstract, and keywords in the search field.
2. Searching using 3 specified query structures as follows:
    - IoT and Cloud and (Healthcare OR smart Health OR e-Health), with the result of 968 papers.
    - IoT and Edge and (Healthcare OR smart Health OR e-Health), with the result of 620 papers.
    - IoT and Fog and (Healthcare OR smart Health OR e-Health), with the result of 516 papers.

We found that the number of extracted papers was relatively large, with 2104. Manually, we removed duplicate papers on the title of each paper. After identifying and removing duplicate papers, 850 papers remained among which the inclusion/exclusion criteria were applied.

3. Include papers based on specific criteria as follows:
   (a) Publication year of research between 2011 and 2019 as shown in Figure 3.
   (b) Papers that have Q1 or Q2 Journal rank or conference papers with a high citation number.
   (c) Papers that have an experimental or case study in the healthcare IoT system field.

From ScimagoJR site Lab, 2022 we got rank for all paper then sort them descending and take the highest Q1, Q2 and conference paper. At the same time, we check each paper to see if we have experimental or case study in the healthcare IoT systems, by reading abstract, introduction and conclusion of each paper.

After applying these steps and inclusion criteria, we ended up with 100 papers used in our research. We found that the highest amount of research has a Q1 rate with 51 papers out of 100, Q2 with 31 paper, and conference paper with 18 papers, as shown in the Figure 4.

1.4.2 Investigation Phase

In this phase, we classify articles using two criteria, type of solved issues and type of computing technology in the healthcare IoT system.

Figure 3. Number of annual publications on healthcare IoT systems

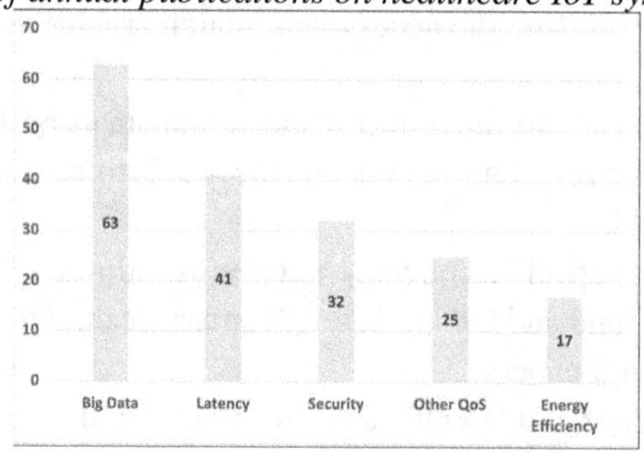

Figure 4. Number of paper classifications (Q1, Q2, Conference)

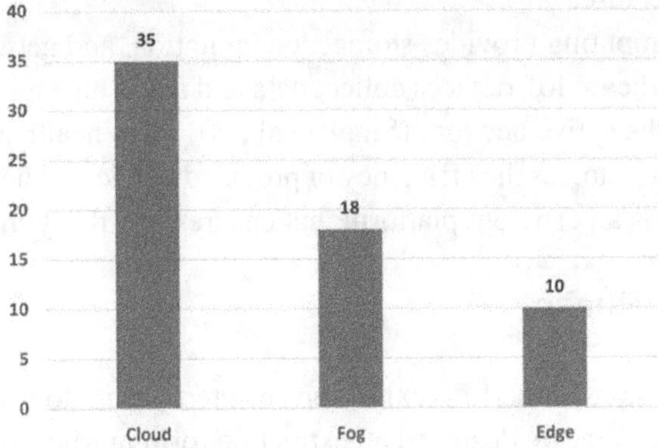

Main Research Topics Classification

This study considers different healthcare IoT research areas with the different computing technologies Cloud, Fog, and Edge. First, we define the main research topics that are considered in each paper. Then, we discuss how to solve each topic that affects healthcare IoT systems when combined with Cloud, Fog, or Edge computing technologies. Finally, we discuss the related concepts, services, and applications.

Computing Technologies Classifications

There are different technologies in the computing environment for healthcare IoT system, including Cloud computing, Fog computing, and Edge computing (Maksimović and Vujović, 2017). In Cloud computing, patients and doctors can connect directly to the cloud using the Internet. Transmission of a huge amount of data in a short time is not efficient in a typical cloud computing architecture. To overcome these problems new computing paradigms such as Fog computing, and Edge computing have been applied which process the data in the local gateways or connected devices (Manogaran et al., 2018).

Fog computing nodes process the request from IoT devices using local resources or transmit it to the cloud server's resources. Therefore, fog computing can manage delay sensitive computation and decrease power consumption while reducing traffic congestion (Monteiro et al., 2018). Generally, the main characteristics of fog computing with healthcare IoT systems are low latency, location awareness, real-time processing, wireless and mobile access, scalability, and geographical distribution support (Bhatia and Sood, 2019). To improve the accuracy of diagnosis and analysis of diseases in healthcare IoT systems, many researchers applied Fog computing architecture.

Also, Edge computing provides storage, computation, and networking services to IoT users. Healthcare IoT devices collect data and act as an edge node to provide an entry point to the active network (Singh et al., 2017). In healthcare IoT systems, edge computing guarantees the efficiency of provided services. The data processing of the patient needs an efficient platform that ensures less delay in response time.

1.4.3 Analysis Phase

In this phase, we read the full text of the selected papers to extract the critical data. To gather the data, we designed an extraction form in Microsoft Excel. Then, we collected the data from 100 selected papers manually.

For each paper, the following data were collected: type of computing technology (Cloud, Fog, Edge), main issues that considered in each article, how to solve these issues, type of network protocols, type of communication technologies, type of disease, system place, data collected technologies, data storage techniques, authors country, funding country/university agency, publication year, citation number, cloud provider type, and the main participated stakeholders in the system.

In this phase, we try to interpret the collected data, including the type of computing technologies and the main issues in healthcare IoT systems. In each studied issue, we used different graphs and views to present the number of studies that were solved by different types of computing technologies (Cloud, Fog, and Edge). The findings can show differences in the data which should be considered. Also, the following section shows the main findings and results.

REFERENCES

Aazam, M., Zeadally, S., & Harras, K. A. (2020). Health fog for smart healthcare. *IEEE Consumer Electronics Magazine*, *9*(2), 96–102. DOI: 10.1109/MCE.2019.2953749

AbdElnapi., Noha M M et al. (2018). "A survey of internet of things technologies and projects for healthcare services". In: *2018 International Conference on Innovative Trends in Computer Engineering (ITCE)*. IEEE, pp. 48–55.

Alasmari, S., & Anwar, M. (2016). "Security & privacy challenges in IoT-based health cloud". In: *2016 International Conference on Computational Science and Computational Intelligence (CSCI)*. IEEE, pp. 198–201. DOI: 10.1109/CSCI.2016.0044

Atlam, Hany F et al. (2017). "Integration of cloud computing with internet of things: challenges and open issues". In: *2017 IEEE International Conference on Internet of Things (iThings) and IEEE Green Computing and Communications (GreenCom) and IEEE Cyber, Physical and Social Computing (CPSCom) and IEEE Smart Data (SmartData)*. IEEE, pp. 670–675.

Bhatia, M., & Sood, S. K. (2019). Exploring temporal analytics in fog-cloud architecture for smart office healthcare. *Mobile Networks and Applications*, *24*(4), 1392–1410. DOI: 10.1007/s11036-018-0991-5

Bonomi, F.. (2014). Fog computing: A platform for internet of things and analytics. In *Big data and internet of things: A roadmap for smart environments* (pp. 169–186). Springer. DOI: 10.1007/978-3-319-05029-4_7

Darwish, A., Hassanien, A. E., Elhoseny, M., Sangaiah, A. K., & Muhammad, K. (2019). The impact of the hybrid platform of internet of things and cloud computing on healthcare systems: Opportunities, challenges, and open problems. *Journal of Ambient Intelligence and Humanized Computing*, *10*(10), 4151–4166. DOI: 10.1007/s12652-017-0659-1

Demir, E., Köseoğlu, E., Sokullu, R., & Şeker, B. (2017). Smart home assistant for ambient assisted living of elderly people with dementia. *Procedia Computer Science*, *113*, 609–614. DOI: 10.1016/j.procs.2017.08.302

Dhanvijay, Mrinai M and Shailaja C Patil (2019). "Internet of Things: A survey of enabling technologies in healthcare and its applications". In: *Computer Networks* 153, pp. 113–131.

Dubey, H.. (2015). "Fog data: Enhancing telehealth big data through fog computing". In: *Proceedings of the ASE bigdata & socialinformatics 2015*, pp. 1–6. DOI: 10.1145/2818869.2818889

Fanjiang, Gary et al. (2005). "Building a better delivery system: a new engineering/ health care partnership". In.

Farahani, B., Firouzi, F., Chang, V., Badaroglu, M., Constant, N., & Mankodiya, K. (2018). Towards fog-driven IoT eHealth: Promises and challenges of IoT in medicine and healthcare. *Future Generation Computer Systems*, *78*, 659–676. DOI: 10.1016/j.future.2017.04.036

Ghosal, P., Das, D., & Das, I. (2018). "Extensive survey on cloud-based IoT-healthcare and security using machine learning". In: *2018 Fourth International Conference on Research in Computational Intelligence and Communication Networks (ICRCICN)*. IEEE, pp. 1–5. DOI: 10.1109/ICRCICN.2018.8718717

Gia, T. N.. (2015). Fog computing in healthcare internet of things: A case study on ecg feature extraction. In *In: 2015 IEEE international conference on computer and information technology; ubiquitous computing and communications; dependable, autonomic and secure computing; pervasive intelligence and computing* (pp. 356–363). IEEE.

Holst, A. (Aug. 2021). *IOT connected devices worldwide 2019-2030*. url: https:// www.statista.com/statistics/1183457/iot-connected-devices-worldwide/

Hossain, M Shamim and Ghulam Muhammad (2016). "Cloud-assisted industrial internet of things (iiot)–enabled framework for health monitoring". In: *Computer Networks* 101, pp. 192–202.

Ida, I. B., Jemai, A., & Loukil, A. (2016). "A survey on security of IoT in the context of eHealth and clouds". In: *2016 11th International Design & Test Symposium (IDT)*. IEEE, pp. 25–30.

Islam, SM Riazul et al. (2015). "The internet of things for health care: a comprehensive survey". In: *IEEE access* 3, pp. 678–708.

Kumar, P. M., & Gandhi, U. D. (2018). A novel three-tier Internet of Things architecture with machine learning algorithm for early detection of heart diseases. *Computers & Electrical Engineering*, *65*, 222–235. DOI: 10.1016/j.compeleceng.2017.09.001

Lab, S. (Oct. 2022). *ScimagoJR, SJR: Scientific Journal Rankings*. url: https: //www .scimagojr.com/journalrank.php%20/

Mahmoud, Mukhtar ME, Joel JPC Rodrigues, and Kashif Saleem (2019). "Cloud of Things for Healthcare: A Survey from Energy Efficiency Perspective". In: *2019 International Conference on Computer and Information Sciences (ICCIS)*. IEEE, pp. 1– 7.

Maksimović, M., & Vujović, V. (2017). Internet of things based e-health systems: ideas, expectations and concerns. In *Handbook of large-scale distributed computing in smart healthcare* (pp. 241–280). Springer. DOI: 10.1007/978-3-319-58280-1_10

Manogaran, G., Varatharajan, R., Lopez, D., Kumar, P. M., Sundarasekar, R., & Thota, C. (2018). A new architecture of Internet of Things and big data ecosystem for secured smart healthcare monitoring and alerting system. *Future Generation Computer Systems*, *82*, 375–387. DOI: 10.1016/j.future.2017.10.045

Martn, A.. (2021). Google Scholar, Microsoft Academic, Scopus, Dimensions, Web of Science, and OpenCitations' COCI: A multidisciplinary comparison of coverage via citations. *Scientometrics*, *126*(1), 871–906. DOI: 10.1007/s11192-020-03690-4 PMID: 32981987

Monteiro, K.. (2018). "Developing an e-health system based on IoT, fog and cloud computing". In: *2018 IEEE/ACM International Conference on Utility and Cloud Computing Companion (UCC Companion)*. IEEE, pp. 17–18. DOI: 10.1109/UCC-Companion.2018.00024

Moosavi, S. R., Gia, T. N., Nigussie, E., Rahmani, A. M., Virtanen, S., Tenhunen, H., & Isoaho, J. (2016). End-to-end security scheme for mobility enabled healthcare Internet of Things. *Future Generation Computer Systems*, *64*, 108–124. DOI: 10.1016/j.future.2016.02.020

Muhammed, T., Mehmood, R., Albeshri, A., & Katib, I. (2018). UbeHealth: A personalized ubiquitous cloud and edge enabled networked healthcare system for smart cities. *IEEE Access : Practical Innovations, Open Solutions*, *6*, 32258–32285. DOI: 10.1109/ACCESS.2018.2846609

Oueida, S., Kotb, Y., Aloqaily, M., Jararweh, Y., & Baker, T. (2018). An edge computing based smart healthcare framework for resource management. *Sensors (Basel)*, *18*(12), 4307. DOI: 10.3390/s18124307 PMID: 30563267

Pace, P., Aloi, G., Gravina, R., Caliciuri, G., Fortino, G., & Liotta, A. (2018). An edge-based architecture to support efficient applications for healthcare industry 4.0. *IEEE Transactions on Industrial Informatics*, *15*(1), 481–489. DOI: 10.1109/TII.2018.2843169

Pathinarupothi, R. K. P Durga, and Ekanath Srihari Rangan (2018). "Iot-based smart edge for global health: Remote monitoring with severity detection and alerts transmission". In: *IEEE Internet of Things Journal* 6.2, pp. 2449–2462.

Qi, J., Yang, P., Min, G., Amft, O., Dong, F., & Xu, L. (2017). Advanced internet of things for personalised healthcare systems: A survey. *Pervasive and Mobile Computing*, *41*, 132–149. DOI: 10.1016/j.pmcj.2017.06.018

Rahmani, A. M., Gia, T. N., Negash, B., Anzanpour, A., Azimi, I., Jiang, M., & Liljeberg, P. (2018). Exploiting smart e-Health gateways at the edge of healthcare Internet-of-Things: A fog computing approach. *Future Generation Computer Systems*, *78*, 641–658. DOI: 10.1016/j.future.2017.02.014

Rahmani, A. M., & Liljeberg, P.. (2017). *Fog computing in the internet of things: Intelligence at the edge*. Springer.

Sawand, A., Djahel, S., Zhang, Z., & Naït-Abdesselam, F. (2015). Toward energy-efficient and trustworthy eHealth monitoring system. *China Communications*, *12*(1), 46–65. DOI: 10.1109/CC.2015.7084383

Scarpato, N., ... (2017). "E-health-IoT universe: A review". In: *management* 21.44, p. 46. DOI: 10.18517/ijaseit.7.6.4467

Singh, D.. (2017). Semantic edge computing and IoT architecture for military health services in battlefield. In *In: 2017 14th IEEE Annual Consumer Communications & Networking Conference (CCNC)* (pp. 185–190). IEEE.

Stergiou, C., Psannis, K. E., Kim, B.-G., & Gupta, B. (2018). Secure integration of IoT and cloud computing. *Future Generation Computer Systems*, *78*, 964–975. DOI: 10.1016/j.future.2016.11.031

Suciu, G., Suciu, V., Martian, A., Craciunescu, R., Vulpe, A., Marcu, I., Halunga, S., & Fratu, O. (2015). Big data, internet of things and cloud convergence–an architecture for secure e-health applications. *Journal of Medical Systems*, *39*(11), 1–8. DOI: 10.1007/s10916-015-0327-y PMID: 26345453

Wang, T., Bhuiyan, M. Z. A., Wang, G., Rahman, M. A., Wu, J., & Cao, J. (2018). Big data reduction for a smart city's critical infrastructural health monitoring. *IEEE Communications Magazine*, *56*(3), 128–133. DOI: 10.1109/MCOM.2018.1700303

Yang, G., Jiang, M., Ouyang, W., Ji, G., Xie, H., Rahmani, A. M., Liljeberg, P., & Tenhunen, H. (2017). IoT-based remote pain monitoring system: From device to cloud platform. *IEEE Journal of Biomedical and Health Informatics*, *22*(6), 1711–1719. DOI: 10.1109/JBHI.2017.2776351 PMID: 29990259

Zhang, X. M., & Zhang, N. (2011). An open, secure and flexible platform based on internet of things and cloud computing for ambient aiding living and telemedicine. In *In: 2011 international conference on computer and management (CAMAN)* (pp. 1–4). IEEE.

Chapter 11
Research Trends in Healthcare IoT Software Systems

Mahmoud M. Hammad
https://orcid.org/0000-0003-2891-0463
Ajman University, UAE & Jordan University of Science and Technology, Jordan

Sajeda Banat
https://orcid.org/0009-0003-1653-6707
Jordan University of Science and Technology, Jordan

Qanita Bani Baker
https://orcid.org/0000-0003-4722-6632
Jordan University of Science and Technology, Jordan

Mohammed Al-Refai
https://orcid.org/0000-0001-7297-7695
Jordan University of Science and Technology, Jordan

Bara'a Abudehais
Jordan University of Science and Technology, Jordan

Salma Suleiman
Jordan University of Science and Technology, Jordan

ABSTRACT

This chapter describes the results and findings of our comprehensive study, discussed in the previous chapter, which focuses on finding the main research trends in cloud, fog, and edge computing technologies within the domain of healthcare IoT systems. In summary, our investigation concluded that the researchers mainly focused on the following five research topics: big data, security, network latency, energy efficiency, and QoS. However, some research topics are well studied while others are poorly investigated and need more attention. We found that the highest number of research papers focused on big data, i.e., 63% of the papers studied, while the energy efficiency topic had the lowest number of papers, i.e., 17% of the papers.

DOI: 10.4018/979-8-3693-9851-7.ch011

1.1 MAIN RESEARCH TRENDS

We found that the most investigated and studies research trends in the cloud computing-based healthcare IoT systems are big data, security, energy efficiency, latency, and other QoS aspects. Based on our study, Figure 2 shows these main research trends and topics. Figure 3 shows the number of papers in each research topic. We found that the highest number of research papers focused on big data, i.e., 63 out of 100 research papers, while the energy efficiency topic had the lowest number of papers, i.e., 17 papers.

Figure 1. Number of annual publication trends of healthcare IoT systems using different computing technologies

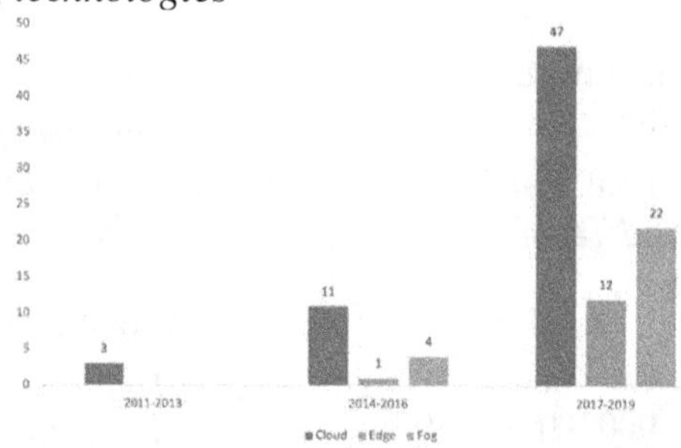

Figure 2. Our taxonomy, the main research topics in healthcare IoT system

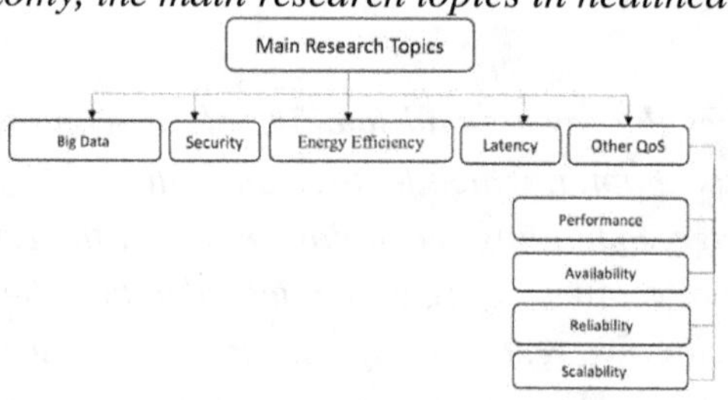

Figure 3. Number of papers that address each research topic

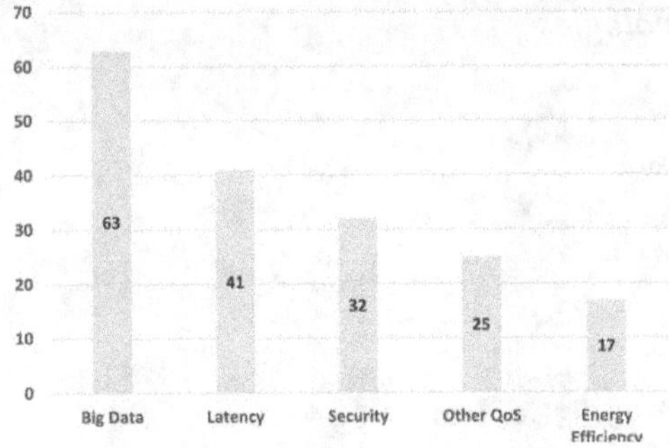

1.2 BIG DATA RESEARCH AREA

Recently, huge data was collected from sensors and wearable IoT devices in the healthcare IoT systems. This data is varied and often unstructured, and requires huge resources for processing, which raised a concern in the computing resources and time needed to analyze the collected data (P. M. Kumar et al., 2018). Therefore, healthcare providers had to employ new technologies like cloud computing and fog computing to deal with such varied and big data streams. A set of choices are used to overcome some of the big data issues by reducing the processing cost and supporting early diagnosis of illnesses (G. Yang et al., 2017; Quwaider and Jararweh, 2016). To get helpful information from big data streams, an essential step is required to reduce data complexity, and this step includes data cleaning such discarding unnecessary and redundant parts of the data.

In the following subsections, we present how cloud computing, edge computing, and fog computing technologies addressed the ability to process huge and complex healthcare data flows. Figure 4 shows the number of papers that addressed the big data aspect using cloud, fog, and edge computing technologies. For example, 55.56% of studied papers used cloud computing technology to solve big data issues, 28.57% used Fog computing, and 15.78% used Edge computing.

Figure 4. Number of papers that addressed the big data topic using cloud, fog, and edge computing technologies

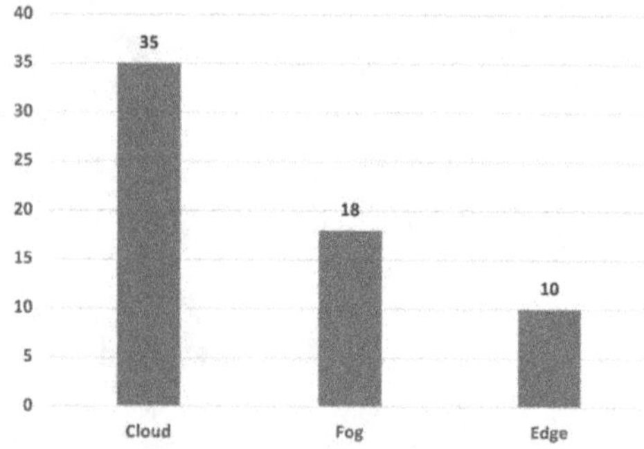

1.2.1 Big Data Processing in Cloud Computing

One of the main advantages of cloud computing is saving a huge amount of data and various resources in a huge data center on the Internet. Moreover, current cloud computing architectures provide effective execution enhancement by combining different environments to execute the applications at different levels. Also, cloud computing offers pay-as-you-go to services that include virtualization, networking, big data analytics, and data-parallel processing on customized servers (Amin et al., 2019; Xie et al., 2018).

Moreover, advanced healthcare providers are improving their infrastructure to deal with a huge amount of data produced by WBAN IoT sensors by using multi-cloud data computing to ensure the highest level of cost-efficiency, data availability, and reliability (Quintero and Lee, 2019). The multi-cloud computing architecture enables the deployment of tasks to the proper environment (public, private or hybrid cloud), which speeds up the processing steps. The authors of Ullah et al., 2017; Jusak, Pratikno, and Putra, 2016 used Microsoft Azure and Google as multi-cloud computing with OpenIoT structure. Furthermore, the survey conducted in Akulov, 2019 found that 86% of respondents are dealing with current cloud computing as multi-cloud.

1.2.2 Big Data Processing in Fog Computing

Cloud computing sources were extended to the edge network, known as the Fog computing layer. Both Cloud and Fog layers provide data processing, storage, and application features to the users. Data processing on the fog computing layer performs an essential role in healthcare monitoring systems. This layer is necessary especially for medical scenarios that involve emergency cases, which require taking critical decisions and sending notifications to the specialists at the least possible time. In Gia, Jiang, et al., 2015; Manogaran et al., 2018; Ahmad et al., 2016, they used fog computing, which is placed in the patient's home, to decrease the processing time, increase efficiency, reduce the amount of data required to send to the cloud, and avoid more latency. In Ray, Thapa, and Dash, 2019; Rani, Ahmed, and Shah, 2018, they used fog computing to improve the healthcare system and enhanced the fog computing layer with distributed data storage and data mining techniques.

1.2.3 Big Data Processing in Edge Computing

Big data processing using edge computing power and storage near the healthcare IoT devices allows data cleaning and analysis in low response time before sending data to the centralized cloud system, which improves data transmission efficiency. In Rani, Ahmed, and Shah, 2018, they deployed edge servers at the already known places of a city to collect the Chikungunya virus data from users and make the processing of the data, then transmitting it to the Cloud. In Azimi, Takalo-Mattila, et al., 2018; Geman et al., 2018, they found that the use of edge computing to process data has a better effect on disease detection when compared to cloud computing and found that edge computing helped in sending earlier notification announcements to the medical service provider compared to cloud computing.

1.3 SECURITY RESEARCH AREA

Combining IoT devices in the healthcare field with Cloud, Fog, and/or Edge computing technologies led to a lot of security issues that need to be resolved Sarkar et al., 2017; Manikandan et al., 2020. These issues can happen at different phases, such as the security of the collected data from healthcare IoT devices, either during sending data to (cloud, Fog, and Edge) to make processing, or while saving data in computing storage (Y. Yang et al., 2018; Yeh et al., 2015.) This section concentrates on the security issue related to the data flow of healthcare IoT systems with the different computing technologies (Cloud, Fog, and Edge).

Figure 5 provides the number of studies that consider security issues by computing technologies. According to Figure 5, the most percentage, including 59.4% of studies used cloud computing technology architecture to solve security issues, 31.3% used Fog computing architecture, and 9.3% used Edge computing architecture.

Depending on Figure 1, cloud computing is the most used layer to solve security issues in healthcare IoT systems. However, as will be described in the following sections, the fog computing layer plays an essential role in the confidentiality and the security of healthcare IoT systems.

Figure 5. Number of studies consider security issues by computing technologies

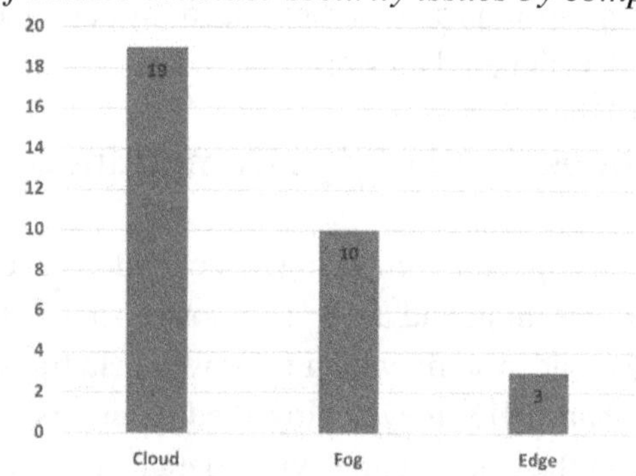

1.3.1 Security Issue for Healthcare IoT System in Cloud Computing

In healthcare IoT systems, the cloud architecture can enhance healthcare services and improve the frequent updating of the healthcare system (Hossain and Muhammad, 2016; Muhammad et al., 2017; Benadda et al., 2018). However, security is one of the main issues when integrating cloud computing with the healthcare IoT system because of the high level of data interoperability, integration, and sharing of these data between healthcare providers and organizations (Sharma, Choudhury, and P. Kumar, 2018). Distinguishing between the actual user and the attacker at the cloud level is a complex process. There are many security threats in the cloud as Denial of Services attack (DOS/DDoS), Man-in-the-Middle attack, and Sleep Deprivation attack (Farahani et al., 2018; Moosavi et al., 2016; Manogaran et al., 2018). To mitigate these threats, cloud computing technologies process and save collected data in distributed cloud servers privately (Yeh et al., 2015; X. M. Zhang and N. Zhang, 2011), and only allows authorized users to securely use patient data by authenticating themselves using robust authentication algorithms. However, most used security techniques in practice are overlooked at the cloud level because of the trade-off between the efficiency, speed up of the system, and security problems in healthcare IoT systems (Doukas and Maglogiannis, 2012).

1.3.2 Security Issue for Healthcare IoT System in Fog Computing

Compared to the cloud layer, fog nodes use more powerful encryption schemes, access control policies, isolation measures, and integrity checks to preserve the security of patient sensitive data (Moosavi et al., 2016). The fog computing paradigm is qualified to overcome the security issues that typical cloud computing architecture is exposed to (Ahmad et al., 2016). Providing fog computing as a middle layer and acting on the edge-side improves data security, consistency, accuracy, minimizes the latency rate, and improves service quality. Because fog nodes spread near the end-users and some places with relatively weak monitoring, it is more vulnerable to malicious attacks. Furthermore, Man-in-the-middle attacks can stop sending patient data from the healthcare IoT devices to the healthcare provider, which leads to life loss in some cases (Pace et al., 2018; Hu et al., 2017; Jia et al., 2019). As a solution to these issues, the multi-layer communication approach was used, which helped in solving many security and privacy issues, including authentication and authorization, identity management, data sharing policy, quality of services, etc.

1.3.3 Security Issue for Healthcare IoT System in Edge Computing

The edge computing layer is very close to the end-users, and therefore, it introduces a platform at the application layer for protecting the data collected by various IoT sensors (Gia, Dhaou, et al., 2019). For example, in Pace et al., 2018; Devarajan and Ravi, 2019, they proposed techniques for encrypting the patients' data at the application layer before sending the data to the cloud servers. Furthermore, to ensure availability while receiving denial of services (DoS) attacks, the edge architecture uses backup systems and redundancy techniques.

1.4 LATENCY RESEARCH AREA

The latency issues vary depending on the nature of healthcare IoT applications. It differs with the type of application and the healthcare IoT systems field. Some applications have more constraints than others. Some healthcare IoT applications are authorized to have some delays while others are not. For instance, sending blood pressure can allow delays up to 2 to 4 seconds (La et al., 2019). While ICU applications, ambulance applications, and emergency applications allow less delay. Surgery applications need to send multimedia data as interactive video and audio to remotely and the allowed latency for these applications must not beat more than 300ms (Feng, Liang, and Zhao, 2010).

If cloud computing is used, normally raw data is sent from IoT nodes to the cloud to be processed and stored. While transferring the data, unpredictable network circumstances may cause delayed responses. The case is even more dangerous when transferring streaming-based data as EEG or ECG signals. To overcome this possible delay for critical data, the analysis of such data is done in the distributed edge gateway and (i.e., the local network level) using time-sensitive procedures (Wac et al., 2009). Then, the data analyzed is transferred to the cloud server for further processing and permanent storage. Healthcare IoT sensors produce a huge amount of data. Processing and analyzing these data need more time, leading to delays in the services provided to the patient, especially in the cloud environment. Recently, traditional services of cloud environments have been unable to obtain the latency requirements of healthcare IoT systems. To solve this problem, in Suciu et al., 2015, they used near edge devices to process and store data locally, to overcome latency problems and provide better QoS. In Hassanalieragh et al., 2015, to execute healthcare monitoring applications using BAN, they used cloudlet computing as a solution to solve high latency problems, especially in critical tasks. They used WiFi direct communication between concentrator and cloudlet to reduce data transmission latency, or LTE to transfer data from the concentrator to the cloud without using cloudlet technology. In Quwaider and Jararweh, 2016; Mahmoud, Rodrigues, Saleem, et al., 2018, to minimize the time of data processing and the number of communications, they used a local cloud or cloudlet with the MapReduce technique which leads to reduce the overall processing delay.

In Farahani et al., 2018; Gia, Jiang, et al., 2015; Ahmad et al., 2016; Verma and Sood, 2018; Bibani et al., 2016; Fernández-Caramés et al., 2019; Ozdemir, Tunc, and Hariri, 2017, wearable IoT sensors can produce a huge amount of raw data within a short time. But it is not necessary and not feasible to transfer these data from many patients to the cloud. Therefore, fog computing is reasonable to filter, process, and compress the data before moving it to the cloud, which is crucial for better visualization, low latency, and context awareness in emergency and ICU rooms.

Consequently, the latency can be reduced because of the shorter physical distance. In Vilela et al., 2019, when applied fog computing concept, they decreased 90% of exchange data from patients to the cloud and reduced up to 20% of the processing time. As provided in Figure 6, we found that most researchers used the Fog computing paradigm to solve latency issues.

In conclusion, based on our findings, we need to reduce latency in the cloud environment

Figure 6. Number of studies that consider high latency issues using different computing technologies

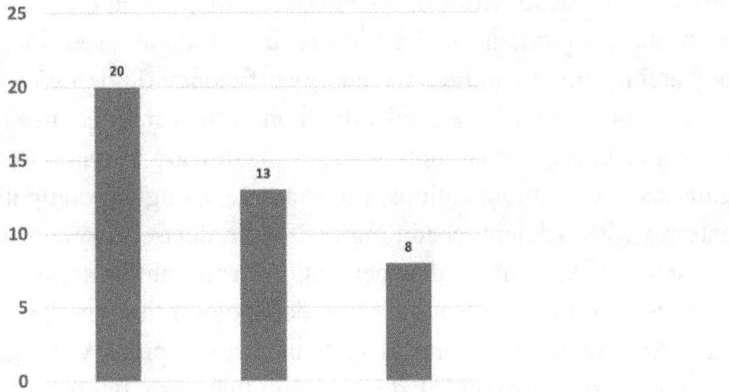

between healthcare IoT sensors and patients, the fog computing techniques are integrated with the cloud environment. Fog computing is designed to be close to IoT sensors, which provide quicker responses to patients in emergency cases compared to cloud computing.

1.5 Energy Efficiency Research Area

Energy efficiency is one of the most important aspects in the field of healthcare IoT systems due to its impact on the environment, operating expenses, and service quality. Healthcare wearable sensors generate a high amount of data that needs high energy and leads to a short lifetime of the battery. In terms of resource consumption due to data processing, the most resource consumption techniques are speech and image processing techniques (La et al., 2019). Depending on our study, to obtain energy efficiency in healthcare IoT systems, researchers used different optimization algorithms, different computing techniques such as Edge or Fog computing, different types of communication technologies, and appropriate hardware according to the type of system. To decrease the usage of energy, optimization algorithms were also applied. An efficient energy architecture for healthcare IoT systems is proposed in Mahmoud, Rodrigues, Ahmed, et al., 2018. This approach uses sleep mode method to reduce the energy consumption depending on turning IoT sensors to sleep mode in three cases: the battery level is low when the area size covering overrides the battery level, the situation of battery level, and the demand of collecting data from patients in a specific interval of time. Therefore, Cloud resources allocated to the system are saved when IoT sensors changed to sleep mode. In Jusak, Pratikno, and Putra, 2016; Yacchirema et al., 2018, they used Raspberry Pi because it has features of having less power consumption of nearly one-tenth when compared with other hardware.

Data transmission and computational tasks are the most energy consuming processes in healthcare IoT system. According to Figure 1.7, the most significant percentage comprising 47.1% of the reviewed studies used cloud computing technology architecture to address the energy efficiency field, 35.3% used Fog computing architecture, and 17.6% used Edge computing architecture. In general, the work to reduce energy consumption in IoT healthcare systems focuses on eliminating unnecessary communications. For example, using fog computing in the intelligent gateway with efficient scheduling tasks can reduce energy consumption in healthcare IoT sensors. Also, in the data centers, determining the appropriate place to process collected data in the Cloud or Fog depends on the type and amount of collected data. Also, most healthcare IoT systems focus on privacy and security protocols that consume less energy in IoT devices, and therefore, lightweight protocols are used.

Figure 7. Number of studies that address the high energy efficiency topic

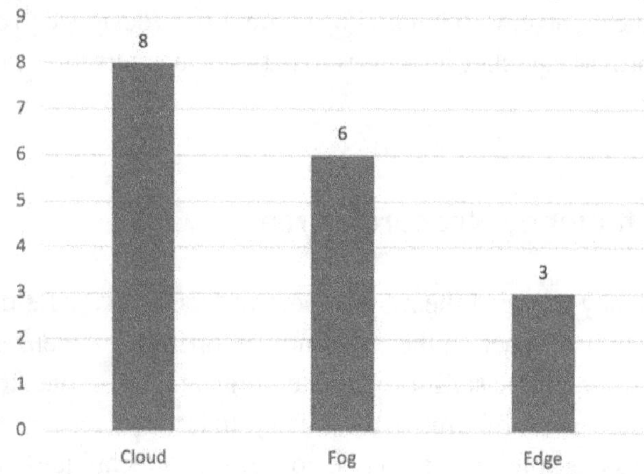

1.6 QUALITY OF SERVICES RESEARCH AREA

In IoT healthcare systems, providing quality of Service (QoS) requirements is one of the critical aspects. Quality of Service (QoS) controls the network's capabilities and resources to afford a reliable backbone to healthcare IoT services. For example, QoS controls latency, delay variations, packet loss, and bandwidth and communication protocols. IoT healthcare systems that are based on cloud, edge, and fog computing technologies have multiple QoS aspects to be controlled, such as performance, reliability, scalability, and availability. The following subsections discuss those aspects.

1.6.1 Performance

Performance is a very important aspect to address in healthcare IoT systems because they include a wide variety of heterogeneous tools that collect huge amounts of medical and health data for acute and chronic cases, and such data needs to be processed quickly using high performance computing technologies. Therefore, healthcare IoT systems must contain improved methods to ensure high-performance results. Scalability and interoperability play the main role in the performance of IoT healthcare systems. Furthermore, IoT big data should be processed in a distributed and parallel way to enhance the performance of data analysis.

Many techniques were introduced in different domains to obtain high-performance healthcare IoT systems (Manogaran et al., 2018; Pace et al., 2018; Muhammed et al., 2018; X. M. Zhang and N. Zhang, 2011; Mohammed et al., 2014). For example, correct interaction and connection between different IoT healthcare devices guarantee that both the tools and patient personal information are under suitable care. Furthermore, a low power WBAN device gives reliable and efficient infrastructure to all embedded, non-embedded, and wearable sensor devices for the patient body. In Pace et al., 2018; Sood and Mahajan, 2017; Oueida et al., 2018; Bibani et al., 2016; Singh et al., 2018, the tasks between fog computing nodes and cloud computing system must be coordinated, so high computational tasks are performed permanently in the cloud computing resources, but other analytical tasks are performed in the fog nodes to reduce the load and enhance the performance of different healthcare activities.

1.6.2 Availability

IoT availability is defined as the reachability of IoT services when network link or device failures occur. A minor interruption of critical healthcare services, especially for older people or in an emergency, may disrupt that service's provisioning and lead to patient death. The availability of IoT healthcare services in a cloud-based computing network is the first major demand. Cloud computing platforms include data storage and computing resources that are distributed on large networks. These networks must be consistent in healthcare IoT performance and availability services.

Healthcare IoT systems require interoperability, and therefore, these systems must use protocols, such as 6LoWPAN, and IPv6 which are significant for healthcare systems where availability always must be provided. In Devarajan and Ravi, 2019, they proposed a service placement algorithm to increase the service availability and the quality of service (QoS) satisfaction rate by mapping applications to the nearest fog devices and then pass the services of the applications to other fog devices depend on the available fog nodes.

1.6.3 Scalability

Healthcare IoT systems must be developed to help many patients. Also, doctors and other healthcare specialists must use the devices and troubleshoot any problem remotely. This requires transacting with a huge number of connections from wearable IoT sensors and devices to the healthcare servers. Scalability is defined as the ability of the healthcare IoT system to keep meeting system requirements in case of an increase in demand for its services. In Farahani et al., 2018, they used a clustering approach to improve scalability with more efficient communication among sensors, and to increase the duration of the network connections by decreasing the number of directors between the IoT nodes and their corresponding coordinators.

In Gomes et al., 2017, they used a load balancing algorithm with cloud computing to improve the scalability of the IoT network. This algorithm enhances energy consumption and processing abilities and reduces the time consumption of data processing.

1.6.4 Reliability

The reliability of healthcare IoT systems has absolute importance. Any problem with such a system availability often has direct consequences on patients and end users, so the system must operate without any failure. Unpredictable reliability could lead to many problems in obtaining reliable health monitoring and transferring important signals from patients to healthcare services.

Recently, many researchers addressed the reliability aspect using fog computing techniques. This gateway can offer a lot of features such as local data processing, local storage, secure data mining, etc. (Ahmad et al., 2016; Azimi, Anzanpour, et al., 2017; Rawashdeh et al., 2018; Jia et al., 2019). The reasons for using fog computing and local data processing are: (1) for long-range remote monitoring of patients suffering from chronic diseases, Internet disconnection may happen frequently.

Therefore, local data processing and local data storage improve system consistency and reliability Moosavi et al., 2016, and (2) fog computing allows preserving the system's operation locally in the local storage of the fog layer.

1.7 CONCLUSION

Healthcare IoT systems use medical sensors, mobile computing, and cloud computing technologies to manage patients' conditions and use communication technologies to transfer collected patient data to cloud computing storage. With the rapid increase of using IoT devices in the healthcare field, combining IoT with different Cloud, Fog, and Edge computing technologies improved healthcare IoT systems. Cloud computing technology significantly emerged in various healthcare IoT systems to enhance the platform and infrastructure of services. However, healthcare IoT sensors produce a huge amount of data, so processing and analyzing this data needs more time, especially in the cloud computing environment. Fog and Edge computing technologies transform computing power and processing to the end-user and resolve many data processing challenges including latency and performance.

In this study discussed in this chapter and the previous chapter, we conducted a survey to identify the main research topics that have been addressed in the domain of healthcare IoT systems when used with cloud, fog, and edge computing technologies. We applied a large-scale comprehensive study by analyzing the related research papers based on the exclusion and inclusion criteria that are described previously. Our investigation found that healthcare IoT systems address mainly five research topics, namely: big data, security, latency, energy efficiency, and QoS. We found that the highest number of research papers focused on big data, i.e., 63% of the studied research papers, while the energy efficiency topic had the lowest number of papers, i.e., 17% of the papers. Most of the papers that focused on the big data topic used cloud computing technology to solve big data processing issues, i.e., 55.5% of the research papers that address big data used cloud computing. Likewise, 59.4% of the security-related papers addressed the security aspect in the cloud layer. Most of the papers that address the latency topic used the edge and fog layers, i.e., 68% of the latency-related papers, to reduce latency in healthcare IoT systems. Most of the papers that address energy efficiency used cloud computing, i.e., 47% of the papers, and fog computing, i.e., 35% of the papers, to improve energy efficiency. Overall, we found that the Fog computing layer has better performance, less latency, and better security protocols compared to the cloud layer. The edge and fog layers also enhance the cloud layer by applying early data cleaning and processing tasks to the received raw data before the data is finally transmitted to the cloud layer for further processing and storage. An empirical study of the tools utilized in each discovered topic is an avenue for future work.

REFERENCES

Ahmad, M., Amin, M. B., Hussain, S., Kang, B. H., Cheong, T., & Lee, S. (2016). Health fog: A novel framework for health and wellness applications. *The Journal of Supercomputing*, *72*(10), 3677–3695. DOI: 10.1007/s11227-016-1634-x

Akulov, D. (July 2019). *The benefits of using a multi-cloud strategy for IoT platforms*. url: https://www.itproportal.com/features/the-benefits-of-using-a-multi-cloud-strategy-for-iot-platforms/

Amin, S. U., Hossain, M. S., Muhammad, G., Alhussein, M., & Rahman, M. A. (2019). Cognitive smart healthcare for pathology detection and monitoring. *IEEE Access : Practical Innovations, Open Solutions*, *7*, 10745–10753. DOI: 10.1109/ACCESS.2019.2891390

Azimi, I., Anzanpour, A., Rahmani, A. M., Pahikkala, T., Levorato, M., Liljeberg, P., & Dutt, N. (2017). HiCH: Hierarchical fog-assisted computing architecture for healthcare IoT [TECS]. *ACM Transactions on Embedded Computing Systems*, *16*(5s), 1–20. DOI: 10.1145/3126501

Azimi, I., & Takalo-Mattila, J.. (2018). "Empowering healthcare iot systems with hierarchical edge-based deep learning". In: *Proceedings of the 2018 IEEE/ACM International Conference on Connected Health: Applications, Systems and Engineering Technologies*, pp. 63–68. DOI: 10.1145/3278576.3278597

Benadda, B., ... (2018). "Secure IoT solution for wearable health care applications, case study Electric Imp development platform". In: *International Journal of Communication Systems* 31.5, e3499. DOI: 10.1002/dac.3499

Bibani, O.. (2016). "A demo of IoT healthcare application provisioning in hybrid cloud/fog environment". In: *2016 IEEE International Conference on Cloud Computing Technology and Science (CloudCom)*. IEEE, pp. 472–475. DOI: 10.1109/CloudCom.2016.0081

Devarajan, M., & Ravi, L. (2019). Intelligent cyber-physical system for an efficient detection of Parkinson disease using fog computing. *Multimedia Tools and Applications*, *78*(23), 32695–32719. DOI: 10.1007/s11042-018-6898-0

Doukas, C., & Maglogiannis, I. (2012). "Bringing IoT and cloud computing towards pervasive healthcare". In: *2012 Sixth International Conference on Innovative Mobile and Internet Services in Ubiquitous Computing*. IEEE, pp. 922–926. DOI: 10.1109/IMIS.2012.26

Farahani, B., Firouzi, F., Chang, V., Badaroglu, M., Constant, N., & Mankodiya, K. (2018). Towards fog-driven IoT eHealth: Promises and challenges of IoT in medicine and healthcare. *Future Generation Computer Systems*, *78*, 659–676. DOI: 10.1016/j.future.2017.04.036

Feng, S., Liang, Z., & Zhao, D. (2010). Providing telemedicine services in an infrastructure-based cognitive radio network. *IEEE Wireless Communications*, *17*(1), 96–103. DOI: 10.1109/MWC.2010.5416356

Fernández-Caramés. Tiago M et al. (2019). "Enabling the internet of mobile crowdsourcing health things: A mobile fog computing, blockchain and IoT based continuous glucose monitoring system for diabetes mellitus research and care". In: *Sensors* 19.15, p. 3319.

Geman, O.. (2018). Ubiquitous healthcare system based on the sensors network and android internet of things gateway. In *In: 2018 IEEE SmartWorld, Ubiquitous Intelligence & Computing, Advanced & Trusted Computing, Scalable Computing & Communications, Cloud & Big Data Computing, Internet of People and Smart City Innovation (SmartWorld/SCALCOM/UIC/ATC/CBDCom/IOP/SCI)* (pp. 1390–1395). IEEE.

Gia, T. N., & Ben Dhaou, I.. (2019). Energy efficient fog-assisted IoT system for monitoring diabetic patients with cardiovascular disease. *Future Generation Computer Systems*, *93*, 198–211. DOI: 10.1016/j.future.2018.10.029

Gia, T. N., & Jiang, M.. (2015). Fog computing in healthcare internet of things: A case study on ecg feature extraction. In *In: 2015 IEEE international conference on computer and information technology; ubiquitous computing and communications; dependable, autonomic and secure computing; pervasive intelligence and computing* (pp. 356–363). IEEE.

Gomes, Berto de Tácio Pereira et al. (2017). "A comprehensive and scalable middleware for ambient assisted living based on cloud computing and internet of things". In: *Concurrency and Computation: Practice and Experience* 29.11, e4043.

Hassanalieragh, M.. (2015). "Health monitoring and management using Internet-of-Things (IoT) sensing with cloud-based processing: Opportunities and challenges". In: *2015 IEEE International Conference on Services Computing*. IEEE, pp. 285–292. DOI: 10.1109/SCC.2015.47

Hossain, M Shamim and Ghulam Muhammad (2016). "Cloud-assisted industrial internet of things (iiot)–enabled framework for health monitoring". In: *Computer Networks* 101, pp. 192–202.

Hu, J.-X., ... (2017). "An intelligent and secure health monitoring scheme using IoT sensor based on cloud computing". In: *Journal of Sensors* 2017. DOI: 10.1155/2017/3734764

Jia, X., He, D., Kumar, N., & Choo, K.-K. R. (2019). Authenticated key agreement scheme for fog-driven IoT healthcare system. *Wireless Networks*, *25*(8), 4737–4750. DOI: 10.1007/s11276-018-1759-3

Jusak, J., Pratikno, H., & Putra, V. H. (2016). "Internet of Medical Things for cardiac monitoring: Paving the way to 5G mobile networks". In: *2016 IEEE International Conference on Communication, Networks and Satellite (COMNETSAT)*. IEEE, pp. 75–79. DOI: 10.1109/COMNETSAT.2016.7907420

Kumar, P. M., Lokesh, S., Varatharajan, R., Chandra Babu, G., & Parthasarathy, P. (2018). Cloud and IoT based disease prediction and diagnosis system for healthcare using Fuzzy neural classifier. *Future Generation Computer Systems*, *86*, 527–534. DOI: 10.1016/j.future.2018.04.036

La, Q. D., Ngo, M. V., Dinh, T. Q., Quek, T. Q. S., & Shin, H. (2019). Enabling intelligence in fog computing to achieve energy and latency reduction. *Digital Communications and Networks*, *5*(1), 3–9. DOI: 10.1016/j.dcan.2018.10.008

Mahmoud, Mukhtar ME, Joel JPC Rodrigues, Kashif Saleem, et al. (2018). "Towards energy-aware fog-enabled cloud of things for healthcare". In: *Computers & Electrical Engineering* 67, pp. 58–69.

Mahmoud, Mukhtar ME, Joel JPC Rodrigues, Syed Hassan Ahmed, et al. (2018). "Enabling technologies on cloud of things for smart healthcare". In: *IEEE Access* 6, pp. 31950–31967.

Manikandan, R., Patan, R., Gandomi, A. H., Sivanesan, P., & Kalyanaraman, H. (2020). Hash polynomial two factor decision tree using IoT for smart health care scheduling. *Expert Systems with Applications*, *141*, 112924. DOI: 10.1016/j.eswa.2019.112924

Manogaran, G., Varatharajan, R., Lopez, D., Kumar, P. M., Sundarasekar, R., & Thota, C. (2018). A new architecture of Internet of Things and big data ecosystem for secured smart healthcare monitoring and alerting system. *Future Generation Computer Systems*, *82*, 375–387. DOI: 10.1016/j.future.2017.10.045

Mohammed, J.. (2014). Internet of Things: Remote patient monitoring using web services and cloud computing. In *In: 2014 IEEE international conference on internet of things (iThings), and IEEE green computing and communications (GreenCom) and IEEE cyber, physical and social computing (CPSCom)* (pp. 256–263). IEEE.

Moosavi, S. R., Gia, T. N., Nigussie, E., Rahmani, A. M., Virtanen, S., Tenhunen, H., & Isoaho, J. (2016). End-to-end security scheme for mobility enabled healthcare Internet of Things. *Future Generation Computer Systems*, *64*, 108–124. DOI: 10.1016/j.future.2016.02.020

Muhammad, G., Rahman, S. K. M. M., Alelaiwi, A., & Alamri, A. (2017). Smart health solution integrating IoT and cloud: A case study of voice pathology monitoring. *IEEE Communications Magazine*, *55*(1), 69–73. DOI: 10.1109/MCOM.2017.1600425CM

Muhammed, T., Mehmood, R., Albeshri, A., & Katib, I. (2018). UbeHealth: A personalized ubiquitous cloud and edge-enabled networked healthcare system for smart cities. *IEEE Access : Practical Innovations, Open Solutions*, *6*, 32258–32285. DOI: 10.1109/ACCESS.2018.2846609

Oueida, S., Kotb, Y., Aloqaily, M., Jararweh, Y., & Baker, T. (2018). An edge computing based smart healthcare framework for resource management. *Sensors (Basel)*, *18*(12), 4307. DOI: 10.3390/s18124307 PMID: 30563267

Ozdemir, A. T., Tunc, C., & Hariri, S. (2017). Autonomic fall detection system. In *In: 2017 IEEE 2nd International Workshops on Foundations and Applications of Self* Systems (FAS* W)* (pp. 166–170). IEEE.

Pace, P., Aloi, G., Gravina, R., Caliciuri, G., Fortino, G., & Liotta, A. (2018). An edge-based architecture to support efficient applications for healthcare industry 4.0. *IEEE Transactions on Industrial Informatics*, *15*(1), 481–489. DOI: 10.1109/TII.2018.2843169

Quintero, Dino and Frank N Lee (2019). *IBM Reference Architecture for High Performance Data and AI in Healthcare and Life Sciences.*

Quwaider, M., & Jararweh, Y. (2016). A cloud supported model for efficient community health awareness. *Pervasive and Mobile Computing*, *28*, 35–50. DOI: 10.1016/j.pmcj.2015.07.012

Rani, S., Ahmed, S. H., & Shah, S. C. (2018). Smart health: A novel paradigm to control the chickungunya virus. *IEEE Internet of Things Journal*, *6*(2), 1306–1311. DOI: 10.1109/JIOT.2018.2802898

Rawashdeh, M., AL Zamil, M. G. H., Hossain, M. S., Samarah, S., Amin, S. U., & Muhammad, G. (2018). Reliable service delivery in Tele-health care systems. *Journal of Network and Computer Applications*, *115*, 86–93. DOI: 10.1016/j.jnca.2018.04.015

Ray, P. P., Thapa, N., & Dash, D. (2019). Implementation and performance analysis of interoperable and heterogeneous IoT-edge gateway for pervasive wellness care. *IEEE Transactions on Consumer Electronics*, *65*(4), 464–473. DOI: 10.1109/TCE.2019.2939494

Sarkar, S., Chatterjee, S., Misra, S., & Kudupudi, R. (2017). Privacy-aware blind cloud framework for advanced healthcare. *IEEE Communications Letters*, *21*(11), 2492–2495. DOI: 10.1109/LCOMM.2017.2739141

Sharma, A., Choudhury, T., & Kumar, P. (2018). "Health monitoring & management using IoT devices in a Cloud Based Framework". In: *2018 International Conference on Advances in Computing and Communication Engineering (ICACCE)*. IEEE, pp. 219–224. DOI: 10.1109/ICACCE.2018.8441752

Singh, H., Mallaiah, R., Yadav, G., Verma, N., Sawhney, A., & Brahmachari, S. K. (2018). iCHRCloud: Web & mobile based child health imprints for smart healthcare. *Journal of Medical Systems*, *42*(1), 1–12. DOI: 10.1007/s10916-017-0866-5 PMID: 29188446

Sood, Sandeep K and Isha Mahajan (2017). "Wearable IoT sensor based healthcare system for identifying and controlling chikungunya virus". In: *Computers in Industry* 91, pp. 33–44.

Suciu, G., Suciu, V., Martian, A., Craciunescu, R., Vulpe, A., Marcu, I., Halunga, S., & Fratu, O. (2015). Big data, internet of things and cloud convergence–an architecture for secure e-health applications. *Journal of Medical Systems*, *39*(11), 1–8. DOI: 10.1007/s10916-015-0327-y PMID: 26345453

Ullah, F., Habib, M. A., Farhan, M., Khalid, S., Durrani, M. Y., & Jabbar, S. (2017). Semantic interoperability for big-data in heterogeneous IoT infrastructure for healthcare. *Sustainable Cities and Society*, *34*, 90–96. DOI: 10.1016/j.scs.2017.06.010

Verma, P., & Sood, S. K. (2018). Fog assisted-IoT enabled patient health monitoring in smart homes. *IEEE Internet of Things Journal*, *5*(3), 1789–1796. DOI: 10.1109/JIOT.2018.2803201

Vilela, Pedro H et al. (2019). "Performance evaluation of a Fog-assisted IoT solution for e-Health applications". In: *Future Generation Computer Systems* 97, pp. 379–386.

Wac, K., Bargh, M., Van Beijnum, B., Bults, R., Pawar, P., & Peddemors, A. (2009). Power-and delay-awareness of health telemonitoring services: The mobihealth system case study. *IEEE Journal on Selected Areas in Communications*, *27*(4), 525–536. DOI: 10.1109/JSAC.2009.090514

Xie, R., Khalil, I., Badsha, S., & Atiquzzaman, M. (2018). Fast and peer-to-peer vital signal learning system for cloud-based healthcare. *Future Generation Computer Systems*, *88*, 220–233. DOI: 10.1016/j.future.2018.05.042

Yacchirema, D., Sarabia-Jácome, D., Palau, C. E., & Esteve, M. (2018). System for monitoring and supporting the treatment of sleep apnea using IoT and big data. *Pervasive and Mobile Computing*, *50*, 25–40. DOI: 10.1016/j.pmcj.2018.07.007

Yang, G., Jiang, M., Ouyang, W., Ji, G., Xie, H., Rahmani, A. M., Liljeberg, P., & Tenhunen, H. (2017). IoT-based remote pain monitoring system: From device to cloud platform. *IEEE Journal of Biomedical and Health Informatics*, *22*(6), 1711–1719. DOI: 10.1109/JBHI.2017.2776351 PMID: 29990259

Yang, Y., Zheng, X., Guo, W., Liu, X., & Chang, V. (2018). Privacy-preserving fusion of IoT and big data for e-health. *Future Generation Computer Systems*, *86*, 1437–1455. DOI: 10.1016/j.future.2018.01.003

Yeh, L.-Y., Chiang, P.-Y., Tsai, Y.-L., & Huang, J.-L. (2015). Cloud-based fine-grained health information access control framework for lightweightiot devices with dynamic auditing andattribute revocation. *IEEE Transactions on Cloud Computing*, *6*(2), 532–544. DOI: 10.1109/TCC.2015.2485199

Zhang, X. M., & Zhang, N. (2011). An open, secure and flexible platform based on internet of things and cloud computing for ambient aiding living and telemedicine. In *In: 2011 international conference on computer and management (CAMAN)* (pp. 1–4). IEEE.

Compilation of References

Aazam, M., Zeadally, S., & Harras, K. A. (2020). Health fog for smart healthcare. *IEEE Consumer Electronics Magazine*, *9*(2), 96–102. DOI: 10.1109/MCE.2019.2953749

Abbas, R., Afolabi, R., Eleweke, I., Adesokan, A., Akinsola, A., & Elijah, L. (2025). Adopting Secure Software Development Practices to Improve Financial Transactions in the Banking Sector.

AbdElnapi., Noha M M et al. (2018). "A survey of internet of things technologies and projects for healthcare services". In: *2018 International Conference on Innovative Trends in Computer Engineering (ITCE)*. IEEE, pp. 48–55.

Abiona, O. O., Oladapo, O. J., Modupe, O. T., Oyeniran, O. C., Adewusi, A. O., & Komolafe, A. M.Oluwatosin Oluwatimileyin AbionaOluwatayo Jacob OladapoOluwole Temidayo ModupeOyekunle Claudius OyeniranAdebunmi Okechukwu AdewusiAbiola Moshood Komolafe. (2024). The emergence and importance of DevSecOps: Integrating and reviewing security practices within the DevOps pipeline. *World Journal of Advanced Engineering Technology and Sciences*, *11*(2), 127–133. DOI: 10.30574/wjaets.2024.11.2.0093

Abu Al-Haija, Q., Altamimi, S., & AlWadi, M. Analysis of Extreme Learning Machines (ELMs) for intelligent intrusion detection systems: A survey, Expert Systems with Applications, Volume 253, 2024, 124317, ISSN 0957-4174, https://doi.org/ DOI: 10.1016/j.eswa.2024.124317

Acharya, N., Shrivastava, N. A., Panigrahi, B. K., & Mohanty, U. C. (2014). Development of an artificial neural network based multi-model ensemble to estimate the northeast monsoon rainfall over south peninsular India: An application of extreme learning machine. *Climate Dynamics*, *43*(5-6), 1303–1310. DOI: 10.1007/s00382-013-1942-2

Adewole, S. A. (2024). *Navigating the Complexities ofDevSecOps: A Comprehnsive Exploration of Organizational.* Cultural & SocioTechnical Factors.

Afroz, S., Yamaguchi, F., & Wang, D. (2020). Investigating Bias in AI-Powered Phishing Detection Models. *Proceedings of the IEEE Symposium on Security and Privacy*, 107-120.1

Agarwal, Y. (2022). Apache log4j logging framework and its vulnerability.

Agarwal, A., Tiwari, V., & Al-Hamami, A. (2021). Cloud computing and cybersecurity: A survey. *Computers & Security, 110*, 102424.

Aggarwal, K., Mijwil, M. M., Al-Mistarehi, A.-H., Alomari, S., Gök, M., Alaabdin, A. M. Z., & Abdulrhman, S. H. (2022). Has the future started? The current growth of artificial intelligence, machine learning, and deep learning. *Iraqi Journal for Computer Science and Mathematics*, *3*(1), 115–123.

Ahmad, A. A.-S., & Andras, P. (2018). Measuring and testing the scalability of cloud-based software services. *2018 Fifth International Symposium on Innovation in Information and Communication Technology (ISIICT)*, 1–8. IEEE.

Ahmad, A. A.-S., & Andras, P. (2022). Scalability resilience framework using application-level fault injection for cloud-based software services. *Journal of Cloud Computing (Heidelberg, Germany)*, *11*(1), 1. Advance online publication. DOI: 10.1186/s13677-021-00277-z

Ahmad, M., Amin, M. B., Hussain, S., Kang, B. H., Cheong, T., & Lee, S. (2016). Health fog: A novel framework for health and wellness applications. *The Journal of Supercomputing*, *72*(10), 3677–3695. DOI: 10.1007/s11227-016-1634-x

Ajiga, D., Okeleke, P. A., Folorunsho, S. O., & Ezeigweneme, C. (2024). Designing cybersecurity measures for enterprise software applications to protect data integrity.

Ajiga, D., Okeleke, P. A., Folorunsho, S. O., & Ezeigweneme, C. (2024). Enhancing software development practices with AI insights in high-tech companies. IEEE Software Engineering Institute, Technical Report TR-2024-003.

Ajiga, Daniel. (2024). Navigating ethical considerations in software development and deployment in technological giants. .DOI: 10.53430/ijeru.2024.7.1.0033

Akulov, D. (July 2019). *The benefits of using a multi-cloud strategy for IoT platforms*. url: https://www.itproportal.com/features/the-benefits-of-using-a-multi-cloud-strategy-for-iot-platforms/

AlAfnan, M. A., Dishari, S., Jovic, M., & Lomidze, K. (2023). Chatgpt as an educational tool: Opportunities, challenges, and recommendations for communication, business writing, and composition courses. *Journal of Artificial Intelligence and Technology*, *3*(2), 60–68. DOI: 10.37965/jait.2023.0184

Alanazi, F., & Alenezi, M. (2023). Software engineering techniques for building sustainable cities with electric vehicles. *Applied Sciences (Basel, Switzerland)*, *13*(15), 8741. DOI: 10.3390/app13158741

Alasmari, S., & Anwar, M. (2016). "Security & privacy challenges in IoT-based health cloud". In: *2016 International Conference on Computational Science and Computational Intelligence (CSCI)*. IEEE, pp. 198–201. DOI: 10.1109/CSCI.2016.0044

Alberts, C. J., & Dorofee, A. J. (2002). *Managing Information Security Risks: The OCTAVE Approach*. Carnegie Mellon University.

Albrecht, T., *Machine Learning in Business: A Process and Project Perspective*. 2023.

Alert, C. (2020). *Advanced persistent threat compromise of government agencies, critical infrastructure, and private sector organizations*. CISA.

Al-Haija, Q. A., & Al-Salameen, S. O. (2024). Biometric Authentication System on Mobile Environment: A Review. *Computer Systems Science and Engineering*, *48*(4), 1–10. DOI: 10.32604/csse.2024.050846

Aljabri, M., Aldossary, M., Al-Homeed, N., Alhetelah, B., Althubiany, M., Alotaibi, O., & Alsaqer, S. (2022). *Testing and exploiting tools to improve owasp top ten security vulnerabilities detection.* Paper presented at the 2022 14th International Conference on Computational Intelligence and Communication Networks (CICN). DOI: 10.1109/CICN56167.2022.10008360

Aljedaani, B., & Babar, M. A. (2021). Challenges with developing secure mobile health applications: Systematic review. *JMIR mHealth and uHealth*, *9*(6), e15654. DOI: 10.2196/15654 PMID: 34152277

Alloghani, M. A. (2024). Criteria for Sustainable AI Software: Development and Evaluation of Sustainable AI Products. In *Signals and Communication Technology: Vol. Part F1802*. DOI: 10.1007/978-3-031-45214-7_2

Almorsy, M., Grundy, J., & Müller, I. (2014). An Analysis of the Cloud Computing Security Problem. *Proceedings of the 2014 Asia-Pacific Software Engineering Conference*, 50-59.

Alnafessah, A., Gias, A. U., Wang, R., Zhu, L., Casale, G., & Filieri, A. (2021). Quality-aware DevOps research: Where do we stand? *IEEE Access : Practical Innovations, Open Solutions*, *9*, 44476–44489. DOI: 10.1109/ACCESS.2021.3064867

Alonso, J., Orue-Echevarria, L., Casola, V., Torre, A. I., Huarte, M., Osaba, E., & Lobo, J. L. (2023). Understanding the challenges and novel architectural models of multi-cloud native applications–A systematic literature review. *Journal of Cloud Computing (Heidelberg, Germany)*, *12*(1), 1–34. DOI: 10.1186/s13677-022-00367-6

Alshra'a, A. S., Al Sardy, L., & German, R. (2024). Penetration testing in agile cybersecurity environments. In *Agile Security in the Digital Era* (pp. 126–161). CRC Press. DOI: 10.1201/9781003478676-6

Al-Tamimi, S., & Abu Al-Haija, Q. (2025). Security and Privacy of Educational Computational Intelligence. In M. Ouaissa, M. Ouaissa, H. Lamaazi, M. El Hamlaoui, & K. Reddy C. (Eds.), *Internet of Behavior-Based Computational Intelligence for Smart Education Systems* (pp. 301-328). IGI Global Scientific Publishing. https://doi.org/DOI: 10.4018/979-8-3693-8151-9.ch011

Al-Tamimi, S., Al-Haija, Q. A., & Alrawashdeh, K. "Zero-Trust Architecture for Securing Internet of Things (IoT) Networks: A Review," 2024 5th International Conference on Communications, Information, Electronic and Energy Systems (CIEES), Veliko Tarnovo, Bulgaria, 2024, pp. 1-6, DOI: 10.1109/CIEES62939.2024.10811176

Altamimi, S., & Abu Al-Haija, Q. (2024). Maximizing intrusion detection efficiency for IoT networks using extreme learning machines. *Discover Internet of Things*, *4*(1), 5. DOI: 10.1007/s43926-024-00060-x

Althar, R. R., Samanta, D., Purushotham, S., Sengar, S. S., & Hewage, C. (2023). Design and development of artificial intelligence knowledge processing system for optimizing the security of software systems. *SN Computer Science*, *4*(4), 331. DOI: 10.1007/s42979-023-01785-2

Amaro, R., Pereira, R., & da Silva, M. M. (2024). Mapping DevOps capabilities to the software life cycle: A systematic literature review. *Information and Software Technology*, •••, 107583.

Ambati, S. (2023). *Security and Authenticity of AI-generated code*. University of Saskatchewan.

Amershi, S., Begel, A., Bird, C., DeLine, R., Gall, H., Kamar, E., Nagappan, N., Nushi, B., & Zimmermann, T. (2019). Software engineering for machine learning: A case study. *2019 IEEE/ACM 41st International Conference on Software Engineering: Software Engineering in Practice (ICSE-SEIP)*, 291–300.

Amin, S. U., Hossain, M. S., Muhammad, G., Alhussein, M., & Rahman, M. A. (2019). Cognitive smart healthcare for pathology detection and monitoring. *IEEE Access : Practical Innovations, Open Solutions*, *7*, 10745–10753. DOI: 10.1109/ACCESS.2019.2891390

Anand, S., Burke, E. K., Chen, T. Y., Clark, J., Cohen, M. B., Grieskamp, W., Harman, M., Harrold, M. J., McMinn, P., Bertolino, A., Jenny Li, J., & Zhu, H. (2013). An orchestrated survey of methodologies for automated software test case generation. *Journal of Systems and Software*, *86*(8), 1978–2001. DOI: 10.1016/j.jss.2013.02.061

Androutsopoulou, A., Karacapilidis, N., Loukis, E., & Charalabidis, Y. (2019). Transforming the communication between citizens and government through AI-guided chatbots. *Government Information Quarterly*, *36*(2), 358–367. DOI: 10.1016/j.giq.2018.10.001

Ankalaki, S., Rajesh, A. A., Pallavi, M., Hukkeri, G. S., Jan, T., & Naik, G. R. (2025). Cyber Attack Prediction: From Traditional Machine Learning to Generative Artificial Intelligence. *IEEE Access*.

Anwar Mohammad, M. N., Nazir, M., & Mustafa, K. (2019). A systematic review and analytical evaluation of security requirements engineering approaches. *Arabian Journal for Science and Engineering*, *44*(11), 8963–8987. DOI: 10.1007/s13369-019-04067-3

Arora, V., Vargas, E., Aniche, M., & Deursen, A. (2021). Secure Software Engineering in the Financial Services: A Practitioners' Perspective. 10.48550/arXiv.2104.03476.

Artac, M., ... (2017). DevOps: Introducing infrastructure-as-code. 2017 IEEE/ACM 39th International Conference on Software Engineering Companion (ICSE-C), 497–498. IEEE.

Atlam, Hany F et al. (2017). "Integration of cloud computing with internet of things: challenges and open issues". In: *2017 IEEE International Conference on Internet of Things (iThings) and IEEE Green Computing and Communications (GreenCom) and IEEE Cyber, Physical and Social Computing (CPSCom) and IEEE Smart Data (SmartData)*. IEEE, pp. 670–675.

Atlas, S. (2023). *ChatGPT for higher education and professional development: A guide to conversational AI.*

AYNALEM, S. Y. (2022). A FRAMEWORK FOR SOFTWARE SECURITY TESTING IMPROVEMENT FOR WEB-BASED APPLICATIONS.

Ayotunde Alaba, F., Sulaimon, H. A., Ifeyinwa Marisa, M., & Najeem, O. (2024). Smart Contracts Security Application and Challenges: A Review. *Cloud Computing and Data Science, 5*(1).

Azimi, I., Anzanpour, A., Rahmani, A. M., Pahikkala, T., Levorato, M., Liljeberg, P., & Dutt, N. (2017). HiCH: Hierarchical fog-assisted computing architecture for healthcare IoT [TECS]. *ACM Transactions on Embedded Computing Systems, 16*(5s), 1–20. DOI: 10.1145/3126501

Azimi, I., & Takalo-Mattila, J.. (2018). "Empowering healthcare iot systems with hierarchical edge-based deep learning". In: *Proceedings of the 2018 IEEE/ACM International Conference on Connected Health: Applications, Systems and Engineering Technologies*, pp. 63–68. DOI: 10.1145/3278576.3278597

Azizi, M., & Do, H. (Oct. 2018). "ReTEST: A Cost Effective Test Case Selection Technique for Modern Software Development". In: *Proceedings of the 29th International Symposium on Software Reliability Engineering (ISSRE'18)*. Ed. by Ghosh, Sudipto, & Natella, Roberto. Memphis, TN, USA: IEEE, pp. 144–154. DOI: 10.1109/ISSRE.2018.00025

Babu, C. V. S., & Andrew, S. P. (2024). Adaptive AI for Dynamic Cybersecurity Systems: Enhancing Protection in a Rapidly Evolving Digital Landscape. In Zhihan, Lv., & Global, I. G. I. (Eds.), *Principles and Applications of Adaptive Artificial Intelligence* (pp. 52–72)., DOI: 10.4018/979-8-3693-0230-9.ch003

Bakhshi, T., Ghita, B., & Kuzminykh, I. (2024). A Review of IoT Firmware Vulnerabilities and Auditing Techniques. In *Sensors* (Vol. 24, Issue 2). DOI: 10.3390/s24020708

Baldassarre, M. T., Barletta, V. S., Caivano, D., & Scalera, M. (2020). Integrating security and privacy in software development. *Software Quality Journal, 28*(3), 987–1018. DOI: 10.1007/s11219-020-09501-6

Baluta, T., Chua, Z. L., Meel, K. S., & Saxena, P. (2021). Scalable quantitative verification for deep neural networks. In *Proceedings of the 2021 IEEE/ACM 43rd International Conference on Software Engineering (ICSE)* (pp. 1-10). IEEE.

Barkaoui, K., Outamazirt, A., & Aissani, D. (2019). A new analytical model for calculating elasticity in cloud computing. MSR 2019-12ème Colloque sur la Modélisation des Systèmes Réactifs.

Bass, L., Weber, I., & Zhu, L. (2015). *DevOps: A Software Architect's Perspective*. Addison-Wesley.

Beck, K., Beedle, M., van Bennekum, A., Cockburn, A., Cunningham, W., & Jeffries, R. (2001). *Manifesto for Agile Software Development.*

Behutiye, W., Karhapää, P., López, L., Burgués, X., Martínez-Fernández, S., Vollmer, A. M., Rodríguez, P., Franch, X., & Oivo, M. (2020). Management of quality requirements in agile and rapid software development: A systematic mapping study. *Information and Software Technology*, *123*, 106225. DOI: 10.1016/j.infsof.2019.106225

Benadda, B., ... (2018). "Secure IoT solution for wearable health care applications, case study Electric Imp development platform". In: *International Journal of Communication Systems* 31.5, e3499. DOI: 10.1002/dac.3499

Bentaleb, O., Belloum, A. S. Z., Sebaa, A., & El-Maouhab, A. (2022). Containerization technologies: Taxonomies, applications and challenges. *The Journal of Supercomputing*, *78*(1), 1144–1181. DOI: 10.1007/s11227-021-03914-1

Berman, M., Triki, A. R., & Blaschko, M. B. (2018). The Lovasz-Softmax loss: A tractable surrogate for the optimization of the intersection-over-union measure in neural networks. In *Proceedings of the 2018 IEEE/CVF Conference on Computer Vision and Pattern Recognition (CVPR)* (pp. 1-10). IEEE. DOI: 10.1109/CVPR.2018.00464

Bernardino, N. A., Sequeira, B., Piza, E., Henriques, F., Neves, F., & Reis, C. I. (2024). *Enhancing DevSecOps: Three Custom Tools for Continuous Security.* Paper presented at the 2024 IEEE 11th International Conference on Cyber Security and Cloud Computing (CSCloud). DOI: 10.1109/CSCloud62866.2024.00017

Bertolino, A. (2007). Software Testing Research: Achievements, Challenges, Dreams. In *In: 2007 Future of Software Engineering* (pp. 85–103). IEEE Computer Society.

Bhatia, M., & Sood, S. K. (2019). Exploring temporal analytics in fog-cloud architecture for smart office healthcare. *Mobile Networks and Applications*, *24*(4), 1392–1410. DOI: 10.1007/s11036-018-0991-5

BHATORE. (2020). *S., Software Engineering practices for building MLware applications-credit risk evaluation case study*. International Institute of Information Technology Hyderabad.

Bhat, S. A., & Huang, N.-F. (2021). Big data and ai revolution in precision agriculture: Survey and challenges. *IEEE Access : Practical Innovations, Open Solutions*, *9*, 110209–110222. DOI: 10.1109/ACCESS.2021.3102227

Bibani, O.. (2016). "A demo of IoT healthcare application provisioning in hybrid cloud/fog environment". In: *2016 IEEE International Conference on Cloud Computing Technology and Science (CloudCom)*. IEEE, pp. 472–475. DOI: 10.1109/CloudCom.2016.0081

Boda, V. V. R. (2022). Zero Trust in Healthcare: Building a Secure Future with DevOps. *Advances in Computer Sciences, 5*(1).

Bonde, B. (2024). Edge, Fog, and Cloud Against Disease: The Potential of High-Performance Cloud Computing for Pharma Drug Discovery. In *Methods in molecular biology (Clifton, N.J.)* (Vol. 2716). DOI: 10.1007/978-1-0716-3449-3_8

Bonomi, F.. (2014). Fog computing: A platform for internet of things and analytics. In *Big data and internet of things: A roadmap for smart environments* (pp. 169–186). Springer. DOI: 10.1007/978-3-319-05029-4_7

Boopathi, S. (2023). Deep Learning Techniques Applied for Automatic Sentence Generation. In *Promoting Diversity, Equity, and Inclusion in Language Learning Environments* (pp. 255–273). IGI Global. DOI: 10.4018/978-1-6684-3632-5.ch016

Brataas, G.. (2017). Scalability analysis of cloud software services. *2017 IEEE International Conference on Autonomic Computing (ICAC)*, 285–292. IEEE. DOI: 10.1109/ICAC.2017.34

Briand, L. C., Labiche, Y., & He, S. (2009, January). Automating Regression Test Selection Based on UML Designs. *Information and Software Technology, 51*(1), 16–30. DOI: 10.1016/j.infsof.2008.09.010

Brundage, M., ... *The malicious use of artificial intelligence: Forecasting, prevention, and mitigation.* arXiv preprint arXiv:1802.07228, 2018.

Brundage, M., Avin, S., & Clark, J.. (2020). Toward Trustworthy AI Development: Mechanisms for Supporting Verifiable Claims. *Journal of AI Research, 69*, 365–412.

Buczak, A. L., & Guven, E. (2016). A Survey of Data Mining and Machine Learning Methods for Cyber Security Intrusion Detection. *IEEE Communications Surveys and Tutorials, 18*(2), 1153–1176. DOI: 10.1109/COMST.2015.2494502

Bulla, S., Reddy, C. V. R., Padmavathi, P., & Padmasri, T. (2020). Analytical evaluation of resource estimation in web application services. *Ingénierie des Systèmes d'Information, 25*(5), 683–690. DOI: 10.18280/isi.250516

Caracciolo, M. (2023). *Policy as Code, how to automate cloud compliance verification with open-source tools.* Politecnico di Torino, Chung, J. (2024). *DevSecOps Metrics, Benefits, and Improvements.* National University, Cybersecurity, C. I. (2018). Framework for improving critical infrastructure cybersecurity. *URL:https:// nvlpubs. nist. gov/nistpubs/CSWP/NIST. CSWP, 4162018*(7).

Carriles, S. C., Martínez, J. V. B., Bernabéu, J. M. S., & Pérez, F. M. (2024). S-SCRUM—Methodology for Software Securitisation at Agile Development. Application to Smart University. *Lecture Notes in Networks and Systems, 789 LNNS.* DOI: 10.1007/978-981-99-6586-1_3

Casola, V., De Benedictis, A., Mazzocca, C., & Orbinato, V. (2024). Secure software development and testing: A model-based methodology. *Computers & Security*, *137*, 103639. Advance online publication. DOI: 10.1016/j.cose.2023.103639

Chafik, N. and D.A. Benchekroun, *Integrating artificial intelligence in software engineering: Enhancements and challenges in the development lifecycle.* 2020.

Chandramouli, R., Xie, S., & Bhatia, S. (2019). Leveraging machine learning for cyber threat intelligence. *Journal of Cybersecurity and Privacy*, *1*(1), 84–101.

Chassignol, M., Khoroshavin, A., Klimova, A., & Bilyatdinova, A. (2018). Artificial Intelligence trends in education: A narrative overview. *Procedia Computer Science*, *136*, 16–24. DOI: 10.1016/j.procs.2018.08.233

Cheng, L., Liu, F., & Yao, D. (2020). Enterprise Threat Modeling: Threat Model Analysis and Management with Open-Source Tools. *ACM Transactions on Privacy and Security*, *23*(1), 1–28.

Chen, H., & Babar, M. A. (2024). Security for Machine Learning-based Software Systems: A Survey of Threats, Practices, and Challenges. *ACM Computing Surveys*, *56*(6), 1–38. Advance online publication. DOI: 10.1145/3638531

Chen, H., Chan-Olmsted, S., Kim, J., & Mayor Sanabria, I. (2022). Consumers' perception on artificial intelligence applications in marketing communication. *Qualitative Market Research*, *25*(1), 125–142. DOI: 10.1108/QMR-03-2021-0040

Chen, S.. (2011). "Using semi-supervised clustering to improve regression test selection techniques". In: *2011 Fourth IEEE International Conference on Software Testing, Verification and Validation*. IEEE, pp. 1–10. DOI: 10.1109/ICST.2011.38

Chen, X., Xie, H., & Hwang, G.-J. (2020). A multi-perspective study on artificial intelligence in education: Grants, conferences, journals, software tools, institutions, and researchers. *Computers and Education: Artificial Intelligence*, *1*, 100005. DOI: 10.1016/j.caeai.2020.100005

Chen, Y., Probert, R. L., & Paul Sims, D. (Sept. 2002). "Specification-Based Regression Test Selection with Risk Analysis". In: *Proceedings of the Conference of the Centre for Advanced Studies on Collaborative Research (CASCON'02)*. Ed. by Stewart, Darlen A., & Howard Johnson, J.. IBM Press, pp. 1–14.

Chittimalli, P. K., & Harrold, M. J. (2009). Recomputing Coverage Information to Assist Regression Testing. *IEEE Transactions on Software Engineering*, *35*(4), 452–469. DOI: 10.1109/TSE.2009.4

Choudhury, L. K. (2022). STUDY ON LOGIC AND ARTIFICIAL INTELLIGENCE SUBSETS OF ARTIFICIAL INTELLIGENCE. *Innovative Research Thoughts*, *8*(1), 127–134.

Ciresan, D.. (2012). Deep neural networks segment neuronal membranes in electron microscopy images. *Advances in Neural Information Processing Systems*, ●●●, 25.

Coleman, A. (2024). Integrating MLOps Pipelines with DevOps for Seamless Model Deployment and Continuous Delivery. *Australian Journal of Machine Learning Research & Applications*, *4*(2), 87–94.

Collier, M., & Shahan, R. (2015). *Microsoft Azure essentials—Fundamentals of Azure*. Microsoft Press.

Dahl, H., Tøndel, I., & Beisheim, E. (2020). Integrating Security in Agile Development: A Case Study. *Journal of Systems and Software*, *166*, 110594.

Dakić, P. (2024). Software compliance in various industries using ci/cd, dynamic microservices, and containers. *Open Computer Science*, *14*(1), 20240013. DOI: 10.1515/comp-2024-0013

Darwish, A., Hassanien, A. E., Elhoseny, M., Sangaiah, A. K., & Muhammad, K. (2019). The impact of the hybrid platform of internet of things and cloud computing on healthcare systems: Opportunities, challenges, and open problems. *Journal of Ambient Intelligence and Humanized Computing*, *10*(10), 4151–4166. DOI: 10.1007/s12652-017-0659-1

Dawoud, A., Finster, S., Coppik, N., & Ashiwal, V. (2024). *Better Left Shift Security! Framework for Secure Software Development.* Paper presented at the 2024 IEEE European Symposium on Security and Privacy Workshops (EuroS&PW). DOI: 10.1109/EuroSPW61312.2024.00078

Dean, J., Grove, D., & Chambers, C. (Aug. 1995). "Optimization of ObjectOriented Programs Using Static Class Hierarchy Analysis". In: *Proceedings of the 9th European Conference on Object-Oriented Programming (ECOOP'95)*. Ed. by Walter G. Olthoff. LNCS 952. Åarhus, Denmark: Springer, pp. 77–101. DOI: 10.1007/3-540-49538-X_5

Demir, E., Köseoğlu, E., Sokullu, R., & Şeker, B. (2017). Smart home assistant for ambient assisted living of elderly people with dementia. *Procedia Computer Science, 113*, 609–614. DOI: 10.1016/j.procs.2017.08.302

Demi, S., Colomo-Palacios, R., & Sanchez-Gordon, M. (2021). Software engineering applications enabled by blockchain technology: A systematic mapping study. *Applied Sciences (Basel, Switzerland), 11*(7), 2960. DOI: 10.3390/app11072960

Devarajan, M., & Ravi, L. (2019). Intelligent cyber-physical system for an efficient detection of Parkinson disease using fog computing. *Multimedia Tools and Applications, 78*(23), 32695–32719. DOI: 10.1007/s11042-018-6898-0

Dhanvijay, Mrinai M and Shailaja C Patil (2019). "Internet of Things: A survey of enabling technologies in healthcare and its applications". In: *Computer Networks* 153, pp. 113–131.

Diaz Rivera, J. J., Akbar, W., Khan, T. A., Muhammad, A., & Song, W. C. (2024). Zt &t: Secure service session management using blockchain-based tokens in zero trust networks. *Annales Des Telecommunications. Annales des Télécommunications, 79*(7–8), 487–505. Advance online publication. DOI: 10.1007/s12243-023-01008-y

Dodson, D., Souppaya, M., & Scarfone, K. (2020). *Mitigating the risk of software vulnerabilities by adopting a secure software development framework (SDF)*. NIST.

Dotsenko, S., Kharchenko, V., Morozova, O., Rucinski, A., & Dotsenko, S. (2022). Heuristic self-organization of knowledge representation and development: Analysis in the context of explainable artificial intelligence. *Radioelectronics and Computer Systems, 1*(1), 50–66. DOI: 10.32620/reks.2022.1.04

Doukas, C., & Maglogiannis, I. (2012). "Bringing IoT and cloud computing towards pervasive healthcare". In: *2012 Sixth International Conference on Innovative Mobile and Internet Services in Ubiquitous Computing*. IEEE, pp. 922–926. DOI: 10.1109/IMIS.2012.26

Dubey, H.. (2015). "Fog data: Enhancing telehealth big data through fog computing". In: *Proceedings of the ASE bigdata & socialinformatics 2015*, pp. 1–6. DOI: 10.1145/2818869.2818889

Duddu, V., Rajesh Pillai, N., Rao, D. V., & Balas, V. E. (2020). Fault tolerance of neural networks in adversarial settings. *Journal of Intelligent & Fuzzy Systems*, *38*(5), 5897–5907. DOI: 10.3233/JIFS-179677

Ehlers, R. (2017). Formal verification of piece-wise linear feed-forward neural networks. In *Automated Technology for Verification and Analysis* (pp. 269–286). Springer International Publishing. DOI: 10.1007/978-3-319-68167-2_19

Engström, E., & Runeson, P. (2010). "A Qualitative Survey of Regression Testing Practices". In: *International Conference on Product Focused Software Process Improvement*. Springer, pp. 3–16. DOI: 10.1007/978-3-642-13792-1_3

Engström, E., Runeson, P., & Skoglund, M. (2010, January). A Systematic Review on Regression Test Selection Techniques. *Information and Software Technology*, *52*(1), 14–30. DOI: 10.1016/j.infsof.2009.07.001

Eniola, J., & Barnty, W. (2025). Agile Development and Cybersecurity: Balancing Speed with Data Security.

Eshraghian, F., Hafezieh, N., Farivar, F., & de Cesare, S. (2024). AI in software programming: Understanding emotional responses to GitHub Copilot. *Information Technology & People*. Advance online publication. DOI: 10.1108/ITP-01-2023-0084

Esteva, A., et al., *Dermatologist-level classification of skin cancer with deep neural networks.* nature, 2017. **542**(7639): p. 115-118.

European Commission. (2021). The Artificial Intelligence Act: A Regulatory Proposal for AI Systems. Available at: https://digital-strategy.ec.europa.eu/en/library/proposal-regulation-laying-down-harmonised-rules-artificial-intelligence-ai-act

Fanjiang, Gary et al. (2005). "Building a better delivery system: a new engineering/health care partnership". In.

Farahani, B., Firouzi, F., Chang, V., Badaroglu, M., Constant, N., & Mankodiya, K. (2018). Towards fog-driven IoT eHealth: Promises and challenges of IoT in medicine and healthcare. *Future Generation Computer Systems*, *78*, 659–676. DOI: 10.1016/j.future.2017.04.036

Farooq, Qurat-ul-ann et al. (Mar. 2010). "A Model-Based Regression Testing Approach for Evolving Software Systems with Flexible Tool Support". In: *Proceedings of the 17th IEEE International Conference and Workshops on Engineering of Computer-Based Systems (ECBS'10)*. Oxford, UK: IEEE, pp. 41–49.

Faruk, M. J. H., Subramanian, S., Shahriar, H., Valero, M., Li, X., & Tasnim, M. (2022, May). Software engineering process and methodology in blockchain-oriented software development: A systematic study. In *2022 IEEE/ACIS 20th International Conference on Software Engineering Research, Management and Applications (SERA)* (pp. 120-127). IEEE. DOI: 10.1109/SERA54885.2022.9806817

Feng, S., Liang, Z., & Zhao, D. (2010). Providing telemedicine services in an infrastructure-based cognitive radio network. *IEEE Wireless Communications*, *17*(1), 96–103. DOI: 10.1109/MWC.2010.5416356

Fernández-Caramés. Tiago M et al. (2019). "Enabling the internet of mobile crowdsourcing health things: A mobile fog computing, blockchain and IoT based continuous glucose monitoring system for diabetes mellitus research and care". In: *Sensors* 19.15, p. 3319.

Feurer, M., & Hutter, F. (2019). Hyperparameter optimization. In *Automated Machine Learning* (pp. 3–33). Springer International Publishing. DOI: 10.1007/978-3-030-05318-5_1

Forsgren, N., Humble, J., & Kim, G. (2018). *Accelerate: The science of lean software and devops: Building and scaling high performing technology organizations*. IT Revolution.

Fowler, M., & Highsmith, J. (2001). The Agile Manifesto. *Software Development Magazine*, *9*(8), 28–35.

Fred, N., & Temkin, I. *A Systematic Literature Review on the Use of Machine Learning in Software Engineering*. arXiv preprint arXiv:2406.13877, 2024.

Friman, O. (2024). Agile and DevSecOps Oriented Vulnerability Detection and Mitigation on Public Cloud.

G., Shilpa R. et al. (2024). "Strengthening Web Application Security: A Penetration Regression Test Selection Algorithm for Early Detection of Buffer Overflow Vulnerability". In: *International Journal of Intelligent Systems and Applications in Engineering* 12.21s, pp. 3073–3079.

Gadani, N. N. (2024). The Future of Software Development: Integrating AI and Machine Learning into the SDLC. *International Journal of Engineering and Management Research*, *14*(1), 308–315.

Gasiba, T., Lechner, U., Pinto-Albuquerque, M., & Porwal, A. (2020, September). Cybersecurity awareness platform with a virtual coach and automated challenge assessment. In *International Workshop on the Security of Industrial Control Systems and Cyber-Physical Systems* (pp. 67-83). Cham: Springer International Publishing. DOI: 10.1007/978-3-030-64330-0_5

Gehr, T., Mirman, M., Drachsler-Cohen, D., Tsankov, P., Chaudhuri, S., & Vechev, M. (2018). AI2: Safety and robustness certification of neural networks with abstract interpretation. In *Proceedings of the 2018 IEEE Symposium on Security and Privacy (SP)* (pp. 1-10). IEEE. DOI: 10.1109/SP.2018.00058

Geman, O.. (2018). Ubiquitous healthcare system based on the sensors network and android internet of things gateway. In *In: 2018 IEEE SmartWorld, Ubiquitous Intelligence & Computing, Advanced & Trusted Computing, Scalable Computing & Communications, Cloud & Big Data Computing, Internet of People and Smart City Innovation (SmartWorld/SCALCOM/UIC/ATC/CBDCom/IOP/SCI)* (pp. 1390–1395). IEEE.

Germán Márquez, A., Varela-Vaca, Á. J., Gómez López, M. T., Galindo, J. A., & Benavides, D. (2024). Vulnerability impact analysis in software project dependencies based on Satisfiability Modulo Theories (SMT). *Computers & Security*, *139*, 103669. Advance online publication. DOI: 10.1016/j.cose.2023.103669

Gershfeld, I., & Sturm, A. (2024). Evaluating the effectiveness of a security flaws prevention tool. *Information and Software Technology*, *170*, 107427. Advance online publication. DOI: 10.1016/j.infsof.2024.107427

Ghosal, P., Das, D., & Das, I. (2018). "Extensive survey on cloud-based IoT-healthcare and security using machine learning". In: *2018 Fourth International Conference on Research in Computational Intelligence and Communication Networks (ICRCICN)*. IEEE, pp. 1–5. DOI: 10.1109/ICRCICN.2018.8718717

Gia, T. N.. (2015). Fog computing in healthcare internet of things: A case study on ecg feature extraction. In *In: 2015 IEEE international conference on computer and information technology; ubiquitous computing and communications; dependable, autonomic and secure computing; pervasive intelligence and computing* (pp. 356–363). IEEE.

Gia, T. N., & Ben Dhaou, I.. (2019). Energy efficient fog-assisted IoT system for monitoring diabetic patients with cardiovascular disease. *Future Generation Computer Systems*, *93*, 198–211. DOI: 10.1016/j.future.2018.10.029

Gkortzis, A., Feitosa, D., & Spinellis, D. (2021). Software reuse cuts both ways: An empirical analysis of its relationship with security vulnerabilities—. *Journal of Systems and Software*, *172*, 110653. DOI: 10.1016/j.jss.2020.110653

Gligoric, M., Eloussi, L., & Marinov, D. (July 2015). "Practical Regression Test Selection with Dynamic File Dependencies". In: *Proceedings of the 2015 International Symposium on Software Testing and Analysis (ISSTA'15)*. Baltimore, MD, USA: ACM, pp. 211–222. DOI: 10.1145/2771783.2771784

Gokarna, M. (2023). DevOps phases across software development lifecycle. *Authorea Preprints*.

Gomes, Berto de Tácio Pereira et al. (2017). "A comprehensive and scalable middleware for ambient assisted living based on cloud computing and internet of things". In: *Concurrency and Computation: Practice and Experience* 29.11, e4043.

Gomes, M., Pereira, R., Silva, M., de Vasconcelos, J. B., & Rocha, Á. (2022). *KPI's for Evaluation of DevOps Teams*. Paper presented at the World Conference on Information Systems and Technologies. DOI: 10.1007/978-3-031-04829-6_13

Goodfellow, I. (2016). *Deep learning*. MIT press.

Guo, L., Liang, J., & Li, D. (2016). Understanding ineffectiveness of the application-level fault injection. Poster in ACM/IEEE International Conference for High Performance Computing, Networking, Storage and Analysis (SC).

Guzman, A. L., & Lewis, S. C. (2020). Artificial intelligence and communication: A human–machine communication research agenda. *New Media & Society*, *22*(1), 70–86. DOI: 10.1177/1461444819858691

Gyori, A.. (Oct. 2018). "Evaluating Regression Test Selection Opportunities in a Very Large Open-Source Ecosystem". In: *Proceedings of the 29th International Symposium on Software Reliability Engineering (ISSRE'18)*. Ed. by Ghosh, Sudipto, & Natella, Roberto. Memphis, TN, USA: IEEE, pp. 112–122. DOI: 10.1109/ISSRE.2018.00022

Hancock, J. T., Naaman, M., & Levy, K. (2020). AI-mediated communication: Definition, research agenda, and ethical considerations. *Journal of Computer-Mediated Communication*, *25*(1), 89–100. DOI: 10.1093/jcmc/zmz022

Hanif, H., Nasir, M. H. N. M., Ab Razak, M. F., Firdaus, A., & Anuar, N. B. (2021). The rise of software vulnerability: Taxonomy of software vulnerabilities detection and machine learning approaches. *Journal of Network and Computer Applications*, *179*, 103009. DOI: 10.1016/j.jnca.2021.103009

Harkai, A., & Ciurea, C. E. (2024). Economic impact of IOT and conventional data breaches: Cost analysis and statistical trends. *Control and Cybernetics*, *53*(2), 385–404. DOI: 10.2478/candc-2024-0017

Harrold, M. J. (July 1999). "Testing Evolving Software". In: *Journal of Systems and Software* 47.2-3, pp. 173–181. DOI: 10.1016/S0164-1212(99)00037-0

Harrold, M. J.. (Oct. 2001). "Regression Test Selection for Java Software". In: *Proceedings of the 16th Conference on Object-Oriented Programming, Systems, Languages, and Applications (OOPSLA'01)*. Ed. by Vlissides, John. Tampa, FL, USA: ACM, pp. 312–326.

Hasnain, M., ... (2019). "Recurrent neural network for web services performance forecasting, ranking and regression testing". In: *2019 Asia-Pacific Signal and Information Processing Association Annual Summit and Conference (APSIPA ASC)*. IEEE, pp. 96–105. DOI: 10.1109/APSIPAASC47483.2019.9023052

Hassanalieragh, M.. (2015). "Health monitoring and management using Internet-of-Things (IoT) sensing with cloud-based processing: Opportunities and challenges". In: *2015 IEEE International Conference on Services Computing*. IEEE, pp. 285–292. DOI: 10.1109/SCC.2015.47

Hemani, Singh, D., & Dwivedi, R. K. (2024). Designing blockchain based secure autonomous vehicular internet of things (IoT) architecture with efficient smart contracts. *International Journal of Information Technology (Singapore)*. DOI: 10.1007/s41870-023-01712-x

Henning, S., & Hasselbring, W. (2021). How to measure scalability of distributed stream processing engines? Companion of the ACM/SPEC International Conference on Performance Engineering (ICPE '21), 85–88. Association for Computing Machinery. DOI: 10.1145/3447545.3451190

Henning, S., & Hasselbring, W. (2022). A configurable method for benchmarking scalability of cloud-native applications. *Empirical Software Engineering*, *27*(6), 143. DOI: 10.1007/s10664-022-10162-1

Hettiarachchi, C., Do, H., & Choi, B. (2014). "Effective regression testing using requirements and risks". In: *2014 Eighth International Conference on Software Security and Reliability (SERE)*. IEEE, pp. 157–166. DOI: 10.1109/SERE.2014.29

Holmes, W. (2020). Artificial intelligence in education. In *Encyclopedia of education and information technologies* (pp. 88–103). Springer. DOI: 10.1007/978-3-030-10576-1_107

Holst, A. (Aug. 2021). *IOT connected devices worldwide 2019-2030*. url: https://www.statista.com/statistics/1183457/iot-connected-devices-worldwide/

Hossain, M Shamim and Ghulam Muhammad (2016). "Cloud-assisted industrial internet of things (iiot)–enabled framework for health monitoring". In: *Computer Networks* 101, pp. 192–202.

Hou, X., Zhao, Y., Liu, Y., Yang, Z., Wang, K., Li, L., Luo, X., Lo, D., Grundy, J., & Wang, H. (2024). Large language models for software engineering: A systematic literature review. *ACM Transactions on Software Engineering and Methodology*, *33*(8), 1–79. DOI: 10.1145/3695988

Hsia, P.. (1997, July). A Technique for the Selective Revalidation of OO Software. *Journal of Software (Malden, MA)*, *9*(4), 217–233.

Hsu, T. H.-C. (2018). *Hands-On Security in DevOps: Ensure continuous security, deployment, and delivery with DevSecOps*. Packt Publishing Ltd.

Hu, J.-X., ... (2017). "An intelligent and secure health monitoring scheme using IoT sensor based on cloud computing". In: *Journal of Sensors* 2017. DOI: 10.1155/2017/3734764

Huang, C., Zhai, S., Guo, P., & Susskind, J. (2021). MetricOpt: Learning to optimize black-box evaluation metrics. In *Proceedings of the IEEE/CVF Conference on Computer Vision and Pattern Recognition* (pp. 1-10). DOI: 10.1109/CVPR46437.2021.00024

Huang, X., Kroening, D., Ruan, W., Sharp, J., Sun, Y., Thamo, E., Wu, M., & Yi, X. (2020). A survey of safety and trustworthiness of deep neural networks: Verification, testing, adversarial attack and defence, and interpretability. *Computer Science Review*, *37*, 100270. DOI: 10.1016/j.cosrev.2020.100270

Huang, Y., Tang, Z., Chen, D., Su, K., & Chen, C. (2020). Batching soft IoU for training semantic segmentation networks. *IEEE Signal Processing Letters*, *27*, 66–70. DOI: 10.1109/LSP.2019.2956367

Huber, N., Brosig, F., & Dingle, N.. (2012). Providing dependability and performance in the cloud: Case studies. In Katinka, W. (Eds.), *Resilience assessment and evaluation of computing systems* (pp. 391–412). DOI: 10.1007/978-3-642-29032-9_19

Humayun, M., Jhanjhi, N., Almufareh, M. F., & Khalil, M. I. (2022). Security threat and vulnerability assessment and measurement in secure software development. *Computers, Materials & Continua*, *71*(3), 5039–5059. DOI: 10.32604/cmc.2022.019289

Hutchinson, B., Smart, A., Hanna, A., Denton, E., Greer, C., Kjartansson, O., & Mitchell, M. (2021, March). Towards accountability for machine learning datasets: Practices from software engineering and infrastructure. In *Proceedings of the 2021 ACM Conference on Fairness, Accountability, and Transparency* (pp. 560-575). DOI: 10.1145/3442188.3445918

Huynh-The, T., Pham, Q.-V., Pham, X.-Q., Nguyen, T. T., Han, Z., & Kim, D.-S. (2023). Artificial intelligence for the metaverse: A survey. *Engineering Applications of Artificial Intelligence, 117*, 105581. DOI: 10.1016/j.engappai.2022.105581

Hwang, JeeHyun et al. (2012). "Selection of regression system tests for security policy evolution". In: *Proceedings of the 27th IEEE/ACM international conference on automated software engineering*, pp. 266–269.

ICO. (2020). British Airways Fined £20m for Data Breach Affecting Over 400,000 Customers. Available at: https://ico.org.uk/

Ida, I. B., Jemai, A., & Loukil, A. (2016). "A survey on security of IoT in the context of eHealth and clouds". In: *2016 11th International Design & Test Symposium (IDT)*. IEEE, pp. 25–30.

Idowu, S., Osman, O., Strüber, D., & Berger, T. (2024). Machine learning experiment management tools: A mixed-methods empirical study. *Empirical Software Engineering, 29*(4), 1–35. DOI: 10.1007/s10664-024-10444-w

Imanbayev, A., Tynymbayev, S., Odarchenko, R., Gnatyuk, S., Berdibayev, R., Baikenov, A., & Kaniyeva, N. (2022). Research of machine learning algorithms for the development of intrusion detection systems in 5G mobile networks and beyond. *Sensors (Basel), 22*(24), 9957. DOI: 10.3390/s22249957 PMID: 36560333

Inouye, B. D., Brosi, B. J., Le Sage, E. H., & Lerdau, M. T. (2021). Trade-offs among resilience, robustness, stability, and performance and how we might study them. *Integrative and Comparative Biology, 61*(6), 2180–2189. DOI: 10.1093/icb/icab178 PMID: 34355756

Islam, SM Riazul et al. (2015). "The internet of things for health care: a comprehensive survey". In: *IEEE access* 3, pp. 678–708.

Jacob, E. S. of R. (ESR) communications@ myesr org N. E. de S. N. B. A. B. A. A. B. C. D. C. F. V. (2019). What the radiologist should know about artificial intelligence–an ESR white paper. *Insights into Imaging, 10*(1), 44.

Jahan, H., Feng, Z., & Hasan Mahmud, S. M. (2020). Risk-based test case prioritization by correlating system methods and their associated risks. *Arabian Journal for Science and Engineering, 45*(8), 6125–6138. DOI: 10.1007/s13369-020-04472-z

Jakeri, M. M., Hassan, M. F., Sarlan, A., & Wahab, A. A. (2024). Adaptive Security Activities Selection Model Using Multi-Criteria Decision-Making Methods. *Journal of Advanced Zoology*, *45*(S1), 65–78. Advance online publication. DOI: 10.17762/jaz.v45iS1.3404

Jang, Y. K., Munro, M., & Kwon, Y. R. (2011, September). An Improved Method of Selecting Regression Tests for C++ Programs. *Journal of Software Maintenance and Evolution: Research and Practice*, *13*(5), 331–350. DOI: 10.1002/smr.236

Jawed, M. (2019). *Continuous security in DevOps environment: Integrating automated security checks at each stage of continuous deployment pipeline.* Wien, Joshi, H. (2024). *A Secure Software Development Methodology for Enterprise Business Applications.* Paper presented at the 2024 IEEE International Conference on Data and Software Engineering (ICoDSE).

Jiang, Q., Adigun, O., Narasimhan, H., Fard, M. M., & Gupta, M. (2018). Optimizing black-box metrics with adaptive surrogates. In *Proceedings of the International Conference on Machine Learning* (pp. 1-10).

Jia, X., He, D., Kumar, N., & Choo, K.-K. R. (2019). Authenticated key agreement scheme for fog-driven IoT healthcare system. *Wireless Networks*, *25*(8), 4737–4750. DOI: 10.1007/s11276-018-1759-3

Johnson Sunday OlihaPreye Winston BiuOgagua Chimezie Obi. (2024a). Securing the smart city: A review of cybersecurity challenges and strategies. *Open Access Research Journal of Multidisciplinary Studies*, *7*(1), 094–101. Advance online publication. DOI: 10.53022/oarjms.2024.7.1.0013

Johnson Sunday OlihaPreye Winston BiuOgagua Chimezie Obi. (2024b). SECURING THE SMART CITY: A REVIEW OF CYBERSECURITY CHALLENGES AND STRATEGIES. *Engineering Science & Technology Journal*, *5*(2), 496–506. Advance online publication. DOI: 10.51594/estj.v5i2.827

Johnson, R. B., & Onwuegbuzie, A. J. (2004). Mixed methods research: A research paradigm whose time has come. *Educational Researcher*, *33*(7), 14–26. DOI: 10.3102/0013189X033007014

Jones, A., & Ashenden, D. (2005). *Risk Management for Computer Security: Protecting Your Network and Information Assets*. Elsevier Digital Press.

Jusak, J., Pratikno, H., & Putra, V. H. (2016). "Internet of Medical Things for cardiac monitoring: Paving the way to 5G mobile networks". In: *2016 IEEE International Conference on Communication, Networks and Satellite (COMNETSAT)*. IEEE, pp. 75–79. DOI: 10.1109/COMNETSAT.2016.7907420

Karim, N. S. A., Albuolayan, A., Saba, T., & Rehman, A. (2016). The practice of secure software development in SDLC: An investigation through existing model and a case study. *Security and Communication Networks*, *9*(18), 5333–5345. DOI: 10.1002/sec.1700

Karmakar, S., *Artificial Intelligence (AI) Chatbots and Customer Experience: Developing a.* 2024.

Karthik, S., Hemalatha, R., Aruna, R., Deivakani, M., Reddy, R. V. K., & Boopathi, S. (2023). Study on Healthcare Security System-Integrated Internet of Things (IoT). In *Perspectives and Considerations on the Evolution of Smart Systems* (pp. 342–362). IGI Global.

Katz, G., Barrett, C., Dill, D. L., Julian, K., & Kochenderfer, M. J. (2017). Reluplex: An efficient SMT solver for verifying deep neural networks. In Computer Aided Verification (pp. 97-117). Springer International Publishing.

Khalifa, M., Albadawy, M., & Iqbal, U. (2024). Advancing clinical decision support: The role of artificial intelligence across six domains. *Computer Methods and Programs in Biomedicine Update*, *5*, 100142. DOI: 10.1016/j.cmpbup.2024.100142

Khan, S. A., Oshin, N. T., Nizam, M., Ahmed, I., Musfique, M. M., & Hasan, M. (2023). *AI-Based Software Testing.* Paper presented at the World Conference on Information Systems for Business Management.

Khan, R. A., Khan, S. U., Akbar, M. A., & Alzahrani, M. (2024). Security risks of global software development life cycle: Industry practitioner's perspective. *Journal of Software (Malden, MA)*, *36*(3), e2521. DOI: 10.1002/smr.2521

Khan, R. A., Khan, S. U., Khan, H. U., & Ilyas, M. (2022). Systematic literature review on security risks and its practices in secure software development. *IEEE Access : Practical Innovations, Open Solutions*, *10*, 5456–5481. DOI: 10.1109/ACCESS.2022.3140181

Kharchenko, V., Fesenko, H., & Illiashenko, O. (2022). Quality models for artificial intelligence systems: Characteristic-based approach, development and application. *Sensors (Basel)*, *22*(13), 4865. DOI: 10.3390/s22134865 PMID: 35808361

Kim, G., Humble, J., Debois, P., & Willis, J. (2016). *The DevOps Handbook: How to Create World-Class Agility, Reliability, & Security in Technology Organizations.* IT Revolution.

Kodakandla, N. (2024). Securing Cloud-Native Infrastructure with Zero Trust Architecture. *Journal of Current Science and Research Review*, *2*(02), 18–28.

Korel, B., Tahat, L. H., & Vaysburg, B. (Oct. 2002). "Model Based Regression Test Reduction Using Dependence Analysis". In: *Proceedings of the International Conference on Software Maintenance (ICSM'02)*. Ed. by Antoniol, Giuliano, & Baxter, Ira D.. Montréal, Quebec, Canada: IEEE, pp. 214–223. DOI: 10.1109/ICSM.2002.1167768

Kotłowski, W., & Dembczyński, K. (2016). Surrogate regret bounds for generalized classification performance metrics. *Machine Learning*, *106*(4), 549–572. DOI: 10.1007/s10994-016-5591-7

Kotyan, S., & Vargas, D. (2022). Adversarial robustness assessment: Why in evaluation both L0 and L∞ attacks are necessary. *PLoS One*, *17*(4), e0265723. DOI: 10.1371/journal.pone.0265723 PMID: 35421125

Krasner, H. (2021). The cost of poor software quality in the US: A 2020 report. *Proc. Consortium Inf. Softw.* [CISQTM]. *QualityTM*, 2, 3.

Kudriavtseva, A., & Gadyatskaya, O. (2022). Secure software development methodologies: a multivocal literature review. *arXiv preprint arXiv:2211.16987*.

Kumar, P. M., & Gandhi, U. D. (2018). A novel three-tier Internet of Things architecture with machine learning algorithm for early detection of heart diseases. *Computers & Electrical Engineering*, *65*, 222–235. DOI: 10.1016/j.compeleceng.2017.09.001

Kumar, P. M., Lokesh, S., Varatharajan, R., Chandra Babu, G., & Parthasarathy, P. (2018). Cloud and IoT based disease prediction and diagnosis system for healthcare using Fuzzy neural classifier. *Future Generation Computer Systems*, *86*, 527–534. DOI: 10.1016/j.future.2018.04.036

Kung, D. C., Gao, J., Hsia, P., Toyoshima, Y., & Chen, C. (1996, January). On Regression Testing of Object-Oriented Programs. *Journal of Systems and Software*, *32*(1), 21–40. DOI: 10.1016/0164-1212(95)00047-X

Kushwah, J. S., Gupta, M., Shrivastava, S., Saxena, N., Saini, R., & Boopathi, S. (2024). Psychological Impacts, Prevention Strategies, and Intervention Approaches Across Age Groups: Unmasking Cyberbullying. In *Change Dynamics in Healthcare, Technological Innovations, and Complex Scenarios* (pp. 89–109). IGI Global.

Lab, S. (Oct. 2022). *ScimagoJR, SJR: Scientific Journal Rankings*. url: https://www.scimagojr.com/journalrank.php%20/

Langstrof, T., & Sabau, A. R. (2024). The current state of security—Insights from the German software industry. arXiv preprint arXiv:2402.08436.

La, Q. D., Ngo, M. V., Dinh, T. Q., Quek, T. Q. S., & Shin, H. (2019). Enabling intelligence in fog computing to achieve energy and latency reduction. *Digital Communications and Networks*, *5*(1), 3–9. DOI: 10.1016/j.dcan.2018.10.008

Latha, V. P., Reddy, N. S., & Babu, A. S. (2022). On optimizing scalability and availability of cloud-based software services using scale rate limiting algorithm. Theoretical Computer Science. https://api.semanticscholar.org/CorpusID:251079287

Legunsen, O., Shi, A., & Marinov, D. (Oct. 2017). "STARTS: STAtic Regression Test Selection". In: *Proceedings of the 32nd IEEE/ACM International Conference on Automated Software Engineering (ASE'17)*. Ed. by Massimiliano Di Penta and Tien N. Nguyen. Urbana-Champaign, IL, USA: IEEE Press, pp. 949–954. Leung, Hareton K. N. and Lee J. White (Oct. 1989). "Insights into Regression Testing". In: *Proceedings of Conference on Software Maintenance*. Miami, FL, USA: IEEE, pp. 60–69.

Legunsen, O., & Hariri, F.. (Nov. 2016). "An Extensive Study of Static Regression Test Selection in Modern Software Evolution". In: *Proceedings of the 2016 24th ACM SIGSOFT International Symposium on Foundations of Software Engineering (FSE'16)*. Ed. by Cleland-Huang, Jane, & Su, Zhendong. Seattle, WA, USA: ACM, pp. 583–594. DOI: 10.1145/2950290.2950361

Lehmann, C., Bilke, L., Buchwald, J., Graebling, N., Grunwald, N., Heinze, J., Meisel, T., Lu, R., Naumov, D., Rink, K., Özgür Sen, O., Selzer, P., Shao, H., Wang, W., Zill, F., Nagel, T., & Kolditz, O. (2024). OpenWorkFlow—Development of an open-source synthesis-platform for safety investigations in the site selection process. *Grundwasser*, *29*(1), 31–47. Advance online publication. DOI: 10.1007/s00767-024-00566-9

Li, K., Zhu, A., Zhao, P., Song, J., & Liu, J. (2024). Utilizing deep learning to optimize software development processes. *arXiv preprint arXiv:2404.13630.*

Li, Z., Ji, J., Ge, Y., & Zhang, Y. (2022). AutoLossGen: Automatic loss function generation for recommender systems. In Proceedings of the SIGIR '22: The 45th International ACM SIGIR Conference on Research and Development in Information Retrieval (pp. 1-10). ACM.

Li, G., Pattabiraman, K., & DeBardeleben, N. (2018). TensorFI: A configurable fault injector for TensorFlow applications. In *Proceedings of the IEEE International Symposium on Software Reliability Engineering Workshops (ISSREW)* (pp. 1-8). IEEE. DOI: 10.1109/ISSREW.2018.00024

Lima, Jackson A Prado and Silvia Regina Vergilio (2020). "A multi-armed bandit approach for test case prioritization in continuous integration environments". In: *IEEE Transactions on Software Engineering* 48.2, pp. 453–465.

Linden, G., Smith, B., & York, J. (2003). Amazon. com recommendations: Item-to-item collaborative filtering. *IEEE Internet Computing*, *7*(1), 76–80. DOI: 10.1109/MIC.2003.1167344

Lin, G., Wen, S., Han, Q.-L., Zhang, J., & Xiang, Y. (2020, October). Software Vulnerability Detection Using Deep Neural Networks: A Survey. *Proceedings of the IEEE*, *108*(10), 1825–1848. DOI: 10.1109/JPROC.2020.2993293

Lity, S.. (June 2016). "Applying Incremental Model Slicing to Product-Line Regression Testing". In: *Proceedings of the 15th International Conference on Software Reuse (ICSR'16)*. Ed. by Kapitsaki, Georgia M., & Santana de Almeida, Eduardo. Lecture Notes in Computer Science 9679. Limassol, Cyprus: Springer, pp. 3–19. DOI: 10.1007/978-3-319-35122-3_1

Liu, L., Wang, M., & Deng, J. (2020). A unified framework of surrogate loss by refactoring and interpolation. In *Computer Vision–ECCV 2020* (pp. 278–293). Springer International Publishing. DOI: 10.1007/978-3-030-58580-8_17

Liu, Q., & Lai, J. (2020). Stochastic loss function. *Proceedings of the AAAI Conference on Artificial Intelligence*, *34*(4), 4884–4891. DOI: 10.1609/aaai.v34i04.5925

Liu, Q., Li, P., Zhao, W., Cai, W., Yu, S., & Leung, V. C. M. (2018). A survey on security threats and defensive techniques of machine learning: A data driven view. *IEEE Access : Practical Innovations, Open Solutions*, *6*, 12103–12117. DOI: 10.1109/ACCESS.2018.2805680

Lorenzoni, G., . . . *Machine learning model development from a software engineering perspective: A systematic literature review.* arXiv preprint arXiv:2102.07574, 2021.

Lu, H., Li, Y., Chen, M., Kim, H., & Serikawa, S. (2018). Brain intelligence: Go beyond artificial intelligence. *Mobile Networks and Applications*, *23*(2), 368–375. DOI: 10.1007/s11036-017-0932-8

Mahmoud, Mukhtar ME, Joel JPC Rodrigues, and Kashif Saleem (2019). "Cloud of Things for Healthcare: A Survey from Energy Efficiency Perspective". In: *2019 International Conference on Computer and Information Sciences (ICCIS)*. IEEE, pp. 1– 7.

Mahmoud, Mukhtar ME, Joel JPC Rodrigues, Kashif Saleem, et al. (2018). "Towards energy-aware fog-enabled cloud of things for healthcare". In: *Computers & Electrical Engineering* 67, pp. 58–69.

Mahmoud, Mukhtar ME, Joel JPC Rodrigues, Syed Hassan Ahmed, et al. (2018). "Enabling technologies on cloud of things for smart healthcare". In: *IEEE Access* 6, pp. 31950–31967.

Maksimović, M., & Vujović, V. (2017). Internet of things based e-health systems: ideas, expectations and concerns. In *Handbook of large-scale distributed computing in smart healthcare* (pp. 241–280). Springer. DOI: 10.1007/978-3-319-58280-1_10

Malz, C., Jazdi, N., & Göhner, P. (Apr. 2012). "Prioritization of Test Cases Using Software Agents and Fuzzy Logic". In: *Proceedings of the 5th International Conference on Software Testing, Verification and Validation (ICST'12)*. Ed. by Bertolino, Antonia, & Labiche, Yvan. Montréal, BC, Canada: IEEE, pp. 483–486. DOI: 10.1109/ICST.2012.131

Manda, J. K. (2023). DevSecOps Implementation in Telecom: Integrating Security into DevOps Practices to Streamline Software Development and Ensure Secure Telecom Service Delivery. *Journal of Innovative Technologies*, *6*(1).

Manikandan, R., Patan, R., Gandomi, A. H., Sivanesan, P., & Kalyanaraman, H. (2020). Hash polynomial two factor decision tree using IoT for smart health care scheduling. *Expert Systems with Applications*, *141*, 112924. DOI: 10.1016/j.eswa.2019.112924

Manogaran, G., Varatharajan, R., Lopez, D., Kumar, P. M., Sundarasekar, R., & Thota, C. (2018). A new architecture of Internet of Things and big data ecosystem for secured smart healthcare monitoring and alerting system. *Future Generation Computer Systems*, *82*, 375–387. DOI: 10.1016/j.future.2017.10.045

Marchany, R. C., & Tront, J. G. (2002). *E-commerce security issues.* Paper presented at the Proceedings of the 35th Annual Hawaii International Conference on System Sciences. DOI: 10.1109/HICSS.2002.994190

Martínez-Fernández, S., Bogner, J., Franch, X., Oriol, M., Siebert, J., Trendowicz, A., Vollmer, A. M., & Wagner, S. (2022). Software engineering for AI-based systems: A survey. [TOSEM]. *ACM Transactions on Software Engineering and Methodology*, *31*(2), 1–59. DOI: 10.1145/3487043

Martn, A.. (2021). Google Scholar, Microsoft Academic, Scopus, Dimensions, Web of Science, and OpenCitations' COCI: A multidisciplinary comparison of coverage via citations. *Scientometrics*, *126*(1), 871–906. DOI: 10.1007/s11192-020-03690-4 PMID: 32981987

McCarthy, J., *What is artificial intelligence.* 2007.

Mendoza Juan, Y. (2024). *Development of a multi-agent, LLM-driven system to enhance human-machine interaction: integrating DSPy with modular agentic strategies and logical reasoning layers for the autonomous generation of smart contracts*. Universitat Politècnica de Catalunya.

Meyer, M., Schmidt, D., & John, M. (2017). Proactive Risk Management in Software Development: Bridging Security and Quality. *ACM Transactions on Software Engineering and Methodology*, *26*(4), 24.

Mishra, S., & Chaurasiya, V. K. (2024). Hybrid deep learning algorithm for smart cities security enhancement through blockchain and internet of things. *Multimedia Tools and Applications*, *83*(8), 22609–22637. Advance online publication. DOI: 10.1007/s11042-023-16406-6

Mohammed, J.. (2014). Internet of Things: Remote patient monitoring using web services and cloud computing. In *In: 2014 IEEE international conference on internet of things (IThings), and IEEE green computing and communications (GreenCom) and IEEE cyber, physical and social computing (CPSCom)* (pp. 256–263). IEEE.

Molakatala, N., Kumar, D. A., Patil, U., Mhatre, P. J., Sambathkumar, M., & Boopathi, S. (2024). Integrating 5G and IoT Technologies in Developing Smart City Communication Networks. In *Blockchain-Based Solutions for Accessibility in Smart Cities* (pp. 147–170). IGI Global. DOI: 10.4018/979-8-3693-3402-7.ch006

Monteiro, K.. (2018). "Developing an e-health system based on IoT, fog and cloud computing". In: *2018 IEEE/ACM International Conference on Utility and Cloud Computing Companion (UCC Companion)*. IEEE, pp. 17–18. DOI: 10.1109/UCC-Companion.2018.00024

Moosavi, S. R., Gia, T. N., Nigussie, E., Rahmani, A. M., Virtanen, S., Tenhunen, H., & Isoaho, J. (2016). End-to-end security scheme for mobility enabled healthcare Internet of Things. *Future Generation Computer Systems*, *64*, 108–124. DOI: 10.1016/j.future.2016.02.020

Moskalenko, V., Kharchenko, V., Moskalenko, A., & Petrov, S. (2022). Model and training method of the resilient image classifier considering faults, concept drift, and adversarial attacks. *Algorithms*, *15*(10), 384. DOI: 10.3390/a15100384

Moyón, F., Méndez, D., Beckers, K., & Klepper, S. (2020). How do we integrate security compliance requirements with agile software engineering at scale? In *Product-Focused Software Process Improvement: 21st International Conference, PROFES 2020, Turin, Italy, November 25–27, 2020* [Springer International Publishing.]. *Proceedings*, *21*, 69–87.

Muccini, H., Dias, M. S., & Richardson, D. J. (2005). "Towards Software Architecture-Based Regression Testing". In: *ACM SIGSOFT Software Engineering Notes*. Vol. 30. ACM, pp. 1–7. DOI: 10.1145/1083217.1083223

Muccini, H., Dias, M., & Richardson, D. J. (2005). "Reasoning about Software Architecture-Based Regression Testing Through a Case Study". In: *29th Annual International Computer Software and Applications Conference (COMPSAC'05)*. Vol. 2. IEEE, pp. 189–195. DOI: 10.1109/COMPSAC.2005.127

Muhammad, G., Rahman, S. K. M. M., Alelaiwi, A., & Alamri, A. (2017). Smart health solution integrating IoT and cloud: A case study of voice pathology monitoring. *IEEE Communications Magazine*, *55*(1), 69–73. DOI: 10.1109/MCOM.2017.1600425CM

Muhammad, T. (2022). A comprehensive study on software-defined load balancers: Architectural flexibility & application service delivery in on-premises ecosystems. *International Journal of Computer Science and Technology*, *6*(1), 1–24.

Muhammed, T., Mehmood, R., Albeshri, A., & Katib, I. (2018). UbeHealth: A personalized ubiquitous cloud and edge enabled networked healthcare system for smart cities. *IEEE Access : Practical Innovations, Open Solutions*, *6*, 32258–32285. DOI: 10.1109/ACCESS.2018.2846609

Munn, Z., Peters, M. D. J., Stern, C., Tufanaru, C., McArthur, A., & Aromataris, E. (2018). Systematic review or scoping review? Guidance for authors when choosing between a systematic or scoping review approach. *BMC Medical Research Methodology*, *18*(1), 143. DOI: 10.1186/s12874-018-0611-x PMID: 30453902

Mustonen, J. (2024). Designing a security framework for enhanced monitoring and secure development during the software life cycle.

Myagmar, S., Lee, A. J., & Yurcik, W. (2005). Threat Modeling as a Basis for Security Requirements. In *Proceedings of the 2005 ACM Workshop on Storage Security and Survivability* (pp. 94–102). Association for Computing Machinery.

Nallapati, R., & Manning, C. D. *Legal docket classification: Where machine learning stumbles*. in *Proceedings of the 2008 conference on empirical methods in natural language processing*. 2008. DOI: 10.3115/1613715.1613771

Narodytska, N. (2018). Formal analysis of deep binarized neural networks. In *Proceedings of the Twenty-Seventh International Joint Conference on Artificial Intelligence (IJCAI-18)* (pp. 1-10). International Joint Conferences on Artificial Intelligence Organization. DOI: 10.24963/ijcai.2018/811

Narodytska, N. (2018). Formal verification of deep neural networks. In *Proceedings of the 2018 Formal Methods in Computer Aided Design (FMCAD)* (pp. 1-10). IEEE.

Nascimento, E., ... *Software engineering for artificial intelligence and machine learning software: A systematic literature review.* arXiv preprint arXiv:2011.03751, 2020.

Nayaka Sheetakallu Krishnaiah, P., Narayan, D. L., & Sutradhar, K. (2024). A survey on secure metadata of agile software development process using blockchain technology. *Security and Privacy*, *7*(2), e342. Advance online publication. DOI: 10.1002/spy2.342

Neapolitan, R. E., & Jiang, X. (2018). *Artificial intelligence: With an introduction to machine learning*. CRC press. DOI: 10.1201/b22400

Ngai, E. W., Hu, Y., Wong, Y. H., Chen, Y., & Sun, X. (2011). The application of data mining techniques in financial fraud detection: A classification framework and an academic review of literature. *Decision Support Systems*, *50*(3), 559–569. DOI: 10.1016/j.dss.2010.08.006

Nguyen-Duc, A., ... *Generative Artificial Intelligence for Software Engineering—A Research Agenda.* arXiv preprint arXiv:2310.18648, 2023.

Nguyen, T., Gupta, S., & Chandrasekaran, K. (2021). AI in Cybersecurity: A Double-Edged Sword. *ACM Computing Surveys*, *54*(3), 1–28. DOI: 10.1145/3501296

Nugroho, A. Y., Gunawan, H., & Sari, R. E.Adnan Buyung Nasution. (2024). Development of an IoT Based Smart Door System with Access Control via WhatsApp. [ESA]. *Indonesian Journal of Applied and Industrial Sciences*, *3*(1), 87–94. Advance online publication. DOI: 10.55927/esa.v3i1.7815

Núñez, J. C. S., Lindo, A. C., & Rodríguez, P. G. (2020). A Preventive Secure Software Development Model for a Software Factory: A Case Study. *IEEE Access : Practical Innovations, Open Solutions*, *8*, 77653–77665. DOI: 10.1109/ACCESS.2020.2989113

Olpadkar, K., & Gavas, E. (2021). Center loss regularization for continual learning. arXiv, arXiv:2110.11314.

Oueida, S., Kotb, Y., Aloqaily, M., Jararweh, Y., & Baker, T. (2018). An edge computing based smart healthcare framework for resource management. *Sensors (Basel)*, *18*(12), 4307. DOI: 10.3390/s18124307 PMID: 30563267

OWASP. (2021). *OWASP Threat Modeling Cheat Sheet.*

Oyeniran, O. C., Modupe, O. T., Otitoola, A. A., Abiona, O. O., Adewusi, A. O., & Oladapo, O. J.Oyekunle Claudius OyeniranOluwole Temidayo ModupeAanuoluwapo Ayodeji OtitoolaOluwatosin Oluwatimileyin AbionaAdebunmi Okechukwu AdewusiOluwatayo Jacob Oladapo. (2024). A comprehensive review of leveraging cloud-native technologies for scalability and resilience in software development. *International Journal of Science and Research Archive*, *11*(2), 330–337. Advance online publication. DOI: 10.30574/ijsra.2024.11.2.0432

Ozdemir, A. T., Tunc, C., & Hariri, S. (2017). Autonomic fall detection system. In *In: 2017 IEEE 2nd International Workshops on Foundations and Applications of Self* Systems (FAS* W)* (pp. 166–170). IEEE.

Pace, P., Aloi, G., Gravina, R., Caliciuri, G., Fortino, G., & Liotta, A. (2018). An edge-based architecture to support efficient applications for healthcare industry 4.0. *IEEE Transactions on Industrial Informatics*, *15*(1), 481–489. DOI: 10.1109/TII.2018.2843169

Palombo, H., Tabari, A. Z., Lende, D., Ligatti, J., & Ou, X. (2020). An Ethnographic Understanding of Software ({In) Security} and a {Co-Creation} Model to Improve Secure Software Development. In *Sixteenth Symposium on Usable Privacy and Security (SOUPS 2020)* (pp. 205-220).

Pan, R., Bagherzadeh, M., Ghaleb, T. A., & Briand, L. (2022). Test case selection and prioritization using machine learning: A systematic literature review. *Empirical Software Engineering*, *27*(2), 29. DOI: 10.1007/s10664-021-10066-6

Patel, S. K., Rathod, V. R., & Parikh, S. (2011). Joomla, Drupal, and WordPress—A statistical comparison of open source CMS. *3rd International Conference on Trendz in Information Sciences & Computing (TISC2011)*, 182–187. DOI: 10.1109/TISC.2011.6169111

Pathinarupothi, R. K. P Durga, and Ekanath Srihari Rangan (2018). "Iot-based smart edge for global health: Remote monitoring with severity detection and alerts transmission". In: *IEEE Internet of Things Journal* 6.2, pp. 2449–2462.

Paulson, S. (2024). *Epistemic Reasons & Cognitive Self-Monitoring*. Northwestern University.

Pautov, M., Tursynbek, N., Munkhoeva, M., Muravev, N., Petiushko, A., & Oseledets, I. (2022). CC-CERT: A probabilistic approach to certify general robustness of neural networks. *Proceedings of the AAAI Conference on Artificial Intelligence*, *36*(7), 7975–7983. DOI: 10.1609/aaai.v36i7.20768

Pelluru, K., *Advancing software development in 2023: the convergence of MLOps and DevOps.* Advances in Computer Sciences, 2023. **6**(1): p. 1– 14-1– 14.

Perepelitsyn, A., Kulanov, V., & Zarizenko, I. (2022). Method of QoS evaluation of FPGA as a service. *Radioelectronics and Computer Systems*, *4*(4), 153–160. DOI: 10.32620/reks.2022.4.12

Potter, B., & McGraw, G. (2004). Software security testing. *IEEE Security and Privacy*, *2*(5), 81–85. DOI: 10.1109/MSP.2004.84

Prasha Microsoft. (2023, June). What is Azure Chaos Studio? Microsoft Learn. https://learn.microsoft.com/en-us/azure/chaos-studio/chaos-studio-overview

Prince, N. U.. (2024). AI-Powered Data-Driven Cybersecurity Techniques: Boosting Threat Identification and Reaction. *Nanotechnology Perceptions*, •••, 332–353.

Puranik, T. A., Shaik, N., Vankudoth, R., Kolhe, M. R., Yadav, N., & Boopathi, S. (2024). Study on Harmonizing Human-Robot (Drone) Collaboration: Navigating Seamless Interactions in Collaborative Environments. In *Cybersecurity Issues and Challenges in the Drone Industry* (pp. 1–26). IGI Global.

Qaraqe, M., Elzein, A., Basaran, E., Yang, Y., Varghese, E. B., Costandi, W., Rizk, J., & Alam, N. (2024). PublicVision: A Secure Smart Surveillance System for Crowd Behavior Recognition. *IEEE Access : Practical Innovations, Open Solutions*, *12*, 26474–26491. Advance online publication. DOI: 10.1109/ACCESS.2024.3366693

Qian, C., ... *Communicative agents for software development.* arXiv preprint arXiv:2307.07924, 2023. **6**.

Qian, C., Cong, X., Yang, C., Chen, W., Su, Y., Xu, J., Liu, Z., & Sun, M. (2023). Communicative agents for software development. *arXiv Preprint arXiv:2307.07924*, *6*(3).

Qian, C., Liu, W., Liu, H., Chen, N., Dang, Y., Li, J., Yang, C., Chen, W., Su, Y., & Cong, X. (2024). Chatdev: Communicative agents for software development. *Proceedings of the 62nd Annual Meeting of the Association for Computational Linguistics(*Volume 1*: Long Papers)*, 15174–15186. DOI: 10.18653/v1/2024.acl-long.810

Qi, J., Yang, P., Min, G., Amft, O., Dong, F., & Xu, L. (2017). Advanced internet of things for personalised healthcare systems: A survey. *Pervasive and Mobile Computing*, *41*, 132–149. DOI: 10.1016/j.pmcj.2017.06.018

Quintero, Dino and Frank N Lee (2019). *IBM Reference Architecture for High Performance Data and AI in Healthcare and Life Sciences.*

Qureshi, J. N., & Farooq, M. S. (2024). ChainAgile: A framework for the improvement of Scrum Agile distributed software development based on blockchain. *PLoS ONE, 19*(3 March). DOI: 10.1371/journal.pone.0299324

Quwaider, M., & Jararweh, Y. (2016). A cloud supported model for efficient community health awareness. *Pervasive and Mobile Computing*, *28*, 35–50. DOI: 10.1016/j.pmcj.2015.07.012

Rahmani, A. M., Gia, T. N., Negash, B., Anzanpour, A., Azimi, I., Jiang, M., & Liljeberg, P. (2018). Exploiting smart e-Health gateways at the edge of healthcare Internet-of-Things: A fog computing approach. *Future Generation Computer Systems*, *78*, 641–658. DOI: 10.1016/j.future.2017.02.014

Rahmani, A. M., & Liljeberg, P.. (2017). *Fog computing in the internet of things: Intelligence at the edge*. Springer.

Rajawat, A. S., Goyal, S., Verma, C., & Singh, J. (2025). Advancing network security paradigms integrating quantum computing models for enhanced protections. In *Applied Data Science and Smart Systems* (pp. 517–528). CRC Press.

Ramaj, X., Sánchez-Gordón, M., Gkioulos, V., & Colomo-Palacios, R. (2024). *On DevSecOps and Risk Management in Critical Infrastructures: Practitioners' Insights on Needs and Goals.* Paper presented at the Proceedings of the 2024 ACM/IEEE 4th International Workshop on Engineering and Cybersecurity of Critical Systems (EnCyCriS) and 2024 IEEE/ACM Second International Workshop on Software Vulnerability. DOI: 10.1145/3643662.3643954

Rane, J., et al., *Artificial intelligence, machine learning, and deep learning in cloud, edge, and quantum computing: A review of trends, challenges, and future directions.* Future Research Opportunities for Artificial Intelligence in Industry 4.0 and, 2024. **5**: p. 2-2.

Rani, S., Ahmed, S. H., & Shah, S. C. (2018). Smart health: A novel paradigm to control the chickungunya virus. *IEEE Internet of Things Journal*, *6*(2), 1306–1311. DOI: 10.1109/JIOT.2018.2802898

Rapos, E. J., & Dingel, J. (Apr. 2015). "Using Fuzzy Logic and Symbolic Execution to Prioritize UML-RT Test Cases". In: *Proceedings of the 8th International Conference on Software Testing, Verification and Validation (ICST'15).* Ed. by Fraser, Gordon, & Marinov, Darko. IEEE. Graz, Austria. DOI: 10.1109/ICST.2015.7102610

Rawashdeh, M., AL Zamil, M. G. H., Hossain, M. S., Samarah, S., Amin, S. U., & Muhammad, G. (2018). Reliable service delivery in Tele-health care systems. *Journal of Network and Computer Applications*, *115*, 86–93. DOI: 10.1016/j.jnca.2018.04.015

Ray, P. P., Thapa, N., & Dash, D. (2019). Implementation and performance analysis of interoperable and heterogeneous IoT-edge gateway for pervasive wellness care. *IEEE Transactions on Consumer Electronics*, *65*(4), 464–473. DOI: 10.1109/TCE.2019.2939494

Reagen, B., Gupta, U., Pentecost, L., Whatmough, P., Lee, S. K., Mulholland, N., Brooks, D., & Wei, G.-Y. (2018). Ares. In Proceedings of the DAC '18: The 55th Annual Design Automation Conference 2018 (pp. 1-10). ACM.

Rhmann, W., & Saxena, V. (2017, January). Fuzzy Expert System Based Test Cases Prioritization from UML State Machine Diagram using Risk Information. *International Journal on Mathematical Sciences and Computing*, *3*(1), 17–27. DOI: 10.5815/ijmsc.2017.01.02

Ribeiro, V. V., Cruzes, D. S., & Travassos, G. H. (2022). Moderator factors of software security and performance verification. *Journal of Systems and Software*, *184*, 111137. DOI: 10.1016/j.jss.2021.111137

Rindell, K., Ruohonen, J., Holvitie, J., Hyrynsalmi, S., & Leppänen, V. (2021). Security in agile software development: A practitioner survey. *Information and Software Technology*, *131*, 106488. DOI: 10.1016/j.infsof.2020.106488

Romano, S., Scanniello, G., Antoniol, G., & Marchetto, A. (2018, July). SPIRITuS: A SimPle Information Retrieval RegressIon Test Selection Approach. *Information and Software Technology*, *99*, 62–80. DOI: 10.1016/j.infsof.2018.03.004

Ronanki, D., & Karneddi, H. (2024). Electric Vehicle Charging Infrastructure: Review, Cyber Security Considerations, Potential Impacts, Countermeasures, and Future Trends. *IEEE Journal of Emerging and Selected Topics in Power Electronics*, *12*(1), 242–256. Advance online publication. DOI: 10.1109/JESTPE.2023.3336997

Rothermel, G., & Harrold, M. J. (1996, August). Analyzing Regression Test Selection Techniques. *IEEE Transactions on Software Engineering*, *22*(8), 529–551. DOI: 10.1109/32.536955

Rothermel, G., Harrold, M. J., & Dedhia, J. (2000, June). Regression Test Selection for C++ Software. *Software Testing, Verification & Reliability*, *10*(2), 77–109. DOI: 10.1002/1099-1689(200006)10:2<77::AID-STVR197>3.0.CO;2-E

Saeed, H., Shafi, I., Ahmad, J., Khan, A. A., Khurshaid, T., & Ashraf, I. (2025). Review of Techniques for Integrating Security in Software Development Lifecycle. *Computers, Materials & Continua*, *82*(1), 139–172. DOI: 10.32604/cmc.2024.057587

Saeid, H. (2020). Revolutionizing Software Engineering: Leveraging AI for Enhanced Development Lifecycle. *International Journal of Innovative Research in Engineering & Multidisciplinary Physical Sciences*, *8*(1).

Said, A., Ang, Z. E., & Iskandar, Y. H. P. (2024). Assessing Consumers' Acceptance of AR Wayfinding for Indoor Shopping Navigation in Singapore. *WSEAS Transactions on Computer Research*, *12*, 44–61. Advance online publication. DOI: 10.37394/232018.2024.12.4

Salmani, A., *An AI-Based Human-Centered Approach to Support Multidisciplinary Requirements Engineering*. 2023.

Samuel, A. L. (1959). Some studies in machine learning using the game of checkers. *IBM Journal of Research and Development*, *3*(3), 210–229. DOI: 10.1147/rd.33.0210

Sangeetha, M., Kannan, S. R., Boopathi, S., Ramya, J., Ishrat, M., & Sabarinathan, G. (2023). Prediction of Fruit Texture Features Using Deep Learning Techniques. *2023 4th International Conference on Smart Electronics and Communication (ICOSEC)*, 762–768.

Sanyal, A., Kumar, P., Kar, P., Chawla, S., & Sebastiani, F. (2018). Optimizing non-decomposable measures with deep networks. *Machine Learning*, *107*(8-10), 1597–1620. DOI: 10.1007/s10994-018-5736-y

Sarkar, S., Chatterjee, S., Misra, S., & Kudupudi, R. (2017). Privacy-aware blind cloud framework for advanced healthcare. *IEEE Communications Letters*, *21*(11), 2492–2495. DOI: 10.1109/LCOMM.2017.2739141

Sarker, I. H. (2021). Machine learning: Algorithms, real-world applications and research directions. *SN Computer Science*, *2*(3), 160. DOI: 10.1007/s42979-021-00592-x PMID: 33778771

Sawand, A., Djahel, S., Zhang, Z., & Naït-Abdesselam, F. (2015). Toward energy-efficient and trustworthy eHealth monitoring system. *China Communications*, *12*(1), 46–65. DOI: 10.1109/CC.2015.7084383

Scarpato, N., ... (2017). "E-health-IoT universe: A review". In: *management* 21.44, p. 46. DOI: 10.18517/ijaseit.7.6.4467

Seelaboyina, R., Vadla, S. P. C., Teerthala, S. A., & Pedduri, V. V. (2024). Secure Software Development Life Cycle: An Approach to Reduce the Risks of Cyber Attacks in Cyber Physical Systems and Digital Twins. *Lecture Notes in Electrical Engineering*, *1106*, 153–161. Advance online publication. DOI: 10.1007/978-981-99-7954-7_15

Shabina., ... *Ensuring Securing PII Data in the AWS Cloud: A Comprehensive Guide to PCI DSS Compliance*, in *Cybersecurity and Artificial Intelligence: Transformational Strategies and Disruptive Innovation*. 2024, Springer. p. 185-216. DOI: 10.1007/978-3-031-52272-7_8

Shadabfar, M., Mahsuli, M., Zhang, Y., Xue, Y., Ayyub, B. M., Huang, H., & Medina, R. A. (2022). Resilience-based design of infrastructure: Review of models, methodologies, and computational tools. *ASCE-ASME Journal of Risk and Uncertainty in Engineering Systems. Part A, Civil Engineering*, *8*(1), 03121004. DOI: 10.1061/AJRUA6.0001184

Shafik, W. (2024e). Shaping the Next Generation Smart City Ecosystem: An Investigation on the Requirements, Applications, Architecture, Security and Privacy, and Open Research Questions. In *Smart Cities: Innovations, Challenges and Future Perspectives* (pp. 3–52). Springer. DOI: 10.1007/978-3-031-59846-3_1

Shafik, W., & Kalinaki, K. (2023). Smart city ecosystem: An exploration of requirements, architecture, applications, security, and emerging motivations. In *Handbook of Research on Network-Enabled IoT Applications for Smart City Services*. DOI: 10.4018/979-8-3693-0744-1.ch005

Shafik, W. (2024a). Agile Security Strategies. In *Smart and Agile Cybersecurity for IoT and IIoT Environments* (pp. 82–101). IGI Global., DOI: 10.4018/979-8-3693-3451-5.ch004

Shafik, W. (2024b). Cyber Attacker Profiling and Cyberbullying Overview. In *Cyber Space and Outer Space Security* (pp. 125–149). River Publishers., DOI: 10.1201/9781003558118-5

Shafik, W. (2024c). Data Privacy and Security Safeguarding Customer Information in ChatGPT Systems. In *Revolutionizing the Service Industry Wth OpenAI Models* (pp. 52–86). IGI Global., DOI: 10.4018/979-8-3693-1239-1.ch003

Shafik, W. (2024d). Navigating Emerging Challenges in Robotics and Artificial Intelligence in Africa. In *Examining the rapid advance of digital technology in Africa* (pp. 126–146). IGI Global., DOI: 10.4018/978-1-6684-9962-7.ch007

Shafik, W., Kalinaki, K., Fahim, K. E., & Adam, M. (2024). Safeguarding Data Privacy and Security in Federated Learning Systems. In *Federated Deep Learning for Healthcare* (pp. 170–190). CRC Press., DOI: 10.1201/9781032694870-13

Shafik, W., Kalinaki, K., & Zakari, R. Y. (2024). Blockchain's Motivation for IoT-Enabled Smart City. In *Secure and Intelligent IoT-Enabled Smart Cities* (pp. 195–221). IGI Global., DOI: 10.4018/979-8-3693-2373-1.ch010

Shafin, R., Liu, L., Chandrasekhar, V., Chen, H., Reed, J., & Zhang, J. C. (2020). Artificial intelligence-enabled cellular networks: A critical path to beyond-5G and 6G. *IEEE Wireless Communications*, *27*(2), 212–217. DOI: 10.1109/MWC.001.1900323

Shah, V. (2019). Towards Efficient Software Engineering in the Era of AI and ML: Best Practices and Challenges. *International Journal of Computer Science and Technology*, *3*(3), 63–78.

Sharma, R., & Singh, J. *Systematic Literature Review and Comparative Studies on Human Centred Software Development*. in *2022 4th International Conference on Advances in Computing, Communication Control and Networking (ICAC3N)*. 2022. IEEE. DOI: 10.1109/ICAC3N56670.2022.10074154

Sharma, A., Choudhury, T., & Kumar, P. (2018). "Health monitoring & management using IoT devices in a Cloud Based Framework". In: *2018 International Conference on Advances in Computing and Communication Engineering (ICACCE)*. IEEE, pp. 219–224. DOI: 10.1109/ICACCE.2018.8441752

Sheridan, C., & Whigham, D., & Artacˇ, M. (2016). DICE fault injection tool. Proceedings of the 2nd International Workshop on Quality-Aware DevOps (pp. 36–37). ACM. DOI: 10.1145/2945408.2945415

Shi, A.. (Nov. 2014). "Balancing Trade-offs in Test-suite Reduction". In: *Proceedings of the 22nd International Symposium on Foundations of Software Engineering (FSE'14)*. Ed. by Orso, Alessandro, & Storey, Margaret-Anne. Hong Kong, China: ACM, pp. 246–256.

Shin, Y., & Jeon, S. (2024). MQTree: Secure OTA Protocol Using MQTT and MerkleTree. *Sensors (Basel)*, *24*(5), 1447. Advance online publication. DOI: 10.3390/s24051447 PMID: 38474983

Shi, X., Liang, X., & Ansari, S. S. (2024). Bricks without straw: Overcoming resource limitations to architect ecosystem leadership. *Academy of Management Journal*, *67*(4), 1084–1123. Advance online publication. DOI: 10.5465/amj.2021.1440

Shostack, A. (2014). *Threat Modeling: Designing for Security*. Wiley.

Simpson, R. L., Lee, J. A., Li, Y., Kang, Y. J., Tsui, C., & Cimiotti, J. P. (2024). Medicare meets the cloud: The development of a secure platform for the storage and analysis of claims data. *JAMIA Open*, *7*(1), ooae007. Advance online publication. DOI: 10.1093/jamiaopen/ooae007 PMID: 38344670

Singh, D.. (2017). Semantic edge computing and IoT architecture for military health services in battlefield. In *In: 2017 14th IEEE Annual Consumer Communications & Networking Conference (CCNC)* (pp. 185–190). IEEE.

Singh, H., Mallaiah, R., Yadav, G., Verma, N., Sawhney, A., & Brahmachari, S. K. (2018). iCHRCloud: Web & mobile based child health imprints for smart healthcare. *Journal of Medical Systems*, *42*(1), 1–12. DOI: 10.1007/s10916-017-0866-5 PMID: 29188446

Singh, P. (2024). Transforming Healthcare through AI: Enhancing Patient Outcomes and Bridging Accessibility Gaps. *Journal of Artificial Intelligence Research*, *4*(1), 220–232.

Skoglund, M., & Runeson, P. (2007, June). Improving Class Firewall Regression Test Selection by Removing the Class Firewall. *International Journal of Software Engineering and Knowledge Engineering*, *17*(3), 359–378. DOI: 10.1142/S0218194007003306

Smith, J., & Wei, R. (2024). *Implications of Artificial Intelligence in the Software Development Life Cycle*. EasyChair.

Soetens, Q. D., Demeyer, S., Zaidman, A., & Pérez, J. (Nov. 2015). "Change-Based Test Selection: An Empirical Evaluation". In: *Empirical Software Engineering*, pp. 1–43.

Soetens, Q. D., Demeyer, S., & Zaidman, A. (Mar. 2013). "ChangeBased Test Selection in the Presence of Developer Tests". In: *Proceedings of the 17th European Conference on Software Maintenance and Reengineering (CSMR'13)*. Ed. by Cleve, Anthony, & Ricca, Filippo. Genoa, Italy: IEEE, pp. 101–110.

Soni, A., et al., *Integrating AI into the Software Development Life Cycle: Best Practices, Tools, and Impact Analysis*. Tools, and Impact Analysis (June 10, 2023), 2023.

Sood, Sandeep K and Isha Mahajan (2017). "Wearable IoT sensor based healthcare system for identifying and controlling chikungunya virus". In: *Computers in Industry* 91, pp. 33–44.

Souppaya, M., Scarfone, K., & Dodson, D. (2022). Secure software development framework (SDF) version 1.1. *NIST Special Publication*, *800*, 218.

Sreedhar, P. S. S., Sujay, V., Rani, M. R., Melita, L., Reshma, S., & Boopathi, S. (2024). Impacts of 5G Machine Learning Techniques on Telemedicine and Social Media Professional Connection in Healthcare. In *Advances in Medical Technologies and Clinical Practice* (pp. 209–234). IGI Global. DOI: 10.4018/979-8-3693-1934-5.ch012

Srisakthi, S., & Suresh Babu, C. V. (2024). Cybersecurity: Protecting Information in a Digital World. In Saeed, S., Azizi, N., Tahir, S., Ahmad, M., & Almuhaideb, A. (Eds.), *Strengthening Industrial Cybersecurity to Protect Business Intelligence* (pp. 1–25). IGI Global., DOI: 10.4018/979-8-3693-0839-4.ch001

Stavdas, A., Kosmatos, E., Maple, C., Hugues-Salas, E., Epiphaniou, G., Fowler, D. S., Razak, S. A., Matrakidis, C., Yuan, H., & Lord, A. (2024). Quantum Key Distribution for V2I communications with software-defined networking. *IET Quantum Communication*, *5*(1), 38–45. Advance online publication. DOI: 10.1049/qtc2.12070

Steck, H. (2007). Hinge rank loss and the area under the ROC curve. In Machine Learning: ECML 2007 (pp. 347-358). Springer. DOI: 10.1007/978-3-540-74958-5_33

Stergiou, C., Psannis, K. E., Kim, B.-G., & Gupta, B. (2018). Secure integration of IoT and cloud computing. *Future Generation Computer Systems*, *78*, 964–975. DOI: 10.1016/j.future.2016.11.031

Subha, S., Inbamalar, T., Komala, C., Suresh, L. R., Boopathi, S., & Alaskar, K. (2023). A Remote Health Care Monitoring system using internet of medical things (IoMT). *IEEE Explore*, 1–6.

Suciu, G., Suciu, V., Martian, A., Craciunescu, R., Vulpe, A., Marcu, I., Halunga, S., & Fratu, O. (2015). Big data, internet of things and cloud convergence–an architecture for secure e-health applications. *Journal of Medical Systems*, *39*(11), 1–8. DOI: 10.1007/s10916-015-0327-y PMID: 26345453

Sulich, A., Rutkowska, M., Krawczyk-Jezierska, A., Jezierski, J., & Zema, T. (2021). Cybersecurity and sustainable development. *Procedia Computer Science*, *192*, 20–28. DOI: 10.1016/j.procs.2021.08.003

Sun, L., Jiang, X., Ren, H., & Guo, Y. (2020). Edge-cloud computing and artificial intelligence in internet of medical things: Architecture, technology and application. *IEEE Access : Practical Innovations, Open Solutions*, *8*, 101079–101092. DOI: 10.1109/ACCESS.2020.2997831

Suresh Babu, C. V., & Yadavamuthiah, K. (2023). Cyber Physical Systems Design Challenges in the Areas of Mobility, Healthcare, Energy, and Manufacturing. In Thanigaivelan, R., Kaliappan, S., & Jegadheesan, C. (Eds.), *Cyber-Physical Systems and Supporting Technologies for Industrial Automation* (pp. 131–151). IGI Global., DOI: 10.4018/978-1-6684-9267-3.ch007

Susanty, A., Puspitasari, N. B., Rosyada, Z. F., Pratama, M. A., & Kurniawan, E. (2024). Design of blockchain-based halal traceability system applications for halal chicken meat-based food supply chain. *International Journal of Information Technology : an Official Journal of Bharati Vidyapeeth's Institute of Computer Applications and Management*, *16*(3), 1449–1473. Advance online publication. DOI: 10.1007/s41870-023-01650-8

Swartout, P. (2018). *Continuous Delivery and DevOps–A Quickstart Guide: Start your journey to successful adoption of CD and DevOps*. Packt Publishing Ltd.

Taherdoost, H., Drazenovic, G., Farhaoui, Y., Madanchian, M., Mohamed, N., & Kumar, D. (2025). Navigating the AI Era in Startup Business Development. In *Future Tech Startups and Innovation in the Age of AI* (pp. 191–208). CRC Press.

Tashtoush, Y. M., Darweesh, D. A., Husari, G., Darwish, O. A., Darwish, Y., Issa, L. B., & Ashqar, H. I. (2021). Agile approaches for cybersecurity systems, IoT, and intelligent transportation. *IEEE Access : Practical Innovations, Open Solutions*, *10*, 1360–1375. DOI: 10.1109/ACCESS.2021.3136861

Theodoropoulos, T., Rosa, L., Benzaid, C., Gray, P., Marin, E., Makris, A., & Girolamo, M. D. (2023). Security in cloud-native services: A survey. *Journal of Cybersecurity and Privacy*, *3*(4), 758–793. DOI: 10.3390/jcp3040034

Tomašev, N., Cornebise, J., Hutter, F., Mohamed, S., Picciariello, A., Connelly, B., Belgrave, D. C., Ezer, D., van der Haert, F. C., & Mugisha, F. (2020). AI for social good: Unlocking the opportunity for positive impact. *Nature Communications*, *11*(1), 2468. DOI: 10.1038/s41467-020-15871-z PMID: 32424119

Ullah, F., Habib, M. A., Farhan, M., Khalid, S., Durrani, M. Y., & Jabbar, S. (2017). Semantic interoperability for big-data in heterogeneous IoT infrastructure for healthcare. *Sustainable Cities and Society*, *34*, 90–96. DOI: 10.1016/j.scs.2017.06.010

Ural, H., & Yenigün, H. (2013). Regression Test Suite Selection Using Dependence Analysis. *Journal of Software (Malden, MA)*, *25*(7), 681–709. DOI: 10.1002/smr.1559

Vacca, A., Di Sorbo, A., Visaggio, C. A., & Canfora, G. (2021). A systematic literature review of blockchain and smart contract development: Techniques, tools, and open challenges. *Journal of Systems and Software*, *174*, 110891. DOI: 10.1016/j.jss.2020.110891

Vashishtha, R., Agrawal, A., & Haldar, R. (2019). Behavioral Analytics for Threat Detection: A Comprehensive Survey. *Journal of Information Security and Applications*, *45*, 61–73.

Venkateswaran, N., Kunduru, K. R., Ashwin, N., Sundar Ganesh, C. S., Hema, N., & Boopathi, S. (2024). Navigating the Future of Ultra-Smart Computing Cyberspace: Beyond Boundaries. In *Advances in Computational Intelligence and Robotics* (pp. 170–199). IGI Global. DOI: 10.4018/979-8-3693-2399-1.ch007

Venkateswaran, N., Vidhya, R., Naik, D. A., Raj, T. M., Munjal, N., & Boopathi, S. (2023). Study on Sentence and Question Formation Using Deep Learning Techniques. In *Digital Natives as a Disruptive Force in Asian Businesses and Societies* (pp. 252–273). IGI Global. DOI: 10.4018/978-1-6684-6782-4.ch015

Verma, P., & Sood, S. K. (2018). Fog assisted-IoT enabled patient health monitoring in smart homes. *IEEE Internet of Things Journal*, *5*(3), 1789–1796. DOI: 10.1109/JIOT.2018.2803201

Viega, J., & McGraw, G. R. (2001). *Building secure software: how to avoid security problems the right way*. Pearson Education.

Vilela, Pedro H et al. (2019). "Performance evaluation of a Fog-assisted IoT solution for e-Health applications". In: *Future Generation Computer Systems* 97, pp. 379–386.

Vinuesa, R., Azizpour, H., Leite, I., Balaam, M., Dignum, V., Domisch, S., Felländer, A., Langhans, S. D., Tegmark, M., & Fuso Nerini, F. (2020). The role of artificial intelligence in achieving the Sustainable Development Goals. *Nature Communications*, *11*(1), 1–10. DOI: 10.1038/s41467-019-14108-y PMID: 31932590

Vokolos, F., & Frankl, P. G. (Nov. 1998). "Empirical Evaluation of the Textual Differencing Regression Testing Technique". In: *Proceedings of the International Conference on Software Maintenance (SM'98)*. Bethesda, MD, USA, pp. 44–53. DOI: 10.1109/ICSM.1998.738488

Von Solms, S., & Futcher, L. A. (2020). Adaption of a Secure Software Development Methodology for Secure Engineering Design. *IEEE Access : Practical Innovations, Open Solutions*, *8*, 125630–125637. DOI: 10.1109/ACCESS.2020.3007355

Votipka, D., Abrokwa, D., & Mazurek, M. L. (2020, April). Building and validating a scale for secure software development self-efficacy. In *Proceedings of the 2020 CHI Conference on Human Factors in Computing Systems* (pp. 1-20). DOI: 10.1145/3313831.3376754

Wac, K., Bargh, M., Van Beijnum, B., Bults, R., Pawar, P., & Peddemors, A. (2009). Power-and delay-awareness of health telemonitoring services: The mobihealth system case study. *IEEE Journal on Selected Areas in Communications*, *27*(4), 525–536. DOI: 10.1109/JSAC.2009.090514

Wah, B. W., Huang, T. S., Joshi, A. K., Moldovan, D., Aloimonos, J., Bajcsy, R. K., Ballard, D., DeGroot, D., DeJong, K., Dyer, C. R., Fahlman, S. E., Grishman, R., Hirschman, L., Korf, R. E., Levinson, S. E., Miranker, D. P., Morgan, N. H., Nirenburg, S., Poggio, T., & Weems, C. (1993). Report on workshop on high performance computing and communications for grand challenge applications: Computer vision, speech and natural language processing, and artificial intelligence. *IEEE Transactions on Knowledge and Data Engineering*, *5*(1), 138–154. DOI: 10.1109/69.204098

Wang, X., Li, L., Yan, B., & Koyejo, O. M. (2019). Consistent classification with generalized metrics. arXiv, arXiv:1908.09057.

Wang, P., Liu, S., Liu, A., & Jiang, W. (2024). Detecting security vulnerabilities with vulnerability nets. *Journal of Systems and Software*, *208*, 111902. Advance online publication. DOI: 10.1016/j.jss.2023.111902

Wang, T., Bhuiyan, M. Z. A., Wang, G., Rahman, M. A., Wu, J., & Cao, J. (2018). Big data reduction for a smart city's critical infrastructural health monitoring. *IEEE Communications Magazine*, *56*(3), 128–133. DOI: 10.1109/MCOM.2018.1700303

Wang, Y.. (2012). "Using weighted attributes to improve cluster test selection". In: *2012 IEEE Sixth International Conference on Software Security and Reliability*. IEEE, pp. 138–146. DOI: 10.1109/SERE.2012.18

Weng, T.-W., Zhang, H., Chen, P.-Y., Yi, J., Daniel, L., Hsieh, C.-J., Gao, Y., & Su, D. (2018). Evaluating the robustness of neural networks: An extreme value theory approach. arXiv, arXiv:1801.10578.

Wheeler, D. A., & McClure, S. (2017). Integrating Security into the Software Development Lifecycle: A Practical Approach. *IEEE Software*, *34*(4), 50–56.

White, L. J., & Abdullah, K. (May 1997). "A Firewall Approach for Regression Testing of Object-Oriented Software". In: *Proceedings of the 10th International Software Quality Week (QW'97)*. San Francisco, CA, USA.

Wicker, M., Huang, X., & Kwiatkowska, M. (2018). Feature-guided black-box safety testing of deep neural networks. In *Tools and Algorithms for the Construction and Analysis of Systems* (pp. 408–426). Springer International Publishing. DOI: 10.1007/978-3-319-89960-2_22

Wikstrand, G.. (2009). "Dynamic regression test selection based on a file cache an industrial evaluation". In: *2009 International Conference on Software Testing Verification and Validation*. IEEE, pp. 299–302. DOI: 10.1109/ICST.2009.42

Wired. (2024). DeepSeek's Safety Guardrails Failed Every Test Researchers Threw at Its AI Chatbot. Retrieved from https://www.wired.com/story/deepseeks-ai-jailbreak-prompt-injection-attacks

Wong, M.-F., Guo, S., Hang, C.-N., Ho, S.-W., & Tan, C.-W. (2023). Natural language generation and understanding of big code for AI-assisted programming: A review. *Entropy (Basel, Switzerland), 25*(6), 888. DOI: 10.3390/e25060888 PMID: 37372232

Wu, M., Wicker, M., Ruan, W., Huang, X., & Kwiatkowska, M. (2020). A game-based approximate verification of deep neural networks with provable guarantees. *Theoretical Computer Science*, *807*, 298–329. DOI: 10.1016/j.tcs.2019.05.046

Xiang, W., Tran, H.-D., & Johnson, T. T. (2018). Output reachable set estimation and verification for multilayer neural networks. *IEEE Transactions on Neural Networks and Learning Systems*, *29*(11), 5777–5783. DOI: 10.1109/TNNLS.2018.2808470 PMID: 29993822

Xie, X., Ma, L., Juefei-Xu, F., Xue, M., Chen, H., Liu, Y., Zhao, J., Li, B., Yin, J., & See, S. (2019). DeepHunter: A coverage-guided fuzz testing framework for deep neural networks. In Proceedings of the ISSTA '19: 28th ACM SIGSOFT International Symposium on Software Testing and Analysis (pp. 1-12). ACM. DOI: 10.1145/3293882.3330579

Xie, J., Zheng, Y., & Wu, M. (2022). Hybrid Explainable AI Models for Threat Intelligence Analysis. *Journal of Cybersecurity Research*, *7*(1), 45–62.

Xie, R., Khalil, I., Badsha, S., & Atiquzzaman, M. (2018). Fast and peer-to-peer vital signal learning system for cloud-based healthcare. *Future Generation Computer Systems*, *88*, 220–233. DOI: 10.1016/j.future.2018.05.042

Xu, Z., Gao, K., Khoshgoftaar, T. M., & Seliya, N. (2014). System Regression Test Planning with a Fuzzy Expert System. *Information Sciences*, *259*, 532–543. DOI: 10.1016/j.ins.2010.09.012

Yacchirema, D., Sarabia-Jácome, D., Palau, C. E., & Esteve, M. (2018). System for monitoring and supporting the treatment of sleep apnea using IoT and big data. *Pervasive and Mobile Computing*, *50*, 25–40. DOI: 10.1016/j.pmcj.2018.07.007

Yadi Paembonan, A., & Darma Wijaya Waruwu, F. (2024). Subsurface Utility Identification at ITERA Campus Using Multi-frequency Ground Penetrating Radar. *Jurnal Teori Dan Aplikasi Fisika*, *12*(01). Advance online publication. DOI: 10.23960/jtaf.v12i1.14174

Yan, F., et al. *Performance modeling and scalability optimization of distributed deep learning systems*. in *Proceedings of the 21th ACM SIGKDD International Conference on Knowledge Discovery and Data Mining*. 2015.

Yang, G., Jiang, M., Ouyang, W., Ji, G., Xie, H., Rahmani, A. M., Liljeberg, P., & Tenhunen, H. (2017). IoT-based remote pain monitoring system: From device to cloud platform. *IEEE Journal of Biomedical and Health Informatics*, *22*(6), 1711–1719. DOI: 10.1109/JBHI.2017.2776351 PMID: 29990259

Yang, Y., Zheng, X., Guo, W., Liu, X., & Chang, V. (2018). Privacy-preserving fusion of IoT and big data for e-health. *Future Generation Computer Systems*, *86*, 1437–1455. DOI: 10.1016/j.future.2018.01.003

Yaseen, A. (2023). AI-driven threat detection and response: A paradigm shift in cybersecurity. *International Journal of Information and Cybersecurity*, *7*(12), 25–43.

Yeh, L.-Y., Chiang, P.-Y., Tsai, Y.-L., & Huang, J.-L. (2015). Cloud-based fine-grained health information access control framework for lightweightiot devices with dynamic auditing andattribute revocation. *IEEE Transactions on Cloud Computing*, *6*(2), 532–544. DOI: 10.1109/TCC.2015.2485199

Ye, N.. (June 2011). "Automatic Regression Test Selection Based on Activity Diagrams". In: *Proceedings of the 5th International Conference on Secure Software Integration & Reliability Improvement Companion (SSIRI-C'11)*. Jeju Island, South Korea: IEEE, pp. 166–171. DOI: 10.1109/SSIRI-C.2011.31

Yoo, S., & Harman, M. (Mar. 2012). "Regression Testing Minimization, Selection and Prioritization: A Survey". In: *Journal of Software Testing, Verification and Reliability* 22.2, pp. 67–120.

Younas, M., Jawawi, D. N. A., Ghani, I., Fries, T., & Kazmi, R. (2018). Agile development in the cloud computing environment: A systematic review. *Information and Software Technology*, *103*, 142–158. DOI: 10.1016/j.infsof.2018.06.014

Yu, T., & Wang, T. (Oct. 2018). "A Study of Regression Test Selection in Continuous Integration Environments". In: *Proceedings of the 29th International Symposium on Software Reliability Engineering (ISSRE'18)*. Ed. by Ghosh, Sudipto, & Natella, Roberto. Memphis, TN, USA: IEEE, pp. 135–143. DOI: 10.1109/ISSRE.2018.00024

Zech, P., & Felderer, M.. (Oct. 2012). "A Generic Platform for ModelBased Regression Testing". In: *Proceedings of the 5th International Symposium on Leveraging Applications of Formal Methods, Verification and Validation (ISoLA'12)*. Ed. by Margaria, Tiziana, & Steffen, Bernhard. Lecture Notes in Computer Science 7609. Heraclion, Crete: Springer, pp. 112–126.

Zech, P., Kalb, P., Felderer, M., Atkinson, C., & Breu, R. (2017, February). Model-Based Regression Testing by OCL. *International Journal of Software Tools for Technology Transfer*, *19*(1), 115–131. DOI: 10.1007/s10009-015-0408-8

Zhang, L., Zhou, Y., & Zhang, L. (2021). On the robustness of domain adaption to adversarial attacks. arXiv, arXiv:2108.01807.

Zhang, L. (May 2018). "Hybrid Regression Test Selection". In: *Proceedings of the 40th International Conference on Software Engineering (ICSE'18)*. Ed. by Chechik, Marsha, & Harman, Mark. Gotheburg, Sweden: IEEE, pp. 199–209. DOI: 10.1145/3180155.3180198

Zhang, Q., Cheng, L., & Boutaba, R. (2010). Cloud computing: State-of-the-art and research challenges. *Journal of Internet Services and Applications*, *1*(1), 7–18. DOI: 10.1007/s13174-010-0007-6

Zhang, S., Pandey, A., Luo, X., Powell, M., Banerji, R., Fan, L., Parchure, A., & Luzcando, E. (2022). Practical adoption of cloud computing in power systems—Drivers, challenges, guidance, and real-world use cases. *IEEE Transactions on Smart Grid*, *13*(3), 2390–2411. DOI: 10.1109/TSG.2022.3148978

Zhang, X. M., & Zhang, N. (2011). An open, secure and flexible platform based on internet of things and cloud computing for ambient aiding living and telemedicine. In *In: 2011 international conference on computer and management (CAMAN)* (pp. 1–4). IEEE.

Zhao, Z., Xu, J., & Zhang, Y. (2020). Artificial Intelligence in Cybersecurity: A Review. *Journal of Information Security and Applications*, *50*, 102420.

Zografopoulos, I., Ospina, J., Liu, X., & Konstantinou, C. (2021). Cyber-physical energy systems security: Threat modeling, risk assessment, resources, metrics, and case studies. *IEEE Access : Practical Innovations, Open Solutions*, *9*, 29775–29818. DOI: 10.1109/ACCESS.2021.3058403

About the Contributors

Qasem Abu Al-Haija received his Ph.D. from Tennessee State University (TSU), USA, in 2020. He is an Assistant Professor at the Department of Cybersecurity, Faculty of Computer & Information Technology, Jordan University of Science and Technology, Irbid, Jordan. He authorizes more than 250 scientific research papers and book chapters. His research interests include Artificial Intelligence (AI), Cybersecurity and Cryptography, the Internet of Things (IoT), Cyber-Physical Systems (CPS), Time Series Analysis (TSA), and Computer Arithmetic. Recently, he was listed as one of the world's top 2% of scientists list released publicly by Stanford University and Elsevier Publisher.

***

Adeyinka Kehinde Iyioluwa is a dedicated student pursuing a degree in Information and Communication Engineering. With a strong passion for artificial intelligence and technology, Adeyinka has authored several academic papers, focusing on topics such as AI applications and data security. Currently, Adeyinka is actively involved in research related to privacy and security management practices in computer science

Adeyinka Taye Iyinoluwa is a passionate researcher and academic with a strong background in Information and Communication Engineering. Known for a deep interest in technology and its transformative impact, Adeyinka is driven by a commitment to advancing innovative solutions in the field of education and beyond.

Mohammad Alauthman Received PhD degree from Northumbria University Newcastle, UK in 2016. He received a B.Sc. degree in Computer Science from Hashemite University, Jordan, in 2002, and received M.Sc. degrees in Computer Science from Amman Arab University, Jordan, in 2004. Currently, he is Assistant Professor and senior lecturer at Department of Information Security, Petra University,

Jordan. His main research areas cyber-security, Cyber Forensics, advanced machine learning and data science applications.

Amjad Aldweesh is a computer associate professor interested in the Blockchain and Smart contracts technology as well as cyber security. Amjad has a Bachelor degree in computer science. He has a MSc degree in advanced computer science and security from the University of Manchester with distinction. Amjad is the second in the UK and the first in the middle east to have a PhD in the Blockchain and Smart contracts technology from Newcastle University.

Ghaith Al-Refai is an Assistant Professor in the Department of Mechatronics and Artificial Intelligence at the German Jordanian University (Amman, Jordan). He earned his PhD and Master's degrees in Electrical and Computer Engineering from Oakland University (Rochester, MI, USA) and holds a Bachelor's degree in Electrical and Electronics Engineering from Jordan University of Science and Technology (Irbid, Jordan). Dr. Ghaith teaches several course in the mechatronics department, including, control systems, microcontrollers and machine intelligence. His research interests include artificial intelligence, computer vision, machine learning, autonomous driving applications and robotics. In addition to his academic experience, Dr. Al-Refai has several years of professional experience in the U.S. automotive industry, serving as a systems and electrical engineer at renowned companies such as Robert Bosch. His expertise lies predominantly in Advanced Driver Assistance Systems (ADAS) and autonomous driving technologies.

Mohammed Al-Refai is an Assistant Professor in the Computer Science Department within the Computer and Information Technology School at the Jordan University of Science and Technology (JUST). Al-Refai's research focuses on various areas within software engineering, including model-driven development, model-based testing, software architecture, software testing, regression test selection and prioritization, software security, and the integration of fuzzy logic and machine learning in software engineering applications. Al-Refai earned his Ph.D. in Computer Science from Colorado State University, Fort Collins, Colorado, under the supervision of Prof. Sudipto Ghosh. He also holds M.S. and B.S. in Computer Science from Jordan University of Science and Technology. Al-Refai is a member of the Association for Computing Machinery (ACM) and the Institute of Electrical and Electronics Engineers (IEEE).

Ahmad Alzu'bi (SMIEEE, MACM) received the M.Sc. degree in computer science from the Jordan University of Science and Technology, Jordan, in 2009, and the Ph.D. degree in computer science from the University of the West of Scotland (UWS), U.K., in 2016. He is currently an Associate Professor with the Department of

Computer Science, Jordan University of Science and Technology, Jordan. He has many publications in reputed journals and conferences. His research interests include computer vision, cybersecurity, and artificial intelligence.

Qanita Bani Baker is an Associate Professor of Computer Science at Jordan University of Science and Technology (JUST) with more than 16 years of experience in teaching, training, and doing research. She was awarded a scholarship to pursue a Ph.D. at Utah State University, USA and she got her Ph.D. in 2015. Dr. Baker has worked at JUST since 2015. Dr.Baker also has supervised students' innovation through graduation projects and Master theses. Her research interests include Problem Optimization, Artificial Intelligence, Machine Learning, IoT, sensor technology, Health Informatics, and capacity-building of Computer science education. Dr.Baker has co-authored many technical papers in specialized peer-reviewed international journals and conferences.

Mahmoud Hammad is an Associate Professor in the Department of Information Technology within the College of Engineering and Information Technology at Ajman University. Before joining Ajman University, Dr. Hammad worked as Associate Professor in the Software Engineering Department within the Computer and Information Technology School at the Jordan University of Science and Technology (JUST). He also served as the director of the Center for E-Learning and Open Educational Resources at JUST. Hammad's research interests are in the field of software engineering, specifically in the area of software architecture, self-adaptive software systems, mobile computing, software analysis, software security, natural language processing and machine learning. Hammad received his Ph.D. in Software Engineering from the University of California, Irvine (UCI) under the supervision of Prof. Sam Malek . During his Ph.D., Hammad developed a self-protecting Android software system, an Android software system that can monitor itself and adapt (change) its behavior at runtime to keep the system secure and protected from Inter-Component Communication attacks at all times. Hammad received his M.S. in Software Engineering from George Mason University, VA, USA and B.S. in Computer Science from Yarmouk University, Jordan . Hammad is a member of the Association of Computing Machinery (ACM), ACM Special Interest Group on Software Engineering (SIGSOFT), and the Institute of Electrical and Electronics Engineers (IEEE).

Hatem Mosa is a PhD researcher at Princess Sumaya University for Technology (PSUT) in Jordan, specializing in cybersecurity and blockchain security. He holds a Bachelor's in Information Technology from the Arab Open University, Bahrain, and a Master's in Cybersecurity from Arizona State University, USA. With over

10 years of industrial experience across multiple domains, Hatem is also the co-founder of several tech companies in Bahrain. His research focuses on advancing cybersecurity and blockchain solutions, and he has published multiple papers in his field.

Abdallah Qusef is a professor at PSUT in Jordan. He's a co-founder of the National Software Quality Assurance Center at RSS and he offers consultation services for a number of firms and ministries Inside and outside Jordan. He participates in the program committee of many conferences and a reviewer of many SE journals. His research interests including Agile Software Development, Traceability Recovery, Empirical Software Engineering, and e-business topics.

Wasswa Shafik (Member, IEEE) received a Bachelor of Science degree in information technology from Ndejje University, Uganda, a Master of Engineering degree in Information Technology (Computer and Communication Networks) from Yazd University, Iran, and a PhD in Computer Science with the School of Digital Science, Universiti Brunei Darussalam, Brunei Darussalam. He is also the Founder and Research Director of the Dig Connectivity Research Laboratory (DCRLab) after serving as a Research Associate at the Network Interconnectivity Research Laboratory at Yazd University. Prior to this, he worked as a Community Data Analyst at Population Services International (PSI-Uganda), a Community Data Officer at the Programme for Accessible Health Communication (PACE-Uganda), a Research Assistant at the Socio-Economic Data Centre (SEDC-Uganda), Uganda, an Assistant Data Officer at TechnoServe, Kampala, Uganda, and Asmaah Charity Organization as Cheif Executive Officer. He has hundreds of publications with renowned publishers. His research interests include Artificial Intelligence, Smart Agriculture, Digital Health, Nature-inspired Computing, Security and Privacy.

C.V. Suresh Babu is a pioneer in content development. A true entrepreneur, he founded Anniyappa Publications, a company that is highly active in publishing books related to Computer Science and Management. Dr. C.V. Suresh Babu has also ventured into SB Institute, a center for knowledge transfer. He holds a Ph.D. in Engineering Education from the National Institute of Technical Teachers Training & Research in Chennai, along with seven master's degrees in various disciplines such as Engineering, Computer Applications, Management, Commerce, Economics, Psychology, Law, and Education. Additionally, he has UGC-NET/SET qualifications in the fields of Computer Science, Management, Commerce, and Education. Currently, Dr. C.V. Suresh Babu is a Professor in the Department of Information Technology at the School of Computing Science, Hindustan Institute of Technology and Science (Hindustan University) in Padur, Chennai, Tamil Nadu,

India. For more information, you can visit his personal blog at https://sites.google.com/view/cvsureshbabu/.

Index

A

C

D

E

F

H

I

L

M

N

P

R

S

T

V

www.ingramcontent.com/pod-product-compliance
Lightning Source LLC
LaVergne TN
LVHW080340011026
849161LV00009B/2134